CLASSICAL PRESENCES

General Editors
Lorna Hardwick   James I. Porter

CLASSICAL PRESENCES

Attempts to receive the texts, images, and material culture of ancient Greece and Rome inevitably run the risk of appropriating the past in order to authenticate the present. Exploring the ways in which the classical past has been mapped over the centuries allows us to trace the avowal and disavowal of values and identities, old and new. Classical Presences brings the latest scholarship to bear on the contexts, theory, and practice of such use, and abuse, of the classical past.

Tragedy and the Idea of Modernity

Edited by
JOSHUA BILLINGS
AND MIRIAM LEONARD

OXFORD
UNIVERSITY PRESS

OXFORD
UNIVERSITY PRESS

Great Clarendon Street, Oxford, OX2 6DP,
United Kingdom

Oxford University Press is a department of the University of Oxford.
It furthers the University's objective of excellence in research, scholarship,
and education by publishing worldwide. Oxford is a registered trade mark of
Oxford University Press in the UK and in certain other countries

© Oxford University Press 2015

The moral rights of the author have been asserted

First Edition published in 2015

Published in the United States of America by Oxford University Press
198 Madison Avenue, New York, NY 10016, United States of America

British Library Cataloguing in Publication Data

Data available

ISBN 978-0-19-872779-8

Acknowledgements

We are very grateful to colleagues for the support we have received at Oxford, Cambridge, Yale, and University College London. In particular, we would like to thank UCL for hosting the initial conference that launched this book. Thanks are also due to Constanze Güthenke, Bonnie Honig, Edith Hall, Katherine Harloe, Katherine Ibbett, Fiona Macintosh, Glenn Most, Martin Ruehl, Oliver Taplin, and Vanda Zajko for their input at various stages in the project. We would especially like to thank Dylan Kenny for his excellent editorial assistance. We are grateful to Jim Porter and Lorna Hardwick and to Hilary O'Shea for their editorial advice. The advice of the anonymous readers has also been invaluable. Finally we would like to thank our contributors for lively discussions and cheerful cooperation.

Contents

Part III. Tragic Canons

List of Contributors

Ian Balfour is Professor of English at York University. He is the author of *Northrop Frye* (1988) and *The Rhetoric of Romantic Prophecy* (2002) and the editor or co-editor of collections on film, human rights, Walter Benjamin, and Jacques Derrida. He has taught at Cornell as the M. H. Abrams Distinguished Visiting Professor of English and held visiting professorships at Williams College, Stanford, UC Santa Barbara, and the Johann Wolfgang Goethe University in Frankfurt. He is currently completing a book on the sublime.

Andrew Benjamin is Professor of Philosophy and Jewish Thought at Monash University, Melbourne, and Distinguished Anniversary Professor of Philosophy and Humanities at Kingston University. His books include *Towards A Relational Ontology* (2015), *Working with Walter Benjamin: Recovering a Political Philosophy* (2013), *Place, Commonality and Judgment: Continental Philosophy and the Ancient Greeks* (2010), and *Of Jews and Animals* (2010).

Joshua Billings is Assistant Professor of Classics and Humanities at Yale University. His first book, *Genealogy of the Tragic: Greek Tragedy and German Philosophy* (Princeton), appeared in 2014.

Simon Critchley is Hans Jonas Professor at the New School for Social Research. His books include *Very Little . . . Almost Nothing* (1997), *Infinitely Demanding* (2007), *The Book of Dead Philosophers* (2008), *The Faith of the Faithless* (2012), *The Mattering of Matter: Documents from the Archive of the International Necronautical Society* (with Tom McCarthy) (2012), and *Stay, Illusion! The Hamlet Doctrine* (with Jamieson Webter) (2013). An experimental new work, *Memory Theatre*, and a book called *Bowie* were published in 2014. He is moderator of 'The Stone', a philosophy column in the *New York Times*, to which he is a frequent contributor.

Katie Fleming is Lecturer in the Department of English, QMUL. She has written articles on the politics of reception, fascism, Anouilh's *Antigone*, Horkheimer and Adorno's *Dialectic of Enlightenment*, Heidegger and humanism, and Ted Hughes's translation of Seneca's *Oedipus*.

Simon Goldhill is Professor of Greek at Cambridge, where he is also Director of CRASSH and the John Harvard Professor in the Humanities. His most recent books are *Victorian Culture and Classical Antiquity: Art, Opera, Fiction and the Proclamation of Modernity* (2011), which won the Robert Lowry Patten Prize for the best book on Victorian literature for 2010–12, and *Sophocles and the Language of Tragedy*, which won the Runciman Prize (2012) for the best book on a Greek subject, ancient or modern. His new book, *The Buried Life of Things*, was published in 2014.

Rüdiger Görner is Professor of German with Comparative Literature at Queen Mary University of London. He is Director of the Centre for Anglo-German Cultural Relations and Senior Research Fellow at the Morphomata Institute, University of Cologne, and currently Distinguished Visiting Professor at the University of Salzburg. Recent publications include monographs on European Romanticism, Nietzsche's aesthetics, and Heinrich von Kleist. His study on the poetry and poetics of Georg Trakl will appear in July with Hanser/Zsolnay.

John T. Hamilton is Professor of German and Comparative Literature, and Chair of the Department of Germanic Languages and Literatures, at Harvard University. Publications include *Soliciting Darkness: Pindar, Obscurity, and the Classical Tradition* (2004), *Music, Madness, and the Unworking of Language* (2008), and *Security: Politics, Humanity, and the Philology of Care* (2013).

Miriam Leonard is Professor of Greek Literature and its Reception at University College London. She is author of *Athens in Paris: Ancient Greece and the Political in Postwar French Thought* (2005) and *Socrates and the Jews: Hellenism and Hebraism from Moses Mendelssohn to Sigmund Freud* (2012).

Christoph Menke is Professor of Practcial Philosophy, Goethe Universität, Frankfurt am Main. Book publications in English include *The Sovereignty of Art: Aesthetic Negativity after Adorno and Derrida* (1998), *Reflections of Equality* (2006), *Tragic Play: Tragedy. Irony and Theater from Sophocles to Beckett* (2009), and *Force: A Fundamental Concept of Aesthetic Anthropology* (2012).

Terry Pinkard is Professor of Philosophy at Georgetown University in Washington, DC, and *Ehrenprofessor* at Tübingen University in Germany. In 2003–4, he was a Humboldt *Preisträger* in Berlin.

Significant Publications include *Hegel's Phenomenology: The Sociality of Reason* (1994), *Hegel: A Biography* (2000), *German Philosophy 1760–1860: The Legacy of Idealism* (2002), and *Hegel's Naturalism: Mind, Nature and the Final Ends of Life* (2012).

Robert B. Pippin is the Evelyn Stefansson Nef Distinguished Service Professor in the Committee on Social Thought, the Department of Philosophy, and the College at the University of Chicago. He is the author of several books on modern German philosophy, and several on philosophy and various arts. He is a past winner of the Mellon Distinguished Achievement Award in the Humanities, and is a fellow of the American Academy of Arts and Sciences, and of the American Philosophical Society.

James I. Porter is Professor of Classics and Comparative Literature at UC Irvine. He works in the history of classical philology and in Greek and Roman aesthetics, and is author, most recently, of *The Origins of Greek Aesthetic Thought: Matter, Sensation, and Experience* (2010). His book *The Sublime in Antiquity* is forthcoming.

Michael Silk is Professor of Classical and Comparative Literature at King's College London, Adjunct Professor in the Department of English and Comparative Literature at UNC, Chapel Hill, and a Fellow of the British Academy. His books include *Nietzsche on Tragedy* (co-authored with J. P. Stern, 1981/3), *Tragedy and the Tragic: Greek Theatre and Beyond* (ed., 1996/8), *Aristophanes and the Definition of Comedy* (2000), and *The Classical Tradition: Art, Literature, Thought* (co-authored with Ingo Gildenhard and Rosemary Barrow, 2014).

Samuel Weber studied with Paul de Man and Theodor Adorno, and taught at the Free University of Berlin, Johns Hopkins, and UCLA before becoming Avalon Foundation Professor of Humanities at Northwestern University. His most recent publications are *Theatricality as Medium* (2004), *Targets of Opportunity* (2005), *Benjamin's -abilities* (2008), and *Inquiétantes singularités* (2013).

Introduction

Joshua Billings and Miriam Leonard

'What does tragedy mean for us?' (*Was bedeutet die Tragödie für uns?*), Friedrich Nietzsche asks in a note dated 1871.[1] The fragment presents two questions—What is tragedy? Who are we?—that are no less pressing today. These two questions, for Nietzsche as for much of the modern philosophical tradition, are interrelated: thinking about tragedy has been a means of thinking about our identity and our place in time. To ask what tragedy means for us is to ask not only what the works of Sophocles or Shakespeare teach us about ourselves, but what value an ancient form and past culture can have in the present. Nietzsche's question implies that tragedy can be meaningful for us, can transcend its historical moment and speak directly to ours—perhaps, as in another fragment, it could be 'a means *for understanding ourselves*, for judging our own time, and thereby overcoming it' (*ein Mittel uns zu verstehen, unsre Zeit zu richten, und dadurch zu überwinden*).[2]

This conjunction of tragedy and identity is, in the history of thinking about art, a relatively recent phenomenon. Around 1800, the meaning of tragedy was substantially refounded, as thinkers associated with German Idealism came to view Greek tragedy in relation to metaphysical, existential, ethical, aesthetic, and psychological questions.[3] The tradition of philosophical appropriations of Greek tragedy encompasses many of the most important thinkers of

---

[1] Nietzsche (1980: vii. 373).   [2] Nietzsche (1980: viii. 97).
[3] For classic treatment, see Szondi (2002). See also Schmidt (2001), Krell (2005), Lambropoulos (2006), and Billings (2014).

the nineteenth, twentieth, and twenty-first centuries, including Hegel, Kierkegaard, Nietzsche, Freud, and Heidegger.[4] For these figures and many others, thinking about tragedy has been a means of articulating their view of the world, and these articulations have changed our own sense of what tragedy is and means. Discourse on the tragic has spread far beyond philosophy and conditioned many of the ways that tragedy is viewed by scholars and those outside the academy. As a philosophical concern, 'the tragic' is an invention of modernity, and a significant factor in modern philosophical thought.

Yet, as much as modern culture created the concept of the tragic, so too has tragedy created a certain modernity—modernity understood not as a temporal category but as a philosophical idea.[5] The idea of modernity encompasses a related series of questions, all of which are substantially rethought in the wake of the French Revolution and Kantian philosophy: the question of enlightenment, of the subject, of religion, of politics, of the temporal gulf between the present and the past. None of these questions, to be sure, is new, but all of them take on a self-consciously modern form around 1800, defined by a sense of rupture and novelty. The idea of modernity is an idea of categorical difference from the past and radical openness in the future. Tragedy, for reasons both intrinsic and extrinsic, has often been the ground for the elaboration of such concepts. From Hegel's description of the 'tragic fate' of *Geist* to Walter Benjamin's play of mourning to Judith Butler's protest against normative family structures, tragedy has played a leading role in the project of understanding modernity.

Tragedy and the Idea of Modernity considers the way that tragedy and modernity have been intertwined in intellectual life over the past two centuries. Approaching these questions from the discipline of Classics, it seeks to create a dialogue between the concerns of classicists and those of scholars of philosophy and modern literatures.[6] Much of the material considered has been extensively investigated in these latter disciplines, but often remains shadowy to scholars of the ancient world. Yet we believe that classicists have a distinctive voice within debates concerning the tragic, and that the questions raised by

---

[4] See Silk and Stern (1981), Rudnytsky (1987), Georgopoulos (1993), de Beistegui and Sparkes (2000), and Porter (2000).

[5] For a recent discussion of this concept of 'modernity' in relation to antiquity, see Morley (2008). On the philosophical problem of modernity, see Pippin (1999).

[6] Silk (1996) is formative for this dialogue.

this tradition of reflection in turn demand attention from classicists. We suggest that the 'philosophy of the tragic' (in Peter Szondi's influential formulation) can usefully be understood as a phenomenon of classical reception—indeed, as one of the most influential appropriations of classical texts in history. For the past two centuries, theoretical enquiry into tragedy has not simply represented one reception of antiquity among others, but has proven a uniquely powerful engine and provocation for thinking about what it means to read the ancients. Understanding the modernity of our antiquity (and the antiquity of our modernity), then, requires considering the role of tragedy in forming and expressing historical consciousness.

To describe the philosophy of tragedy as a phenomenon of classical reception is to place it in dialogue with a series of concerns different from—though by no means excluding—its place in German intellectual history or the history of western philosophy. On the one hand, the perspective implies a greater continuity with previous receptions of tragedy than is often acknowledged, whether in the eighteenth century or reaching back to antiquity. This longer perspective has often gone lost in discussions of the tragic as a product of modern German thought or post-Kantian philosophy, which has tended to obscure the persistence of certain questions and approaches. On the other hand, viewing the philosophy of the tragic as a phenomenon of classical reception implies a potentially broader context for the concerns raised by the tradition, reflecting not only on literature and philosophy in the modern German tradition, but on cultural politics, the history of classical scholarship, theatre, and music across European cultures. The perspective, finally, implies that recognizing the close relation between ancient literary texts and modern philosophical concepts is crucial to an adequate understanding of both—that we cannot isolate the development of philosophical concepts of the tragic from a history of reading, nor disentangle ancient texts from the categories through which they have been understood.

The chapters collected here propose a dialogue between works of (mainly) ancient Greek tragedy and modern philosophical thought. The anachrony of this conversation, we insist, is part of its value. Both parties are full partners—tragedy is not drowned out by conceptual thought, nor is philosophy rendered mute by tragic theatre. Rather, the application of modern concepts to Greek tragedy, and of ancient drama to philosophy, creates a condition of productive tension that has the power to shed a light different from that of the investigation of tragedy within its own time. We propose to take seriously the elective affinity between tragedy and ideas of modernity and consider their *mutual* implication—philosophy in our understanding of tragedy, and tragedy in the project of philosophy. In investigating this affinity we gain, on the one hand, a more reflective insight into what tragedy means today, and, on the other hand, an understanding of the ways that modernity grasps itself through tragedy. Where much research into Greek tragedy has sought to hold ancient and modern apart, we suggest that their interpenetration is a valuable subject in itself.

It is easy to be sceptical of the project of considering Greek tragedy through modern ideas of tragedy. The pitfalls of an uncritical application of modern concepts to ancient texts are all too obvious, and it is easy to find readings of ancient literature that simply repeat modern concerns in Greco-Roman garb. But equally possible is an engagement that finds ancient literature and modern philosophy to challenge one another, to resist too-easy assimilation, and in the process to broaden the bounds of both sides. This is the effort suggested by Schelling's interrogation of tragic freedom, by Kierkegaard's struggle to comprehend the ambiguity of *Antigone*, by Luce Irigaray's reading of Sophocles as the origin of patriarchy. Whatever their value for understanding what tragedy meant in antiquity, they speak directly to what tragedy means for us. They suggest that the meaning of ancient texts can be found in difference as much as in similarity, in the foreign as much as in the familiar. They offer approaches to antiquity as a site of provocation and challenge for modernity.

Ever since Aristotle, tragedy has been seen to have a distinctive and, some would say, privileged relationship to universalism. Classical scholarship today displays an ambivalent relation to this perceived universalism. On the one hand, the inheritance of radically historicizing positions associated with the aftermath of structuralism in figures such as Jean-Pierre Vernant has made viewing tragedy in terms of a transhistorical philosophical content suspect.[7] On the other hand, some more recent trends, especially those associated with performance and reception studies, have tended to introduce a more circumscribed form of universalism in their investigation of

---

[7] Vernant/Vidal-Naquet (1981). See also Winkler/Zeitlin (1990) and Carter (2011).

historical appropriations of the texts and stories of Greek tragedy.[8] Much of this ambivalence, we suggest, can be understood not just as the legacy of Aristotle but also in terms of a conflicted relation to the history of thought on tragedy, and particularly to the tradition of philosophical appropriations of 'the tragic'.[9] Classical scholarship since the 1960s has often sought, implicitly or explicitly, to dismantle such philosophical universalisms. Yet the historicism of recent years can be as unreflective as the universalism it supplanted, and neither approach can claim to resolve the inevitable tension between tragedy's undeniable power across history and its equally evident situation within history. After thesis and antithesis, an analysis of the tradition of philosophical thought on tragedy offers the chance of a more reflective interplay between theory and history.

Despite a certain ambivalence, the significance of this theoretical perspective is acknowledged by many classicists. Scholars of tragedy have found it difficult to avoid engaging with the tradition of German thought that stretches from the eighteenth to the twentieth centuries. Hegel's analysis of Sophocles' *Antigone* has become a standard reference point. Indeed, it would be difficult to imagine a discussion of the play today that did not touch on the questions that Hegel's reading put on the agenda, whether one thinks of the tensions between the *oikos* and the *polis*, the conflict between divine and human law, or the relationship between the sexes. Similarly, the concepts of the Apollonian and the Dionysiac that emerge from Nietzsche's *Birth of Tragedy* have become crucial to understanding the interplay between sage reflection and violent irrationalism that marks the most powerful Greek tragedies. The continuing impact of Freud's reading of Sophocles' *Oedipus Tyrannus* can be felt in theatrical productions and scholarly articles alike.[10] Hegel, Nietzsche, and Freud, to a greater or lesser extent, form part of the armature of tragic criticism, whether or not they are explicitly invoked. While classical reception studies have uncovered the impact of German philosophical approaches on the performance history of tragedy, work in the history of scholarship has illustrated its influence on philological practice: Jebb was certainly reading Hegel while he prepared his Sophocles edition and Nietzsche

---

[8] Important works on the performance history of tragedy include Hall/Macintosh/Wrigley (2004), Hall/Macintosh (2005), and Foley (2012).

[9] See Judet de la Combe (2010) and Goldhill (2012).

[10] See Goux (1993), Armstrong (2005), and Bowlby (2007).

and Freud both cast a long shadow over E. R. Dodds's commentary of the *Bacchae*.[11] An understanding of German Idealism and its aftermath, we contend, is central to getting to grips with both the generalities and the details of tragic criticism.

As a substantial body of secondary literature within the Classics already exists on Hegel's and Nietzsche's writings on tragedy, one of the aims of this volume is to provide a broader intellectual context for their readings.[12] Much of this context is well known to Germanists and philosophers, but has not received the attention it deserves from classicists. Hegel's conceptions of tragedy were formed in dialogue with Hölderlin and Schelling, while Nietzsche and early twentieth-century thinkers such as Freud, Heidegger, Benjamin, and Carl Schmitt formulated their ideas in dialogue not just with one another but also with the earlier traditions of German Idealism. At another level, we track the circulation of ideas between different spheres. Jakob Bernays's philological analysis of *catharsis* looks back to Kant and Lessing and forward to Nietzsche and Freud. Jean Pierre Vernant's historicist evangelism takes on a different perspective when it is understood as a reaction to Freudian psychoanalysis and Nietzschean aestheticism. Wagner's and Hebbel's tragic performances took their inspiration both from ancient texts and from their modern philosophical readers, while Pascal Quignard's engagement with both the philological and philosophical traditions contributes to the unique quality of his understanding of the tragic voice. Enlarging the canon of philosophical appropriations of tragedy reveals unexpected influences, alliances, and divergences, and contributes to a picture of a substantially more lively and controversial intellectual field than has often been acknowledged.

Looking beyond the philosophical canon of the tragic, the volume also looks beyond the tragic canon of philosophy, to works that have often been neglected or marginalized by the most important theorists. Again and again, thinkers in this tradition have raised the question of what constitutes tragedy: is there something specifically *Greek* about tragedy, and does philosophical thought reflect this quality? Should Greek works be differentiated from other traditions of tragic writing such as Shakespeare's plays and baroque *Trauerspiel*? Underlying much of this questioning of tragic canons is a persistent concern

---

[11] Goldhill/Hall (2009: 1).

[12] See Silk and Stern (1981), Porter (2000), Goldhill (2012), and Billings (2014).

with modern tragedy: is tragedy still possible in modernity?[13] Was it
in the Renaissance? In the late fifth century BCE, even? These questions substantially animate many of the theorists discussed in the
chapters collected here, and the volume pays particular attention to
the way that readings of individual works contribute to general
theories of tragedy. Such an investigation is especially salutary, we
believe, given the tendency of critics to read theories of tragedy in
isolation from the works in which they are in dialogue. We seek to
restore some of the dialectic of the particular and the general that
animates philosophical approaches to tragedy.

It was with tragedy in mind that Plato ruminated in the *Republic* on
the 'the old quarrel between philosophy and poetry', and, when
Aristotle later turned his attention to the tragedians in the *Poetics*,
he established tragedy as a concern for philosophy. Within the
ancient context, this relationship is not arbitrary—Jean-Pierre Vernant argues that it was in tragedy that the most difficult conceptual
and ethical questions of the fifth century BCE were formulated prior to
the advent of Platonic philosophy. Given the continuity in their
preoccupations, it does not seem surprising that philosophy should
show an interest in tragic drama. For Nietzsche, it was precisely the
turn towards abstraction and intellectual self-consciousness that he
saw instantiated in Euripides' plays that sounded the death knell of
tragedy. Conceptual thought sapped the life out of the living art
form of drama and relegated it to empty philosophical speculation.
Nietzsche saw it as his task to liberate tragedy from the philosophical
tradition that had parasitically attached itself to it. That Nietzsche was
himself part of a new philosophical tradition that was enlivened by its
engagement with Greek tragedy is just one of the many ironies of the
Birth of Tragedy. In fact, despite Plato and Nietzsche's oppositional
rhetoric, it is the symmetries and synergies between literature and
philosophy that the history of reading tragedy best exemplifies. Greek
tragedy gives one a unique vantage point from which to observe 'the
literary turn' within philosophy across the *longue durée*.[14]

Tragedy and the Idea of Modernity is divided into three thematic
parts: 'Tragic Poetics', 'Tragic Cultures', and 'Tragic Canons'. Each
part seeks to explore the multiple ways that tragedy has animated the
aesthetic and cultural debates of modernity. In arguing that, 'since

---

[13] See Steiner (1961) and Williams (1979).
[14] See de Beistegui and Sparkes (2000).

Aristotle, there has been a poetics of tragedy. Only since Schelling has there been a philosophy of the tragic,'[15] Peter Szondi sought to create a distinction between the formal and the philosophical approaches to tragedy. According to Szondi, where antiquity understood tragedy in generic terms, modernity approached tragedy as a metaphysical question. The chapters in the first part, by contrast, demonstrate the persistence of poetics within the philosophy of the tragic. Indeed, German Idealism's turn to tragedy is perhaps one of the most significant examples of the imbrication of philosophical and literary discourses. Reacting to the influence of Kant's Third Critique, Schelling, Hegel, and Hölderlin place poetry at the heart of their philosophical enquiries. Hegel's engagement with tragedy determines not merely the content, but also the form, of his philosophy, while Hölderlin's writings could best be described as a philosophical poetics. Nietzsche's *Birth of Tragedy* is a truly hybrid genre: part philological analysis, part poetic fiction, and part metaphysical treatise. In the twentieth century, Benjamin's 'philosophico-historical' enquiry is also a formalist analysis of genre.

Poetological and aesthetic categories have played an important role in grasping abstract concepts across the history of philosophy. When Aristotle, for instance, introduced the notion of *catharsis* into his analysis of tragedy, he could not have known that it would dominate literary and philosophical debates for centuries to come. Indeed, the modern philosophical engagement with tragedy from Schelling to Nietzsche and Freud would look unrecognizable without it. This is why Jakob Bernays's treatment is so paradigmatic. Bernays's philological work situates itself at the intersection of multiple philosophical and literary controversies. His insistence on a 'pathological' reading of *catharsis* simultaneously overturned the dominant moral reading of tragedy and anticipated the new tragic philosophies of Nietzsche and Freud. We are including the first English translation of the final section of Bernays's work as an appendix to allow readers access to a crucial missing link in the modern development of tragic poetics. Where terms like *catharsis* were reimagined, tragic criticism also acquired a new lexicon. The notion of 'the sublime' underwent a substantial reformulation around 1800 and became inextricably tied to the tragic. The engagements of philologists and philosophers with

---

[15] Szondi (2002: 1).

these much-disputed ancient concepts point to the complex inter-penetration of academic exegesis and conceptual analysis. In this section, Friedrich Hölderlin's engagement with, on the one hand, the category of the sublime and, on the other, notions of tragic temporality provides the basis for a reappraisal of his importance and originality as a thinker of tragic poetics. Moving from general questions of the value of philosophical concepts for thought on tragedy through specific nexuses in the ancient vocabulary to a central text in the history of modern thought on tragedy, the first part of the volume demonstrates that concerns with tragic poetics have remained strong in modernity, even as they have been compre-hensively reformulated by the Idealist tradition.

If modern thought on tragedy demonstrates both a continuity and a rupture with ancient poetics, its relationship to the cultural politics of ancient drama is equally complex. There has been a tendency in recent scholarship on tragedy to identify philosophical engagements as apolitical. The increasing emphasis on the social contexts of Greek tragedy and a greater awareness of the civic function of the original performances have led scholars to be suspicious of the perceived abstraction and universalism of philosophical readings. Nevertheless, many of the thinkers explored in this volume had strong political commitments, and the development of Idealist thinking on tragedy emerged, in part at least, from the cultural and political debates of the French Revolution. As tragedy came to be associated with a mode of existence rather than just a literary genre, writers and theorists began to use its vocabulary to explore cultural, ethical, and political themes. While questions of ethical subjectivity and religious identity were central to the Idealists, later readers turned to tragedy with a different set of ideological preoccupations. Our second part, 'Tragic Cultures', focuses on the productive interaction between political and aesthetic debates that arose from the philosophical reading of tragedy. As the opening chapter in this part demonstrates, both Marx and Wagner, in their different ways, placed tragedy at the heart of their explorations of social and cultural revolution in the nineteenth century. In the twentieth century, by contrast, tragedy became implicated in the difficult arguments about resistance and collaboration with Nazism. In highlighting the importance of history for understanding the essence of tragedy, Carl Schmitt also called for a repoliticization of the genre. Schmitt saw himself turning his back both on the aestheti-cism of the nineteenth century and on the bad faith of German critics in the wake of the Second World War. Schmitt's historical reading of tragedy can thus be contrasted to Heidegger's decontextualized exegesis of the language of Sophocles' *Antigone*, which consciously gestures back to Hölderlin while the ethical and political questions it invokes look forward to the preoccupations of poststructuralism and deconstruction. Pascale Quignard's more recent writings engage more explicitly with the historicizing readings of tragedy that emerged in the second half of the twentieth century, particularly in France. But his idiosyncratic approach demonstrates how aesthetic, political, and philosophical approaches need not be mutually exclusive. At a time when historicist criticism claims a monopoly on the cultural politics of tragedy, it seems apt to remember that some of the most import ideological struggles from the social revolutions of the nineteenth century to the sexual revolution of the twentieth took their inspiration from a philosophical tradition that was steeped in Greek tragedy.

Differing canons of tragedy contribute to different theories of tragedy, and the final part of the volume, 'Tragic Canons', considers the ways in which works and thinkers at the margins of the philosophical canon of tragedy might illuminate central issues. Beginning with Aristotle's elevation of *Oedipus Tyrannus*, certain works have been considered more central to the understanding of genre than others. Idealism inherited this canon, but reformed it substantially, most notably through its strong interest in the *Antigone* (which is unprecedented in the Aristotelian tradition), but also with an increasing attention to Aeschylus and general lack of interest in Euripides. At the same time, certain modes of interpretations became canonical: reading tragedy as the representation of a struggle of freedom and necessity (modelled on the *Oedipus Tyrannus*) or as a conflict of the equal rights (modelled on the *Antigone*). The psychoanalytic tradition's Oedipus complex reinforced the play's canonical quality, even while founding a new (and no more flexible) mode of approach. This concentration on a few works has certainly occluded avenues for further thought, but it has also created them, as the margins of these canons gain a power to unsettle the centre and provoke new engagements.

Papers investigate the *Oedipus at Colonus*, *Hamlet*, and German baroque drama, which reflect importantly on concepts of the tragic from a place just outside the core of the tradition, while thinkers such as Walter Benjamin and Bernard Williams engage with previous theories in order to remake them in a post-Idealist and post-Nietzschean context. These chapters illustrate various kinds of uneasiness with the near-hegemonic discourse of the tragic that prevailed through much of the modern era. Engaging critically with this tradition could be a means of declaring one's own modernity, and remains an important way for contemporary readers of tragedy to stake out their own claims in opposition to Idealism. At the same time, these chapters show the continuing value of a serious confrontation with Idealism—if only to reject it. Twenty-first-century readers of tragedy may well need a new canon of tragedy and the tragic, but this will not come *ex nihilo*. Addressing the shortcomings of the philosophical tradition requires also an appreciation of its merits for reading tragedy, and the possibilities it has opened. Nietzsche's question 'Was does tragedy mean to us?' implies an interrogation of how we create and in turn are created by tragedy's meaning. Understanding what tragedy could mean for us requires an understanding of what tragedy has meant.

Part I

Tragic Poetics

1

Jacob Bernays and the Catharsis of Modernity

James I. Porter

In 1857, Jacob Bernays, the German philologist from the Jewish Theological Seminar in Breslau, published an article some seventy pages long that would create an upheaval in the academic world of tragedy. The essay, *Outlines of Aristotle's Lost Work on the Effects of Tragedy*, is one that every study in the same area must reckon with today. Taking on the established view of catharsis, which hung on a single obscure sentence from Aristotle's *Poetics*, he argued that catharsis was not to be understood as a purification of tragic emotions, as the cliché on everyone's lips would have it. This misreading of Aristotle had turned tragedy into a 'moral house of correction', and a 'branch and rival institute of the Church'.[1] Bernays's response to the reigning view was threefold: he demonstrated the absurdities of the existing translations of Aristotle's remark (which meant embarrassing the likes of Lessing and Goethe); he underscored the medical meaning of the term

The rudiments of this chapter were first presented at the Languages of Emotion Cluster of Excellence workshop on Jacob Bernays, organized by Bernd Seidensticker and Martin Vöhler and held at the Free University of Berlin in December of 2008. My thanks to both of these organizers and to the participants in that stimulating event, and to audiences at the APA panel in San Antonio, University College London, Northwestern University, and UCLA, where more developed versions of this essay were read. I further wish to thank Ian Balfour, Josh Billings, Bonnie Honig, Marianne Hopman, and Miriam Leonard for invaluable comments.

[1] Bernays (1970 [1857]: 4/136, 8/140. References to Bernays (1970 [1857]) give two sets of page numbers, the first corresponding to the 1970 reprint, the second to the 1857 original.

katharsis elsewhere in Aristotle's corpus; and he insisted on a pathological interpretation of catharsis. The results were both shocking and sobering. Catharsis had to be understood as a process that involved a violent discharge and not, as his predecessors held, a purification of the affections and emotions. What Aristotle had in mind, Bernays claimed (or appeared to claim), was a process that was closer to an orgiastic reaction, to vomiting, or to evacuation. If Bernays was right, then in contrast to popular and academic belief catharsis could serve no higher purpose, be it moral or pedagogical, and not even any obvious aesthetic purpose. It must be a physiological event, pure and simple.

Bernays's demolition of a cherished commonplace was comparable to Friedrich August Wolf's rude dismantling of the genius of Homer in 1795. Like Wolf, Bernays had both Greek and philology on his side, and in his rebuttal he brought to bear the entire Olympian machinery of the German seminar and every scrap of available evidence from antiquity. What could not be proved directly in Aristotle could be inferred from hints in later sources attesting to a lost treatment, by Aristotle, of a full-blown theory of catharsis, which is meagerly referenced in our *Poetics*, and which in turn is but a pitiful excerption of this longer, lost work—a loss that was all the more regrettable, as the thrust of that entire work was devoted to the effects of tragedy on the spectator and her emotional states (that is, their catharsis), and not to its aesthetic construction or form, as the treatise in its preserved form misleadingly suggests.[2] Modern science, materialism, and rationality triumphed over bourgeois sentimentality. Or so it seemed.[3]

This is how Bernays was and is remembered, and not only because of his later reception by Nietzsche and Freud. He was attacked at the time for his crass reduction of art to a form of pathology, above all in the first half of his article, despite the contrary indications of the later parts of this same document: it was here, in the first two sections (out of four), the most narrowly philological of the treatise, but also the easiest to grasp, that the primary thrust of his argument was felt to lie—a thrust that scholars for the most part ignored or else, more rarely, noted and then condemned as either excessive, misconceived,

---

[2] Bernays (1970 [1857]: 5/137). See Bernays (1970 [1857]: 13/145) on the original, now lost, work of the *Poetics* in two books (Diogenes Laertius 5.24).

[3] For a quick survey of the first reactions to Bernays, see Gründer (1991: 371–2), Stahr being a case in point: he attacked Bernays for his 'materialistic banality' (Stahr 1859: 29).

or contradictory.[4] This same first portion is all that the editor of the only existing translation in any language saw fit to see into English for readers today.[5] And more recent scholarship for the most part follows suit, typically giving Bernays a nod before dismissing him out of hand, and opting instead for a view that blends purgation with purification in the name of emotional and ethical 'balance', alignment, and amelioration.[6] But Bernays did not stop here. On the contrary, he went on to develop a theory of catharsis as an experience of the sublime in the face of nature and the universe, seemingly rejecting his own proposed medical model, but in fact building on the logic of his analysis from the first part of his treatise.

As Bernays develops his idea, he moves well beyond the rather limited (if provocative) theory about the physiological discharge of burdensome affections that he is usually understood to have held, and even beyond tragedy. In the final analysis, his hypothesis amounts to a general theory of affective experience in the Greek world, of which tragic catharsis is only a small subset and to which medicine is irrelevant as an explanatory model: catharsis describes *any* vital encounter in the mind, soul, or body with the outer world of experience, an encounter that Bernays takes to have been ecstatic, for reasons that will emerge. And, as his theory unfolds, it explodes the

---

[4] E.g. Brandis (1860: 171–2): 'We are delighted by this recognition [of the higher goals of catharsis as these are unveiled in the final pages], without asking whether or to what extent it squares with the blunt claim, put forward at the beginning of the treatise, about the purely pathological nature of catharsis.' Further, Baumgart (1875: 92): 'Thank God Aristotle did not know these verses!' ('Shuddering is the best part of mankind,' quoted from Goethe's *Faust* by Bernays at the conclusion of his essay); Egger (1883: 38): Bernays's final arguments are 'obviously not Aristotelian'; they are imported from modern philosophy 'since Spinoza'.

[5] The partial translation by Jennifer Barnes (in Barnes, Schofield, and Sorabji 1975: iv. 154–65) is reprinted and revised as Bernays (2006).

[6] See Janko (1992: 341, 347): tragedy teaches audiences how to regulate their emotions 'in the right way', both affectively and cognitively, through 'the purgation of undesirable emotions'; hence, catharsis is conducive to virtue. This is the current default view, and not far removed from Lessing's view that catharsis is 'the transformation of the passions into virtuous dispositions' (quoted in Bernays (1970 [1857]: 4/136), e.g., Halliwell (1986: 168–201); Belfiore (1992: 348–9); possibly also Lear (1992); Schadewaldt (1970 [1955]) is closer to Bernays. The scholarship on catharsis is astonishingly large. For a rapid survey, see Munteanu (2012: 238–50). Outside of classics, a more Nietzschean paradigm reigns (see n. 110). The most drastic solution on offer is to athetize the very mention of catharsis in the *Poetics* as a textual corruption (see Veloso 2007).

very premisses on which it has been misread for so long. This, at least, is what I hope to demonstrate in what follows.[7]

1. BERNAYS'S THEORY OF VITAL AFFECTIONS

The basic outlines of Bernays's reading of Aristotle are shown in diagrammatic form in Figure 1. His scheme, though quickly brushed in, is fairly complex and closely thought out. (I will leave aside the question whether his reconstruction, so understood, provides us with a better understanding of Aristotle; in some crucial respects I believe it does.) Where readers of Bernays have most of all gone astray is in their assumption that his theory of tragic catharsis is reducible to his view of somatic catharsis, which is to say, to a medical reading of the phenomenon.[8] But, as Figure 1 indicates, neither the orgiastic nor the

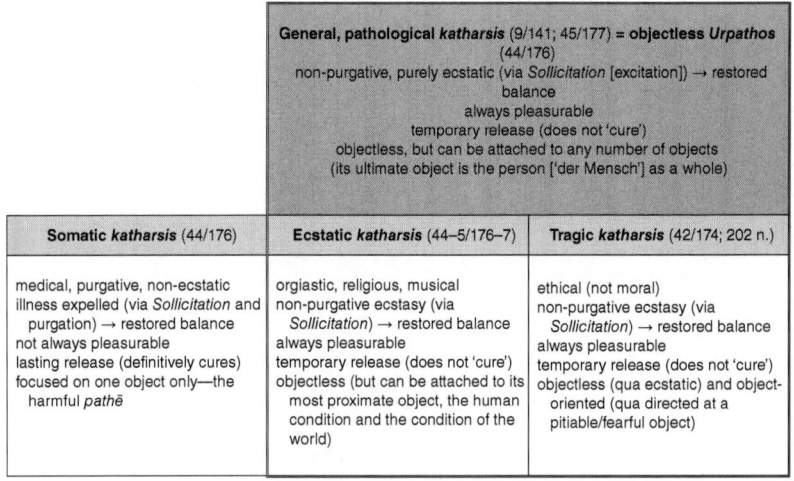

Figure 1. Diagram of Bernays's theory of catharsis.

---

[7] See the translation of section IV provided in the Appendix to this book, the section in which Bernays's theory of affection is most fully developed, as Bernays (1980 [1859]: 121 n.) himself recognizes; we will come back to this bit of evidence at n. 102.

[8] This is almost universally assumed, representatively by Belfiore (1992: 259): 'In arguing for an exclusively medical interpretation of katharsis, Bernays failed...'. Identically, Spengel (1859: 17); Halliwell (2012: 245). Aristotle's Neoplatonist interpreters made the same reduction (Bernays (1970 [1857]: 37–8/169–70).

medical model is sufficient to exhaust the meaning of catharsis.[9] Bernays foresaw the charge of reduction,[10] but he also knew that he was immune to the charge. Most significantly, he recognized, as most modern readers of Aristotle do, that the only relationship between catharsis and medical therapy is that of an analogy, as Aristotle explicitly states in *Politics* 8:[11] the medical model is no more than an analogy or a metaphor for psychological relief (*Erleichterung*).[12] Bernays relishes the shock value of the analogy,[13] but the analogy is merely a stepping stone in his argument. After all, the reductive medical (somatic) model is not that different from the moral model that Bernays sets out to refute. Both models ultimately involve purification and (selective) eradication, a 'cure' and a normalization, as was long recognized,[14] whereas Bernays goes a different way. He reads catharsis as involving a positive heightening and expansion, and not a removal, let alone normalization, of emotional and

---

[9] The third and fourth traits of somatic catharsis ('lasting release' and 'not always pleasurable') follow from Bernays (1970 [1857]: 44–5/176–7), where he draws a distinction between somatic and ecstatic catharsis: 'ecstatic catharsis is distinguished [from somatic catharsis] by the fact that it is capable of generating merely temporary but never lasting relief [unlike somatic catharsis], and by the fact that it is always accompanied by the feeling of pleasure, as is consistent with the nature of ecstasy,' whereas somatic catharsis, though it results in lasting relief (it heals), is evidently not ecstatic, and hence is not predominantly pleasurable. It is conceivable that somatic catharsis is a mere physiological reflex that involves no intentional object at all, even if it has a clear somatic object (harmful *pathē*). Cf. also Aristotle, *Nicomachean Ethics* 1154b17–19, 1173b8–9.

[10] Bernays (1970 [1857]: 11/143).

[11] Aristotle *Politics* 8.7.1342[a]10–11; rendered in Bernays (1970 [1857]: 10/142): '"Those in ecstasy who have been calmed down," Aristotle says ... "have undergone as it were [*hōsper*] a medical cure and a catharsis...".'. *As it were*, therefore not actually; thus, a metaphor underlies *katharsis* just as it does *iatreia* [medical treatment].' Contrast Halliwell (1986: 193, 197), who claims that Aristotle's insistence that medicine is only an analogy refutes Bernays. Similarly, Destrée (2013).

[12] *Erleichterung* Bernays (1970 [1857]: 16/148); *Gleichniss*, 12/144; *Vergleich*, 10–11/142–3; *Metapher*, 16/148 (also Bernays 1880 [1859]: 122). Cf. *ästhetische Terminus*, 6/138; *parallalisiert*, 12/144; *wie*, 44/176. At issue is '*only* a way of rendering [the problem] concrete [*nur eine Versinnlichung*] by pointing to *analogous* bodily experiences' (11/143; emphasis added)—a slippage that Bernays decries as all too 'seductively easy' (30/162; cf. 12/144).

[13] 'Let know one look down his nose at this *presumed* dragging of aesthetics down into the realm of medicine' (Bernays 1970 [1857]: 11/143; emphasis added). Bernays (1970 [1857]: 12/144): the analogy should not be rejected 'simply because of its medicinal smell.'

[14] Cf. K. O. Müller (1833: 191): 'läutern und erheben'; Weil (1848: 138): 'eine Arznei [sc., purgation], eine Reinigung'; Spengel (1859: 17): 'purification means elimination,' as in Plato. Contemporary readings tend to conflate these too, e.g., Halliwell (1986: 198); Belfiore (1992: 348–9).

psychological potentials 'that takes in every kind of affection in the soul'[15]—a reading that, he insists, is empirically based and not governed by analogies, at least in Aristotle's mind.[16] Aristotle's theory of catharsis is crucially an insight into the psychology of the soul, an entity that makes itself known through its *pathē* alone.[17] Medicine is merely a graphic way of representing an underlying mental phenomenon that, on its own, is exceedingly difficult to grasp and is irreducible to a physical explanation.[18]

To be sure, emotional heightening was an element of every major treatment of catharsis from Lessing onward.[19] What sets Bernays's theory apart are two related considerations. First, he understands 'discharge' neither as a purgation and quieting of emotions nor as the elimination of undesirable quantities of affect,[20] but as a form of excitation (*Sollicitation*) and release (*Entladung*) of inner states, both physical and psychological, that lie dormant, waiting to be expressed, and that are, moreover, desirable to maintain and even to nurture. This is precisely why the medical understanding of catharsis points the wrong way: its *telos* is a permanent elimination and a radical cure of a troubling affection, unlike discharge, which is temporary and repeatable.[21] Secondly, Bernays uncouples catharsis from tragedy

---

[15] Bernays (1970 [1857]: 6/138; 11/143; 41/171; 44/176).

[16] Bernays (1970 [1857]: 11/43; 44/176).

[17] Aristotle, *On the Soul* 1.1, 402^{a}10–11: 'To attain any knowledge of the soul is one of the most difficult things in the world' (trans. Smith)—hence, Bernays's 'enigmatic': 'The ever enigmatic pathological *mental* symptom . . . is made concrete [*wird versinnlicht*] [in ancient accounts] through *comparison* with pathological *bodily* symptoms' (Bernays 1970 [1857]: 11/143; emphasis in original). Cf. Aristotle, *On the Soul* 1.5, 409^{b}15–16: the affections (*pathē*) of the soul are its functions or operations (*erga*).

[18] The soul cannot act or be conceived 'without involving the body', to which it is nonetheless irreducible (Aristotle, *On the Soul* 1.1, 403^{a}5–6, etc.; Bernays 1970 [1857]: 63/195 n. 9, and *passim*).

[19] Lessing (1985: vi. 563, §76: 'so ist es doch unstreitig, daß unser Mitleid, wenn jene Furcht dazu kömmt, weit *lebhafter und stärker und anzüglicher* wird, als es ohne sie sein kann,' etc. Similarly, Goethe (1999 [1827]: 338).

[20] See Bernays (1970 [1857]: 6/138), where Bernays objects to the notion that catharsis resembles housecleaning or the separation and flushing of unwanted chemicals. For the same reason, it is wrong to believe, with Kommerell (1957: 265), and virtually all others, that Bernays construes Aristotle's *katharsis tōn pathēmatōn* as a *genitivus separativus*. For Bernays it is a *genitivus objectivus* (it specifies the object of the act of 'heightening' and 'discharging'), while the 'true', '*logical*' (and internal) object of catharsis is 'the person' (Bernays 1970 [1857]: 17/149).

[21] Bernays (1970 [1857]: 45/177). Nietzsche uses *Entladung* in a similar way in *The Birth of Tragedy*, as will be shown. Freud understands catharsis in the same fashion (e.g. Freud 1953–74 [1905–6]: 305): 'it is a question of opening up [*Eröffnung*] sources

so as to arrive at a larger theory of emotional response, one that is not morbidly pathological, but is rather a kind of pathology in the most general sense of the term—in the sense of involving the *pathē*, whereby these are understood as 'predominantly *psychological* affections'.[22] The ultimate thrust of Bernays's analysis is thus, surprisingly, psychological, not medical or somatic. Once this is seen, the rest of his theory falls into place.

Reasoning from Aristotle's views of natural ends, Bernays rails against what he called a 'transcendental teleology' of catharsis (one that postulated an end outside of itself—most objectionably, a moral *telos*) in favour of Aristotle's 'immanent teleology', which discovers final ends within the processes of both nature and art. Such intrinsic purposiveness has no outer object; it is more like what happens when you light a cigar (Bernays's metaphor): it 'feeds on its own flame' and burns naturally.[23] But a process like this required a few postulates of its own: the notion of a psychological state to accompany the physiological symptoms, a subject properly attuned to both, and the ideal outer conditions for the flame to catch and for the cathartic event to take place (those provided by Greek culture in general, and tragedy in particular). An anthropology of the Greeks is invoked to explain the Greeks' susceptibility to *ekstasis*: their Oriental traits, their proneness to excitation (*Erregbarkeit*), their comparative lack of self-control, their cognitive immaturity, which is to say their

of pleasure or enjoyment in our emotional life [*Affektleben*]' and of psychic 'heightening' (*Höherspannung*), etc.

[22] Bernays (1970 [1857]: 29/161; emphasis added). This usage of *pathologisch* was standard for the day. Cf. Goethe, letter to Schiller, 9 December 1797: 'Ohne ein lebhaftes pathologisches Interesse ist es auch mir niemals gelungen irgend eine tragische Situation zu bearbeiten' (Goethe 1887: iv, pt 12. 373). But the ambivalence of the term in German allowed for misconstruals, and the whole of Bernays's reception is premissed on one such misconstrual, e.g. Spengel (1859: 17): catharsis is 'a spiritual ["intellectual": *geistige*] and moral effect, not a reductively [*bloß*] medical and pathological effect.'

[23] Bernays (1970 [1857]: 42/174; 44/176). Possibly an oblique allusion to Lessing (1985: vi. 563, §76 ('Flamme')). Bernays is picking up an earlier thread. Three pages into his essay he approvingly cites Goethe (1999 [1827]: 336), who rejected the validity of extrinsic 'teleology in nature and art', and who noted that Aristotle's interest lay in 'the [inner aesthetic] construction of tragedy', not in some 'remote effect' such as a moral catechism would represent (Bernays 1970 [1857]: 5/137). This formal, aesthetic notion is central to Bernays's theory from start to finish (cf. 48/180: 'inner economy of tragedy'; 51/183: 'construction of tragedy'), and only the first of many indications of his argument's own inner coherence.

lack of a firmly formed self-consciousness,[24] all of which enabled the Greeks to step outside themselves and to be susceptible to rapturous and ecstatic states of mind (*das Aussersichsein*) in a way that is no longer quite possible in the modern world. The fundamental processes remain psychologically valid today;[25] they simply transpire along more domesticated routes—typically secular ones—and hence are no longer taken for 'holy and divine' states of mind.[26]

Bernays targets first and foremost the human capacity for an *Ur-pathos*, or a general response to sensations and experiences that gives rise to motions and emotions in the soul (*Sollicitationen*—Bernays's gloss on κίνησις τῶν παθῶν, or the stirring-up of the affections).[27] His theory is rooted in this primitive level of experience (the whole realm of sentience and perception, as is outlined in Aristotle's *On the Soul*), and not in medicine, which at most inspired Aristotle's choice of the term *catharsis*,[28] nor does Bernays ever actually leave this domain behind: the primordial nature of affection informs all cathartic experiences and is the ultimate source of their value as well. But in order to see all this, we need to look closely at his starting premiss.

'*All forms of* pathos [*affection*] *are essentially ecstatic; in all of them a person is put outside of himself*'.[29] Bernays's premiss, which is based on a rather free reading of Aristotle, is that the primary response to the world of experience (feeling, sensation, emotion), activated whenever any experience is had (whenever a subject is affected), is one of ecstasy. Such responses are invariably pleasurable, even if they also necessarily entail pain; and they are pleasurable in virtue of the primary conditions of sensate experience, which, as we just saw, are ecstatic. They are, we might say, vital pleasures—painful pleasures that are taken in the sheer vitality of life—though ultimately the labels 'pleasure' and 'pain' are too impoverished to capture the experience that Bernays is seeking to name. That is perhaps best described as the ecstasy of sensation and feeling *simpliciter*.

---

[24] Bernays (1970 [1857]: 43/175).

[25] 'Catharsis emerges as a broadly conceived universal, one that is congenial to both ancient and modern poetry' (Bernays 1970 [1857]: 43/175).

[26] Bernays (1970 [1857]: 43/175).

[27] Bernays (1970 [1857]: 32/164). The phrase κίνησις τῶν παθῶν is a calque on Aristotle's κίνησις τῆς ψυχῆς (Aristotle, *Rhetoric* 1.11, 1369^b33–4; Aristotle, *Politics* 8.6.1337^b42, 8.7.1342^a8: pity and fear are *kinēseis*; etc.): it derives from Proclus' discussion of catharsis in Proclus, *Commentary on Plato's Republic* (1:42.14 Kroll).

[28] Bernays (1970 [1857]: 38/170).

[29] Bernays (1970 [1857]: 44/176, emphasis added).

According to Bernays, any experience I have is bound to be both painful and pleasurable—painful in that it disturbs me within, pleasurable in that it opens my world to a richer world beyond, though I could as easily describe things in the opposite way. I am simultaneously disturbed and expanded, and the one because the other. Such is the nature of ecstasy. 'Every affection, because it contains an ecstatic element, also contains a hedonic element, however painful the object that elicits it may appear to be.'[30] Temporarily thrown out of my normal state of equilibrium by the (ecstatic) experience of being affected from without, I eventually return to myself. There is a pleasure to this return, which Bernays calls an assuagement (*Erleichterung, Beschwichtigung*) of the original and painful disturbance.[31] The effects of discharge persist as a feeling of painful–pleasurable release (rather than relief).[32] What is more, there is a pleasure to be found in the very sources of pain.[33] Finally, though equilibrium is regained, it is wrong to imagine that the subject is restored to the same state as that in which she started out. The subject is permanently altered, not restored; and that alteration is neither a moral one 'nor is it even a return to a normal condition'.[34] Involved is, rather, an *expansion* in the subject's perceptual awareness, one that exhibits 'intrinsic purposiveness' and obeys no extrinsic teleologies. It describes what a human creature does in virtue of its nature whenever it undergoes an affection that originates from within or without.[35] And such an expansion is unquestionably valuable; it is repeatedly sought after; and it puts a subject in touch with the largest (most heightened) dimensions of reality.

Bernays is at once basing his theory on Aristotle while also elaborating freely on his view of pleasure and pain. Pleasure, Bernays says, 'depends upon a sudden disturbance [*eine plötzliche Erschütterung* ("jarring, convulsing")] and [a] restoration of psychic equilibrium

---

[30] Bernays (1970 [1857]: 46/178).

[31] Bernays (1970 [1857]: 11/143; 44/176).

[32] Bernays (1970 [1857]: 11/143): momentary *Erleichterung* is 'intrinsically unhedonic'.

[33] Cf. Bernays (1970 [1857]: 41/173): 'a reveling ["voluptuous ecstasy"] in things being torn apart and in the act of disruption itself [*eine Wollust des Zerreissens und der Zerrissenheit*], an ecstatic despair...'. Contrast Schelling, *Philosophie der Kunst* (1985: ii. 525), which typifies German Idealism's posture on the problem: 'nicht zerrissen, sondern geheilt, und wie Aristoteles sagt, gereingt.'

[34] Bernays (1970 [1857]: 11/143).

[35] 'A *pathos* ... designates the unexpected and momentary outbreak of an affection [*Affekt*]' (Bernays 1970 [1857]: 17/149).

[*Gleichgewicht*]',[36] and the process occurs whenever a force within the soul (or mind) 'erupts for brief moments in pleasurable shuddering [*lustvolles Schaudern*]'.[37] Bernays has introduced the notion of 'pleasurable shuddering' into Aristotle's account.[38] Departing still further from Aristotle, he adds that the experience described is an ecstatic one, and, to the degree that it provides a powerful discharge and release for the experiencing subject, it is also cathartic—a term that Bernays nowhere defines independently of this ecstatic process, which describes 'the general, pathological [form of] catharsis'.[39]

Ecstatic pleasure is for Bernays the primary and predominant state of all affections. Hence, such pleasure describes the primary condition of the human soul in both a tendential and a normative sense: the soul strives to attain the purest form of pleasure, which, according to Aristotle, is available only to God in his unprecedented 'self-sufficiency [*Selbstgenügen*] and self-satisfaction [*Selbstgenuss*]'.[40] Pain, by contrast, has one basic function in Bernays's eyes: it serves to heighten the excitement one ordinarily and ultimately feels in the face of the world.[41] A strong thread of optimism and affirmation towards the self

---

[36] Bernays (1970 [1857]: 46/178).   [37] Bernays (1970 [1857]: 52/184).

[38] The account is borrowed from Aristotle, *Rhetoric* (1.11, 1369^{b}33–5), which is partially translated at Bernays (1970 [1857]: 46/178). For Aristotle, the sudden psychic disturbance is a source of pain, not pleasure. Bernays may be conflating this account from the *Rhetoric* with the account from the *Poetics*. Cf. *phrittein* (Aristotle, *Poetics* 14, 1453^{b}5), translated as *Schaudern* at Bernays (1970 [1857]: 50/182).

[39] Bernays (1970 [1857]: 45/177). The closest that Bernays comes to providing a focused definition of catharsis is in his comment that 'the catharsis of tragedy, correctly understood, designates nothing other than an effect that is indissolubly linked to intrinsic purposiveness' (Bernays 1970 [1857]: 42/174), which brings us back to the natural teleologies of emotion.

[40] Bernays (1970 [1857]: 48/180). Bernays adds the Greek term *autarkeia* in parentheses. He appears to be combining two discussions: Aristotle, *Metaphysics* 12, chs 7–9 (on God's autarkic pleasure) and Aristotle, *Magna Moralia* 2.15, 1212^{b}38–9 (God possesses all goods and is self-sufficing). Very likely, his thought here is that God's pleasure is intrinsic but not ecstatic (and hence, too, not painful), while individuals are driven outside themselves into the arms of a pleasure that at best appears to have a divine sanction, but that they can only ever experience in the form of (or combined with) pain.

[41] Analogously, for Lessing fear intensifies pity (fellow-feeling) (Lessing (1985: vi. 559, §75): 'gleichsam zur Reife bringe'), though Bernays drives the discussion down to a more primitive and general level of painful and pleasurable sensations. For the same reason, 'discharge' does not involve 'a transformation [*Verwandlung*] of pain into pleasure' (the term is Lessing's: Bernays (1970 [1857]: 6/138, 30/162), quoting Lessing (1985: vi. 574, §78); cf. Bernays (1970 [1857]: 12/144): 'nicht zu verwandlen'), which would yield a purely 'hedonic' reading of catharsis, a reading that Bernays roundly

and the world runs Bernays's vision of human psychology. But there is more than a hint of the same in Aristotle's ethical and psychological theory.[42] Bernays is considering the feelings of pain and pleasure as they relate to the most vital functions of a living creature, whose stance towards the world is fundamentally ecstatic. At the most primary level of experience, and of life itself, pleasure and pain name the experience that a subject undergoes when she is exposed to an outer sensation, registers its surroundings, and 'erupts' in a feeling of psychic intensity. There is a suddenness to these events. They come and go like a squall. Were they to endure any longer, ecstasy would not occur. Occurring as briefly as do, the experience is all that much more intense.

Bernays calls these experiences 'primary affections': they are instances of an *Urpathos*.[43] They are also said to be 'objectless'. Directed to nothing in particular but available to everyone in general, an *Urpathos* is a universal affection that enjoys 'the objectlessness of pure ecstasy', whereby 'objectlessness' (*Objektlosigkeit*) is to be understood in the widest possible sense: in such conditions, what is sensed is not this or that object, but only the experience of being affected itself—one experiences sentience, pure and simple. Primordial affection is the basic condition of sentience and of the general receptiveness to the outside world that is universally had by all sensate subjects: it is the shocking pleasure one takes in the mere state of being affected, which is to say, in the sheer experience of experience. For the same reasons, the idea of 'primordial *pathos*' is intended to cover emotions in their universal (generic) character—not qua determinate emotions, but rather qua a fundamental stirring within.[44] What these describe are the motions of the emotions, insofar as these resonate with 'the lively power of movement in the universe at large'.[45] This last concept is vaguely Aristotelian, but it ultimately points in some other direction, as we shall see. And in fact, in generalizing 'the

---

rejects (Bernays 1970 [1857]: 9/141; 11/143, quoted earlier). See also Bernays (1880 [1853]: 143): a 'blend of pleasure and pain.'

[42] This is not well noticed, but see Broadie (1991), 329; 353: 'pleasure is a dimension of vital activity as such' and 'a kind of affirmation'. Also Porter (2010: 50–6), where I label this a broadly aesthetic stance in which the emphasis is on affirmation and intensity of focus and attention to the inner objects of experience rather than on pleasure *per se*.

[43] Bernays (1970 [1857]: 44/176).   [44] Bernays (1970 [1857]: 45/177).

[45] Bernays (1970 [1857]: 47/179).

possibility of a similar cathartic treatment *for all other movements of the mind*,[46] Bernays is clearly overreaching the authority of Aristotle that he claims in order to license his reading of 'the universality of catharsis'.[47] Nevertheless, it is mainly in his creative reading, not in his exegesis of Aristotle, that Bernays's theory is of interest to us here.

Every experience, Bernays claims, begins with this kind of undirected and objectless focus before it turns into a determinate affection. Indeed, it is the very precondition of a *pathos* that it should first pass through this stage before being transferred onto determinate objects.[48] And, while purely ecstatic events like these are commonplace in the world of the senses, attending to them is not. What gives such experiences their power is the form of attention they command. It is in lingering on the threshold of indeterminacy that the responses of the subject are at their most vehement: at such moments, objectlessness is made into an object in its own right.[49] The popular imagination (Bernays reasons) attributed holy, religious connotations to such states of mind (these were called instances of ecstatic *katharsis*);[50] the philosophical imagination sought rational explanations in medical analogues to orgiastic phenomena, what Bernays calls somatic *katharsis*,[51] while beneath the first but not the second form of catharsis lay the more primary phenomenon just described.[52] Philosophers also saw a potential for discovering universal emotions in the tragic genre.[53] And Bernays, in turn, is taking the philosophical account a stage further by offering an explanation of how one should characterize these universal phenomena prior to their insertion into one context or another. In short, catharsis is nothing other than the (ecstatic) pleasure of sensible

---

[46] Bernays (1970 [1857]: 9/141).   [47] Bernays (1970 [1857]: 43/175).

[48] 'The primary form of *pathos* [*Urpathos*] that is bound up with *no* object at all . . . must also allow itself to be successfully transferred onto a *pathos* that is kindled by [a] determinate object' if the ecstatic process in cases of conditioned experiences is to succeed at all (Bernays 1970 [1857]: 44/176).

[49] It is here that 'we find the most violent of all ecstatic manifestations' (Bernays 1970 [1857]: 44/176).

[50] Scholars today include under this category 'musical catharsis', though the term is not Aristotle's, nor is it Bernays's.

[51] Bernays (1970 [1857]: 44/176).

[52] The somatic model is adduced for being historically relevant (inasmuch as it was used in antiquity to help account for the primary *pathos*), but it is theoretically irrelevant to Bernays's theory: it is at most an incomplete if interesting parallel, in part because Bernays is looking at psychological phenomena, but also because somatic catharsis is a form of purgation, while the ecstatic and tragic forms of catharsis are not.

[53] Bernays (1970 [1857]: 47/179).

experience, pure and simple, a pleasure that is to be found in every encounter with the world that we have, regardless of the object, though obviously some pleasures will be more powerful than others. Simply to attend to such effects is to enhance the pleasure they yield.

2. TRAGIC CATHARSIS

Tragic catharsis is a species of this *Urpathos*, existing alongside two other forms of catharsis, ecstatic and somatic catharsis—though somatic catharsis has to be deemed either an incomplete form of the *Urpathos* or else an experience that merely resembles it in some but not in all respects.[54] Tragic catharsis represents a later development, genetically speaking, and an aestheticization and ennobling (cf. *veredelte*[55]), of a more primary form of experience, which is to say, of both the *Urpathos* and its 'Bacchic' expressions. But it is also a return to this *Urpathos* in its primordial and universal character. Tragedy's cathartic power resides exactly in its capacity to deliver an *Urpathos* to the spectator—that is, in its capacity to induce, or simply to heighten, this state in her.

In tragedy, viewers are put in touch with a universal humanity (*d[ie] Urform des allgemein menschlichen Charakters*) in a particularly jarring way, through identification with the sufferings of others. While the experience is painful, the very process of identification, facilitated by fellow-feeling (*sympatheia*), serves to assuage and then diminish the viewer's pain, and it opens the way to pleasurable release—not to a self-regarding form of pleasure (for example, mere self-satisfaction), but to a release that stems from self-dissolution. Pity eliminates the particularity of the affection and ensures its universality: the viewer steps out of herself and enters into another—or better, another's—condition altogether.[56] Here,

---

[54] Bernays (1970 [1857]: 47/179).

[55] Bernays (1970 [1857]: 47/179). This is the immediate point of access to the *Urpathos* that was also the proximate object of ecstatic catharsis (the 'representation of universal and human destiny', which is to say the condition of the universe and of mankind as these are experienced at any given time (Bernays 1970 [1857]: 47/179)). It is here that Bernays finds the genetic link between tragic and ecstatic catharsis to be revealed.

[56] Bernays (1970 [1857]: 49–50/181–2).

the protective boundaries of the self are breached and larger psychic unities are formed as the psyche expands to take in more of the world than it originally did.[57]

Tragic catharsis returns the tragic subject to the primordial condition of experience *tout court*. Tragedy renders a subject directly capable of an expanded sensation—that is, capable of participating in the ecstatic nature of the 'primary *pathos*'. This latter is the true source and power of tragic catharsis. For it is the very same 'shuddering' that tragedy unleashes that is present '[in] *any* intense physical or mental pleasure'.[58]

Consequently, tragedy can claim no special privileges: it is not the only, nor even necessarily the most efficacious, form of ecstatic perception. Tragedy merely exposes the nature of the affections and emotions in their primary form, albeit in a particularly visible way. It is in approaching a general *Urpathos* and a kind of universal affection (the original form of pure ecstasy that lacks any concrete object) that tragedy achieves its catharsis. For the same reason, tragedy's effects are not, strictly speaking, aesthetic. Aristotle, after all, arrived at his insight into pity and fear 'independently of aesthetic theory'. That is, he took a 'pathological' approach to these two emotions and glimpsed their deepest nature, which is to say, he recognized that they were both 'supremely universal and ecstatic–hedonic emotions' capable of releasing the soul to the universe and of surrendering it, trembling, to 'the tumultuous chaos of strange and threatening things'.[59] In this way, Bernays gives the inherited theory of catharsis a universal character. Any affection contains an ecstatic element and an element of pleasure ('the hedonic element in every affection').[60] This pleasure is essentially ecstatic and cathartic, which is to say it forces an *expansion of the personality* by virtue of its contact with the self, quite literally *driving the self out of itself*, and exposing it to the source of sensate experience and to the world at large. Medicine has no explanatory value here, while tragedy is only of secondary interest. Far from being a reductionist, Bernays is in fact an anti-reductionist

---

[57] One wonders whether Freud had any of this in mind in, say, *Beyond the Pleasure Principle*, which operates on the same speculative principles of psychic breaching. On some of the more immediate points of contact between Bernays's and Freud's theories, see Treml (1997) and Gödde (2009).

[58] Bernays (1970 [1857]: 50/182, emphasis added).

[59] Bernays (1970 [1857]: 48–9/180–1).   [60] Bernays (1970 [1857]: 46/178).

and an *expansionist*: for him, catharsis is a primary fact of sensation that is available to everyone, but also one that leads to a heightened sense of reality.

3. CATHARSIS BEYOND THE MEDICAL MODEL

There is a social contingency to this process that I will touch on momentarily. But also, the entire process describes an ethical (*sittlich*) and psychological (*psychisch*) rather than moral (*moralisch*) form of self-cultivation, one that aims to create an enlarged sense of the self.[61] This is in fact the ultimate direction that Bernays's theory takes, for it is in virtue of this deepest capacity to be moved and affected and to attain a heightened sense of reality that humanity shares a common ground of experience. Such an experience is by definition not limited to pathological individuals (they are not 'aberrant', or rather 'degenerate' (*entartete*) individuals[62]), as Bernays's theory is still imagined to have restricted itself:[63] catharsis and ecstasy are an essential element of *all* human experience—and consequently of all feeling and emotion, which in turn have no proper object. They have no such object, because in Bernays's generous view of things the motions and emotions of the soul are 'universal' and can be so conceived only if they are not limited to any particular object. This is not to say that the emotions in their primary character cannot attach themselves to objects. It simply means that a multitude—in Bernays's words, a 'sheer abundance [*Häufigkeit*]'—of objects can and do fulfil this function.[64] That they do proves the universality of catharsis all over again: such affections 'repeatedly flare up around the most diverse objects, and therefore *are present in every normal human nature* as

---

[61] Bernays (1880 [1859]: 127; 131); Bernays (1970 [1857]: 7/139, 45/177): 'sittliche Stimmung (ethische)' ('his most cherished psychological and ethical principles'); Bernays (1970 [1857]: 52/184): *hamartia* is a sign of 'sittliche Schuld', not evil. Cf. Goethe's *Nachlese* (1999 [1827]: 337).

[62] Bernays (1970 [1857]: 52/184).

[63] See Bernays (1970 [1857]: 47/179): 'the ordinary spectator in the audience'; 42/174: 'any spectator who is endowed with a natural constitution'; 48/180: 'even the most ordinary spectator'; 52/184: 'not an aberrant [or "degenerate": *entartet*] individual.' Contemporary scholars tend to prefer this kind of inclusivity (e.g., Lear 1992: 317; Halliwell 2003: 506; 2012: 245), while objecting (wrongly) to Bernays's failure to do the same.

[64] Bernays (1970 [1857]: 47/179).

affections [and] are ready to erupt at any time, simply because *they belong to the constitution of human beings generally*'.[65]

Catharsis affects the whole person as a whole and in the core of her being. Hence, 'the proper object' of catharsis is 'not the pathological matter, but the individual who has been thrown off-balance'.[66] It is 'referred to the person' (*der Mensch*)[67] and the unfolding of her potentialities—that is, to 'any spectator [and, indeed, any subject generally] who is endowed with a natural constitution'.[68] But then, in this view the object is really not an object: it is merely the subject of the experience itself. We might call this the 'inner object' of catharsis, which captures its intrinsic value for Bernays. For all these reasons, catharsis, whenever it occurs, invariably approaches 'the objectlessness of pure ecstasy'.[69]

Bernays arrives at this view by reaffirming a version of Aristotle's theory of natural ends, which looks for final ends within the 'immanent teleology' that is displayed in both nature and art. A process of this kind 'feeds on its own flame'[70] and unfolds 'all by itself' (*von selbst*).[71] For, in the final analysis, catharsis (in any form), whether it occurs in the everyday traffic with objects of experience or in more specialized settings (ritual or tragic), is a means to a much larger end. It maps the shattering of the self's boundaries—through a diffuse and swarming apprehension or intuition (*Ahnung*) rather than fear. It is objectless for this exact reason: its source and cause elude conceptualization. Additionally, fear does not transpire in the face of singular things: it 'can never be aroused directly or through a [lifeless] thing',[72] but only by means of (the image of) another subject. It is a mirroring of the self in another. More precisely, it is the mirroring in one's own *pathos* of another's *pathos*.

Catharsis brings about a universalization of the self as the self expands (*erweitert*) in two distinct ways: first, through *ek-stasis* (by being 'placed outside itself' (*ausser sich gesetzt*)[73]), and then by an identification with 'the whole of humanity' (*die ganze Menschheit*).[74]

---

[65] Bernays (1970 [1857]: 47/179, emphasis added).

[66] Bernays (1970 [1857]: 13/145). Contrast Barnes's translation (Bernays 2006: 167), which prejudicially offers '*morbid* matter' and 'the *unbalanced* man'). Cf. Bernays (1970 [1857]: 44/176): 'equilibrium is restored after it has been [*momentarily*] lost.'

[67] Bernays (1970 [1857]: 17/149).

[68] Bernays (1970 [1857]: 42/174).

[69] Bernays (1970 [1857]: 42/173).

[70] Bernays (1970 [1857]: 44/176).

[71] Bernays (1970 [1857]: 50/182).

[72] Bernays (1970 [1857]: 49/181).

[73] Bernays (1970 [1857]: 44/176).

[74] Bernays (1970 [1857]: 50/182).

Indeed, simply to undergo the one is to undergo the other: ecstasy is an 'excitation of universal human affections', which are experienced at the deepest level, that of 'the primordial form [*Urform*] of the universally human character', which is to say, that of an *Urpathos* (Bernays's term).[75] In tragedy, this last stage is achieved by reaching out to others through identification *via* pity, and then by 'recogniz-[ing] [one's] position vis-à-vis the universe'[76] as the self 'stands face to face with the frightfully sublime [*furchtbar erhabene*] laws of the universe and its . . . incomprehensible power'.[77] This vision of the universe, which is in principle available to all forms of cathartic ecstasy, produces not fear (φοβεῖσθαι) but trembling (or shuddering: *Schauder*, φρίττειν) and shock (*Erschütterung*), which releases pleasure (*Lust*).[78] The language recalls Longinus, Lucretius, and Kant, and with good reason. Bernays's theory of *katharsis* is a theory of the ecstatic sublime, a theory that in its own way participates in the ecstasy that it describes.[79]

4. FROM CATHARSIS TO THE SUBLIME

We have come a long way from the medical, pathological reading, and from Aristotle too. If we have left the medical and pathological reading behind, it is in good part because we have passed through Kant, as Bernays's language betrays. The final pages of his 1857 essay are sprinkled with Kantianisms. Kant too talks about the feeling of sublimity that comes from the expansion (*Erweiterung*) of the mind in the face of the idea of an absolute whole, with its attendant mixture of displeasurable and pleasurable sensations, not to mention the language of frightful sublimity, loss of self, and unfathomable power.[80] Tragedy

[75] Bernays (1970 [1857]: 47/179; 49/181).

[76] Bernays (1970 [1857]: 52/184).

[77] Bernays (1970 [1857]: 50/182). Hence, too, Bernays can speak of 'an awareness that comes neither by observing individual actions nor through conceptual understanding, but from intuition alone' (Bernays 1970 [1857]: 52/184).

[78] Bernays (1970 [1857]: 50/182).

[79] Longinus, *On the Sublime* 1.4, 35.3; Lucretius, *On the Nature of Things* 3.29–30. The partnering of Longinus, Lucretius, Kant, and the sublime is a natural one (Porter 2007 and Porter 2015).

[80] The correspondences in phrasing between *The Critique of Judgment* and Bernays are surprisingly exact, but too many to name here. Bernays knew Kant at first

for Bernays leaves one with a *feeling*,[81] not with an understanding or cognition—a mere (if baffled) intuition (*blosse Anschauung*) that is had in the face of the overwhelming universe itself.[82] At once fleeting and affecting, the experience is a powerful, (all-too) human, even plebeian,[83] glimpse of it all, indeed of *das All*.[84] From here, or rather in the same breath, Bernays's language passes into a form of life-affirming hedonism: the glimpse of the universe, for all its terrors and oppressiveness, 'is at the same time a source of unrivalled and unadulterated pleasure'.[85] The reason is self-evident: the experience describes a vital

hand (Bernays (1880 [1853]: 184); letter to P. Heyse from 4 February 1854 in Calder and Günther (2010: 101). A further overlay is Goethe, whose *Faust* pt. 1 ('Studierzimmer'), ll. 1764–74, is seemingly quoted by Bernays, above all: 'Und was *der ganzen Menschheit* zugeteilt ist, | Will ich in meinem Selbst genießen [cf. Bernays on God's *Selbstgenuss*: Bernays (1970 [1857]: 48/180)] . . . | *Und so mein eigen Selbst zu ihrem Selbst erweitern* [where Bernays writes, "*das eigene Selbst zum Selbst der ganzen Menschheit erweitert*"].'

[81] And an 'immediate' one at that. Immediacy further guarantees universality, for 'everyone' (Bernays 1970 [1857]: 39/171).

[82] Bernays (1970 [1857]: 52/184).

[83] Cf. 'the ordinary spectator in the audience, endowed with the simple capacity to feel' (Bernays 1970 [1857]: 47/179); contrast the 'nobler spirits' who turn to philosophy and religion, 52/184. Cf. 7/139: 'present in all people' (*in allen Menschen vorhanden*); 'in everyone' (*bei Allen*); etc. The momentary emphasis, in both Bernays and Aristotle, on the *pathētikos*, or someone who is constitutionally predisposed to an affection such as pity and fear (17/149), is qualified and ultimately erased by these generalizations. (For one thing, everyone is predisposed to such emotions.) Bernays is quoting from Aristotle, *Politics* 8.7, 1342ᵃ4–6: 'For, any emotion that strongly affects the souls of some (for example, pity and fear) is present in everyone'; *Politics* 8.7, 1342ᵃ14: 'everyone gets a kind of *katharsis*.'

[84] Bernays (1970 [1857]: 50/182).

[85] Bernays (1970 [1857]: 50/182). The actual source, or sources, of Bernays's affirmative stance remains a mystery, though I suspect that Aristotle may be a significant contributor, as I mentioned earlier. Kant and Schiller are also good candidates. In 'Über die Tragische Kunst', Schiller speaks in Kantian overtones of the value of a 'Lebensphilosophie' in which the self is extinguished by the 'sublime' prospect of a larger universe and its 'universal laws' (Schiller 1943–: xx. 151; cf. Bernays 1970 [1857]: 52/184: the universe and 'its mysterious laws'). Spinoza is another possible candidate. See Bernays (1885: ii. 342–50), an essay from 1850 on Spinoza's views about Hebrew grammar and the way they bear on his ethical system; also his correspondence in Calder and Günther (2010: 71), etc.; Egger (1883: 38). The oppressiveness of the universe's dimly sensed logic—'die von dorther auf ihn [sc., the subject of the catharsis] drückende Empfindung' (Bernays(1970 [1857]: 52/184); 'die Gewalt des von aussen her die Persönlichkeit gleichsam zusammendrückend . . . Objects' (Bernays 1970 [1857]: 46/178); 'die Menschheit umfassenden unbegreiflichen Macht' (Bernays 1970 [1857]: 50/182); this is the meaning behind 'ein Beklommener' (Bernays 1970 [1857]: 12/144): a person oppressed or overcome with anxiety—recalls Goethe's essay on catharsis: 'durch eine dustere Heftigkeit [des] Daseins'; 'den ewig

sensation, one that produces a heightened sense of one's own reality. That is the ultimate criterion of what a *pathos* is and does.[86]

By the end of his treatise it might seem that Bernays has come dangerously close to adopting his own version of abstruse, quasi-transcendent metaphysics and a higher purpose. Nevertheless, his conclusions are consistent with his starting premisses: he has indeed come full circle, albeit in a surprising way. His initial purpose was to descend to an empirical level and to reject 'the heaven of Ideas' and 'all forms of febrile spirituality'[87] as not only un-Aristotelian but also as un-Greek. With both phrases Bernays is taking a swipe at Platonism,[88] while simultaneously presenting his contemporaries with a provocative challenge. True, the self that emerges from Bernays's account of tragic and all other forms of cathartic ecstasy is one that is ready to acquire (or reaffirm) an ethical disposition and to undergo spiritual reflection of the highest order.[89] But his theory remains what it always was—namely, committed to the *logic of human reality* and 'empirical principles [that] were drawn up under the *quiet* assumption of a "higher reason"'.[90]

If Bernays has gone astray, it is not in his surrendering to any kind of spiritualism but only in his being too much a creature of his times—too modern a reader of tragedy and of Aristotle, and too

---

unerforschlichen, unbegreiflich folgerechten Gewalten' (Goethe 1999 [1827]: 336–7). Similarly, Grillparzer (1964 [1820]: 301), in a discussion of catharsis: 'einen uns unbegreiflichen Zusammenhang', etc.

[86] Cf. Lessing (1985: iii. 711, letter to Moses Mendelssohn from 1757): the most intense of our passions, 'even the most unpleasant', are the means by which we become 'aware, to a greater extent, of our reality [*daß wir uns eines größeren Grads unserer Realität bewußt sind]*', an awareness that 'cannot help be anything but enjoyable'. That is why, for Lessing, tragic affections resolve into fellow-feeling (Lessing 1985: iii. 711). Bernays would agree with everything but this last qualification.

[87] Bernays (1970 [1857]: 12/144).

[88] A steady but little noticed undercurrent in Bernays's essay is the contrast between Aristotelianism, which he favours, and Platonism, which he rejects and which is in evidence here too: 'Ideas', 'spirituality'; cf. 'spiritual effusiveness' (Bernays 1970 [1857]: 28/160); 'the Platonic striving towards sheer spiritualization' (33/165); 'the ascetic subjection of the sensuous impulses' (38/170); contrast Aristotle's spurning of asceticism (12/144), and his countertendency 'to render humanity human' (33/165).

[89] Cf. Bernays (1970 [1857]: 9/141): once the storm of ecstasy has passed, the self achieves (rather than returns to) 'a more reflective mood' ('einer besonnenern Stimmung'). Further, 45/177: catharsis, as Bernays understands it, would have been coherent with '[Aristotle's] ethical principles'.

[90] Bernays (1970 [1857]: 51/183).

enthusiastic an adherent of contemporary thought, as many of his
contemporaries never tired of complaining.[91] In one respect, however, he could be blamed for not being modern enough. For, in
conducting a private dialogue with Lessing and Goethe, Bernays
ignores, as though it had never occurred, the mountain of scholarship
that had risen in between,[92] most notably an essay from 1848 by the
fellow classicist Heinrich Weil ('On the Effects of Tragedy according
to Aristotle'). At first glance, the two essays share an embarrassing
amount in common, from their titles and language to their findings.
For Weil, catharsis has an effect that is 'similar to a purgative', and
hence tragedy cannot serve as 'a school of morals'.[93] As it turns out,
the coincidences have another explanation. Far from innovating in
this reading of catharsis, Weil is merely reviving it.[94] He was only one
of many classical scholars since the Renaissance who anticipated the
quasi-medical and pathological reading of catharsis for which Bernays would later be given credit (Milton is another example). Bernays
was, of course, well aware of the Renaissance tradition (though not,
apparently, of Weil's short and rather obscurely placed essay),[95] but
then he had more in mind than medical analogies. Nor is this all,
for Weil mentions the sublime turn that Bernays would later take—
and severely critiques it as misguided. It appears that Bernays's
vision of catharsis as sublime was already a commonplace by 1848.
Here is Weil:

> A little later in Germany, Kant and Schiller's ideas were adapted to
> Aristotle and grasped under the undefined label of *catharsis*. The
> purifying power of tragedy now lay in the sublime: fear and pity stir

---

[91] Spengel (1859: 12, 37) calls Bernays too 'modern' and anachronistic in his
methods (cf. Spengel 1859: 46).

[92] The exceptions include a commentary on Aristotle's *Politics* 7–8 by Friedrich
Wolfgang Reiz (1776), a history of Greek aesthetics by Eduard Müller (1834–37), and
a passing mention of Hermann.

[93] Weil (1848: 139): 'eines Purgativs ähnlich'; 133: 'wodurch die Tragödie zu einer
Schule der Moral würde.' Bernays's description of tragedy as 'a moral house of
correction' (*ein moralisches Correctionshaus*) and 'a moral institution' (*eine moralische Veranstaltung*) may recall Weil's 'school of morals'. But it more closely recalls
Stahr (1840: 574) (*Correctionshaus*) and Grillparzer (1964 [1820]: 303) (*Korrektion-
shaus*; *Trivialschule für Unmündige*), and a lecture title by Schiller from 1784 ('Die
Schaubühne als eine moralische Anstalt betrachtet', printed in Schiller (1838:
x. 69–81).

[94] For a convenient summary of Renaissance predecessors, see Bywater (1900).

[95] Bernays (1970 [1857]: 10/142, 60/192 n. 7), on the Renaissance tradition;
Bernays (1880 [1859]: 119–21 n.), on Weil.

us, to be sure, but they cannot get the better of us. They can no longer overwhelm and suppress us once we have been steeled by the influence of the sublime. This would be all well and good if only the slightest trace of such a conception were to be found in Aristotle. But even if he said nothing of the kind, surely he must have had something like this in mind and wanted to say it. He merely expressed himself badly. What Aristotle *thought* is that tragedy purifies us through the sublime; what he *said* is 'through pity and fear'—he obviously misspoke.[96]

Weil is only slightly parodying an interpretative line among earlier and contemporary philosophers of art (he names 'Solger, Bohtz, Vischer, and others') that he felt could be traced back to an earlier piece of classical scholarship—namely, Gottfried Hermann's edition of the *Poetics* from 1802, which actually says what Weil claims it says:

> Aristotle misidentified the cause [of catharsis] because he says that tragedy 'achieves, through pity and fear, the catharsis of such emotions as these'. For this sort of purgation (*purgatio*) of the soul is accomplished *not through pity and fear, but through sublimity*, which, of all the topics that Aristotle ought most to have discussed in his definition of tragedy, he touched on least of all.[97]

Even if Bernays did not know about Weil's essay (he pleads ignorance in an addendum from two years later),[98] his failure to mention Hermann's theory of catharsis is striking but not inexplicable.[99] Hermann devoted a section to the sublime, dotting it with references to Kant.[100] But the thinking is mechanical and uninspired, while the argument is vague: Kant is Hermann's badge of modernity and of his being theoretically *au courant* but little more; and Hermann at most treated the sublime as a way of *shielding* the viewer from the effects of tragedy.[101] Bernays's omission of Hermann is excusable: he goes off

---

[96] Weil (1848: 134–5).

[97] Hermann (1802: 115; emphasis added; cf. 149–50; 247–8, 257): tragedy requires sublime, uplifting action. Hermann is named by Weil on p. 135 n. 9; his successors are named on p. 135 at n. 11.

[98] Bernays (1880 [1859]: 119–21 n.), charging his critics with having committed the same 'sin' of omission, one that Weil himself had to bring to light (Weil 1859).

[99] Hermann's edition was of course familiar to him; see Bernays (1970 [1857]: 54/186), where it is fleetingly mentioned, in a more technical, not aesthetic, context.

[100] Hermann (1802: 202–7), a section entitled 'De sublimitate', though sublimity features elsewhere in his commentary.

[101] On Hermann's familiarity with Kant, see most recently Couturier-Heinrich (2011).

in another direction, which is in ways more Schillerian than Kantian, though in other respects the contrasts with Schiller are more salient and instructive than the similarities.

Bernays's omission of Weil was another story: here the overlaps were undeniable. Nonetheless, even if Bernays had known about Weil's essay, this would have changed nothing, as he himself recognized in a belated acknowledgement from 1859. Defiant and entrenched, he was fully aware of how much more his theory of catharsis had to offer beyond the medical approach, especially in the final sections of his work. Accordingly, a 'coincidence' (*Zusammentreffen*) of views with Weil could be predicated 'only of the first two sections of my essay'— the only sections that attracted any real notoriety: sections III and IV went off in a different direction altogether.[102] Another important predecessor is K. O. Müller's commentary on the *Eumenides* from 1833, which sketches out a view of Greek tragedy as aesthetically sublime owing precisely to its foundation in Dionysian catharsis (understood as intensification, purification, and removal: *läutern und erheben, befreien*), and ultimately appeals to the ever-cheerful (*heiter*), composed, and sublime 'eternal powers' above, the Olympians, whose demeanour provides a higher, moral sanction to human suffering.[103] In effect, Müller gives a ritualistic spin to Lessing, but he makes only two glancing references to Aristotle. Bernays may have known Müller's work, but he does not mention it, and it is not clear that he needed it. Nietzsche drew heavily on Müller, but for all his interest in orgiastic excesses he stood closer to Bernays in his view of tragic discharge (*Entladung*) as a deeply psychological and existential process (*On the Birth of Tragedy*, §§6–8, 22). Schiller is Bernays's most proximate forerunner. Yet the differences are more telling than the similarities. Focusing on the former will help us flesh out the rest of Bernays's theory.

5. CULTURAL CONTINGENCIES OF CATHARSIS

For both Bernays and Schiller, tragic catharsis is a crucial element in the constitution of the self, that is, in any account of how the self

---

[102] Bernays (1880 [1859]: 121 n.).
[103] Müller (1833: 108, 136, 138, 180, 190–2).

finally and fully comes to be. But, for Schiller, modern tragedy can achieve a height that no ancient experience could match, thanks to its grasp of a 'purer stuff' by way of a 'purified', almost cathartically heightened, philosophy. Schiller's view is ultimately teleological and moral.[104] Bernays knows nothing of the kind. First of all, his Greeks (philosophers aside) are not exemplars of humanity: they are historically bound creatures and are cast in a rather unflattering light. They look forward to Nietzsche's Dionysian Greeks more than to Goethe's or Hegel's classically composed and balanced natures, though at bottom they nothing more than common individuals 'endowed with the simple capacity to feel'.[105]

Secondly, catharsis obtains under cultural pressures and it responds to cultural objects, above all to cultural shifts. The cathartic quality of Euripidean tragedy—for Bernays, the most tragic and most cathartic of the canonical three—is a reflex of Euripides' *own* modernity, or rather of his awkward straddling of two worlds: what Athenians pitied and feared on the Euripidean stage was nothing less than a 'fellow-suffering' (*Mitleid*) they shared 'in the face of the collapse of the old world' and 'a delicious fear and shuddering at the prospect of a fast-approaching new age' (*der neuen Zeit*), and indeed at the onset of a new modernity (*Neuzeit*). This cathartic shift to a new age is not one that Bernays laments, unlike Nietzsche, because it describes an enabling, positive response (the birth pangs of a new cultural order), nor is it one whose rebirth he clamours for. Bernays's Euripides, like Nietzsche's later on, is a transitional figure who sits on the cusp between antiquity and modernity. He is a cauldron of passions; he overwhelms, by overpowering, the very idea of morality, blotting it out in a fit of cathartic release: the most

---

[104] 'Über die tragische Kunst, in Schiller (1943–: xx. 157; cf. xx. 151): only advanced, modern, and philosophically adept spirits are susceptible to the highest form of spiritual *ekstasis*. Cf. 'Über das Pathetische', in Schiller (1943–: xx. 196–220, esp. 197–209); cf. p. 201: 'the sublime originates [not in bare passion, but] only in reason'.

[105] See n. 83 above. But note how Bernays anticipates Nietzsche's concept of Apollonian illusion and its (apparent) metaphysical comforts: 'the pain that the bare fact of suffering [*auto to pathos*] can cause on its own, quite independently of the compassion that it causes, will vanish before the rapture that accompanies this stepping outside of one's self—not least because the awareness one has of the [theatrical] illusion, which is never entirely dormant, already serves to mitigate this empirical pain' (Bernays 1970 [1857]: 50/182).

tragic of the three poets, he is 'the most cathartic'[106]—another controversial reading of Aristotle, but also a slap in the face for the
German Romantics who had 'outrageously' defamed Euripides,
the way Nietzsche later would.[107]

As it turns out, catharsis is most symptomatic of such contingencies, which are man-made rather than naturally occurring (let alone
divine): 'social life, with its never-ending reversals [*Umschwunge*],
offers an all too ready supply' of objects that can cause cathartic
disturbances in the soul.[108] This too has a very different feel from
Schiller's view, which takes its cue from an ideal of human nature.
Schiller knows *some* sort of contingency, but it is not a social one. He
recognizes at most a moral evolution that takes place in the human
soul. Such change follows an inner teleology but not one that is
susceptible to the hazards of communal or social life, even if the
end results—the psychological states described by both Schiller and
Bernays and the kinds of identifications envisioned by both—appear
to be so deeply compatible with one another, at least on the surface. In
the end, Bernays's reading is empirical and particularistic rather than
universalizing, all of his many appeals to 'universal affections' not-
withstanding, while his theory of catharsis is notably free of nostalgia.

Why Bernays chose to read the Greeks as he did in 1857 is
something of a mystery, but no more so than why his contemporaries
failed to penetrate his meanings, for the most part overlooking his
culminating cultural and metaphysical theory and his far-reaching
expansion of catharsis theory, and canonizing him instead for his
pathological, medical reading of catharsis as purgation. Why a cath-
arsis-frenzy seized philology for half a century after Bernays is likewise a mystery. Classical philology underwent a veritable paroxysm as
it tried to establish its modern credentials through the lens of tragic
catharsis.[109] But why tragedy? Why did this genre attract the attention it did, as it continues to do—albeit more so outside classics than
within it, for example, in the work of Eagleton, Loraux, and Kristeva,

---

[106] Bernays (1970 [1857]: 41/173).
[107] Bernays (1970 [1857]: 41/173); see Behler (1986) for the background.
[108] Bernays (1970 [1857]: 46/179); 'nie rastenden Umschwunge' (47/179).
[109] See Stahr (1859: 28–9), where the very term 'modernity' is at stake (as it was for Bernays).

and often in conjunction with ecstasy and the sublime?[110] The last question is of particular interest, especially when we consider how any other number of aesthetic categories were and still are available: beauty, the symbolic, plastic form (sculpture), even epic.

Whatever the answers may be, we can be sure that they will be bound up with the cultural contingencies of modernity itself and with its own preconceptions about Greece, tragedy, and catharsis. Finding a way back to the Greeks in the era of secular Enlightenment was a tantalizing imperative, not least because Christianity stood in the way. Just as tragedy, and catharsis in particular, promised an immediate conduit to ancient, and indeed primordial, sensibilities in their most intense form imaginable, so too did they crystallize the issues in a way that no other genre or medium could. Lessing led the way to an enlightened view of tragedy with his *Hamburg Dramaturgy* (1767–68), which was in the first instance a critique of Christian tragedy and some of its later avatars.[111] He concluded that Christian dramas could in no way be staged ('Isn't the character of the true Christian entirely untheatrical?') and that the idea of a Christian catharsis was a contradiction in terms: Christian serenity and meekness were incompatible with tragic pity and fear.[112] Bernays largely agrees: his theory of catharsis is resolutely un-Christian. Recall how he objects to the way his contemporaries had made Greek tragedy into a 'branch and rival institute of the Church'. The concepts of evil, fate, and divine providence are for him alien to the spirit of Greek tragedy. The latter two concepts originated in the Orient, were taken on board by the Stoics, and blossomed only in modern thought.[113] Religion as a whole fares badly in Bernays's essay,[114] and instead his focus is, like Lessing's, entirely on the inner life of mankind, a perspective that he finds confirmed by Aristotelian psychology and

---

[110] Eagleton (2003: 154): 'tragedy is a blending of beauty and sublimity'; cf. p. 176; Loraux (1999: 123–37), giving catharsis a collective political twist; Kristeva (1980: 11, 22, 28, 210): catharsis reveals the sublime abject, not object, of 'the powers of horror'.

[111] Above all, Cronegk's failed *Olint and Sophronia*, a contemporary German revival of the Christian martyr play (it is set in twelfth-century Jerusalem and turns on a stolen crucifix), which Lessing savages.

[112] Lessing (1985: vi. 187–96, §§1–2).

[113] Bernays (1970 [1857]: 51/183).

[114] Compare his complaint: 'the seductive ease with which a theory of psychological excitation can slip over to the sensuous domain is plain from the history of sects of all ages and, alas, of all religions too' (Bernays 1970 [1857]: 30/162). The specific reference is to Iamblichus' 'apologetics'.

contradicted by the proto-Christian spiritualism of the Neoplaton-ists.[115] If Bernays's metaphysical indulgences appear to be ultimately secular (there is no trace of the divine in them), in other respects his vision of a hoary and inscrutable universe governed by 'mysterious laws' and meeting out rewards and punishments, albeit free of the determinations of fate, could veil a distinctively Jewish outlook, one that may well have been mediated by Spinozism.[116] Is God absent or merely hidden—and if so, why? The very uncertainty of the question suggests its own answer.[117] As a Jew in the age after Hegel, Bernays has even more reasons to adopt such a carefully aggressive stance than Lessing ever had—more reasons to adopt it, and more reasons to be discreet in doing so.[118]

The quandaries surrounding Mendelssohn's *Antigone* production in 1841 showed that these issues were still burning fiercely in the middle of the century (was Antigone a Christian martyr or a symbol of ethical agency rejecting the imperatives of the modern state?),[119] as did the demand in some quarters that 'something more and higher', capable of 'lifting [*erheben*] man beyond the world of the senses and brings him closer to the divine', should be extracted from Aristotle's theory of catharsis than Bernays's pathological reading

---

[115] According to Porphyry and other Neoplatonists, as ventriloquized by Bernays, everything involved in catharsis is 'natural, human, and the work of man [*natürlich und menschlich und Menschenwerk*], but... without a trace of the divine'; hence their frowning disparagement of 'the godless medicine of Aristotle' (Bernays 1970 [1857]: 37/169). Bernays is more than happy to side with Aristotle, all of whose theories tend towards the 'rendering of humanity human' [(*die*) *Vermenschlichung des Menschen*] (Bernays 1970 [1857]: 33/165). On Plato's proto-Christian morality, see Bernays (1885: ii. 364: 'die christliche Moral vorbereitet').

[116] This could be true even given the echoes with Goethe and Grillparzer noted earlier, which could themselves reflect the direct or indirect influence of Spinoza. Some partial hints may be found in 'Die Gottesfürchtigen bei Juvenal', in Bernays (1885: ii. 71–80) and in 'Ueber das phokylideische Gedicht', in Bernays (1885: i. 203–4, 249–50, 254). See also n. 85 above.

[117] Historically, the trope of *Deus absconditus* functions either as an allusion to the sublimely inscrutable Yaweh or as a figure for the dilemmas of staging his presence in a Christian world. See Biale (2011); Kessler and Nirenberg (2011), esp. Neer (2011: 335, 342–3). Spinozism may in this case be relevant after all.

[118] Hegel famously denied tragedy and catharsis to the Jewish race (the reverse argument of Lessing's). See Leonard (2012: 94–104). Bernays's theory of catharsis is implicitly un-Hegelian.

[119] See Steinberg (1991, 2004); Geary (2006). Thanks to Bonnie Honig for pointing me to this debate.

permitted.[120] As for the question why sublimity achieved the prominence it did in modern tragic theory, the answer surely has to do with the brighter and darker associations of the sublime—which could underwrite either spiritual reconciliation in a Christianizing Idealist mould[121] or rupture and dislocation in an un- or anti-Christian mould—and with the way these associations tend to resonate in modern historical consciousness whenever it ponders ancient Greece and itself, each time classical antiquity is, so to speak, being staged in the modern imagination. But these larger issues are best left for another day.[122]

---

[120] Spengel (1859: 18 (citing Plato, *Phaedo* 67), 22; cf. 24). Similarly, von Berger in Gomperz (1897: esp. 84–97).

[121] See n. 33.

[122] It has been claimed that Aristotle's notion of catharsis was 'to a great extent supplanted in the eighteenth-century tradition by the turn towards Longinian sublimity' (Ashfield and De Bolla 1996: 11), but it is likelier that, on the Continent, at least, catharsis became sublime in this period under the influence of German Idealism. I suspect that a similar trend could be charted out in Britain starting with Burke's *On the Sublime* (1757), which has much to say about the effects of tragedy. On Idealism and tragedy, see Krell (2005: 286–8), who briefly signals the significance of Bernays's theory, and esp. now Billings (2014).

2

The Aesthetics of Tragedy: Romantic Perspectives

Christoph Menke

Is there an aesthetics of tragedy? That is to say: can tragedy, in its classical form, be seen in an aesthetic way, or be conceived of as an aesthetic object? Or does the viewing of a tragedy, the understanding of a text or a play as a tragedy, preclude its aesthetic experience?

1. THE PROBLEM OF AESTHETIC AUTONOMY

The question for an aesthetics of tragedy will make sense, or even appear urgent, only to those who are prepared to share one presupposition. This presupposition assumes a particular, demanding determination of both concepts involved: of *aesthetics* and of *tragedy*. The question for an aesthetics of tragedy would not need to be posed, and indeed could not be posed at all, unless the concept of the aesthetic indicates a specific condition or 'regime' (Rancière) of art, and the concept of tragedy indicates a particular type of serious drama: not all (experience of) art is aesthetic and not every serious drama is a tragedy.

Furthermore, the question for an aesthetics of tragedy will be urgent only for those who draw a particular conclusion from this presupposition. The conclusion is made up of the claim that, if one takes the concepts of aesthetics and of tragedy in their specific sense, the connection between the aesthetic and the tragic will appear as a significant problem; they even contradict each other. This does not seem obvious, however, for the concepts of the aesthetic and the tragic do not refer to the same thing. To be sure: both concepts refer to artistic presentations, yet they refer to artistic presentations in different ways. The concept of the *aesthetic*, on the one hand, refers to a specific form of presentation (and its production and reception). The concept of the *tragic*, on the other hand, refers to a specific course of action—that is, the content of that presentation. Why, then, should we not say that an artistic presentation can be aesthetic, with regard to its form, and at the same time tragic, with regard to its content; so that the idea of an 'aesthetics of tragedy' would not pose any problem at all?

The assumption behind the problematization of the idea of an 'aesthetics of tragedy' must be something like the following. The aesthetic form of presentation concerns not only, nor even necessarily, its technique—that is to say, in the case of literature: vocabulary, stylistics, rhetoric, and so on. Aesthetic and non-aesthetic ways of presentation differ not only, nor necessarily, according to their respective means. Even the simple, identical reproduction of a soccer team's composition table can be a poem.[1] Rather, an aesthetic presentation is defined by the specific relation in which it stands to the object—its content—that it presents. While a non-aesthetic presentation aims to make the object present, the relation of an aesthetic presentation to its object is essentially a relation not of re-presentation but of transfiguration. This transfigurative power of aesthetic presentation, however, affects not the properties of its object, but rather its ontological status. Aesthetic transfiguration turns the positive existence of the represented object into something posited. According to this argument, aesthetic transfiguration means: to transform the world of real and thus representable objects, by its presentation, into a world of mere appearances—of semblance.

This argument indicates what is at stake in problematizing the relationship between aesthetics and tragedy: it is concerned with the autonomy of the aesthetic. For the autonomy of the aesthetic does not just mean the *difference* of the aesthetic; it does not mean that presenting in an aesthetic way proceeds somehow differently from presenting in a non-aesthetic way. Rather, the autonomy of the aesthetic means that the presented object undergoes an ontological

---

[1] Cf. Peter Handke, 'Mannschaftsaufstellung des 1. FC Nürnberg vom 27. 1. 1968': Handke (1969: 59).

transformation through its aesthetic presentation, because it is thereby 'present' in a different, 'fractured', way. This also explains why there appears to be a contradiction in talking of a piece of literary presentation as aesthetic in its form and at the same time as tragic in its content, and thus a problem in the idea of an aesthetics of tragedy. For to describe a piece of literary presentation as a tragedy seems to describe it by reference to its content, and thus as the representation of a tragic course of action. However, according to the argument of aesthetic autonomy, an aesthetic presentation, if taken seriously in its aesthetic form, *cannot* be determined by its content; for this would mean to ignore its specifically aesthetic power to transform its content into semblance. This is the objection raised by an aesthetics of autonomy against the possibility of an aesthetics of tragedy: the concept of tragedy is a non- or even anti-aesthetic concept; it is a concept that is constituted by an act of 'abstraction' (Hegel) from aesthetic form.[2]

2. TRAGIC IRONY

When I just said that to problematize the very possibility of an aesthetics of tragedy one has to address the question of aesthetic autonomy, I did so in view of a particular constellation in the history of aesthetics. I mean the objection against the eighteenth-century theory of tragedy that was, at least in Germany, one of the starting points of the discourse of aesthetic modernity in the context of early romanticism. If Friedrich Schlegel anticipated that tragedy properly speaking would one day appear as 'antiquated', and his brother August Wilhelm emphasized the 'comic interruptions' in Shakespeare's theatre that 'prevent the play from becoming business'[3]— then this was directed against a theory of tragedy that assumed that 'true sympathy' (A. W. Schlegel: 'wahre Teilnahme') of the audience with the presented actions and occurrences was not only required for

---

[2] In the following steps, I want to elaborate an argument that is contained in Menke (2009), but has not become sufficiently clear so far. I will draw on various points made throughout the book, without marking the pages in each case. See, in particular, Menke (2009: chs I.3 and II.1) for the crucial statements and further reference.

[3] F. Schlegel (1958–: v. 189); A. W. Schlegel (1923: ii. 141).

the experience of tragedy but was, at the same time, also the qualification of a truly aesthetic attitude. According to this (sentimentalist) theory of tragedy, the tragic and the aesthetic appear as one under the auspices of an affectively intensified identification. The early romantic objection to this theory drives a wedge between the tragic and the aesthetic. And the early romantic name for this aesthetic rupture with sympathy is, as is well known: *irony*.

Whereas it breaks with the traditional theory of tragedy in its definition of the aesthetic, the early romantic declaration of aesthetic autonomy adheres to this theory in another respect: in its assumption that 'true sympathy' is indeed required for the experience of a tragic action. While both Schlegel brothers share this assumption, Adam Müller, another early romantic critic, was the first to oppose this view: he drew together into one idea what was strictly opposed for the Schlegel brothers and invented the concept of 'tragic irony'. While August Wilhelm Schlegel assumes 'with the incipience of the tragical properly, all irony must end' (which implies in reverse that with the incipience of irony all the tragical properly must end), Adam Müller sees in irony, which is distinctive of aesthetic presentation as such, an essential condition of the tragic.[4] Müller thus paved the way for a detachment of the tragic from the non-aesthetic attitude of identification by claiming that, on the contrary, the experience of the tragic *presupposes* an essentially ironic, thus aesthetic, relation to its object. In the following, I will try to reconstruct in three steps how this concept of tragic irony has been (and can be) further developed in order to see what its consequences are for the initial opposition between aesthetic autonomy and tragedy.

The first step was undertaken by Connop Thirlwall, a translator of German Romanticism, in his article 'On the Irony of Sophocles' from 1833. Thirlwall was well aware that some of his readers might be 'surprised to see irony attributed to a tragic poet'.[5] This follows from the still prevailing Aristotelianism in the interpretation of tragedy against which Thirlwall's Romantic idea of its essentially ironic character is directed. Thirlwall develops this idea like all of his successors with reference to *Oedipus the King*, by showing that there are indeed two aspects of irony in (this) tragedy; tragic irony is double irony.

---

[4] A. W. Schlegel (1923: ii. 141); Müller (1967: 240–1).
[5] Thirlwall (1833: 483).

In its first sense, 'tragic irony' refers to an understanding of the tragic as *internally* ironic. Thirlwall calls this 'the irony of the action',[6] which distinguishes the experience of fate in Sophoclean tragedy from myth. In myth, fate appears as 'mere brute force, a blind necessity, effective without any consciousness of its end or means'.[7] Oedipus, by contrast, is no longer 'the victim of a cruel and evil power'; rather, his fate is 'self-inflicted'.[8] 'Fate' means for Oedipus that his own intentions and purposes by being enacted turn against themselves. This is precisely the *irony* of his fate. In speech, irony consists in expressing 'the opposite of what has been stated' (Quintilian). While ironic speech deliberately employs this reversal to the contrary, the irony of fate is 'unconscious'.[9] To suffer from a tragic fate means to be exposed to the force of ironic reversals.

But this alone does not make up for the rupture with the Aristotelian view that Thirlwall claims, for the 'irony of the action' could still be interpreted according to the Aristotelian concept of *peripeteia*. We reach the decisive step of Thirlwall's argument only when we see why irony in the first sense, the irony of the tragic action, presupposes irony in a second sense—namely, the 'poet's irony'. Thus, the irony of (or in) the action combines with irony *in view of* the action. This becomes apparent in *Oedipus* in 'how different everything is from how it appears',[10] in the 'contrast between the appearance of good and the reality of evil'.[11] This contrast refers to the difference between the beginning and the end of Oedipus' fate: the beginning as highly respected king of Thebes, his end as self-blinded exile. The contrast, however, is at the same time and in a more substantial sense a contrast between two perspectives that are present and effective throughout the play. For the 'appearance of good' at the beginning occurs within the play, for its hero. The 'reality of evil', on the other hand, is known to the poet and to the audience right from the start. This superior knowledge makes up what Thirlwall describes as their attitude of 'irony' in view of Oedipus being caught up in his fate: the poet and the audience see the action not from the hero's point of view but from outside and above; their view is of the whole and in particular of the end.

---

[6] Thirlwall (1833: 498).
[7] Thirlwall (1833: 492).
[8] Thirlwall (1833: 500).
[9] Thirlwall (1833: 496).
[10] Thirlwall (1833: 498).
[11] Thirlwall (1833: 500).

The attitude of irony in relation to the presented action, which allows for a detached and knowing overview, is an attitude of freedom from the ironic entanglements of tragic fate in which the hero gets caught up. Furthermore, it is only this freedom from the action that permits the audience to recognize it as tragic. For the Aristotelianism of the German eighteenth-century theory of tragedy, the tragic heroes were not only the victims of an overpowering fate but they were at the same time also the privileged authority of its experience: they are the ones who experience, as victims, the tragedy of their own fate. Therefore, the audience had to try and identify with their point of view. Now, this is just what Thirlwall's title, and argument, of the 'irony of Sophocles' is directed against: only someone who is *not* herself subject to a tragic fate can experience a particular occurrence as an instance of tragic fate. Tragic necessity requires ironic freedom because insight into the irony of fate cannot arise from the internal point of view of the hero within the play, but can come only from ironic detachment, from an external point of view.

Thirlwall tends to ascribe to this ironically detached view not only the insight into the tragic fate of action, but also an insight into a superior truth, a world of 'clearest harmony'[12] above any tragic fate, capable of 'replacing it by the better'.[13] But the superiority in knowledge, which the audience and the author have in contrast to the characters involved in the tragedy, is of a quite different kind. They do not know how it might be done better, but simply how it turns out in the play. And they owe this knowledge not to a superior wisdom, but simply to the theatre. The theatre is a spectacular apparatus, a device that produces a specific structure of viewing that is most crucially characterized by the separation between the spectators and the performance. The theatre creates a detached external position from where the audience can watch the events on stage without being involved. What Thirlwall calls 'irony' is nothing but an implication, or, more precisely, a specific way of using the theatrical viewing apparatus. To claim that irony is the prerequisite of tragedy thus means that the theatre is its prerequisite. Or that the aesthetic is its prerequisite. The aesthetic irony of detached free spectatorship is not the end of tragedy, but, quite to the contrary, its condition of possibility.

---

[12] Thirlwall (1833: 509).   [13] Müller (1967: 242).

3. DRAMATIC AMBIGUITY

The romantic concept of tragic irony yields an important clarification for the idea of the tragic. By demonstrating the ironic condition of the tragic, it exposes at the same time the ironic structure of the tragic that distinguishes fate in tragedy from mythical fate. The limitation of the romantic concept of tragic irony, however, lies in its insufficient understanding of the aesthetic, which is taken as being simply characterized by the attitude of free, detached contemplation—the 'poet's irony'. This is legitimate as far as it dissolves tragic fate from the attitude of sympathy or identification. But it is insufficient for understanding the dependency of tragic fate on its aesthetic mode of presentation.

We reach a more comprehensive understanding of the aesthetic in tragedy as soon as we realize that the two meanings of the concept of irony in Thirlwall presuppose in fact a third one. According to Thirlwall, the ironic reversal of the action happens to the hero and it becomes accessible to the author and the audience in ironic distance. Thirlwall thus ascribes the tragedy of ironic reversal and the irony of aesthetic distance to two separate positions: the irony of tragic fate to the character in the play, the irony of aesthetic distance to the author and the audience outside the play. That this separation of tragic fate and aesthetic distance misses their actual conjunction in tragedy was pointed out by Arnold Hug in an influential article in 1872, in which he examined how Sophocles employed the 'ambiguity' of speech 'for the purpose of the so-called tragic irony':

> That he does wherever he puts an ambiguity into the words uttered by a character, a double sense unknown to the speaker himself and not even suspected by the other characters involved, but only comprehensible to the audience already familiar with the plot of the play. Nowhere has Sophocles applied this tragic ambiguity—like tragic irony in general, of which it is the linguistic application—in a more abundant or, one might feel tempted to say, more cruel way than in *Oedipus the King*. In this most terrible of all tragedies he pursued a tacit, formal dialogue with the audience, not suspected by Oedipus, nor Jocasta or the chorus, yet spoken through their own mouths, so that they often say something completely different from what they think.[14]

---

[14] Hug (1872: 67–8).

The third sense of the concept of 'tragic irony', thus described by Hug, refers to the ambiguity of tragic speech. Tragic speech is an act of the hero; in fact it is the very act by which he himself produces the tragic reversal of his fate. For it is a speech that in its first sense is directed against someone else, which turns in a second, concealed sense against the speaker himself. This second sense, however, which cannot be intended by the speaker himself because it will eventually lead to his destruction, is a sense attached to his speech because it is not merely his own speech. The two meanings of the tragic speech refer to two different positions that have their say at once in this speech. Hug describes this by saying that, in the ambiguous speech of the hero, a 'dialogue' takes place between the author and the audience, over his head. In the hero's own speech it is not just the hero himself who speaks; rather through the hero's speech the poet also speaks with ironic distance. The ironic distance of the poet towards the hero is thus present precisely in the speech from which it is ironically detached.

The classical example of this third and basic type of tragic irony, the irony of ambiguous speech, is the great curse speech of Oedipus. Oedipus directs his curse against the murderers of Laios, who are unknown to him. In his role as royal judge, he curses them in the event that they are not ready to support him with their knowledge in the investigation of the case. Oedipus banishes the culprit from the community:

> I charge you that no resident of this land, which I rule, give shelter to or
> address that murderer, whoever he is, or make him a partner in prayer
> or sacrifice, or give him a share of the lustral rite.[15]

Indeed, that is exactly what Oedipus will eventually do to himself at the end of the play. Actually the fate from which he suffers consists in nothing else than being compelled to carry out against himself the very curse that he had previously directed against the unknown perpetrators. The ironic ambiguity of his curse speech is not merely that he unwittingly predicts his own fate, but that he unknowingly brings it about through his own curse. That is how he himself comes to see it when he comments: 'Unhappy that I am! I think that I have laid myself under a terrible curse without realizing it.'[16] As it turns

---

[15] Sophocles (1887: ll. 236–40).   [16] Sophocles (1887: ll. 744–5).

out, he has cursed himself, and therefore—that is to say: *only*
therefore—he *is* cursed in the end. This is how Oedipus' fate is 'self-
inflicted' (as Thirlwall said). The tragic reversal in Oedipus' fate
originates in the tragic 'derailment' (W. Benjamin) of his speech.

But what is the reason for this derailment, for the tragic ambiguity
of Oedipus' speech? Hug's analysis provides the decisive hint to the
answer to this question by interpreting this ambiguity not only in
terms of semantics, but in terms of dramatics: as an intersection not
just of two meanings—that is to say: of the intended and the actually
realized effect of the speech act—but of two different speakers—of
two positions of spech. In his ambiguous speech through which he
brings about his tragic fate, Oedipus speaks as a character in the play,
while at the same time—as Hug described it—the author and the
audience of the play pursue quite a different 'dialogue'. The positions
of the author and the audience, before and in front of the play, are
thus in this speech present *within* the play. The ambiguity of speech is
due to the double position of the speaker. Indeed, Oedipus has a
double identity: being a character in the play, he speaks at the same
time *as* an author to himself and *as* his own audience. It is this
position: being his own author and audience, and not his alien or
repressed desires, which is the unconscious of Oedipus expressed in
the double meaning of his speech. According to Hug's analysis the
reason for the tragic reversal of Oedipus' fate is the tragic ambiguity
of his speech. Yet the reason for the tragic ambiguity of his speech is
the tragic rift that splits his identity: being a dramatic character he is
at the same time his own author and his audience.

Hug's account thus answers the question 'why does Oedipus
unconsciously curse himself?' by analysing who Oedipus is as he
speaks. In his curse speech, he speaks not (only) as himself, not
(only) as the dramatic character, but (also) like or, in fact, *as* his
author to himself as his audience. But why is that an answer to the
question of Oedipus' fate? It will turn out as an answer if we understand what it means to speak as a dramatic author and what it means
to be a dramatic character.

This requires, first of all, a reminder that these two positions or
functions—dramatic authorship and being a dramatic character—
came into being only with ancient tragedy.[17] For sure, tragedy evolved

---

[17] This was pointed out by recent research in the philology and theory of drama:
see, in particular, Segal (1986) and Wise (1998).

out of a long-standing tradition of performing arts, but it emerged out of this tradition only by a revolutionary rupture. This rupture occurred with the introduction of a written text, the script preceding the performance, which thus became the staging of a play. The consequences of this textual composition of tragedy are revolutionary indeed. They change not only the technical, institutional, and personal structure of the theatre, but also turn the theatre (which thus becomes 'dramatic') into the scene of a new type of action; more precisely: of *two* new types of action that are at the same time two new types of subjectivity. One of these types is the dramatic character: according to Aristotle, dramatic characters are, in contrast to epic figures, individuals acting and talking themselves in person. At the same time, this personal acting and talking are prescribed to the character, down to the last detail, by the script. The dramatic character is pure self-action, yet this action is nothing but an enaction of a textual prescription.[18] To this paradoxical simultaneity of pure self-action and of being completely determined in the dramatic character, there corresponds, on the other hand, the new position of the author. Just as drama is made up of nothing but speech acts, it was made in an act of a person speaking in his own name: in the act of writing of an author. Being a dramatic character means to repeat a script that was prescribed by an author; it means to be an author's character—an individual who speaks and acts in person, but only as it was prescribed to him by the author. Being a dramatic author means to produce a script that determines the speech and acting of characters. Dramatic authorship consists in the superior authority of prescription; being a dramatic character consists in the dependency of re-enacting.

So this is what it means to say that Oedipus speaks like or as an author: he speaks with the authority of an author who does not describe or evaluate the existence of characters, but irrevocably determines their actions. That, however, is exactly what a curse is supposed to do. In cursing, Oedipus speaks as a dramatist writes: he exerts a power to determine that reaches beyond all human authority because it renders its subjects irrevocably determined. In his curse Oedipus condemns just as the author prescribes. But, in contrast to the author of a play, Oedipus does this as a character in the play. In this position,

---

[18] The basic idea here is that the dramatic text does not describe or evaluate character, but makes the characters speak (as or by themselves).

being a character in the play, he cannot control his authority of authorship; he succumbs to it, his curse turns against himself. This is how Arnold Hug's account of dramatic ambiguity would answer the question of Oedipus' fate: the reversal in Oedipus' fate occurs because Oedipus speaks like or as an author, because he claims authorial power to determine the existence of the subject of his conviction, as it becomes evident in his speech act of cursing. However, this authority of authorship, which completely prescribes the speech and the actions of the characters, cannot be exerted by a character in the play. Being a character in the play, Oedipus succumbs to his own determining authority as author. The tragedy of Oedipus tells the story of the ascent of a character into the position of the author and of the fall of the author into the position of the character. The tragic reversal that is the subject of the Oedipus tragedy is the reversal of the authorship claimed by Oedipus in his curse.

4. TRANSCENDENTAL DRAMATICS

What consequences does such a reading of *Oedipus*, if it could be carried out convincingly, bring forth for the problem of an aesthetics of tragedy? The point in question was the relationship between the tragic quality of an action and the aesthetic quality of its presentation. The reading of the tragic fate of Oedipus just outlined yields the insight that this fate stems from the fact that Oedipus, being a dramatic character, speaks at the same time as the author of this very character. To put it in Charles Segal's words, the story of Oedipus is the 'implicit story of the tragic poet'.[19] Such a reading uses the dramatic categories of 'author' and 'character' in order to describe the structure of tragic action. It thus describes the tragic action with categories that are properly applied in the description of the dramatic form of the presentation of this action. The claim of such a reading would be, then, that the formal structure of dramatic presentation is repeated in the structure of the action presented in it. The outlined reading of *Oedipus the King* understands tragedy as a

---

[19] Segal (1986: 80-1).

presentation whose dramatic form is mirrored in its tragic content—
hence as a presentation that is (self-)reflectively structured.

Thus, tragedy is characterized precisely by a trait that stands at the
centre of Friedrich Schlegel's concept of irony and that in another
context he has described under the label of 'transcendental poetry'.
The relevant passage in Schlegel's famous Athenäum-fragment No.
238 reads:

> Just as one . . . would hardly value a transcendental philosophy that was
> not critical, i.e. that would not present the productive together with the
> product and contained within its system of transcendental ideas at once
> a characteristic of transcendental thought [thinking]: so also that poetry
> [the 'transcendental poetry'] should unite the transcendental materials
> and preliminary approaches to a poetic theory of the poetic faculty,
> which are not rare in our modern poets, with an artistic reflection and
> beautiful self-mirroring, as is found in Pindar, in the lyrical fragments of
> the Greeks and in the older elegies, or among our contemporaries in
> Goethe, and thus present itself in each of its presentations, and be at
> once poetry and poetry of poetry throughout.[20]

Schlegel applies the term 'transcendental' first to a philosophy that
'contained within its system of transcendental ideas at once a characteristic of transcendental thought'. Another version of the same
idea, which will allow Schlegel to pass from philosophy to poetry,
states that any presentation that 'presents the productive together
with the product' was 'transcendental'. Hence, 'transcendental' means
'self-reflective': a presentation that is at once 'co-presentation' (*Mit-
Darstellung*) of the productive or the presenting faculty within the
presented content. In view of the reading just presented, this means
that the behaviour of the characters in a tragedy follows certain
structural patterns that determine the tragedy in its form of presentation. Tragedy is a presentation of actions that is at once a 'co-
presentation' of the activity of producing this presentation. In this
Schlegelian sense, tragedy is self-reflective.

That its self-reflection is a constitutive quality of tragedy means
that the tragic quality of the presented content in tragedy results from
the co-presentation of its form. The tragic fate that is shown in
tragedy is therefore the effect of an aesthetic self-reflection: of a
reflection or repetition of the *how* of dramatic presentation in the

---

[20] F. Schlegel (1958–: ii. 204).

what of dramatic action. The fundamental assertion of the romantic concept of tragic irony was that tragic action and aesthetic presentation do not exclude each other but, on the contrary, require each other: without aesthetic irony no tragic fate. As we have seen, Thirlwall could initially sustain this pioneering claim only in a limited sense because he worked with a limited concept of the aesthetic: a concept of the aesthetic that was restricted to the ironically detached freedom of aesthetic contemplation. As we see now, the assertion of the concept of tragic irony cannot realize its full sense until it is tied to the much more demanding definition of the aesthetic contained in Friedrich Schlegel's idea of a transcendental poetry.[21] This definition recognizes as 'aesthetic' in particular a way of presentation that is self-reflective, since it adopts a co-presentation as an inextricable part of the presented content. If the reading of *Oedipus the King* that I have sketched following Arnold Hug is right, then this (Schlegelian) qualification of 'aesthetic' will apply to this tragedy too in a sense that can be summarized by four theses: (1) An essential part of that which carries out the presentation in this tragedy, and hence of that which determines its dramatic form, is the relationship between the author and his dramatic character. (2) As becomes evident with the curse of Oedipus, the tragic fate of the hero originates in his ambiguous speech: the hero *makes* his own fate by his own words. (3) The tragically ironic speech of the hero is the expression of his dramatic ambiguity: the hero is a character in the play and speaks like the author of the play. Hence (4): *What* the tragedy shows—the tragic fate of the hero—originates from its self-reflective co-presenting of *how* (this) tragedy presents. (This) tragedy is the presentation of a tragic action exactly because its presentation has an aesthetically self-reflective form.

This has some bearing, first of all, on (our understanding of) the tragic: the tragic experience of the action is an aesthetic experience—

---

[21] 'In its *form* the older Athenian comedy is quite similar to tragedy. It has adopted from the latter the chorus as well as dramatic–dialogical parts, also the monodies. The only difference lies in the *Parekbasis*, a particular speech that was delivered in the middle of the play by the chorus in the name of the author and directed to the audience. Indeed, this was a complete interruption and cancellation of the play, in which the utmost licentiousness prevailed, as in the play itself, and the audience was addressed most crudely by the chorus, who had moved forward right to the limit of the proscenium. It is from this stepping out [ἐκβασις] that the name was derived' (F. Schlegel 1958–: xi. 88). Hegel has applied this romantic figure of aesthetic self-reflection to tragedy in his *Phenomenology of Spirit*; cf. Menke (1996: 53 ff.).

bound to the aesthetic form of its presentation, since it is bound to its aesthetic, or, more precisely, dramatic, self-reflection. But it also has some bearing on (our understanding of) the aesthetic. The assumption that the relationship between the aesthetic and the tragic poses a fundamental problem, is motivated—as we have seen—by (a certain understanding of) the autonomy of the aesthetic. To experience a presentation in its specifically aesthetic constitution—that was the argument of this objection—excludes perceiving it as a presentation of a tragic action. Now, our reading of the tragic story of Oedipus and the reconception of its basic claim drawing on Schlegel's concept of 'transcendental poetry' (or 'dramatics') can show why this opposition, raised in the name of aesthetic autonomy, misconceives just the autonomy of the aesthetic. Tragedy does not dissolve the tragic quality of the action by its aesthetic self-reflection, but it discovers this tragic quality in the first place. Tragedy makes use of the new dramatic structure, to which it owes its existence and which determines its form, for a critical analysis of the new enlightened legal practice of judging that had only begun to take shape in its distinctly judicial form at this time. By recognizing its own dramatic structure in the pattern of action it presents, tragedy exposes the tragic irony to which this pattern of action is subject from the onset and inexorably. If aesthetic self-reflection is a fundamental trait of aesthetic autonomy, then aesthetic autonomy means precisely not the closure of self-referential form but, rather, the disclosure of the structure of its content through its transfiguration by the aesthetic form.

5. META-THEATRE

Still, the objection against the very possibility of an aesthetics of tragedy is not yet settled. For also against the adjusted understanding of the aesthetic character of tragedy (that I have sketched) the objection against the very possibility of an aesthetics of tragedy can be reiterated. This objection claims: the self-reflection of tragedy can comprehend (at best) its dramatic structure, but it cannot grasp its theatrical constitution. Or, to put it in a shorter and simpler way: (ancient) tragedy does not reflect itself as theatrical play. Despite the self-reflective capacities that are essential for the very possibility of tragic action, there is one thing that no tragedy could integrate: a tragedy cannot 'co-present' the actor performing it on the theatre stage without thereby losing the tragic quality of the presented action. With this argument, the objection against the very possibility of an aesthetics of tragedy returns once again.

This argument is convincing: from the point of view of the theatrical play there is no tragedy. That is to say: whoever assumes the attitude of a theatrical actor towards an action cannot experience this action as actually bringing about a tragic reversal of fate. The theatrical performance of an action consists in showing an action by partly repeating it. The repetition in the play, however, only ever presents isolated elements, certain features of an action, never its purpose. If 'seriousness, taken in the broadest sense [. . .] is the direction of the powers of the soul to a purpose',[22] then the playful quality of acting of the actor consists just in the opposite: in the repetition of an action without actually assuming its purpose. This is the freedom of the play, without which there would not be any tragedy—for nothing could be seen on stage unless some actions are performed by an actor for presentation—but it is a freedom that cannot take place *within* the tragedy. No characters in a drama would suffer from a tragic fate if they would no longer seriously execute their actions but present them as part of a play. According to the concept of tragic irony, 'tragic' is a self-inflicted reversal in the course of an action (or a life). But there can be no 'tragic reversal' without seriously assuming a purpose: the good purpose pursued by the hero turns into a bad one, indeed into the most terrible outcome possible, because of the action of the hero. So, nothing is tragic but a self-made reversal from the good to the most terrible, and good things and bad things exist only in a realm of purposes—that is to say: in the practical sphere, in the world of doing and of suffering. Whenever actions are undertaken as performed in a play, they are no longer part of the practical world, of the world of purposes and judgments; therefore they cannot be subject to a tragic fate any more.

But what happens if the aesthetically playful attitude towards the presented action is actually adopted *within* the play and becomes part of what the play presents? That is to say: what happens to the tragic action if the aesthetically playful form of its presentation is adopted within the presented action itself? If this happens, the theatre turns

---

[22] A. W. Schlegel (1923: i. 30).

into a 'meta-theatre'. This is the term coined by Lionel Abel in order to characterize those peculiar 'theatre pieces about life seen as already theatricalized'[23] that appear with the early modern recommencement of theatre. Abel's paradigm cases are Shakespeare and Calderón. Their characters 'are aware of their own theatricality'.[24] This distinguishes them from the characters of ancient tragedy: if Oedipus could see himself as his own actor, he would no longer see himself in the way a dramatic character must see himself, determined in his existence by the words of his own judgement. Under such conditions, he could deal with his condemnation as freely as actors do who take liberties in changing their part. Only now, in view of this result, can the problem I raised in the beginning be properly phrased: the problem that the idea of an 'aesthetics of tragedy' must raise for a position of aesthetic autonomy. This problem is not—not *only*—that *from* an aesthetic point of view there can be no tragic action. This is true: no matter whether you understand the aesthetic point of view as characterized primarily by a contemplation of beauty or by (taking part in) the performance of a play, from or for such a viewpoint there is no action properly speaking, nothing serious and therefore nothing good or bad, hence no tragic reversal from the one to the other. The problem raised by the idea of an 'aesthetics of tragedy' for a position of aesthetic autonomy concerns, rather, what consequences for the presented action and its tragic quality arise from the aesthetic constitution of its presentation in tragedy. Ancient tragedy could still avoid this problem because it was already self-reflective in a way, but its self-reflection did not include its truly aesthetic, namely theatrical, constitution. Modern meta-theatre, by contrast, raises exactly this problem.

The common answer to this question assumes that the self-reflection of theatrical play leads to a resolution of the tragic quality of the action: as soon as the characters begin to see themselves and their actions as played, they are no longer subject to a tragic fate.[25] This answer is wrong. It would be right only under one condition: the self-reflection of theatrical play could resolve the tragic quality of the action only if it could resolve the world of action altogether. But the co-presentation of theatrical play, which carries out the presentation,

---

[23] Abel (1963: 60–1).   [24] Abel (1963: 60).
[25] This was Abel's thesis. Stanley Cavell in his great *Lear*-Essay pleads for the opposite assumption: Cavell (1976).

as a part of the presented action in the play turns theatrical play itself into a way of action in its own right. To assume the aesthetic point of view, to take part in seeing certain actions as theatrically performed, thus becomes a way of action itself. Like any action properly speaking, this aesthetic way of action will be executed for some purpose, for the sake of some idea of the good, and therefore it is capable, like any action, of undergoing a tragic reversal into the worst outcome. The aesthetic is non-tragical only as long as it maintains its position as the other in contrast to the practical. Taking the juridical metaphor of self-legislation in a literal sense, quite often the 'autonomy' of the aesthetic is understood to refer to the unrelated coexistence of independent states or territories. But there have always been and there will always be transgressive encroachments of the aesthetic into the practical world; one might describe this as the 'sovereignty' of the aesthetic.[26] Inevitably, in such encroachments into the practical sphere, the aesthetic will be subject to the latter's laws—the laws of good and bad—and one of these laws is the law of tragic reversal; characters from Hamlet to Clov have experienced this. The only form of action that suspends tragic fate is the theatrical play-acting of the actor. But, as a form of *action*, the theatrical play-acting of the actor becomes or remains itself subject to the irony of tragic reversals.

To raise the problem of the possibility of an aesthetics of tragedy in the name of the autonomy of the aesthetic means that, wherever there is aesthetic presentation in the genuine sense of the word, there can be no tragedy any more. The counter-argument states that even the aesthetic in its genuine sense is subject to this experience of tragedy, since the aesthetic is itself a form of action. The answer to the initial question whether an aesthetics of tragedy is possible at all is thus that the condition of possibility of an aesthetics of tragedy is the tragedy of the aesthetic.

---

[26] Menke (1991).

3

Paradoxon: On the Sublimity of Tragedy in Hölderlin and Some Contemporaries

Ian Balfour

True tragedy remains in abeyance.

(Jean Epstein)

I am often all the more clumsy and muddled in what I do and say precisely because I stand there in the modern water like geese with their flat fleet and beat my wings helplessly against the Greek sky.

(Friedrich Hölderlin)

Tragedy has tended to solicit thinking in a manner and with an intensity distinct among the literary genres. For a good many philosophers tragedy has held price of place in their speculations, even for some philosophers, such as Hegel and Schelling, committed to account for the entire range of the literary and other arts in their treatments of the aesthetic. Plato legendarily wrote tragedies himself before burning them and going on to the bigger and better thing of philosophy, even if he was to conduct that philosophizing in an oddly dramatic, mimetic mode that denounced mimesis. The paradigmatic status of tragedy for Aristotle is palpable, and its primacy would probably not be countered were his lost treatise on comedy miraculously to turn up. Tragedies attain the status they do in Aristotle not least because they are logical in an exemplary, even proto-philosophical way, and the supreme example, *Oedipus Tyrannus*, places a premium on knowledge and self-knowledge at the expense of the senses, in keeping with the explicit values of Aristotle's philosophy that ranks *dianoia* or thought at the top and (mere) *opsis* or spectacle at the very bottom. That Oedipus, in coming to his 'senses' via the knowledge he attains, gouges out his eyes makes perfect Aristotelian sense. It is a fate more appropriate than death.

In what follows I enquire into how the genre of tragedy can be thought in relation to the aesthetic mode of the sublime 'around 1800' with a focus on Friedrich Hölderlin's thinking about tragedy in the company of some of his contemporaries. Hölderlin, in his readings of Sophocles and in some other texts making broad, grand claims about tragedy, draws on a rhetoric and vocabulary of the sublime (though usually without using the word as such) to help make sense of that which both demands and resists sense-making. His project is caught up in the vexed struggle in late-eighteenth-century 'Germany' (not yet a nation state) to come to terms with the legacy of ancient Greek culture in a pointed instalment of the so-called quarrel between the ancients and the moderns variously fought out in European culture in the preceding several centuries. It is an episode—but not only that— in the history of the loose, baggy monster called 'modernity' and not one that, in Hölderlin's case, is very helpfully thought of in terms of secularity. Its texture is complicated because moments in Hölderlin that are distinctly 'modern' (he uses just this word in addition to his signature category of the 'Hesperian') entail a reading, reworking, or direct translation of texts of ancient Greek literature, philosophy, and mythology. Hölderlin is also interested, in the same breath, in a specifically German modernity, which is nonetheless, only a little paradoxically, to be avowedly cosmopolitan, extending to and par- ticipating in nothing less than the universal.[1]

Together with Hölderlin's intense engagement with the culture of Greek antiquity, the other two most powerful forces driving his thinking—not without their effect on his poetical practice—through the 1790s were the French Revolution and Kant's critical philosophy. The common thread was an impassioned concern for freedom or, more precisely, the recognition of a dialectic of freedom and neces- sity demanding the exercise of freedom. This variously conceived

---

[1] Of his numerous critiques of German narrowness and the need for the Germans to embrace the cosmopolitan, see especially Hölderlin's letter to his half-brother, Karl Gök, of 31 December 1798 (Hölderlin 2009: 118 ff.; all references to the letters and essays are to this edition unless otherwise noted.) Here Hölderlin appeals to the beguiling notion of 'political reading' as a means to cosmopolitanism.

freedom was often thought to be in tandem with a universalizing, even 'infinitizing', impulse, which, despite its fundamentally epistemological character, also had a political thrust (democratic, cosmopolitan, humanitarian).[2] Winckelmann had already argued for the ancient Greeks as models for imitation (*Nachahmung*) but in a mode of freedom, not least because the Greeks constituted—over and against oppressive models of Latinate Christianity—a belated, new source of inspiration that neither called for nor really permitted slavish imitation.[3] In Hölderlin's thinking, the relation of modern German poetry to ancient Greek literature was complex in the extreme, as laid out in the paradoxical, far-reaching formulations from the famous letters to Böhlendorff. The paradigm for the relation charted there cannot be construed as one of mirroring, in that sense of imitation, because, for all of the ways in which Hölderlin draws on the Greeks (from alcaic and asclepiadic metrical schemes to invocations of mythological and historical figures as well as to the protocols of Pindar's odes[4]), he acknowledges a fundamental divide between the Greek and the Hesperian worlds. 'Aside from vital relation and proportion' (*lebendigen Verhältnis und Geschick*), he writes in the first letter to Böhlendorff, 'we can have nothing in common with them'.[5] Given that 'vital relation and proportion' are arguably characteristics of all good art and hardly the exclusive property of the Greeks and the Germans, Hölderlin is positing an almost categorical divide from the Greeks. Yet the very same letter characterizes the Greeks as 'indispensable for us'. The Greeks are necessary and impossible sources of imitation, a double-bind (that produces allegory) whereby the moderns imitate the Greeks by doing the very opposite of them in an analogous way.

If Hölderlin's turn to the Greeks risks seeming backward-looking (but it is not, not even in the translations), the embrace of or the felt need to think through and beyond Kant's aesthetics crystallized in the

---

[2] Something of this constellation can be glimpsed in Hölderlin's 'Becoming in Dissolution' (Holderlin 2009: 271–6), a text mainly about the fatherland, as well as in the letter noted in n. 1.

[3] On the importance of freedom in Winckelmann's historicized aesthetics, see Potts (1994; 2006: 26–7).

[4] Hölderlin nonetheless also urges his friend Neuffer that 'we must abandon the old classical forms, which are so intimately fitted to their subject matter that they are good for no other' (Holderlin 2009: 145).

[5] Hölderlin (2009: 207 (translation modified)).

Critique of Judgment of 1790 was about as cutting-edge as could be, something close to what in philosophy would be the equivalent of the French Revolution in the domain of history. Hölderlin was not just steeped generally in Kant's thinking, as were his philosophically minded co-conspirators at the Tübingen *Stift*; he made a point of studying the *Critique of Judgment* closely just at the moment when he was trying to think about poetry and aesthetic theory together, as is clear in his plans for a fledgling journal to which he invited the likes of Hegel, Schelling, Goethe, and Schiller to contribute. Like Kant, Hölderlin thought judgement was built into the experience of the aesthetic and that that relation bore thinking about. Kant's aesthetics was a transcendental enquiry into the conditions of the possibility of our apprehending and comprehending beauty and sublimity. The texture of his analysis was a far cry from what we would recognize as historicist, but his enquiry had a historical component of sorts built into it, in the sense that utterly singular experiences of nature (or, secondarily, art) as beautiful or sublime are its objects. Is there anything more historical than such singular experience? Such experience, however, is hard to talk about and all the more so in the case of the sublime, one prominent feature of which is the breakdown of an ability to represent just that experience. The Kantian plot of the sublime, however, entails a turn of the subject inward, on the heels of imagination's breakdown, to discover the superiority of reason over nature in its ability to *think* (which is not necessarily to *know*) beyond the realm of the senses to the supersensible and thus to assert and perform the subject's freedom. It is not clear that Hölderlin would, on the far side of the aesthetic experience of excess and incomprehension that is the sublime, share entirely Kant's narrative of the ultimate triumph of reason. But he found in Kant (especially) a new vocabulary of the sublime to bring to bear on the overwhelming experience of compelling examples in ancient Greek literature. The 'sublime' is both an ancient and a modern category, one whose force counts as rather more strange and modern for its discontinuous history, given that the category was rediscovered in modernity long after it had all but disappeared from the scenes of criticism.[6] It was a category (re-)born 'in the modern water', to borrow Hölderlin's

---

[6] For many in the Romantic period, from Rousseau through Volney to Hazlitt, antiquity itself was a source of sublimity. The past garners more and more sublimity as it recedes ever further from the present.

phrase.[7] Though the term *erhaben* ('sublime') surfaces only now and then in Hölderlin's prose writings and just once in his notes on Sophocles, there are any number of clear hallmarks of the sublime conjured in the notes via terms such as *unendlich* ('infinite'), *ungeheuer* ('enormous'), *ungebundenst* ('least restrained'), *grenzenlos* ('without boundaries') as well as a host of superlatives rendering some sort of excess: 'the wildest', 'the most extreme', and the like. Tragedy operates at the extremes. It is not just that tragedy confronts the horrific, the unspeakable, and the unbearable. From Hölderlin's point of view, virtually everything crucial in tragedy is pushed to the limit in ways beyond their invocation in thematic terms and is rendered in forms partly commensurate with that extremity, even if, in the end, reason will—more or less—prevail. Within this renovated discourse of the sublime, Hölderlin, in his readings of Sophocles, is especially and oddly occupied with the motif of infinity. This last term is by no means peculiar to Kant; even the empirically inclined Edmund Burke finds infinity, together with eternity, 'among the most affecting [ideas] we have'.[8] But its prominence in Hölderlin is extreme. Nothing along those lines was at all common in the decades before him.

In this constellation around 1800 tragedy finds its place as an exemplary historical *and*—to some extent—transhistorical phenomenon. When we encounter reflection about genre in Germany in this period, it is more often than not in the form of thought that unfolds within a philosophy or theory of history. One is familiar especially through Hegel with how philosophy tends to assume a historical, narrative form (the lecture courses, the 'spirit' section of the *Phenomenology*), but one also finds across a spectrum of rather diverse thinkers of the time a tendency to a historicizing theory of poetics and genre(s), from Herder's anthropological discourse about poetic origins and folk culture to Friedrich Schlegel's positing of the novel (*Roman*) as the super-genre in relation to all others to Schelling's refashioning of the ancient/modern debate with Dante's faintly subjective epic as the pivot of Western cultural history, at the cusp of

---

[7] It is remarkable that Hölderlin's 'Notes on the *Oedipus*' begins with an analysis of the *modern* poet and the wish for a general return to an artisanal métier of poetry on the model of the ancients.

[8] Burke (1958 [1756]: 61).

ancient and modern.[9] Genres, even when their homogeneity is a little tenuous, are tailor-made for thinking about theory and history at the same time.[10] It is not hard to recognize significant differences between tragedies by, say, Aeschylus, Seneca, Shakespeare, Racine, Schiller, and Baillie at the same time as one acknowledges 'family resemblances', such that we can plausibly term all of them tragedies.[11] The facts of literary history call out for thinking genre, history, and theory together, even when one is trying to get at the (relative) singularity of certain works of art, as Hölderlin does in his wild readings of Sophocles.[12]

Too often the sublime is considered as if it operated transcendently, ethereally, irrespective of genre. Longinus, to be sure, in the great inaugural treatise *On the Sublime* (*Peri hypsous*), educes examples from an expansive array of genres: epic, tragedy, lyric, political oration, even the Book of Genesis, whatever genre that text belongs to, if any. Homeric epic (and *The Iliad* far more than *The Odyssey*, the latter conceived by Longinus to be a slacker work of old—or older—age) garners the preponderance of citations in *On the Sublime*, but one does not sense any strict hierarchy of genres prevailing: it is not epic's excellence but Homer's that accounts for this primacy. For a good many of Hölderlin's contemporaries and near-contemporaries, tragedy often assumes the loftiest place among the genres and stands as the greatest source of the sublime. From Lessing and Mendelssohn and Jacobi through Schiller and Schelling to Hegel and Vischer and ultimately to Nietzsche, tragedy often implicitly and

---

[9] For an extremely lucid and wide-ranging account of this, see Szondi (1974). Walter Benjamin's famous account of the *Trauerspiel* complicates this approach, however, as he posits a series of significant differences between classical tragedy and the modern *Trauerspiel*, principally the very different sense of history entailed.

[10] It is no accident that Marxist criticism, from Lukács through Benjamin and Adorno to Jameson, excels at illuminating matters of genre.

[11] One of the best accounts of the different kinds of tragedy within an overarching identity or even *mythos* of tragedy remains that of Northrop Frye in *Anatomy of Criticism*. Nonetheless, one needs to recognize the perils of generalization, as cautioned by Simon Goldhill (2008) just for the circumscribed corpus of Athenian tragedy. Theories of tragedy tend, notoriously, to promote one shining example over the others (Aristotle's *Oedipus Tyrannus*, Hegel's *Antigone*). It is a beguiling thought experiment to imagine what the theory of tragedy would look like with very different paradigmatic examples—say, Sophocles' *Philoctetes* or *Ajax* or Shakespeare's *Coriolanus*.

[12] Cf. Walter Benjamin: 'A major work will either establish the genre or abolish it: and the perfect work will do both' (Benjamin 1998: 44).

sometimes explicitly gets singled out as *the* genre of the sublime or is coupled with epic in a pairing of two that tower over the other genres.[13]

The articulation of the mode of the sublime with the genre of tragedy took a quantum leap in the wake of Kant's *Critique of Judgement*. It did not matter much that Kant himself, in his earlier text of 1764, the *Observations on the Feeling of Beautiful and the Sublime*, had associated tragedy with sublimity and comedy with beauty.[14] Kant offered, in the *Critique of Judgement*, a newly variegated, profound account of the sublime as crucial to the very constitution of the subject, not just some epiphenomenal, merely aesthetic matter. But tragedy was hardly even evoked in the great critical work where Kant was infinitely, as it were, more interested in nature than in art. Indeed, he rules out that works of art can be considered sublime (even if his rhetoric and examples sometimes belie his claim). Yet he laid the groundwork for any number of intellectuals to transpose what he said about nature to the domain of art, Schiller foremost among them.

Schiller had long had an interest in the practice of tragedy and in reflection on it, but it is only in the wake of Kant's *Critique of Judgement* (1790) that he offers repeated, sustained reflections on the two—tragedy and sublimity—in more or less the same breath. Frederick Beiser can even say: '*Prima facie* Schiller's theory of tragedy seems to be little more than an application of Kant's concept of the sublime.'[15] He emphasizes the former cannot remotely be reduced to the latter, yet he can also maintain: 'Schiller's reflections on the concept of the sublime always took place within the context of his theory of tragedy. While he realized the concept of the sublime is broader than the tragic he made his special concern the sublime in tragedy.'[16] Beiser seems to me to overstate the case, but he is not wrong to stress the intimate articulation of the genre of tragedy with the mode of the sublime in Schiller's intense Kantian phase.[17]

It is hard to summarize Schiller's writings on tragedy, even in the early 1790s, when he writes a handful of essays about tragedy and/or

---

[13] See Reiss (1980: 7).   [14] Kant (2011: 15, 52).
[15] Beiser (2005: 239).   [16] Beiser (2005: 257).
[17] The fullest study of Schiller on the sublime is Barone (2004: 164 ff.), which includes a substantial section on 'theory of tragedy' with a lot of attention to Schiller's own dramatic practice as operating in the mode of the sublime. See also Alt (2000: 78 ff.) and Sharpe (1991: 122–30).

the sublime with a good deal of crossover, essays in which he shifts position or emphasis from one piece to the next. What overarches a good deal of this work, however, is a sense of the sublime as crucial to the very status or destiny of the human subject if he or she is to be fully human:

> Man can no longer be the being that wills if there is even a single case in which he simply must do what he does not will. This single terror, which he simply must do and does not will, will haunt him like a ghost [*ein Gespenst*] and, as is the case in the majority of people, will deliver him up prey to the blind terrors of imagination; his vaunted freedom is absolutely nothing if he is bound in even a single point.[18]

It is one thing to have freedom be *a* or even *the* desideratum of the human being and quite another to make freedom of the will *the* defining characteristic of the human being, much less to do so in a way such that one's humanity would be compromised utterly if this freedom were compromised in even a single point.[19]

Would not virtually every example of tragedy feature the compromise of freedom in at least a single point?

It is perhaps surprising that Schiller makes this case for freedom precisely apropos the sublime, for the overwhelming tendency of the tradition of thinking on the sublime had stressed precisely the unfreedom at work in this aesthetic mode, beginning with Longinus's implicit sense that the sublime is paradigmatically a matter of violence and excess, like a thunderbolt or a conflagration, against which the spectator or reader is powerless to resist. In the 'Kallias Letters', Schiller had glossed beauty in general (which had been the time-honoured model for the aesthetic) as 'freedom in its appearance' (*Freiheit in der Erscheinung*),[20] a formulation that foregrounds the possible elaboration of the ethical more than any of the rival slogans of his near contemporaries. One might think this is more plausible to maintain in the case of the beautiful than the sublime, but for Schiller the latter domain of aesthetics is even more conducive for the exercise of freedom than is the beautiful. Tragedy, the sublime mode par excellence, often showcases heroes and heroines struggling against

---

[18] Schiller (1943–: xx. 38–9; 1993: 71 (translation modified)).

[19] Walter Hinderer (2005) highlights usefully this aspect of Schiller's thinking under the rubric of 'anthropological aesthetics'.

[20] Schiller (1943–: xx. 83, 87).

a fate they are, ultimately, unable to overcome, but the protagonists of his own plays (*Kabale und Liebe, Don Karlos, Wilhelm Tell*) are conspicuous for the exercise of their freedom within the not-quite-inevitable unfolding of events. Numerous theorists (following the example of playwrights) try to carve out a middle ground for the protagonists as free and not free, with the qualified freedom of the hero/heroine precariously balanced against the force of fate. Schiller contends, however, that tragedy should not accord fate all that much power:

> Being blindly subject to fate is . . . always humiliating and debilitating for entities that are free and self-determining. This is why the most splendid plays on the Greek stage leave something to be desired, since in all these plays appeal is ultimately made to necessity and our reason, demanding reason as it does, is always left with some untied knot.[21]

Thus the work of art, in principle free, should display freedom freely, should display freedom at the level of theme or sheer content. It is no accident that so many of Schiller's tragedies or near-tragedies go out of their way to underscore this thematics of freedom so as better to distinguish them from their Greek ancestors. But Greek tragedies do have some features that mark them as conducive to the sublime, such as the distinctive and hard-to-imitate convention of the chorus, about which Schiller struggled as to whether or not he could plausibly include one in a modern play. Schiller will say, years after the flurry of essays on tragedy and the sublime, in an essay on the chorus:

> If the blows with which tragedy meets our heart followed on one another without interruption, suffering would triumph over action. We would become wrapped up in the material and no longer float above it. In that the chorus holds the parts together, and steps between the passions with its calming observations, it gives us back our freedom, which would be lost in the storm of feelings.[22]

The chorus in effect does what tragedy does in general: it contains suffering and passion in a rational form that asserts freedom. (This is not everyone's understanding of tragedy, but it is close to the party line of German aesthetics between 1790 and 1840.) It is a vehicle of

---

[21] Schiller (1943–: xx. 157; 1993: 9).
[22] Schiller (1988–2004: v. 289). For a fine analysis of the vexed status of the Greek chorus and German understandings of it around 1800, see Billings (2013a).

and for the public performance of reason, even in its lyrical, highly figurative moments.

The concern with and operating in the mode of reason is one of numerous indices that tragedy is exemplary of art and its mission. Schiller posits that 'the ultimate purpose of art is to present what transcends the realm of the senses and the art of tragedy in particular accomplishes this by displaying morality's independence, its freedom, in the throes of passion, from nature's laws'.[23] Tragedy's sublimity lies, in good measure, in its presentation of the unrepresentable— namely, freedom (freedom, together with God and immortality were Kant's prime examples of 'ideas' that were unrepresentable). And, once again, freedom asserts itself in the very mode of something usually recognized as antithetical to freedom, the 'throes of passion'. It is one of the permanent paradoxes of tragedy.

Hölderlin (and Hegel) would surely have read his good friend Schelling's early reflections on tragedy set out in the latter's 1795 (thus at age 20!) *Philosophical Letters on Dogmatism and Criticism*, much of which is reworked and raised to a higher level, if that were possible, in the more systematic and extended lectures on the *Philosophy of Art* of 1802–3. Especially in the later text, the idea of the sublime is repeatedly and crucially adduced in the brief account of tragedy towards the end of the *Philosophy of Art*. The earlier text worries the apparent contradictions (*Widersprüche*) for the Greeks and their tragedies, with the resolute commitment to reason and thus to the possibilities of human freedom and yet at the same time cognizant of not just any 'objective power' external to human beings but a power conceived of as fate, working its inevitable work directly against human beings' putative freedom.[24] It is in this dialectic—one can use the word advisedly here—that

> the protagonist had to struggle against fate; otherwise there was no struggle at all, no expression of freedom. He had to succumb within that which is subject to necessity. Yet in order not to allow necessity to overcome him without simultaneously overcoming it, the protagonist also had to atone voluntarily for this guilt—guilt imposed by fate itself. *This is the most sublime idea* and the greatest victory of freedom: voluntarily to bear the punishment for an unavoidable transgression

---

[23] Schiller (1943–: xx. 196; 1993: 45).
[24] For an insightful account of Schelling on tragedy, see Ferris (2000).

in order to manifest his freedom precisely in the loss of that very same freedom, and to perish amid a declaration of free will. (emphasis added)

'It sounds paradoxical', as Holderlin says in a related context, that freedom's great victory is to submit voluntarily to the loss of freedom. This becomes a common gambit in Kant, Schiller, Fichte, Schelling, and Hegel. It is eminently dialectical, of course, and bears some real relation to the texture of tragedies: still it is a hard paradox to swallow, the free sacrifice of freedom as nonetheless a triumph for freedom. This 'most sublime idea', as Schelling phrases it, is summoned via the genre that operates *in extremis*, as is clear especially in the predicament of the tragic hero:

> precisely at the moment of greatest suffering he enters into the greatest liberation and greatest dispassion. From that moment on, the insurmountable power of fate, which earlier appeared in absolute dimensions, now appears merely relatively great, for it is overcome by the will and becomes the symbol of the absolutely great, namely, of the attitude and disposition of *sublimity*.[25]

Yet this fiercely extreme kind of text is governed by a balancing act, managing to contain the forces that push and pull in opposite directions, with Schelling, as before him Schiller, having recourse to the notion of equilibrium (*Gleichgewicht*):

> The Greeks sought in their tragedies this kind of equilibrium between justice and humanity, necessity and freedom, a balance without which they could not satisfy their moral sensibility, just as the highest morality itself is expressed in this balance. Precisely this equilibrium is the ultimate concern of tragedy. It is not tragic that a premeditated, free transgression is punished. That a guiltless person unavoidably becomes increasingly guilty through fate itself, as remarked earlier, is the greatest conceivable misfortune. But that this guiltless guilty person accepts punishment voluntarily—this is the sublimity of tragedy; thereby alone does freedom transfigure itself into the highest identity with necessity.[26]

The sacrifice to a higher power, the loss of freedom, raises one higher. Or that is the idea. And this all unfolds, despite the balanced rhetoric of thematic extremity, in keeping with a principle of balance (*Gleichgewicht*), the principle we found in Schiller and which will return in

---

[25] Schelling (1989: 254).   [26] Schelling (1989: 255).

Hölderlin in a different form. For Schiller and Schelling equilibrium is a matter of opposing forces colliding at the level of the concept, variously embodied in the drama's actors and action, whereas Hölderlin's *Gleichgewicht* is a structure that organizes how the play is put together, with Sophocles' landmark tragedies each divided into two 'halves' of equal weight but unequal length. It is not as if Hölderlin shies away from big metaphysical and ethical categories—hardly—but he is rather more concerned than Schiller and Schelling with the mechanics of tragedy, their formal dynamics, which have their consequences for tragedy's sublime power.

One might vaguely expect that it would be Hegel to whom one could look for a theory of tragedy as sublime, given the lofty status he assigns it in his *Aesthetics* and the philosophical dignity he ascribes to *Antigone*, making it the very model for the dialectics of ethical life as expounded in *The Phenomenology of Spirit*. But, strictly speaking, for Hegel there is, in principle, nothing in classical *art* (which corresponds essentially to the paradigm of ancient Greek art) that is sublime. In Hegel's tripartite, historical division of the arts into the symbolic, the classical, and the romantic, the mode of the sublime inhabits almost only symbolic art, which is to say, primarily ancient Eastern (or Oriental) and Middle Eastern art, whose main object was the representation of the divine or the absolute, which it could render only inadequately.[27] This is art that does not quite even merit the name. It is, rather, 'pre-art' (*Vorkunst*), as Hegel calls it, because it is not characterized by the interpenetration (*Ineinandersein*) of meaning (*Bedeutung*) and form (*Gestalt*) definitive of art in the first place.[28] Hegel, unlike any of his contemporaries, confines the '*art* of the sublime' in the strict sense—in increasingly narrow fashion—almost exclusively to ancient biblical poetry (and in the strictest sense to the Psalms) and then allows for a few epigonal formations that can be called sublime under a more capacious umbrella term, as in Christian mysticism and what he calls Mohammedan poetry. Perhaps the most telling exception occurs in his invocation of *Antigone* as 'one of the most sublime and in every respect most excellent works of art of all time' (*einer der allerhabensten, in jeder Rücksicht vortrefflichsten*

---

[27] See de Man (1996: 92 ff.) on the historical and structural senses of the symbolic in relation to the sign.

[28] Hegel (1970: xiii. 13, 95; 1975a: i. 304).

Kunstwerke aller Zeiten).[29] In any event, it is a counter-example that brings into relief the general rule that ancient Greek tragedy, as classic (al) art, operates in the mode of the beautiful. One might say, not quite in Hegel's terms, that, if there are excesses in the content and texture—prompting awe, terror, or transport—that one would be tempted to call sublime, they are resolutely inscribed within teleological plots of reason, as befitting what is in part the performance of the *polis* before the people of the *polis*.

For the purest account of tragedy as sublime, one rather more Hegelian than Hegel's own, one can turn instead to his disciple, Friedrich Theodor Vischer, who in 1837 published a fascinating treatise, *On the Sublime and the Comic*, when only the first part of Hegel's lectures on *Aesthetics* had been published, thus lacking the analysis of comedy and tragedy that formed the final topics or indeed the culmination of Hegel's lecture courses.[30] Vischer follows Hegel in many things but departs from him in the analysis of the sublime. For Vischer the sublime is not the opposite of the beautiful, as, say, for Burke or for Schelling (*Gegensatz* is his term):[31] it proceeds from beauty. Vischer posits two kinds of sublimity: that of nature (or what he also calls substance, aligning it with objects and objectivity) and that of the subject. In his massive *Aesthetik des Schoenen* (1846), a later work that incorporates a good deal of the 1837 treatise, tragedy emerges as the one and only genre that bridges the opposition between subject and object, all the while operating in the mode of the sublime. It is, thus, the sublime of the sublime, as the transcending of the merely subjective and the merely objective sublime(s): the *ne plus ultra* of the aesthetic.[32] A remarkable feature of texts promulgating theories of the sublime is the charged status of examples in them (given the often meagre general definitions of the sublime), and what

---

[29] Hegel (1970: iv. 60; 1975a: i. 464).

[30] The oddity of the title is worth pausing over. In the categories of the time, one would have expected the title to be either *The Tragic and the Comic* or *The Sublime and the Beautiful*. It is unusual that Vischer invokes together a mode and a genre rather than two modes or two genres. The oddity might be explained by the thoroughness with which Vischer identifies the sublime with the tragic and vice versa.

[31] Schelling, however, sometimes, in Longinian fashion, sees the sublime and the beautiful as *not* in opposition, a point he makes even apropos of tragedy.

[32] Vischer's argument for the sublimity of tragedy is only the most thoroughgoing or extreme identification. Elsewhere one sees fainter versions of the association that variously emphasize the heroic, sacrificial, Dionysian, Apollonian, subjective, objective, modern, or ancient character of tragedy as sublime.

is striking in Vischer is the extent to which he so resolutely promotes, by example, tragedy over all genres. Through the course of the analyses, in the earlier treatise, of both sublimes—of nature and of 'the subject'—it is already striking how prominently tragedy figures as the main source of aesthetic (artistic, non-natural) examples of the sublime before that genre emerges explicitly as the synthesizing category that reconciles and raises to a higher level both nature and the subject, now in the heady domain of the absolute. This for Vischer, unlike for Hegel, is eminently possible even in his own time, as his pointed invocation of the scene featuring the out-of-this-world *Erdgeist* (earth-spirit) in Goethe's *Faust*, a play that even in its earliest published form was recognized by Hegel as 'the absolute philosophical tragedy'.[33]

If there were a good many critics and philosophers who thought of tragedy as sublime, no writing on tragedy, nonetheless, very much resembles Hölderlin's enigmatic, convoluted, and profound reflections. One might broach his thinking on the subject through an isolated fragment, of uncertain date, singled out by Peter Szondi as emblematic of his 'philosophy' of tragedy:

> The significance [*Bedeutung*] of tragedies can be understood most easily by way of paradox. For everything primal, because all potential is divided justly and equally, manifests itself not in original strength but, in fact, in its weakness, so that quite properly the light of life and the appearance attach to the weakness of every whole. Now in the tragic, the sign in itself is insignificant [*unbedeutend*], without effect, yet what is primal is straightforward [*gerade heraus*]. Properly speaking, what is primal can only appear in its weakness; however, to the extent that the sign is posited as insignificant = 0, what is primal, the hidden foundation of any nature, can also present itself. If nature properly presents itself in its weakest gift [*Gabe*], then the sign, if nature presents itself in its most powerful gift, = 0.[34]

---

[33] Hegel (1970: xv. 557). Friedrich Schlegel (2001: 32, 115), discerned a kind of play he called 'philosophical tragedy' (*Hamlet* and *Faust* being prime examples) constituting one pole on a spectrum within the general recognition of tragedy as congenial to or even demanding of philosophy.

[34] Hölderlin (1943–85: iv. 274; 1988: 89; 2009: 315 (translation modified)). 'Die Bedeutung der Tragödien ist am leichtesten aus dem Paradoxon zu begreifen. Denn alles Ursprüngliche, weil alles Vermögen gerecht und gleich geteilt ist, erscheint zwar nicht in ursprünglicher Stärke, sondern eigentlich in seiner Schwäche, so daß recht eigentlich das Lebenslicht und die Erscheinung der Schwäche jedes Ganzen angehört.

It is not a good sign, as it were, that the *easiest* way to understand tragedy lies in a paradox. Moreover, the paradox is not a merely verbal one, a play of figure and letter that is soon easily resolved. It is conceptually complicated and hard to figure out. What exactly is entailed in Hölderlin's paradox or paradoxes? What he claims is definitive of tragedy here—that in *it* the sign is meaningless—would seem to hold for absolutely any language, any non-onomatopoetic or not naturally motivated language, if there were such a thing.[35] Hegel would claim explicitly in his *Aesthetics* that the signs of poetry (that is, not just language, but poetic language) were precisely 'meaningless.'[36] This might not sound so 'positive', though poetry, for Hegel, has the advantage of partaking of and consisting in—as with all language—the meaningless, arbitrary signs of philosophical discourse on the cusp of which poetry, as the highest and most encompassing of the arts, is poised. In this, poetry is unlike the other arts (for example, sculpture, architecture) that dwell un-poetically in signs that are, for Hegel, variously meaningful. But why should Hölderlin say here—and nowhere else—that in tragedy the sign is meaningless, equalling or adding up to zero?

The claim seems bound up with a major paradox of this short text: that the primal or what is original cannot appear in its original strength. It does not appear as such but rather, already divided from the start, in its weakness, something less than the posited original strength, which was always only, in its fullest, potential. Given the necessary diminution of the original force, then the least diminution would be effected via the vehicle of least resistance: hence

---

Im Tragischen nun ist das Zeichen an sich selbst unbedeutend, wirkungslos, aber das Ursprüngliche ist gerade heraus. Eigentlich nämlich kann das Ursprüngliche nur in seiner Schwäche erscheinen, insofern aber das Zeichen an sich selbst als unbedeutend = 0 gesetzt wird, kann auch das Ursprüngliche, der verborgene Grund jeder Natur sich darstellen. Stellt die Natur in ihrer schwächsten Gabe sich eigentlich dar, so ist das Zeichen, wenn sie sich in ihrer stärksten Gabe darstellt, = 0.'

[35] Sometime attributed to Saussure as if it were his invention, the doctrine of the arbitrariness of the sign is found in various guises in Plato, Locke, and Hegel, among others. If linguistic signs were not arbitrary, translation would either be unnecessary or a piece of cake.

[36] Within poetry, drama occupies the highest position, it is thus the highest of the high. Perhaps surprisingly, it is not tragedy with which Hegel's lectures on aesthetics finish but comedy (despite Hegel's having far more to say about tragedy). Perhaps it is because the shape of Hegelian narrative is essentially and ultimately comic and thus the end of the *Aesthetics* features a coincidence of subject matter and plot.

the virtue of the nothingness or meaninglessness of the sign. It is perhaps the lack of meaning of the sign, its pure vehicality, so to speak, that allows the primal nonetheless to appear, with nothing interfering, because the sign equals zero. Nothing. If it meant anything, the sign could be what Rousseau called a 'dangerous supplement', adding something where nothing was required, depriving the primal even more of its putatively unadulterated strength. It is only in empty representation that the primal can appear as such, weak for appearing via meaningless signs but strong for not being altered or undermined in advance by meaningful ones. Only via the nothingness of these signs can the primal present or represent itself. The empty sign is somehow registered as such but then immediately consigned to the status of nothing.

Peter Szondi, one of Hölderlin's most sensitive and sensible readers, rather unexpectedly identifies the tragic sign in the above passage as the *hero*, though there is no mention of a hero or indeed any character or person.[37] Szondi in effect immediately aligns this fragment with something like Hölderlin's unfinished tragedy *The Death of Empedocles*, whose hero obliterates himself by leaping into the volcano of Mount Etna, his suicide reducing him to nothing. This is perhaps an understandable way to make sense of this thorny passage. Yet nothing in the fragment, as far as I can tell, authorizes us to translate from sign to hero, from linguistic mark to person: indeed, it may domesticate Hölderlin's claim to do so. There is little in Hölderlin's writings on tragedy that dwells on characterological or psychological matters. He does often invoke wrath (*Zorn*), a trait common to humans and gods[38] and one notes, for example, the concern about 'a consciousness' in the 'Notes on the *Oedipus*', where Hölderlin contends that one of the titular hero's great errors is 'his foolishly wild search for a consciousness'.[39] To be sure, in the

---

[37] Szondi (2002: 12). Szondi's phrasing is: 'In tragedy, this sign is the tragic hero.' Szondi is not alone in such a determination. Jeremy Adler and Charlie Louth do the same in their introduction to Hölderlin (2009: l). Joshua Billings, in the Hölderlin chapter of his *Genealogy of the Tragic* (2014: 189), offers a differently concrete and more compelling interpretation of the passage than one reducing the sign to the hero: ' "The sign" is the human world, which reveals its transience and fragility in tragedy, but in doing so, gives a glimpse into "the original". The dissolution of the represented world is the negative manifestation of an ontological fullness—a structure Hölderlin takes over from Schiller's and Schelling's theory of the sublime.'

[38] For a probing analysis of the motif and mode of 'wrath', see McCall (1988).

[39] Hölderlin (2009: 321 (modified slightly)).

'Notes on the *Antigone*' Hölderlin speaks of 'persons' such as Antigone and Creon, but even there they are resolved into 'principles'. Yet Hölderlin opts to say 'sign' and not 'hero' or 'person' or the like. He famously wrote, in some versions of the poem 'Mnemosyne': 'Ein Zeichen sind wir, deutungslos' ('A sign we are, without meaning'),[40] which suggests that human beings can be signs and vice versa. Still, the fragment on tragedy avoids any such terms as person or character. The meaningless sign of tragedy is apparently 'just' that: a sign. Whatever that is.

The enigma of the fragment is perhaps clarified—though in another way is redoubled—by aligning it with Hölderlin's 'Remarks on *Oedipus*' and on 'Remarks on *Antigone*', where a certain emptiness of representation recurs in a definitive way. Much attention has been lavished on the beguiling invocation of the so-called caesura of the speculative, the postulate that, at the pivotal moments of the two Sophoclean tragedies, something like a caesura occurs organizing the rhythm of each play, interrupting the action, dividing each play into two unequally extended parts, uneasily if artfully balanced.[41] Just prior to the claim for the organizing caesura, Hölderlin proffers a general formulation about the effect and movement of tragedy in keeping with his invocation of the 'lawful calculus' required (for ancient and now for moderns) of the genre:

> The law, the calculation, the manner in which a sensuous system, man in his entirety develops as if under the influence of the element, and how representation, sensation, and reason appear in different successions yet always according to a certain law, exists in tragedy more as a state of balance [*Gleichgewicht*] than as mere succession.
>
> For indeed, the tragic t r a n s p o r t is actually empty and the least restrained [*ungebundenste*].[42]

The opening paragraphs of the 'Notes on the *Oedipus*' make the case for an artisanal, workmanlike approach to poetry, sounding for a moment, despite the departure from Aristotle toward a principle of balance rather than logical succession, rather like some neoclassical brief for a normative poetics—and this apropos the genre of tragedy

---

[40] Hölderlin (1943–85: ii.1, 195).
[41] See the famous analysis by Philippe Lacoue-Labarthe (1989).
[42] Hölderlin (1943–85: v. 196; 1988: 101). (N.B. Sometimes for the notes I use the Pfau translation (Hölderlin 1988), as the base, sometimes the Adler and Louth version (Hölderlin 2009).

that Hölderlin calls 'the strictest poetic form'.[43] But, in the passage just quoted, things start exploding. And keep exploding. The odd word 'transport' (*Transport*) is enlisted for the most general, basic designation of what is at work and at play in tragedy. Tragedy sends you, in the least restrained way. This subject of transport has no object: it just transports or gets transported. To where, one does not know. Hölderlin's 'transport' links up with a massive discourse of related words—*Übergang* or transition, metaphor, translation—common in his poetological and *geschichtsphilosophisch* texts, each term being itself a translation of the others, all of which attest to how Hölderlin tended to think of language and history in terms of each other, rather as the young Walter Benjamin would.[44] These terms tend to the mobility and the power but also the instability of poetic discourse. Curiously Hölderlin uses here the Latinate word *Transport* where he might easily have used a Greek one, to say nothing of a German equivalent. The paragraphs prior to the exposition of the caesura are peppered with Greek terms such as *mechane* and the like, with some words left in Greek characters. It may well be, as Charles Lewis has recently argued,[45] that Hölderlin had read Boileau's translation of Longinus' treatise on the sublime (a text that his friend Hegel had translated in his youth). The term 'transport/*Transport*'—emphasized typographically in the printed text by doubling the spaces between letters—is, among other things, a rendition of Longinus' *ekstasis*, the term definitive of the effect of the sublime on its unsuspecting reader or auditor, rendering a subject literally beside itself.[46] Sublime transport renders the subject no longer sovereign in her or his subject-hood.

This empty transport is supplemented by an arguably more radical emptiness, what Hölderlin likens to a caesura, usually conceived of as

---

[43] Hölderlin (1943–85: vi. 339; 2009: 146).

[44] In the powerful, enigmatic text called 'Werden im Vergehen' ('Becoming in Dissolution' or known by its first phrase 'The Declining Fatherland') Hölderlin charts how the metaphor, transition, or translation is the paradoxical 'ground' of the nation. The ground moves, that is. I discuss this briefly in Balfour (2002: 241 ff.).

[45] See Vohler (1992–3) and Lewis (2011) for the encompassing situation.

[46] In English translations of the long eighteenth century, 'transport' is commonly used as the equivalent to Longinus' *ekstasis*. On the motif of 'transport' in Hölderlin and his thinking about and translating of Sophocles, see McCall (2014). In German texts of the period the stretched-out typography is often used for foreign words but in the notes to Sophocles all kinds of German words—and whole German sentences—are rendered this way, most likely just for emphasis.

a moment of silence, a moment that Hölderlin nonetheless locates in the *speeches* of Tiresias in *Oedipus Tyrannus* and *Antigone* respectively, speeches that Hölderlin characterizes as instances of 'pure word', where representation as such emerges: representation (re)presenting itself.[47] This representation too—full of itself and yet empty—is paradoxical insofar as representation is not representing anything, nothing other than itself. As a caesura, the interruption seems to have an affinity with the silence of the hero often posited as an eminently sublime moment in tragedy.[48] Yet Hölderlin locates the caesura in both of the plays by Sophocles, again, in the *speeches* of Tiresias, the blind prophet. How can such speeches—nothing but strings of words—constitute caesuras? Hölderlin makes explicit that these ruptures are instances of the 'pure word', which is perhaps another way of underscoring that is a matter of representation *as such*, of representation whose relation to the represented is suspended. These speeches interrupt the action of the plays and divide them into differently unequal 'halves'. The ruptures reframe the horizon of the action unfolding. The import of the seer's speeches, Hölderlin contends, is 'the removal of man from the sphere of life . . . to another world' '[tearing] him off into the eccentric sphere of the dead'.[49] To the extent that the seer's speeches are about the future, they engage 'objects' of representation in a peculiar way: the representation of the future is structurally different from that of the past or the present, since the future, by definition, does not yet exist. Such discourse, with a not-yet-real referent, emphasizes all the more the character of representation with its function of representing the represented at least temporarily suspended.

I gloss over here—instead of glossing—the enigmatic but often suggestively analysed notion of the caesura[50] to turn to the subsequent movement of Hölderlin's 'Remarks' so as to maintain our focus on the sublime, beginning with Hölderlin's novel interpretation of the oracle's pronouncements regarding the problem 'plaguing' Thebes. Hölderlin contends that Oedipus has interpreted the oracle 'too

---

[47] In this text the caesura counts mainly as a 'counter-rhythmical interruption' and so could indeed take the form of actual language as long as it were interrupting the established rhythm of the play or the action.

[48] This motif is important in W. Benjamin (1998) and Rosenzweig (2005).

[49] Hölderlin (1943–85: v. 197; 2009: 318 (translation modified)).

[50] For some of the more searching readings of the caesura, see Lacoue-Labarthe (1989) and Warminski (1987).

infinitely' (*zu unendlich*). He reasons that Oedipus could easily have understood the oracle as calling for the maintenance of good civil order or an upright court. Instead, he sought out a 'man', as Oedipus goes on to say, or, as Hölderlin, translating, says, 'a consciousness', but a man or consciousness whose sinful deeds are themselves 'infinite' (*unendlich*). Oedipus' interpretation is 'too infinite' by zeroing in, as it were, on the utterly finite possibility of a single man or consciousness as the source of the evil, a man whose nefarious deeds are in turn designated 'infinite'. (One zooms in, all the way, only to zoom out again, all the way.) It is remarkable that Hölderlin repeatedly has recourse to the term 'infinite' or some very proximate word to designate matters that could easily be construed otherwise. Why is Oedipus' error not rather called 'serious' or 'catastrophic' and why, say, are his sins not 'egregious' or 'monstrous' instead of 'infinite'? 'Infinity' is perhaps the most characteristic and pervasive of the predicates of the Kantian sublime. The term and concept had been operative in numerous critics of the sublime, as even in the empirically and somatically minded Edmund Burke.[51] But no one makes infinity as central or as crucial as does Kant. For him and some followers, the infinite raises and absolutizes the stakes of experiences that are putatively sublime. 'Infinity' and 'infinite' trip off Hölderlin's tongue or pen in his brief 'Remarks' on Sophocles. Versions of the word or concept occur some ten times in a mere fifteen or so pages. In the most pointed definition of the tragic, Hölderlin casts the forces at work as boundless:

> The representation of the tragic depends primarily on this: that the enormity [*das Ungeheure*] of God and man uniting, and the power of nature becoming boundlessly one with man's innermost being in wrath [*Zorn*] thereby comprehends itself, that the boundless [*grenzenlos*] unification purifies itself through boundless separation.[52]

Aspects of these formulations offer a framework, even if rendered here in extreme fashion, for the unfolding of the action in *Oedipus Tyrannus*, where, as Jean-Pierre Vernant has pointed out, the human

---

[51] A good deal of the discourse on infinity in the eighteenth century has to do with the physical universe or elements of it that suggest infinity. It is with Kant and his contemporaries that sublime infinity becomes as much in the purview of the subject. (There were exceptions beforehand, of course, as in Pascal and even Descartes.)

[52] Hölderlin (1943–85: v. 201; 2009: 323 (translation modified)).

is precariously, indeed ambiguously, poised between the divine and the animal, the divine and the natural, a framework equally applicable to Hölderlin's own *The Death of Empedocles*.[53] The main interest in the above passage lies in the strange force of the unbounded and the infinite, a passage rather typical of the baroque, involuted writings of Hölderlin's on poetry and poetic theory. One can sometimes be seduced, in reading high German Idealist prose, into thinking that the rhetorical balance of the phrasing, the parallel terms or clauses, means that there is or will be some dialectical resolution to the matter at hand. Tragedy is indeed the genre that stages the enormity of god and man 'uniting', but the stipulated unity, multiply invoked in the passage, is predicated in part on these forces bearing upon man and nature as projecting, in unbounded fashion, in opposite directions (unity versus separation). Can the equilibrium of the phrasing overcome the disequilibrium of the content? It is a hard paradox to overcome.

It is notable that Hölderlin's key term in the passage above, translated as enormity (*Ungeheuer*), is the same word used at the outset of *Antigone*'s set-piece that is the 'ode to man':

> Ungeheuer ist viel. Doch nichts
> Ungeheurer, als der Mensch.[54]

Ungeheuer translates the Greek *deina/deinos*, a term that itself pulls in several directions. Redolent of violence and power, the word also suggests an incapacity for moderation.[55] Man is already *deinos* (awesome/enormous/terrifying) before Hölderlin posits the *union* of man and god to be just that: *deinos*. But, again, is there any way to reconcile the limitless unification of the power of nature and man's

---

[53] See Vernant (1978). Tom McCall (2014) has pursued brilliantly the motif and idea of wrath stressed so much by Hölderlin in his understanding of Oedipus: the hero's 'wrathful anticipation', 'wrathful immoderation', and more, fully outdoing Hölderlin's beloved Achilles, his favourite hero, on this score. Wrath or rage is the one thing that humans and God or the gods, it seems for Hölderlin, have most in common.

[54] Hölderlin (1943–85: v. 219). An ultra-literal translation, though 'ungeheuer' is ambiguous, would read: 'Enormous/monstrous [*ungeheuer*] is much. Yet nothing is more enormous/monstrous than man.'

[55] On the polyvalence of the term *deinos/deina*, see Griffith (1999) and Kitzinger (2008). For Heidegger's famous, problematic, and—it is safe to say—non-dramatic reading of the choral ode on man, see Heidegger (2000: 155 ff.).

inmost being when that putative union is based on an infinite separation of the two?[56]

In the very next passage on the 'Notes on the *Oedipus*' following the general characterization of tragedy as *ungeheuer/deinos*, Hölderlin proposes:

> For this reason the ever-oppositional dialogue; for this reason the chorus as antithesis of the latter. For this reason the over-chaste, over mechanical and factually ending interlocking of the various parts; both in the dialogue and between the chorus and the dialogue and between the great sections or episodes which consist of chorus and dialogue. Everything is speech against speech, which mutually cancel each other out. [*Alles ist Rede gegen Rede, die sich gegenseitig aufhebt.*][57]

In the first instance, the reference of 'speech against speech' might well be to stichomythia, the rapid exchange, usually of one-liners, that Sophocles exploits, as Shakespeare and Racine later would, to great effect. But Hölderlin seems to have rather more that just this figure of speech in mind, as the absolute term 'Alles' ('everything') suggests. That speech is conceived as self-cancelling is one way of making sense of the proposition that in tragedy the sign equals zero.[58] I think one has to resist reading the loaded word *aufhebt* in its full Hegelian splendour and understand it, just as Thomas Pfau and other translators do, as 'cancel'. Martha Nussbaum proposes we think of tragedy as a genre that cannot arrive at a resolution 'without remainder'.[59] This seems to be in line with Hölderlin's insight, except that the remainder here is zero. For all of Hölderlin's enigmatic rhetoric, this passage does make possible a conception of tragedy as a discursive process that reduces itself in the end to nothing, in a mode cast in terms of the demise or negation not simply of the 'hero' but of speech itself, without which a tragedy is nothing.

---

[56] Hölderlin returns in the 'Notes on the *Antigone*' to this passage, again stressing the unity of god and man but one in which 'consciousness cancels out consciousness, and the God, in the form of death, is present' (Hölderlin 2009: 329).

[57] Hölderlin (1943–85: v. 201; 2009: 323).

[58] I do not take up here Hölderlin's skeletal remarks on the chorus, which no doubt play an important role in the conception of the dynamics of speech cancelling speech. For a good account of thinking about the chorus in Hölderlin's time, see Billings (2013b). On the functions of the Greek chorus more generally see Billings, Budelman, and Macintosh (2013) and (with special attention to gender dynamics) Foley (2003).

[59] Nussbaum (2001: p. vii).

The ultimate, radical negation to which tragedy tends does not occur in just any genre or form of art. Tragedy unfolds in time and space unlike most literary works. It is usually designed, in principle, to be performed.[60] One cannot press the pause button. The headlong rush, what Tom McCall terms the 'frantic pace' of Sophoclean tragedy, moves relentlessly on, not just in its own verbal terms but also redoubled in the unceasing experience of tragedy, with vertical, figurative complexity at odds with the (Beckettian) need to go on.[61] Tragedy can operate in classic Kantian sublime fashion, whereby comprehension, in its will to totalize and make sense, cannot keep up with apprehension. It can easily break down, even as play proceeds apace.

Hölderlin characterizes the time of Sophoclean tragedy as 'reissende': 'tearing' or 'rending'.[62] This destructive force of time is presided over by Zeus, whom Hölderlin notoriously translates as 'father of time' (*Vater der Zeit*). Numerous readers have wondered, understandably, why a pure transliteration of the Greek name Ζεύς as the German Zeus would not be a perfectly good, obvious choice, bolstered by the familiarity with Zeus as a Greek god for educated Germans.[63] Not only does it seem as if nothing would get 'lost in translation'; normally proper names stand outside the domain of units of language that require translation. One might think that, for the translation of the name of a *god*, one should interfere as little as possible. Hölderlin goes so far as to switch the category from proper name to a phrase made up of common nouns. He opts for a charged, allegorizing 'name' that is hardly a name: it is closer to an epithet or gloss. 'Father of time' renders, improperly, 'Zeus', providing a figuration where none seems required. Of all possible determinations of Zeus,

---

[60] Hölderlin's translations, however, were 'destined' for a long while only to be read, not to be performed. Hölderlin was very concerned about the visual appearance of the letters (in the sense of typeface) of the words on the printed pages, as evidenced in his letters to his publisher, Friedrich Wilmans. For example, 'I think that with letters like these it is easier for the eyes to find the meaning, since with over-pointed letters one is easily tempted just to look at the type' (Hölderlin 2009: 217).

[61] Hölderlin notes the 'rapidity' (Hölderlin 1943–85: v. 196; 2009: 318), the 'rapid concision' (Hölderlin 1988: 142), and the 'irresistible progress' (Hölderlin 1988: 146) of the *Oedipus* and of tragedies more generally.

[62] Hölderlin (1943–85: v. 198, 266; 2009: 320, 326).

[63] Each of the good philologico-critical essays on Hölderlin's Sophocles addresses this notorious translation. I have learned the most from the essays by Reinhardt (1961), Schadewalt (1966), and McCall (2014).

Hölderlin singles out 'father of time'—which is not just any identity when it comes to translation and, for that matter, tragedy. It is in and through time that Zeus becomes the 'father of time'. Zeus stands as the figure who brings things 'down to earth', the infinite god who descends to finitude to make the world what it is. The intervention of time helps Zeus appear as the 'father of time' and the agent of the victory of the Olympians over the Titans.[64] This father of time is all the more just that, in and after (some) time, after and across the chasm that separates Greeks from Hesperians, ancients and moderns. Zeus for 'us', according to Hölderlin, is no longer exactly the same god that he 'always' was: 'now, because we live under the more essential Zeus, who not only pauses between this earth and the wild world of the dead, but, on his way into the other world, *more decidedly forces down to earth* the natural process which is eternally hostile to man . . .'.[65] This now strangely 'more essential' Zeus is transformed, in such a way that it renders it necessary or plausible for Hölderlin to (re)name Zeus 'father of time'. The chasm of time separating antiquity and modernity requires a domesticating, explanatory, transformative translation, which, in trying to help us understand, adds a layer of vertical complexity to the frantic pace, the headlong rush of tragic plots that cannot be stopped.

To this point we have been concentrating more on 'Notes to the *Oedipus*' than on those to *Antigone*. The rhetoric of the sublime not only continues in the latter text but is ratcheted up a notch to something 'more than infinite', in Fichte's impossible phrase.[66] This sort of formulation is not foreign to Hölderlin, who repeatedly has recourse in his 'Fragment of Philosophical Letters' and the 'Ground to *Empedocles*' to the similarly impossible phrasing: 'more infinite' (236, 237, etc.).[67] In the 'Notes to the *Antigone*' Hölderlin attributes to Antigone herself a sublime posture in the sole passage where the word *erhaben* appears. Having just quoted Antigone's speech in which she likens herself to Niobe, a woman turned to stone for defiance of the gods, Hölderlin comments:

---

[64] Hölderlin's short ode 'Natur und Kunst oder Saturn und Jupiter' ('Nature and Art or Saturn and Jupiter') aligns, allegorically, Jupiter/Zeus with art and its difference from nature. One way to conceive of this is that art, as the break from or with nature, marks the beginning of time.

[65] Hölderlin (1943–85: v. 270; 2009: 330).   [66] Fichte (1968 [1807–8]: 123).

[67] Hölderlin (1943–85: iv. 275, 276; 2009: 236, 237).

Probably the highest trait in Antigone. The sublime mockery [*erhabene Spott*] surpasses all her other utterances, insofar as sacred madness is the loftiest human phenomenon and is here more soul than language . . .[68]

At the height of her language and soaring beyond to the loftiest level of the humanity because, on the cusp of and even participating in the divine, Antigone is no ordinary figure, yet Hölderlin goes on to generalize from what one might think is a near-singular situation (she is also, to put it a little crudely, a woman comparing herself to Niobe, who turned to a stone):

> In high consciousness the soul then always compares itself with objects that have no consciousness, but that in their fate take on the form of consciousness. Such an object is a land grown barren, which in its original lush fertility has too greatly intensified the effects of the sun and becomes dry for that reason. The fate of the Phrygian Niobe; as it is everywhere the fate of innocent nature, which everywhere in its virtuosity passes over into the all-too-organic, to just the degree that man approaches the aorgic, in more heroic circumstances and motions of the affects. And Niobe is then quite properly the image of the early genius.[69]

Niobe is not just any character to cut a sublime figure. In the generalized aesthetic sexism of the long eighteenth century, the sublime was almost systematically associated with men and beauty with women.[70] This had to do primarily with the different sexes being the objects associated with these two opposing principles but also often entailed the possibility of each sex being more prone to experience one of the two divergent aesthetic modes over the other: for example, women were not thought as likely to be able to experience the sublime as were men. Yet the great tragic heroines of Greek antiquity as well as Niobe (herself the subject of lost tragedies by Aeschylus and Sophocles) arguably constitute powerful exceptions to this sexist and sometimes misogynist rule.[71] Niobe is strikingly proposed by

---

[68] Hölderlin (1943–85: v. 267; 2009: 327).

[69] Hölderlin (1943–85: v. 267–8; 2009: 328). Paul de Man (2012) draws attention to the importance of Hölderlin's sense, for the Greeks, of the ontological priority of the object and its attendant complications. For a probing reading of de Man's account of Hölderlin, see Chase (2012).

[70] I discuss this problematic in my 'Torso' essay: Balfour (2006). There I am indebted to Alex Potts' analysis of Winckelmann (1994).

[71] I am stressing here the formidable character of these characters, some of them titular heroines of tragedies. This is not to say that these heroines might, at the same time that they are taken with the utmost seriousness, also be undermined by

Winckelmann as a figure who can trigger the full-fledged sublime able to stop us in our tracks, in a small way repeating her fate of being turned from an animate being to an immobile stone.[72] Antigone, who at the outset of Sophocles' play risks the announced punishment of being stoned to death, comes to be buried alive in a cave of stone. She is not so much turned into stone as enveloped within it. Antigone, heightened by the identification with Niobe, is fully operative in the mode of the sublime.

In the high consciousness invoked above, Hölderlin contends, the subject is close to the state of 'highest consciousness' when it 'avoids consciousness', a state of affairs with affinities to at least some moments of the Longinian and Kantian sublimes. In such high consciousness, unlike in the full-blown Kantian sublime where the power of comparison is suspended, the soul, for Hölderlin, 'always compares itself with objects which have no consciousness', a rhetorical form of the negation of consciousness from within it. It is this movement that ushers in, for Hölderlin, the figure of Niobe, in turn a figure for the stone-like Antigone.

The 'drama' internal to the subject unfolds in the more properly dramatic, theatrical encounter of 'two opposing forms of character' to which the chorus, with its great 'impartiality', relates. Somewhat in the spirit of Hegel to come on the matter of *Antigone*, Hölderlin stresses the 'equal balance' of the opposing forces that sets the stage, as it were, for reason, in the end, to enter the analysis in its final phase.[73] Close to the end of the second of the two sets of reflections, Hölderlin in a dense passage foregrounding both a certain infinity and a certain reason, contends:

> So, more Greek or more Hesperian, tragic representation depends on a more violent or uncontrollable dialogue and choruses, more halting and interpreting in the case of the dialogue, give the infinite strife direction or force, being the suffering organs of the divinely struggling body, which are really needed because even in his tragically infinite

---

discursive sexism. On the complicated status of women in tragedy and the tragic heroines in particular, there is formidable array of work by Froma Zeitlin, Nicole Loraux, Helene Foley, and Victoria Wohl, among others.

[72] Edmund Burke's term for one effect of the sublime, 'astonishment', contains the sense of turned to stone.

[73] Karl Reinhardt (1961) insists that Hölderlin was the 'first' to have hit up this sort of account of *Antigone*, which would later come to be known as Hegel's signature argument.

form the god cannot communicate himself properly to the body with absolute immediacy but must be comprehensively grasped, or appropriated in a lively manner; above all, however, tragic representation consists in the factual word, which is a continuum rather than an utterance, and goes fatefully from the beginning to the end; in the nature of the action, in the arrangement of the persons in relation to one another, and in the form of reason which develops in the terrible weariness of a tragic age and which, just as it represented itself in opposites at its wild conception, so afterwards, in a humane age, is accepted as a secure belief, born of divine fate.[74]

Here the tragic and the infinite are most tightly articulated in the 'tragically infinite' form of the god whom Hölderlin had described earlier as becoming one with the body of man, perhaps not far from Nietzsche's contention in *The Birth of Tragedy* that in instances of this genre Dionysus always inhabits the hero. It is easier to imagine a god as infinite than it is a human being, but the tragic god, like Zeus, descends to finitude or becomes one with finite beings, his fall being a prelude to theirs. The nonetheless infinite god must be grasped or comprehended by a finite being, a classic sublime predicament. Order might seem to be restored in the following claim of the protocols of the 'factual' word, proceeding, so its sounds, in Aristotelian fashion from beginning to end. Yet Hölderlin had earlier specified that this factual word is the one that kills, not some beautiful or harmless discourse that offers us education, pleasure, or both. All this, however, is taking shape within what Hölderlin calls a 'form of reason' (*Vernunftform*).

This form of reason has a lot to contend with in *Antigone* because the play contains a revolt wherein

> everyone, being overwhelmed by the infinite reversal [*unendlicher Umkehr*], and thoroughly moved, apprehends himself in the infinite form in which he is moved. For national reversal is the reversal of every mode of understanding and form. But a national total reversal in these, like any total reversal without any check, is not granted to man as a creature endowed with perception.[75]

Hölderlin posits the core of *Antigone*—it is a reading, not a 'theory' of tragedy—as an infinite revolt that is registered and cannot be

---

[74] Hölderlin (1943–85: v. 270; 2009: 330–1 (translation lightly modified)).
[75] Hölderlin (1943–85: v. 271; 2009: 331).

perceived, as such, on the far side of a reversal of all modes of understanding and form.[76] The action is uneasily balanced in the opposing principles (they are characters but more than that) of Creon and Antigone. They are equal but excessively so:

> The form of reason which here takes shape itself tragically [*die hier tragisch sich bildet*] is political, and specifically, republican, because the balance between Creon and Antigone is too equal [*zu gleich*].[77]

The end of Hölderlin's reflections turns insistently to reason as the shaping force of tragedy, as so many tragedies might themselves be said to do, whether it is the divine judgement with which the *Eumenides* culminates or the codas in numerous Shakespearian tragedies where the survivors of the awful excess remain to make sense of it all. Hölderlin seems, to a point, on the same page with so many philosophers who have conscripted the genre of tragedy, with more or less violence, for the demands of reason and even for philosophy. Tragedy comes in the form of reason and reason, in part, in the form of tragedy.

If in the end Hölderlin turns increasingly and then arrives at the category of reason, he follows suit from his philosophical master Kant and is in concert with a good many of his contemporaries and friends, several of whom ranked among the greatest thinkers of the day. The disruptions to the faculties of the mind in the face of the sublime give way, more or less convincingly, to the triumph of reason vaulting, in and via thought, to the realm of the supersensible where reason reigns.[78] Hegel's dialectic, especially, is notoriously able to swallow up any sort of error, one-sidedness, and negativity in the grand story of reason's self-realization. But Hölderlin's reason remains a tragic, unstable reason: the balance (*Gleichgewicht*) of the formalizing and unformalizing principles, Creon and Antigone, is paradoxically 'too equal'. In excess.

Hölderlin's Sophocles remains sublime in the negative mode, scarcely able to contain, within the tragic shaping of reason, the infinitizing forces at work in the two great tragedies. Kant had had

---

[76] Hölderlin's use of the category of infinity seems, contrary to our 'modern' usage, thinkable with that of totality, as if one can conceive of a totality that is infinite even if we could not know it (to borrow a Kantian framework developed partly apropos the sublime).

[77] Hölderlin (1943–85: v. 272; 2009: 332).

[78] Schiller gets there too, only far more precipitously than does Hölderlin.

little to say about tragedy but an awful lot to say about the sublime. The post-Kantians (Schiller, Schelling, Hegel, and Hölderlin) thought far more resolutely about literature, and, when they broached tragedy, they often did so within parameters outlined by Kant: freedom, the zone of the supersensible more generally, and an odd discursive space where representation has somehow been suspended, and yet the imperative to think, if not know, remains in force. Hölderlin relies on a modern vocabulary and framework of the Kantian sublime to help make sense of ancient plays separated from the former's Hesperian modernity by a chasm. Hölderlin responds to the predicament of confronting the 'indispensable' but in some sense inimitable Greeks by providing a critical, modernizing, allegorizing translation that takes account of the passage of time and the world-historical divide between ancient Greece and modern: even Zeus has changed and so needs to have his name changed accordingly. Hölderlin's own attempt to write 'modern' tragedy foundered, and not, I think, because he had chosen, in Empedocles, an antique subject. Modern tragedy had become precarious, unfated, *dysmoron*. It was no longer characterized by the tragic *transport*, the empty and unbounded transport of the Longinian sublime. Rather it found its emblem, as outlined in a famous letter to Böhlendorff, in this:

> For that is the tragic with us, to go away from the kingdom of the living in total silence packed up in some kind of container, not to pay for the flames we have been unable to control by being consumed in fire.[79]

It would be hard to invent an image less unbounded than that of the coffin, an emblem not just of finitude but of negation and framed nothingness. It connotes a different kind of emptiness from the undetermined transport of Sophoclean tragedy—an emptiness, then, in Hölderlin's tragic time and tragic space. If there is generally a resolution to the rational/irrational dialectics of tragedy, it is less a matter of all's well that ends well than—on the heels of all the infinite strife and the negation of 'everything', with speech cancelling speech and the reversal of every mode of understanding and form—much ado about—and under the sign of—nothing.[80]

---

[79] Hölderlin (1943–85: vi. 426; 2009: 208).

[80] I would like to thank Jim Porter, Joshua Billings, and Miriam Leonard for helpful comments and suggestions throughout the process of writing this essay.

4

Tragedy and *Trauerspiel*: Too Alike?

Samuel Weber

'When we say "tragic drama", we know what we are talking about; not exactly, but well enough to recognize the real thing.' So George Steiner towards the end of the introduction to his now classic study, *The Death of Tragedy*.[1]

Whether this is the case in regard to the dramatic works themselves—that is, whether we recognize such works as 'tragic drama' without necessarily knowing what those words mean—I would tend to doubt. But I am quite certain that such recognition was not at work when Walter Benjamin's study *Ursprung des deutschen Trauerspiels* was translated into English under the title *The Origin of German Tragic Drama*.

For, after even a relatively cursory reading of Benjamin's book, one of the few things that should have emerged clearly is the author's conviction that the word 'tragedy' or 'tragic' could not be used legitimately to designate the German Baroque *Trauerspiel*, literally 'mourning' or 'sorrow' plays. Indeed, in the light of Benjamin's discussion one could with considerable justification conclude that the main thing the two theatrical forms have in common is the first three letters of their respective names—in German as in English. Although Benjamin himself never descends to this level of literality, it is arguable that today as well this 'tra-*tra*' assonance may well be one of the factors contributing to making this equation plausible, even in the face of the extended arguments to the contrary deployed by Benjamin. Needless to say, this is too simple, as we will see. But it is not entirely misleading.

---

[1] Steiner (1961).

For, here as elsewhere, Benjamin's arguments weigh little with many of his readers compared to the dominant prejudices that inform their readings.[2] Another such is the tendency to equate value with universality: since 'the tragic' or 'tragedy' generally is understood as a positive value, it is often taken for granted that what it designates persists throughout history, and possibly even across cultures, in a universal manner. And, although Steiner himself begins his book with the well-justified warning that 'tragedy is not universal', but specific to the Western tradition, he too does not resist the temptation to describe it in ways that would transcend or abolish precisely the historical distinctions on which Benjamin was so keen to insist. The result is an appeal to words that become abstract when invoked in an ahistorical manner, for instance, 'catastrophe':

> Any realistic notion of tragic drama must start from the idea of catastrophe. Tragedies end badly. The tragic personage is broken by forces that can be neither fully understood nor overcome by rational prudence. This again is crucial.[3]

It is relatively easy to see, however, that not every drama that 'ends badly' is therefore tragic. Nor, if one thinks of Greek tragedies, is it evident that every 'tragic personage is broken by forces' beyond his (or her) control or comprehension. Two of the greatest Greek tragedies, *Oedipus at Colonus* and the *Eumenides*, do not end with anything like a total breakdown of 'the tragic personage'—unless death *per se* is considered to constitute such a breakdown. But, once again, it is difficult to argue convincingly that the universality of death as such suffices to define tragedy, or even to identify 'the real thing' when we see it. Nevertheless, Steiner is convinced that we find that 'real thing' throughout the Western tradition, albeit not often; and that the reason for this relates to the confrontation of the injustice of human existence, through which the tragic hero 'assumes a new grandeur'.

But even this experience of injustice is qualified and limited by Steiner, who begins his book by asserting that tragedy is alien 'to the

---

[2] Perhaps the most egregious and far-reaching instance of this can be found in the politics of translation: whereas Benjamin, in his own essay on the subject, 'The Task of the Translator', outlines an entirely practicable principle of translation, which he calls 'literalness [*Wörtlichkeit*] of syntax', his own translators into English have, by and large, with some notable exceptions, entirely ignored Benjamin's own syntax in reading, rendering, and interpreting him. See W. Benjamin (1996–2003: i. 260).

[3] Steiner (1961 : 97).

Judaic sense of the world' insofar as this 'sense' presupposes some sort of divine compensation ultimately accorded humans for the suffering imposed upon them—as in the case of Job. Curiously, however, Steiner does not apply this argument to the Christian tradition, from which his own language is drawn:

> Hence, there is in the final moments of great tragedy, whether Greek or Shakespearean or neoclassic, a fusion of grief and joy, of lament over the fall of man and of rejoicing in the resurrection of his spirit. No other poetic form achieves this mysterious effect; it makes of *Oedipus*, *King Lear*, and *Phèdre* the noblest yet wrought by the mind.[4]

Whereas Steiner thus excludes the Judaic 'sense' from the 'mysterious effect' of tragedy, the 'resurrection of (the) spirit' that Steiner celebrates here does not seem for him to fall under the notion of 'compensation'. This allows him to formulate an essence of 'tragic drama' that would justify its continued presence—and indeed, its culmination—in a 'Western' tradition dominated by Christian culture and values.

Thus, Steiner's emphasis on the ennobling confrontation with 'injustice' and 'excess' of human suffering seems informed by the Christian promise of redemption and resurrection, even while he acknowledges that such a hope is alien to the Greek 'spirit' and its tragedies. In short, the 'death of tragedy' is construed on the model of a Christian 'death of God'—which serves as the condition of the resurrection—or spiritual 'ennobling'—of man.

Nothing could be further from the view of tragedy and its relation to modernity developed by Walter Benjamin in his 1924 study of *The Origins of the German Mourning Play*. Benjamin insisted on the historical specificity of Greek tragic drama, which alone for him deserved the name of 'tragedy'. Adopting views developed by Wilamowitz and Franz Rosenzweig, Benjamin constructs a theory that construes Greek tragedy as a unique historical moment marking a decisive break with Greek mythology and its institutions—a break manifested above all in the refusal of the Greek hero to continue speaking the religious-judicial language of 'myth'. Since Benjamin's elaboration of this position is both complex, at times perhaps even somewhat confused, it reveals certain problems that tend to recur in thinking about the relation to Greek tragedy to modernity. Let me try

---

[4] Steiner (1961: 130).

therefore to lay out his position in some detail. From Wilamowitz he takes the idea of Greek tragedy as indelibly linked to myth, to which Benjamin then adds that this link consists above all in a 'tendentious reshaping of the tradition'. In order to identify the precise tendency that informs this 'reshaping', Benjamin invokes Rosenzweig's theory of tragedy outlined in his *Star of Redemption*. According to Rosenzweig, the tragic hero—and he assumes, and Benjamin follows him here and elsewhere, that tragedy necessarily involves individual 'heroes' (and 'heroines')—affirms himself by sacrificing his life in an act of refusal that at the same time is an affirmation of his Self. This refusal takes the form of a refusal to speak, as with Orestes in Aeschylus' *Eumenides*. In this play, Orestes scarcely utters a word throughout his trial, before being acquitted through the intervention of Athena, his protectress.

Although Benjamin's construction of tragedy, like that of Rosenzweig, is clearly based on the *Oresteia*, this play conforms to his notion of the tragic in only one respect: that of the silence of the tragic hero. In order properly to understand the emphasis that Benjamin places on the 'sublime'[5] dimension of this 'silence', a linguistic gloss is required. The German word that Benjamin, following Rosenzweig, uses to describe what in English is translated as *silence* says both more and less than its English equivalent. *Schweigen* is not simply 'silence'. As a noun that is also a verb, it connotes an active, voluntary, and deliberate *refusal* to speak, whereas the English word 'silence' primarily denotes the *absence of sound* as a *state of being*, rather than as the result of a deliberate act. According to Rosenzweig, whom Benjamin quotes at length and almost always approvingly, by refusing to speak the language of his society, the tragic hero withdraws into his isolated Self. What Benjamin then adds to this account of tragedy is a supplement: in addition to manifesting defiant withdrawal into an isolated Self, this act of not speaking fulfils a sublimely *prophetic* function:

> The more tragic words fall behind the situation—and they could no longer be called tragic were they ever to attain it—the more the hero has escaped from the ancient institutions, to whom—when they overtake

---

[5] 'Tragic silence [*Schweigen*], far more than tragic pathos, became the focus of an experience of the sublimity of linguistic expression that was far more intensively alive in antique writing than in that which came later' (W. Benjamin 1980: i. 288). My translation, here and throughout.

him in the end—he abandons only the mute shadow of his being, that Self as sacrifice, while the soul is saved in the words of a distant community.[6]

The paradox of Benjamin's account here—which precisely defends paradox against ambiguity, which he takes to be a feature of mythic demonism—is that, in insisting on the unique and inimitable historicity of Attic tragedy, its significance is precisely to anticipate, indeed to prophesize, a coming community that may well converge with certain essential aspects of Western modernity—for instance, with its emphasis on monotheism. Calling tragedy a 'preliminary stage of prophesy', Benjamin hints elusively at just what is being prophesied: 'In tragedy pagan man realizes that he is better than his gods, but this realization strikes him dumb and it remains unarticulated.'[7]

It would not have been easy for Benjamin himself to articulate just where in Greek tragedy this 'realization' can be seen—it is certainly not obvious in the *Oresteia*, where the struggle is between Gods, Athena, and the Furies, rather than between Orestes—who justifies his murder of Clytemnestra by saying that he was only following Apollo's orders—and the Gods. What then does Benjamin mean by asserting that man 'is better than his gods'? And how does this realization help constitute a preliminary form of prophesy?

About that 'coming community' very little is said, at least in the section of the book devoted to Greek tragedy. What is asserted is that the future significance of his action cannot be anticipated by the tragic hero, beyond his discovery that he is 'better than his gods'. Indeed, Benjamin insists that the historical significance of the hero's tragic silence remain unknown and unknowable to him.[8] This places him in sharp contrast with the death of Socrates. For Benjamin insists on the fact that Socrates knows—or thinks he knows—what he is doing and why he is dying. What thereby disappears in the story of the death of Socrates is precisely what is decisive for tragedy—namely, its agonistic dimension, consisting in a wordless—and one might add, uncomprehending—struggle, which in the Platonic dialogues has been replaced by the eloquent unfolding of speech and of consciousness.

---

[6] W. Benjamin (1980: i. 288).   [7] W. Benjamin (1980: i. 288).

[8] The reading of the *Eumenides* as the exemplary tragic articulation of a redemptive sacrifice goes back at least to Hegel's essay on Natural Law: see the excellent discussion in Thibodeau (2012: 74 ff.).

From the Socratic drama, the agonistic moment has broken free—even philosophical struggle is itself a specific kind of training and all of a sudden the death of the hero has changed into the dying of a martyr. Like the Christian hero of the faith . . .[9]

As in Nietzsche's *The Birth of Tragedy*—to which Benjamin here remains more indebted than he explicitly acknowledges—the death of Socrates marks the end of tragedy, which cannot survive either the certainty of the philosopher or an unshakable faith in the Christian Good News. For the tragic hero, Benjamin asserts, there is no clear consolation for his suffering and death:

He shrinks before death as before a power that is familiar, personal, and inherent [*eingebannten*]. His life unrolls from death, which is not its end but its form. For tragic existence finds its task only because the limits— those of linguistic as of corporeal life—are given it from the beginning.[10]

In this sense of the inevitability of death, which informs his life, 'the tragic hero . . . is soulless'.[11]

And yet, only a few pages earlier, in a passage already quoted, Benjamin can assert that through the sacrifice of his 'self' the tragic hero's 'soul is saved in the words of the distant community'. History, in short, is still the medium of salvation: salvation of the isolated individual, from whose tragic 'silence' 'coming generations' will 'learn their language'.[12]

Now what is truly curious and thought-provoking in Benjamin's study is that the 'coming generations' or 'distant community' that are described at any length in it are those involved in the post- and indeed Counter-Reformation German *Trauerspiel*. And the unique language that this generation speaks through its theatre at least is that of *allegory*. But Benjamin's entire effort in this text will be expended on arguing how remote and contrary that language is from the 'silence' of the tragic hero. 'The *Trauerspiel* can be thought of as a pantomime; tragedy cannot.'[13]

Whereas the authors and contemporary theoreticians of the German baroque Trauerspiel, or 'mourning play', sought from the very start to portray these plays as the legitimate heir and continuation of Greek tragedy, Benjamin interprets this as an effort both to claim a certain

---

[9] W. Benjamin (1980: i. 293).   [10] W. Benjamin (1980: i. 293).
[11] W. Benjamin (1980: i. 293).   [12] W. Benjamin (1980: i. 293).
[13] W. Benjamin (1980: i. 297).

legitimacy, and to obscure the true nature of their enterprise, which he argued had to be radically distinguished from tragedy.

For whereas the point of departure and element of tragedy was myth, that of the German Trauerspiel was 'history'. But not just any history, nor the history of nations, peoples or institutions. Rather the 'history' which provided the point of departure and the element of the Trauerspiel was that of a Christian *Heilsgeschichte*—'salvational history'. The form in which this history had hitherto been propagated had been radically challenged and shaken by the Protestant (especially Lutheran, and hence German) Reformation, which in turn produced as a reaction a movement of Counter-Reformation that Benjamin insists was at work in both Christian confessions, and not simply in Catholicism. The result was the generalization of the 'agonistic' dimension of Greek tragedy, but also its displacement: it now played itself out within a Christian Europe divided against itself, but still informed by the horizon of a promised but uncertain redemption and resurrection. Whereas Greek tragedy was marked by the decisive struggle waged by an isolated tragic hero against the prevailing theological–political–juridical order—which in turn perpetuated its power and authority by enforcing a 'mythological' regime of fate and guilt— for the *Trauerspiel*, by contrast, the struggle was no longer between the individual Self and a mythic order, but rather between different conceptions of 'history': first as a *Heilsgeschichte*—promising redemption; and second as *Naturgeschichte*—a 'natural history'—understood, however, not in terms of the eighteenth century but as the fatal fate of a guilty and unredeemed creation.

In this sense, these two, essentially Christian, conceptions of 'history', far from materializing the coming community that was to learn to speak from the silence of the tragic hero, embodied, paradoxically, the very 'mythical' tendencies against which the tragic hero rebelled. For both pagan myth and Christian 'histories' presuppose 'guilt' as the condition of 'redemption'—even if the redemption is in each case significantly different. The permanence of 'guilt' and 'destiny' thus suggests an underlying continuum linking Greek (pagan) mythology with Christian *Heilsgeschichte*. But precisely this link distinguishes, for Benjamin, tragedy, which seeks to break with guilt (if not redemption), and *Trauerspiel*, which seeks to perpetuate it.

Using broad brushstrokes, reminiscent somewhat of Nietzsche's operation in 'The Birth of Tragedy', especially in their lack of concrete historical or historiographical references, Benjamin sketches out the following sequence:

1. The Lutheran emphasis on *sola fides* marks a decisive break with the established and the historically institutionalized form through which the Christian Good News is administered on earth. Hitherto a universal (Catholic) church had been able to claim that it embodied the worldly link between the trials and tribulations of the mortal life of guilty individuals, and the hope of a redemption and resurrection that would overcome both guilt and mortality. The Lutheran attack on 'good works' called into question not only the authority of the Church and the efficacy of its sacraments, but more generally the ability of all volitional action to fulfil this promise—which was largely experienced as the total loss of meaning of worldly human existence.

2. This emphasis on 'faith alone' that could no longer be reliably measured in terms of worldly action and experience inevitably called into question established institutional structures, the political consequences of which Benjamin interprets through invoking Carl Schmitt's work on the crisis of political sovereignty in the seventeenth century. Thus Benjamin extends the Lutheran attack on 'good works' to apply to all purposive action, and not just to moral or religious acts. It was this tendency that the 'Counter-Reformation' sought to counteract. Benjamin emphasizes that 'Counter-Reformation' in this sense could not be limited to the actions of the Catholic Church: rather, it was at work in all efforts to attenuate or roll back the corrosive implications of the Protestant, and, in particular, Lutheran, Reformation, which in Benjamin's eyes entailed a certain radicalism that was then somewhat attenuated in Calvinism. Here, without referring to Max Weber's *The Protestant Ethic and the Spirit of Capitalism*, his argument continues that developed in chapter three of that book, 'Luther's Conception of the Calling', in which Weber distinguishes the role played by Luther's version of Protestantism from that of Calvinism in promoting the rise of capitalism:

> Although the Reformation is unthinkable without Luther's own personal religious development, and was spiritually long influenced by his personality, without Calvinism his work could not have had permanent concrete success.[14]

---

[14] M. Weber (1992: 47).

3. In his study of the German mourning play, Benjamin notes the following apparent paradox: on the one hand, all of its major authors were Protestants; on the other hand, as employees of local state regimes, they were engaged in an essentially conservative undertaking, which sought to attenuate if not eliminate the corrosive impact of the Lutheran Reformation on contemporary political and social structures, through its questioning of the salvational value of 'good works', which is to say, human initiative and action. It is significant in this perspective that Benjamin would focus on a phenomenon of theatre, instead, for instance, on the lyric poetry or narrative fiction of the same period, both of which could lay claim to greater literary–aesthetic value than the *Trauerspiel*. But Benjamin was no more interested in traditional literary–aesthetic values in this study than the Kant of the Third Critique was in traditional aesthetic values (preferring 'natural beauty' to 'artistic beauty'). His argument, influenced by the work of Alois Riegl, on Late Roman Art Industry (1901), was that certain artistically inferior works could demonstrate more profoundly critical social and political problems and situations than could more consummate aesthetic works.[15] And it was these problems that interested Benjamin more than their ostensible resolutions, no doubt because he was convinced that it was the persistence and evolution of those unresolved problems that had become the motor of subsequent history, at least in the West.

In short, rather than endorsing Max Weber's conviction that Calvinism had contributed to the growth and expansion of Capitalism, Benjamin was concerned to show that driving this historical development was a series of unresolved 'religious' problems grown increasingly problematic; and that their ostensible resolution, qua 'secularization', had to be understood as a defensive reaction rather than as a constructive resolution of an ongoing crisis, involving the loss of faith in a Christian salvational narrative that promised personal redemption and bodily resurrection as the reward for 'good works'.

Western modernity, then, in this view, was dominated by the response of the Counter-Reformation to the radical antinomianism

---

[15] W. Benjamin (1980: i. 235).

of the Lutheran Reformation. And, since Counter-Reformation was a term that Benjamin explicitly refused to limit to 'one of the two Christian confessions'—that is, to Catholicism—there is every reason to argue that he would have included many forms of Protestantism, including Calvinism and perhaps other institutionalized religions as well, under its heading.

His study of the German *Trauerspiel*—plays written by Lutherans but in the spirit of the Counter-Reformation—was thus at the same time an attempt to reconstruct what might be called a genealogy of modernity. But his genealogy stamped 'modernity', at least in its more obtrusive manifestations, as an essentially defensive process in which the accessibility of 'salvation' was relegated to the most internal and elusive experience of 'faith'.

Viewed from this perspective, the theatrical experience of the *Trauerspiel* could be seen as an attempt to counter such internalization. Whereas in Greek tragedy, the audience, qua community, is invited to serve as 'judge' of an 'unrepeatable' and 'decisive cosmic process and trial', the spectators of the *Trauerspiel* find themselves confronted by 'situations presented on a stage in an interior space devoid of any relation to the cosmos'.[16] At the same time it would be wrong to conclude that the German *Trauerspiel*, because of its emphasis on affect and feeling, and because of its distance from any 'cosmic' process, is therefore simply subjective. For 'the *Trauerspiel* knows no heroes, but only constellations',[17] whereas, in tragedy, it is the ability to assume, reflect, and process the notion of 'guilt' that constitutes the individualizing moment. In the *Trauerspiel*, by contrast, because of its Christian origins, guilt is so generalized that it cannot be ascribed or embodied, much less reflected and overcome in a single figure. A historical variation of the *Trauerspiel*, the 'drama of destiny' (*Schicksalsdrama*), presents guilt as the result of an original sin that condemns that 'natural' world to mortality, while preserving the memory of a prelapsarian, paradisiacal state. As Benjamin puts it in one of his most striking images and formulations:

> Destiny . . . fulfils its meaning only as a natural–historical category in the spirit of the restoration theology of the Counter-Reformation. It is the elementary natural force in historical events, which itself is not entirely nature insofar as the state of creation still reflects the rays of

---

[16] W. Benjamin (1980: i. 298–9).   [17] W. Benjamin (1980: i. 311).

the grace-giving sun [*Gnadensonne*]—mirrored, however, in the cess-pool of Adamitic guilt [*Verschuldung*].[18]

It is the tension between the vision of a paradise lost through guilt and sin, and the hope of its recovery through a grace that, however, ever since the Reformation, had become increasingly elusive, that distin-guishes the German *Trauerspiel* not just from Greek tragedy but from its Spanish counterpart, exemplified by the works of Calderon. For, if Benjamin insists on the distinctiveness of the 'German *Trauerspiel*', it is not because of its aesthetic superiority, but rather because, through its lack of artistic perfection, it throws a sharp light upon the specific situation and crisis to which it responds. Thus, in contrast with Calderon, the German *Trauerspiel* is distinguished by its 'great pov-erty of non-Christian ideas'.[19] And, among these ideas, the balance between guilt and grace, fear and hope, has been tilted strongly towards the former of the two terms.

This, in turn, gives a very different interpretation of the 'openness' of the theatrical process in the *Trauerspiel* with respect to the defini-tiveness of the tragic decision.

> Whereas tragedy, even the most uncertain, ends with a decision, there lurks in the essence of the *Trauerspiel* and especially in the death (it stages) an appeal such as that formulated by martyrs. It is appropriate to develop the legal (dimension) further and in the sense of medieval literature of complaint to speak of a trial of the creation, whose accusa-tory complaint [*Klage*] against death—or against whomever else it may be directed—is laid *ad acta* at the end of the *Trauerspiel* after being only partially processed. Its resumption is implicit in the *Trauerspiel*...[20]

This 'unfinished' aspect of the German *Trauerspiel*, in which a final decisive verdict remains forever outstanding, is what stamps it as an exemplary 'originary' historical phenomenon, in the sense attributed to the word origin by Benjamin in his *Epistemo-Critical Preface*:

> In origin what is meant is not the becoming of the emergent, but rather that which emerges out of becoming and passing away. Origin stands in the flux of becoming as a maelstrom [*Strudel*] and tears into its rhyth-mic movement the material of emergence. . . It wants to be recognized, on the one hand, as restoration, as reconstruction, and therefore, on the other, as incomplete and inconclusive. In each originary phenomenon

---

[18] W. Benjamin (1980: i. 308).   [19] W. Benjamin (1980: i. 309).
[20] W. Benjamin (1980: i. 315–16).

the figure is defined in which again and again an idea encounters and resists [*sich auseinandersetzt*] the historical world, until it lies there in the totality of its history.[21]

If this intrinsically restorative, and therefore structurally incomplete, 'idea' of the German *Trauerspiel* were finally to 'lie there in the totality of its history', its significance could only be situated outside of that history. And, indeed, there is every reason to suspect that for Benjamin the history of the German *Trauerspiel*—or what he also calls 'the German drama of the Counter-Reformation'[22]—far from being limited to a particular historical period, converges with the history of Western modernity in general. If this history is, therefore, marked by the essentially defensive and incomplete response to the crisis of the Christian soteriological narrative, one of its major effects is to establish the feeling of *Trauer*—sadness, mourning—and the state of 'melancholy' as the major moods of that history.

The German *Trauerspiel* presupposes this feeling, mood, and state, but attempts to control its more disruptive effects. This process leads to one of the most curious and unusual formulations in all of Benjamin's writing:

> Those who looked deeper saw their existence inserted in a field of ruins composed of partial, inauthentic actions. Against this life itself struck back. It feels profoundly that it is not there only in order to be devalued by faith. Terror overwhelms it at the idea that the whole of existence could play itself out in this way. It is profoundly horrified [*tief entsetzt es sich*] when confronted by the thought of death. Mournfulness is the state of mind, in which feeling reanimates the emptied world as though masked, in order to derive an enigmatic satisfaction from its appearance.[23]

The formulation is unusual insofar as it invokes 'life itself' as the subject of this historical development. This designation operates in his text something like a form of *style indirect libre* in narrative fiction: the term 'life itself' is not so much a designation of an objective 'subject' as an expression of the state of mind that marked the defensive position of the *Trauerspiel*. For what it mourned and the object of its sadness were precisely the loss of a notion of 'life itself', of a life that would be as free of death as was the creation before the fall. It is the nostalgia for this 'life itself' that is mourned by the mourning play and its audience:

---

[21] W. Benjamin (1980: i. 226).   [22] W. Benjamin (1980: i. 229).
[23] W. Benjamin (1980: i. 318).

this is both the source of its sadness and the means of its attenuation. Without claiming to reinstate the Christian Good News, the German drama of the Counter-Reformation aspires to reanimate the visible world, albeit in the form of a 'mask'—*maskenhaft*. Hence the 'affinity between mournful sadness and ostentation':[24] ostentation seeks to divert its audience from the 'emptiness' of a world without visible access to grace. But its revalorization of the phenomenal world as 'allegory' elevates and debases it at the same time. And, in so doing, 'its never-ending repetition secures the disconsolate domination of the melancholic temper's distaste for life'.[25]

Benjamin thus seeks to depict the relation of Greek tragedy to the German *Trauerspiel* as one of mutual exclusion and indeed polar opposition: the one involves the refusal to speak the language of myth and the mute appeal to a coming community; the second involves the reaction of an existing community to the fear of death triggered by the crisis of the Christian soteriological narrative: the *Trauerspiel* is meant both to tranquillize that fear and to perpetuate it qua melancholy. *Trauer* is the experience of this crisis as a loss, but as one that gives rise to a certain play (*Spiel*); melancholy entails the awareness that this loss is endemic in the temporal finitude of living beings.

This awareness ironically—in the Benjaminian perspective, that is—returns to precisely the myths that the tragic hero is said to have overcome: the myths of *Kronos* and the titans, emasculated and devoured by their children, who become the Greek Olympian deities. The death of God results in a return of the saturnine sense of time as the devourer of all beings.

The German Baroque *Trauerspiel* thus involves a community that is very different from that which the heroic and sacrificial silence of the tragic hero seems to portend. It is certainly not a world in which man recognizes that he is 'better than his gods'. Nor is it one that has broken free of the constraints of guilt. And yet in one particular aspect it is profoundly related to Greek tragedy. In both Greek tragedy and the German *Trauerspiel* language signifies more and less than what is said explicitly. In Greek tragedy, as we have seen, the hero—so Benjamin—chooses silence over speech, refusing the dominant language of a myth-based society, but in the process offering that silence as a 'preliminary stage of prophecy' that inserts silence

---

[24] W. Benjamin (1980: i. 319).   [25] W. Benjamin (1980: i. 319).

and ignorance at the heart of language. The Greek hero, therefore, does not and cannot know the meaning of his silence—or his death. The German *Trauerspiel*, by contrast, thinks it knows the meaning of what is said and done, but knows it as pure negation. This is why its basic stance is that not of silent resistance, but of noisy complaint and accusation: not *Trotz* but *Klage*.

Thus, the silence of the tragic hero functions as a resonance board, which allows 'distant, new divine commands' (*Göttergeheiße*)[26] to resound, without his knowing where they are coming from or what they mean. By contrast, the world of the allegorical *Trauerspiel*, despite all its verbiage and ostentation, is also one marked by a certain silence, although it is one very different from that of the tragic hero. And that difference has to do, perhaps, with the fact that those *Göttergeheiße* are no longer all that distant, but in fact all too close—as close as the creator is to the creation. Now, however, instead of *Schweigen* the world of the *Trauerspiel* is marked by *Stummheit*, struck dumb by the history of its own *name*:

> Because it is mute [*Stumm*] fallen nature mourns. But the essence of nature is revealed even more profoundly by the inversion of this proposition: its mournful sadness makes it fall silent [*macht sie verstummen*]. There is in all mourning an inclination to lose language, which is infinitely more than just the inability or unwillingness to communicate. The mournful feels thoroughly recognized by the unrecognizable. To be named—even when the name-giver is like the gods and blessed—always retains perhaps a sense of mourning. How much more, however, when one is not named but only read, uncertainly, through the allegorist and made highly significant [*hochbedeutend*] only through him.[27]

Trauer—mournful sadness and the loss of language (muteness)—are the result not just of the abuse of the allegorist, but of the history whose crisis produces the allegorist in the first place: the history of a creation in which creatures 'feel themselves thoroughly recognized by the unrecognizable'—which is to say, by a creator-god that is entirely heterogeneous to them, but who delegates the function of naming to his privileged creature, prelapsarian Adam. This 'godlike' giver of names thus imposes a certain alterity at the very heart of what is to be the mark of the creature's identity: its name. The allegorist then only continues and exacerbates what is already present in the story of the creation.

---

[26] W. Benjamin (1980: i. 293).   [27] W. Benjamin (1980: i. 398).

Benjamin thereby implicitly disavows the opposition he had sought to construct in his early (1916) essay on 'The Language of Man and Language Overall', where he identified the 'fall' with the fall from a language of divine naming into one of profane judgment. The allegorist embodies an extreme of the language of judgment, in his imposition of 'signification' on creatures that from the start have been 'overnamed'.[28]

Since one of those 'distant divine commands' will be precisely that which assigns Adam the task of naming all the creatures, *Trauer* and indeed the *Trauerspiel* emerges as one of the consequences of that process. The crisis of the Christian salvational narrative is therefore rooted in the creation myth itself.

The allegorist is the master of meanings and of signification, but precisely his mastery entails an experience of the irreducible nullity of his existence—a nullity that is measured in terms of the loss of 'faith' in the promise of redemption and resurrection. What is depicted on stage is history not as the site of future redemption, but as the actual 'production of corpses'.[29] The best that the German *Trauerspiel* can do, according to Benjamin—and it is not trivial—is to provide a certain consolation, by emphasizing the artificiality of the destruction it stages. What Benjamin could not yet know, but what his discussion prepares us to recognize, is that the self-negating strategy of the allegorical *Trauerspiel* is a precursor of today's audiovisual presentation of the 'news' as a series of spectacular catastrophes—which, qua spectacle, serve as distraction and entertainment.

Nothing could seem at first sight more removed from Benjamin's interpretation both of tragedy and of *Trauerspiel* than Hölderlin's 'Remarks on *Oedipus*' and 'Remarks on *Antigone*'. And this distance is all the more remarkable since, in an essay written shortly before his book on the *Trauerspiel*—namely in his essay on 'Goethe's Elective Affinities' (1924–5)—Benjamin refers extensively to what today has become the most quoted term of those 'Remarks', the concept of *caesura*. Benjamin invokes this notion precisely in relation to Greek tragedy, where he equates it with 'the falling silent [*Verstummen*] of the hero' in Greek tragedy.[30]

---

[28] W. Benjamin (1980: ii.1. 155).

[29] Benjamin makes an exception here for *Hamlet*, which in contrast to the German *Trauerspiel*—so he argues—retains the hope of providential salvation: W. Benjamin (1980: i. 335).

[30] W. Benjamin (1980: i. 181–2).

It is significant, however, to note that he uses the word *Verstummen* rather than *Schweigen*. This reflects the impact of Hölderlin's 'Remarks', in which the notion of the tragic 'self' of the hero—indeed, of the hero as subject—plays little or no role. It is not even the speech of the hero that is 'interrupted' by the 'caesura', but rather the succession of ideas, images, and scenes that make up what might be called the 'plot'. Although Hölderlin does not use this word, his 'Remarks' are informed by a very different relation to the tradition and to history from that of Benjamin. This relation is not primarily that of a critic, as in the case of Benjamin, but rather that of a poet and a translator. This puts Hölderlin in a much more interactive relation to the tradition than was the case with Benjamin. Although, like Benjamin, Hölderlin clearly distinguishes ancient Greek tragedy from its more modern, 'Hesperian' and German counterparts, he does not insist on their mutual exclusivity. Benjamin, who does, winds up, as I have tried to argue, by demonstrating—between the lines rather than explicitly—their profound complicity. The German *Trauerspiel*, and the modernity it presages, turns out to be an heir of Greek tragedy, insofar as the 'history' that the latter portends develops as the 'salvational history' of Christian Europe. Myth and this history thus also turn out not to be simply opposed to one another, but to be profoundly interrelated.

Hölderlin's reflections on the relation of Greek to Hesperian cultures will lead in a somewhat different direction, involving the acknowledgement of a profound interaction and even reciprocity obtaining between the two.

Hölderlin's awareness of this reciprocity is in part a result of his own unsuccessful attempt to write a modern tragedy—*Empedocles*. Unable to complete this project, Hölderlin then turns to translation as a way of better articulating the relation of his historical situation to Greek culture and theatre. A note to his publisher, Wilmans, indicates just how he construed this relationship:

> I hope to present to the public Greek art—which is foreign to us through national conventions and errors, through which it has sought to help itself—in a more vivacious manner than usual, by bringing out its suppressed oriental dimension, as well as correcting its artistic errors, wherever they occur.[31]

---

[31] Hölderlin (1943–85: ii. 947, 28 September 1803).

This remark makes clear just how much Hölderlin's practical relation to the Greek text, as its translator, has influenced his approach to tragedy. He seeks not to assimilate it to a modern view, but to strengthen 'its suppressed oriental dimension'. This remark, in turn, has to be read in the context of the more general theory of Greek and modern culture that Hölderlin has sketched in a famous letter to his friend Böhlendorf:

> In the process of cultivation [*Bildung*] the truly national will become increasingly less attractive. Hence the Greeks are less master of sacred pathos because it was innate to them, whereas they excel in their talent for presentation, beginning with Homer, because this exceptional man was sufficiently sensitive to master the Western Junonian sobriety for his Apollonian empire and thus veritably to appropriate what was foreign.
>
> With us it is the reverse. Hence it is also so dangerous to deduce the rules of art for oneself exclusively from Greek excellence . . . With the exception of what must be the highest for the Greeks and for us— namely, the living relationship and destiny—we must not share anything identical [*gleich*] with them. What is familiar must be learned as well as what is alien.[32]

On the one hand, then, Hölderlin, like Benjamin, stresses the differences between ancients and modern: 'we must not share anything identical with them' (*wir nicht wohl etwas gleich mit ihnen haben dürfen*). But the key word here, which Hölderlin sets in italics, and which is translated as 'identical', is not quite identical with its English translation: *gleich* is cognate with the English *like*, and thus can signify not just identity but also difference. Here, to be sure, it is in the sense of being similar or identical that Hölderlin uses the word. But, as we shall see towards the end of this essay, the word is always overdetermined—'overnamed', as Benjamin might have said.

Here, the statement that the moderns should not try to be *gleich* with the Greeks follows one decisive exception: 'With the exception of what must be the highest for the Greeks, namely the living relation and destiny.' Just what the 'living relation and destiny' involves will become clearer when we turn to the 'Remarks'. For the moment let us just note that, despite these historical and cultural differences and similarities, Hölderlin does not exclude the possibility of there being

---

[32] Hölderlin (1943–85: ii. 940). See also the English translation by Pfau in Hölderlin (1988: 149–50). Translation modified.

a 'genuinely modern tragedy',[33] which he congratulates his friend
Böhlendorf at having written. Thus, what Greeks and Germans
share—that 'living relationship and destiny'—is in principle at least,
and despite historical differentiation, sufficient to justify retaining the
same word to describe tragic dramas of both cultures. Nevertheless,
the emphasis, in the passages quoted, is that modern German writers
will be able to fulfil their literary and cultural destinies only if they do
not try to imitate or be 'like' their Greek predecessors. For what
Greeks and Germans share in common—'the living relationship
and destiny'—is shared in different and indeed opposing ways. In
his 'Remarks on *Antigone*', Hölderlin makes this difference explicit:

> For us... the Greek notions [*Vorstellungen*] transform themselves inso-
> far as their main tendency is to get a grasp on themselves, because that
> was their weakness, whereas the main tendency in the notions of our time
> is to hit the target, whatever it may be [*etwas treffen zu können*], to be
> skilful [*Geschick*], since the lack of destiny [*das Schicksallose*], is our
> weakness. This is why the Greek has more skill and athletic prowess,
> whereas with us this is more subordinated to propriety [*Schicklichkeit*].[34]

You will have noticed how much certain key terms in this description
are all built on a single lexical root: *Schick*, from *schicken*, to send. The
three decisive words that Hölderlin employs to relate and differentiate
Greek and German culture are *Geschick*, *Schicksallose*, and *Schicklichkeit*. In each case the root word is combined to mean something
different: skill, lack of destiny, propriety, to describe the contrasting
relation of Greeks and Germans (moderns). But what they all share in
common is what that root word signifies—namely, a movement
originating elsewhere and tending elsewhere. With the exception of
the last word, *Schicklichkeit*, which reduces the notion of 'sending' to
a means–end activity, implying conformity to a programme or set of
rules. The English and French words chic/*chic* are probably both
derived from this use of *schicklich*. *Geschick*, which today means
generally 'skilfulness' or 'artfulness', as a past participle suggests the
ability to respond to the unexpected, and therefore is not reduced to
instrumentalization, as with *Schicklichkeit*. *Schicksal*,[35] commonly

---

[33] Hölderlin (1943–85: ii. 941).   [34] Hölderlin (1943–85: ii. 788).
[35] This word marks perhaps the point of greatest divergence between Hölderlin
and the critic and thinker he has perhaps most inspired—with the exception of
Heidegger—namely, Benjamin, for whom *Schicksal* is linked to the mythical–juridical
regime of guilt (as in the essay *Schicksal und Charakter, Destiny and Character*) (cf.

translated as 'fate', connotes more literally a 'sending', 'mission', or 'destiny'. For Hölderlin it marks the way in which a culture responds to and assumes its historical heterogeneity. Such a heterogeneity derives for Hölderlin from the dependency upon and interaction of man with his environment. At the beginning of his 'Remarks on *Oedipus*' Hölderlin describes human being as a 'system of sensations' (*Empfindungssystem*) that 'develops itself under the influence of the elements'.[36] The way this 'sensation-system' responds to those 'influences' determines its trajectory and its very being. As a temporal being, the system responds with 'notions and sensations and reasoning . . . in different successions, but always following a certain rule'. In 'the tragic'—and it is significant that Hölderlin here writes always of 'the tragic' rather than of 'tragedy', since what constitutes its essence is not peculiar to a work or genre, but to a way of being, something that Benjamin also emphasizes—what prevails is 'equilibrium, rather than pure successivity'.[37]

Hölderlin's emphasis here on *Gleichgewicht*, equilibrium, although absolutely essential to his entire argument about 'the tragic', has been almost totally neglected in favour of the dramatic pathos attached to the notion of 'caesura', 'the counter-rhythmic interruption' of the sequence of notions, of *Vorstellungen* (here rendered as 'notions'), that Benjamin and so many others following him have adapted from Hölderlin. By ignoring the function assigned by Hölderlin to the caesura—namely, that of establishing a certain 'balance' or equilibrium—the notion itself is radically transformed, and/or misunderstood.

Thus, for Benjamin, the function of the caesura qua interruption, whether in his interpretation of the tragedy or, some years later, of Brecht's Epic Theatre, is to disturb a certain homeostasis, to introduce a certain *imbalance*. For Hölderlin, on the contrary, a certain imbalance constitutes the point of departure for Greek tragedy, as it does more generally for the formation of a national culture: the culture, as explained in the letter to Böhlendorf, must move away from what is most familiar, most innate, most immediately identical to itself, in order to fulfil its potential by appropriating what it innately lacks. For

---

W. Benjamin 1980: ii.1, 171–9; i. 308–9). This is precisely not the case for Hölderlin, however, as we will see shortly. I hope in the future to be able to analyse in some detail their divergent uses of this all-important word.

[36] Hölderlin (1943–85: ii. 730).   [37] Hölderlin (1943–85: ii. 730).

the Greeks this was the power to organize and represent, manifest in athletic skill; for the Germans, on the contrary, what is initially lacking is the ability to abandon themselves to the 'fire', to that 'oriental' element that was innate to the Greeks. This is why in his letter to his publisher Hölderlin claims that he has sought to foreground what the Greeks sought to repress—namely, their 'oriental' tendencies, since it is precisely this that is lacking in German culture, which places its priority on being able to 'hit the mark'—to follow rules and be astute (*schicklich*)—or, as Hölderlin also puts it in that letter to Böhlendorf, to remain 'quietly packed into some container':

> This is the tragic for us: that, quietly packed in some container we depart from the realm of the living, rather than atoning for the flame through being consumed by flames we are incapable of taming.[38]

'The realm of the living'—like 'the living relationship' shared with the Greeks, but also like 'the living sense' (*der lebendige Sinn*) that Hölderlin, at the outset of the 'Remarks on *Oedipus*', emphasizes 'cannot be calculated' but must nevertheless be 'brought into relation with the calculable laws' of poetry[39]—this 'realm of the living' entails an openness to everything that cannot be 'contained' in a 'box' or container, although it cannot be simply separated from such laws and rules. It entails an openness to alterity, to the future, and, for living beings, to mortality. Thus, for Hölderlin it falls to 'the tragic', through its caesura, to establish a 'balance' between the desire to contain and comprehend, which is also the desire to know and to survive what cannot be comprehended ('death'), and the necessity of reconciling oneself with 'the living relationship', which is also and perhaps above all a relationship with the incomprehensible fact of mortality. The 'tragic transport', that is 'interrupted' by the 'counter-rhythmic caesura', is for Hölderlin inevitably the manifestation of this drive to overcome alterity, to assert what is familiar, natural, and native over what is foreign, alien, and other, to assert life *against* death rather than to assume their imbrication. It is this drive that the caesura is called upon to interrupt, by re-establishing a 'balance' between 'beginning' and 'end', so that neither prevails over the other and both acknowledge their mutual interdependence.

---

[38] Hölderlin (1943–85: ii. 941).   [39] Hölderlin (1943–85: ii. 730).

In this sense we can see how Hölderlin's conception of 'the tragic' is both transhistorical and historical. It is transhistorical in having its basis in a human being that qua finite transcends the specificities of historical periods and cultures. But it is historical in relating the different ways in which human beings experience their finitude to the manner in which different cultures relate to what is native to them and to what is foreign.

As with Benjamin, the caesura challenges the status quo, the dominant traditions and tendencies of a given society at a given moment; but, unlike Benjamin, it does not manifest itself primarily in the refusal to speak (the existing language), but rather in a dialogical intervention that establishes 'balance'. Hölderlin's notion of 'balance' or 'equilibrium' seems at first sight quite foreign to Benjamin, who thinks far more in terms of explosive or disruptive interventions. But for Hölderlin the shock of the caesura is no less powerful—it is just that its power is conceived of in a different manner. Rather than 'breaking' through a congealed surface or situation, it brings about a more enigmatic transformation, organized around a single word: 'counter' (in German: *gegen*). This is the sense of another formulation often overlooked or neglected by critics: the fact that the 'interruption' of the caesura is repeatedly designated by Hölderlin as 'counter-rhythmic'. Counter-rhythmic has quite a precise meaning here: first of all, it arrests the initial tendency of what might be called the 'plot' in tragedy either to escape its beginning by reaching its goal as quickly as possible (*Oedipus Tyrannus*); or to remain tied to an initial decision and refuse its future transformations (*Antigone*). In each case, the caesura intervenes 'counter-rhythmically' by altering the tendency of the plot either to rush forward towards a conclusion or to arrest all forward movement by remaining fixed on an initial decision or act. In both cases, for Hölderlin it is the appearance of Tiresias that constitutes the caesura, helping to establish a certain 'balance' or equilibrium in the succession of ideas and acts that constitute the plot. Thus, the expression of the caesura will be primarily through the form of the dialogue, although of a highly discontinuous and violent one. Tiresias speaks only with an interlocutor (Oedipus, Hamon), never by himself or on his own. He would like to keep silent, but the circumstances do not allow him to. There is no 'falling silent'—no *Schweigen* or *Stummheit* of the tragic hero in Sophocles.

And it is Sophocles, rather than Aeschylus, that interests Hölderlin most.

This enables us to read the famous formulation from section three of the 'Remarks on *Oedipus*' about the nature of tragic presentation in a somewhat different manner from how it has previously been understood:

> The presentation of the tragic rests primarily on the fact that the enormity of god and man coupling with each other and that nature's power and man's innermost being become one in fury, comprehends itself therein, that limitless unification purges itself through limitless separation.[40]

To understand just what is meant by the often quoted phrase 'the enormity of god and man coupling with each other and... nature's power and man's innermost being becom(ing) one in fury' it suffices to turn to the example given by Hölderlin with respect to Oedipus: 'The understanding of the whole rests primarily on focusing upon the scene where Oedipus interprets the words of the oracle too infinitely . . .'.[41] According to Hölderlin the tragedy takes its point of departure in Oedipus' fateful response to the Oracle: instead of responding pragmatically, and seeking to 'keep good civil order' (*haltet gute bürgerliche Ordnung*), Oedipus responds in too 'priest-like' a manner by 'suspiciously interpreting the general command [of the Oracle] into particulars [*ins Besondere*], applying it to a murderer of Laios and then taking the sin as well to be infinite'.[42] If now we keep in mind just how much Hölderlin's reading here itself runs *counter* to established interpretations of Oedipus—especially his insistence on the possibility of the Oracle being understood to demand 'good civil order'—then we must ask just what it is that his own caesura-like intervention is 'interrupting'—and in what sense might that interruption be considered 'counter-rhythmic'?

There is one word in the passage just quoted that indicates what might be at stake here, and more generally in the 'coupling of man and god': it is the word 'sin'. It is a strange word for Hölderlin, with his acute sense of historical differentiation, to apply to a Greek tragedy. For it takes one of the key words of a biblical tradition that would seem to have absolutely no relevance to Greek culture and

---

[40] Hölderlin (1943–85: ii. 756).   [41] Hölderlin (1943–85: ii. 731).
[42] Hölderlin (1943–85: ii. 732).

makes it a decisive moment in his reading on Oedipus. But it is
precisely the tendency of Oedipus to 'take the sin . . . to be infinite'
that can make him intelligible to modern audiences. And this is, after
all, Hölderlin's professed aim in translating and interpreting the
tragedies. 'We must present the myths namely as everywhere more
demonstrable,' he observes in the 'Remarks on *Antigone*'.[43] Hölderlin's reading of Oedipus' response as 'priest-like', too 'infinite', and,
above all, as moving too quickly from the general to the particular,
demonstrates the 'sin' that afflicts his contemporaries and, even more,
their response to it. The moderns have no destiny because they
enclose themselves in a container, afraid of what might come from
without—afraid of what Hölderlin (and Benjamin in his Hölderlin
essay) identify with a certain 'oriental' element—namely, the 'fire'.
Afraid of contingency, of anything not controllable in advance—of
both freedom and death, the moderns derive mortality from 'sin'—
which is to say from an act of transgression, in which man sought to
be too much *like* his conception of the divine, in whose 'image' he
declares himself to have been 'created'. This 'likeness' would make
death a result of action: a transgression that is then punished, but that
then becomes the basis of the Christian Good News. The path to
salvation is confided to the action of priests, who seek to establish a
certain continuity between immanence and transcendence, between
sin (mortality) and grace (resurrection).

By seeking to retrace the cause of the plague decimating Thebes to
the act of a single human being, to a 'murderer', Oedipus reacts in a
manner that is both all too familiar and effectively 'modern'. Through
such identification he claims for himself the power of purging the
city from illness and death that come from without, rather than that
of 'keeping good civil order' within. Already, Hölderlin's translation
of the Oracle's words, as conveyed by Creon, is couched in terms
that allow for such reading, in contradistinction to most other
translations:

> *Man soll des Landes Schmach, auf diesem Grund genährt,*
> *Verfolgen, nicht Unheilbares ernähren.*

> (The country's shame, nourished on this ground, should be pursued,
> the incurable not nourished.)[44]

---

[43] Hölderlin (1943–85: ii. 786).   [44] Hölderlin (1943–85: ii. 731).

Contrast this with a fairly recent English translation, and you will see how the latter already incorporates and predetermines Oedipus' reaction, thus eliminating effectively the question of interpretation and leaving Oedipus no alternative but merely to echo the words of the Oracle, which the translation renders without any ambiguity:

> There is an unclean thing,
> Born and nursed on our soil, polluting our soil,
> Which must be driven away, not kept to destroy us.[45]

Hölderlin, by contrast, through his translation and especially through his use of the word *verfolgen*—to 'persecute', or more literally, to 'pursue' or 'attend to'—allows for Oedipus' reading but also for other responses as well. He never says what must be, but only what could be: 'Das könnte heißen . . .' ('That *could* mean . . .').[46] And his formulation, that 'the incurable should not be nourished', suggests that behind the plague decimating Thebes lurks the question of the vulnerability and mortality of the living, something that the famous second chorus of *Antigone*, announcing the singular 'uncanniness' of man, will confirm, as well as demonstrating in its final lines the ambivalence of the chorus in confronting this terrifying destiny.

It is this ambivalence that the notion of 'sin' seeks to master and ultimately to do away with—'death, where is thy sting?' (1 Corinthians 15:55), as Paul will put it, in declaring the mission of the Church to be that of destroying its final enemy, death ('The last enemy that will be destroyed is death' (1 Corinthians 15:24–6)).

In thus calling attention to the possibility that Oedipus acts in too 'priest-like' a manner, Hölderlin calls attention to the greatest difference separating Greek tragedy from its modern successors: the Christian notion of mortality as a punishment for a transgressive act—but which, as an act, can therefore be overcome by another action. In this regard, Hölderlin situates himself squarely within the Post-Lutheran context discussed by Benjamin, since it is precisely a certain desire to save through 'good works' that drive Oedipus to his downfall.

---

[45] Sophocles (1947: 28).
[46] Hölderlin (1943–85: ii. 731). This conditionality of phrasing, also in his poetry, is something Heidegger can simply not accept. See his seminar on 'The Ister', where he responds to the last lines of the poem—'Yet what that one does, that river | No one knows'—by insisting: 'What the vocation is of the Ister and what it does . . . it well knows . . .' (Heidegger 1984: 163).

On the other hand—and with this I will have to stop, rather than conclude—Hölderlin also refuses the clear-cut division into Reformative and Counter-Reformative movements that Benjamin uses to situate the German *Trauerspiel,* and by implication much of Western modernity more generally. Hölderlin's insistence that the effort to 'couple' man with the gods results in 'fury' and infinite separation, and that this in turn takes the form of disloyalty (*Untreue*) and forgetfulness of both man and god—this insistence leads to another highly unexpected political conclusion. Having described the 'nature' of the proceeding (*Hergangs*) in *Antigone* as one of an 'uproar', Hölderlin shows how this can be seen as a political consequence of the monstrous—uncanny—coupling of man and god:

> The kind of proceeding in *Antigone* is that of an uproar [*Aufruhr*], in which what counts, insofar as it is a fatherlandic affair, that is, insofar as each thing is seized by infinite overturning [*Umkehr*], and is shaken by it, also feels itself in infinite form. For fatherlandic overturning is the overturning of all kinds of representation and of forms. A total overturning, without anything to hold on to, is not permitted to humans, as cognitive beings [*als erkennendem Wesen*].[47]

A total, permanent 'revolution' is thus impossible, at least for man as a 'cognitive being'. This is why, at the very end of his 'Remarks', Hölderlin notes that 'the form of reason, that here (in Antigone) forms itself tragically, is political, and namely republican'.[48] The same, however, is not necessarily true for man as a *sentient* being. However if this question is left open, the need to establish some sort of 'balance' remains the imperative task of tragedy. But even here no unequivocal certainty is possible. In contradistinction to the Benjamin of the *Trauerspiel* book, at least Hölderlin does not affirm the value of paradox against that of ambiguity, no more than he affirms that of history against myth. For his own practice of writing—in this not unlike that of Benjamin—makes abundant use of ambiguity, as the link that joins and separates man as cognitive and as sentient being. But such ambiguity requires a sharp eye to distinguish, as in the lines that complete the remark just quoted and which insist that the implications of the tragedy are

---

[47] Hölderlin (1943–85: ii. 789).   [48] Hölderlin (1943–85: ii. 790).

political and namely republican, because between Creon and Antigone, formal and counter-formal, the balance is held too equal [*zu gleich gehalten*]. In particular this shows itself at the end, when Creon is almost abused by his servants.

Sophocles was right. It is the destiny of his time and the form of his fatherland.[49]

'Sophocles was right' (*Sophokles hat Recht*). The tragedy that seeks to establish balance achieves it almost too well: in a formulation that is infinitely ambiguous, Hölderlin separates two words that could also be read together: 'zu gleich'—meaning either 'too equal, too like' or 'at the same time': the balance—the *Gleichgewicht*—between Creon and Antigone is at the same time, *gleich* and *zu gleich*, equal, balanced and too balanced: Antigone dies and Creon is abused. Not the same thing, of course, but also not entirely different, if each is seen as standing for an aspect of human finitude that cannot simply be abolished.

There is a final image that sums up perhaps that *about which* Sophocles was *right*, and what at the same time separates him from those Moderns who would encapsulate themselves in containers and always hit the mark, who value *Schicklichkeit*, astuteness, and conformity over meeting their *Schicksal* with *Geschick*—confronting their destiny with virtuosity. If Benjamin compares both tragedy and the *Trauerspiel* to a legal trial and its outcome, Hölderlin, the reader and translator of Pindar, compares *Antigone* to that other Greek form of agonistics, the sporting event, and in particular to a *race*: 'The grouping of persons, (in Antigone), resembles a competition [*Kampfspiel*: literally battle-play] of runners, where the one who first gasps for breath and jostles the opponent [*Gegner*] has lost . . .'.[50] It should be noted that Hölderlin does not say who wins, but rather who 'has lost': the runner who can no longer keep upright and so sustain a certain *separation*—from the other runners as well as from the Gods. The key word, for Hölderlin, remains the word *Gegen-*: 'counter': whether as counter-rhythmic interruption, or as encounter with the adversary (*Gegner*). The relation of Greek tragedy to modernity may also be construed along the lines of a *Begegnung* ('encounter') that invites an *Entgegnung*—a countering that responds, but without either touching

---

[49] Hölderlin (1943–85: ii. 790).   [50] Hölderlin (1943–85: ii. 790).

or avoiding the other. Perhaps this encounter-without-direct-contact, which conserves a certain separateness, is what can be called 'feeling' or sensation—at least in the sense of the word used by Hölderlin to describe the singular systematicity of the human being.

Despite the lack of direct contact—or perhaps because of it—, nothing perhaps could—in the Benjaminian sense of the word at least—come as more of a shock.

5

Leben und Glück: Modernity and Tragedy in Walter Benjamin, Hölderlin, and Sophocles

Andrew Benjamin

Denn Schicksal . . . betrifft das Leben unschuldiger Pflanzen nicht. Nichts ist diesem ferner. Unaufhaltsam dagegen entfaltet es sich im verschuldeten Leben. Schicksal ist der Schuldzusammenhang von Lebendigem.[1]

(Walter Benjamin)

Das Glück ist es vielmehr, welches den Glücklichen aus der Verkettung der Schicksale und aus dem Netz des eignen herauslöst. "Schicksallos" nennt nicht umsonst die seligen Götter Hölderlin.[2]

(Walter Benjamin)

(1) Endings are themselves fraught with difficulties. How is a work to end and to what end? The ending brings with it the possibility of a summation and therefore it would need to be read, though in the case of theatrical performance heard, as pronouncing upon what has already taken place—a pronouncement that in encapsulating what had been read, heard, or experienced brings it to an end by re-creating

---

[1] W. Benjamin (1980: i.1. 138; 1996–2003: i. 307): 'For fate . . . does not affect the life of innocent plants. Nothing is more foreign to it. On the contrary, fate unfolds inexorably in the culpable life. Fate is the nexus of guilt among the living.' This chapter needs to be read as an extension of the interpretation of Walter Benjamin developed in A. Benjamin (2014).

[2] W. Benjamin (1980: ii.1. 174; 1996–2003: i. 203): 'Happiness is, rather, what releases the fortunate man from the embroilment of the Fates and from the net of his own fate. Not for nothing does Hölderlin call the blissful gods "fateless".'

it. These concerns, it can be argued, are at their most emphatic when what occurs at the end, as its end, conditions the preceding in one direction rather than another. Such is the case with Sophocles' *Antigone*. While there are references within the last speech by the Chorus, the speech that brings the play to a close, to both the Gods and a self-referential concern with age, it remains the case that the speech can be read and heard as recasting a number of the play's defining elements. Perhaps the most insistent, and in this instance the most significant, occur in the speech's opening lines.[3] Pursuing the opening provided by the speech as a whole provides the means for tracing an important link between Sophocles, Hölderlin, and Walter Benjamin in regards to a philosophical thinking of life. What is at stake here turns around a number of interrelated questions. What is 'life' and thus the 'living' thought philosophically? Moreover, what would it mean to act for the sake of the living and thus in the name of life? How would such actions be understood philosophically? These questions will announce a project whose major focus is thinking of life philosophically, some of whose defining elements are present here.[4]

---

[3] The full text in Greek follows:

πολλῷ τὸ φρονεῖν εὐδαιμονίας
πρῶτον ὑπάρχει. χρὴ δὲ τά γ᾽ εἰς θεοὺς
μηδὲν ἀσεπτεῖν. μεγάλοι δὲ λόγοι
μεγάλας πληγὰς τῶν ὑπεραύχων
ἀποτίσαντες
γήρᾳ τὸ φρονεῖν ἐδίδαξαν. (Sophocles 1885: 47)

Standard English and German translations are as follows:

Of happiness, far the greatest part
Is Wisdom, and reverence towards the Gods.
Proud words of an arrogant man, in the end,
Meet punishment, great as his pride was great,
Till at last he is schooled in wisdom. (Sophocles 1970: 45)

Besinnung ist von den Gütern des Glücks
bei weitem das höchste: man frevle nicht
gegen Göttergebot! Ja größer der Stolz
der Vermessenen ist, um so tiefer der Sturz,
der die Untat sühnt
und lehrt sie in Alter Besinnung. (Sophocles 2003: 261)

[4] These passages are excised from a work-in-progress provisionally entitled *Life and Luck*—a work whose project pertains to how life is thought philosophically when life cannot be reduced to the biological, on the one hand, while, on the other, neither the biological let alone the neurological provides a model in relation to which the detail and the complexity of human life can be thought. Central to such a project is *Glück* and thus the complexities presented by its translation.

Of central importance within the Chorus's last speech is the relationship between the terms τὸ φρονεῖν and εὐδαιμονία as they stage the concerns of life. Sophocles wrote:

πολλῷ τὸ φρονεῖν εὐδαιμονίας
πρῶτον ὑπάρχει.

At its most elementary Sophocles has the Chorus claim that there is an important connection between τὸ φρονεῖν and εὐδαιμονία. And thus what matters in any subsequent translation of the line is the way in which that relationship is then understood. In Ezio Savino's Italian translation the Chorus states:

ragionevolezza è base, base prima di buona vita.[5]

The translation stages a set of relations: namely, that 'ragionevolezza', as the translation of τὸ φρονεῖν, is the basis of εὐδαιμονία translated here as the 'buona vita'. In other words, τὸ φρονεῖν allows for εὐδαιμονία, in the precise sense of providing that on which it is based. Mark Griffith, in his commentary on the *Antigone*, suggests that the line be understood as claiming that τὸ φρονεῖν 'is laid down as the first principle of happiness' (or 'of the good life').[6] There is, therefore, first, as a conceptual argument, the identification of τὸ φρονεῖν as the *sine qua non* in regards to the possibility of εὐδαιμονία; hence what could be described as 'firstness' (πρῶτον) takes on the quality of an *arché*. Secondly, there is a conceptual compatibility between 'happiness' and the 'good life' that is evidenced by the subsequent translation in which 'happiness' and the 'good life' can be substituted for each other. It should be clear in addition that the 'good life' cannot be equated with 'life' *tout court*. Hence there is a twofold question. What is the 'good life'? How within the life is the 'good life' to be actualized? At work here, therefore, is the implicit identification of the 'good life' as a potentiality within life.

Kitto's earlier and more literary English translation of this line involves a slight shift in emphasis:

> Of happiness far the greatest part
> Is Wisdom.[7]

---

[5] Sophocles (1989: 309). [6] Sophocles (1999: 354).
[7] Sophocles (1970: 45).

Again, there is the suggestion of a form of complementarity. Within Kitto's translation that shift is evidenced by τὸ φρονεῖν now being the major component of 'happiness' (where the latter is the translation of εὐδαιμονία). τὸ φρονεῖν is, of course, now present as 'wisdom'. Wilhelm Willige's contemporary German translation can be read as having introduced a complicating factor.

> *Besinnung ist von den Gütern des Glücks*
> *bei weitem das höchste.*[8]

The complication, at least initially, emerges in the translation of τὸ φρονεῖν as 'Besinnung'. A further part of the complication is that *Besinnung* is not a straightforward translation of Kitto's 'wisdom', even though both 'wisdom' and *Besinnung* may be there in τὸ φρονεῖν. Without there being clear forms of identity between these terms, there is, nonetheless, an overlap of concerns staged by their announced interrelationship.

In all these translations, what emerges are not just possible relations between τὸ φρονεῖν and εὐδαιμονία; of greater significance is that the former is taken as functioning as a necessary precondition for the latter. At this point, acts of translation run into a set of problems that are as much terminological as they are philosophical. The most acute concerns the translation of τὸ φρονεῖν. The problem is clear: τὸ φρονεῖν is not 'wisdom' if wisdom is understood as contrasted to knowledge, as, for example, would be evident in Augustine's distinction between *sapientia* and *scientia* established in the *De Trinitate* (books 12–14). In the Augustinian context, *sapientia* involves turning inward and thus turning from the world. The worldly nature of *scientia* would have an affinity with calculation and to that extent judgement. In the context of Sophocles' *Antigone*, 'wisdom' has to bring with it a concern with judgement and therefore political calculation. This tempers the evocation of the Gods in the second line of the Chorus's final speech, thereby allowing that line to be read as enacting a sustained refusal of the way in which a relation to the Gods is evoked by both Antigone and Creon earlier in the play. The argument for what would amount to piety, or rather the counter to 'sacrilege', in this latter context, in its differentiation from the 'tragic conflict' that the relationship between Creon and Antigone is taken to

[8] Sophocles (2003: 261).

stage, has been delimited in advance. It occurs, therefore, within the already present necessity for judgement, demanding as a consequence a form of political calculation. The latter is necessary for the realization of εὐδαιμονία, the term that has been already announced in the opening lines of the Chorus's final speech. These calculations are not made just in relation to life in the *polis*. More importantly, life in the *polis* is defined as much by the necessity for judgement, as it is by judgement becoming that which delimits in advance the propriety of human being, where the latter is understood as a set-up in which the 'good life' endures as a potential within life and where the object of the polis is the realization of that potentiality. This does, of course, repeat the point made by Aristotle in the *Politics* in which he argues that the *polis* exists initially for 'life'; however, it continues in order to facilitate 'the good life'—γινομένη μὲν τοῦ ζῆν ἕνεκεν, οὖσα δὲ τοῦ εὖ ζῆν.[9]

In the context of the *Antigone*, to be human, and to be in a relation to the Gods, is not to have a relation to the latter that is defined by immediacy, where the immediacy of the law is taken as delimiting and defining human action. There is the possibility for another conception of relationality, where relationality comprises human relations, relations to the law, and finally relations to the Gods. This other conception of relationality, which would also be at work within these three domains, arises from the recognition that the hold of immediacy can always be suspended and thus tragedy is not inevitable. Hence, what matters here is not that Antigone and Creon act but that those actions are themselves the enacting of what they take to ground or determine their actions. That they speak will never be as significant as what it is that is spoken. The division between two modes of speech breaks the link between character and fate insofar as that link not only necessitates the singularity of character but also assumes the indelible nature of the mark of fate on the determination of character.[10] Overcoming the hold of tragedy depends on the refusal of that mark as determining. (With that refusal fate can be rethought

---

[9] Aristotle, *Politics* 1252[b]29: 'while it comes into existence for the sake of life, it exists for the good life.'

[10] In addition, what is at stake here is the possibility of beginning to interpret the writings of Walter Benjamin in terms of a specific relationship to Greek philosophy. And thus to make the claim that, despite their obvious use of motifs from Jewish philosophical sources and despite his recourse to the language of a certain Marxism, what is at work is a series of concerns that are far more Greek in orientation. Two texts that advance similar positions are Birnbaum (2008) and Blumenthal-Barby (2009).

as history.) As such, history becomes the site of contestation rather than that which can be attributed an ineluctable inevitability.

It must always be remembered that both Antigone and Creon hold to the law's immediacy. The difference between them therefore has to be understood in terms of the content of the law and not in the way in which any one individual becomes subject to the law. The implicit suggestion made by the Chorus is that the possibility of an already present connection between τὸ φρονεῖν and εὐδαιμονία entails that any relation to the Gods will have been determined in advance by the location of that connection within life and thus with its having a determining effect on life. Life in this context is not biological life. Nor, however, is it a complete abstraction that denies a relation between human life and biological life. Life needs to be understood as an activity and thus the continuity of activity. In sum, life is—is what it is—in the continuity of its being lived out. It occurs therefore in the place in which it is lived out. In other words, in the place opened and sustained by the necessity of the relation between τὸ φρονεῖν and εὐδαιμονία; life becomes therefore *being-in-place.*[11] The setting is thus provided for the next line of the speech:

χρὴ δὲ τά γ' εἰς θεοὺς
μηδὲν ἀσεπτεῖν.

(It is necessary not
to be sacrilegious in relation to the Gods.)

What this line demands, almost as a form of abstract necessity, which is itself a set-up carried by the impersonal verb form χρή, is that a sacrilegious relation to the Gods has to be refused. As is now inevitable, given the opening of the speech, what matters is the quality of the refusal. The full force of the position advanced by the Chorus can be located in the necessity that this refusal is the result of a judgement that is itself premissed on the interdependence between τὸ φρονεῖν and εὐδαιμονία. Consequently, any such refusal is not an immediate response. The decision to refuse sacrilege would have been mediated from the start. There is the implicit suggestion, therefore, that a response to the law, where the source of law is identified with either the Gods or the *polis*, and where that response is immediate, becomes, as a consequence, a form of sacrilege. In other words, what is at work

---

[11] I have tried to develop a sustained conception of *being-in-common*, as it is at work in Ancient Greek philosophy and literature, in A. Benjamin (2010).

is a conception of 'sacrilege' (ἀσεπτέω) whose avoidance is ground in the mediacy of judgement rather than the immediacy of the law (or laws as the site of immediacy). In a sense the suggestion here is that 'sacrilege' concerns a relation to the Gods and not one to the actual presence of the Gods. In more general terms, therefore, the opening lines of the final speech by Chorus function both as a conclusion and, equally, as the staging of the play's other possibility.

Within the context of the play as a whole, the possibility for it to end in this way will have already been noted by the play's audience. (Moreover, such an ending marks a return to τὸ φρονεῖν as an element integral to life.) The evocation of the centrality of τὸ φρονεῖν has occurred at an earlier stage in the play. The positioning is deliberate. At the play's centre, Haemon, as part of a heated exchange with Creon, his father, says the following to the latter:

If you were not my father [μὴ πατὴρ] I would say that you had no wisdom [οὐκ φρονεῖν]. (l. 755)

The significance of this line is twofold. In the first instance it locates the centrality of τὸ φρονεῖν within the play as a whole. In the second it means that any possible attribution of centrality to τὸ φρονεῖν locates τὸ φρονεῖν as standing in opposition to the law on the condition that the latter is itself defined in terms of immediacy—a form of definition that, on the one hand, notes the radical difference between the conceptions of law evoked by Creon and Antigone and yet, on the other, elides that difference insofar as both conceptions of law are defined in terms of immediacy insofar as law is held apart from justice.[12] (τὸ φρονεῖν is positioned between law and justice mediating the relationship such that justice as a result takes on the quality of a decision.) Consequently, while always allowing for another relation to the law, such a relation would necessitate a reworking of the law such that the law was of necessity interarticulated, from the start, with the

---

[12] The *Antigone* will always mark a clash as much between family and the *polis* as it does between female and male. There is an obviously gendered dimension to the play. And yet, the recourse made to law's immediacy—the twofold recourse in terms of Antigone and Creon—while involving gender is not explicable in gendered terms. Were that to be the case, then gender would be linked to the immediacy of the law and thus relations between the genders would be inevitably tragic. The play can be read as suggesting that the relationship between genders—a relationship that allow for conflict but resists tragedy—is a relationship that is always already mediated in advance by the complex operation(s) of judgement.

possibility of judgement (where judgement marks the inescapability of mediacy; mediacy is the precondition for justice). Consequently, law would have an importantly different status. Rather than, as would be the case were law to be posited in relation to immediacy, within this other setting law could not be separated easily from life. Hence the full force of Haemon's utterance is to be found in the suggestion that, despite the reality of the relation between a father and son, and thus by extension family relations in general, such relations cannot be understood as comprising that which is intrinsically necessary to the formation and effective functioning of the *polis*. As a result, not only should there be a disjunctive relation between the familial and the social (where the latter names the concerns of the *polis* and where one of those concerns would be the security of families), familial relations can form only part of the 'good life' to the extent they are themselves mediated in advance by an already present relation to τὸ φρονεῖν. (What counts as acts of judgement will always be the decisive question here.) Moreover, this is the point at which any attempt to take the family as the central element, insofar as the family's coherence and therefore obligations stemming from it would have a determining effect on actions that had implications beyond the family, would have ceded its place to the presence of a more abstract set of relationships structured by τὸ φρονεῖν. Within that set of abstract relations there would need to be the cessation of the effect of kinship precisely because that effect could only ever be immediate. Haemon's riposte to Creon undoes the immediacy of both the law of the family (as a law within a kinship structure that both unites and separates Antigone and Creon) while undoing, in addition, the immediacy of the application of the law that Creon claims to enact—namely, the law of the *polis*. The law itself is not undone: the contention νόμος βασιλεύς endures. Rather, there is a twofold undoing at work here. In the first instance the equation of both law and justice with practices of immediacy is undone. Secondly, and simultaneously, this calls into question the basis of the structures that sustain those practices—that is, the family or the *polis* as the bearers of immediacy.

Haemon opens up, as a possibility, the suspension of immediacy in the name of τὸ φρονεῖν. (What can be suggested in addition is that this suspension of immediacy is the moment at which the possibility of εὐδαιμονία emerges.) What this means is that, from line 775 on, τὸ φρονεῖν names the possible suspension of the twofold determination of the law's immediacy. That this mooted suspension of immediacy does not dominate any further registration of law as the play unfolds reinforces the point that the mooted suspension of immediacy is there both as the named as well as the unnamed possibility that always accompanies the claims of immediacy. What is checked therefore is what can be described as the immediacy of immediacy. What matters is that, even if the effect of τὸ φρονεῖν remains unactualized, it is there as an ever present possibility. In other words, from line 775 onwards the suspension of the law is there as that other possibility for law once law is no longer defined by its continual oscillation between various forms of immediacy. Mediacy takes on the quality of that which is intrinsic to relationality. It is already there within human being as *being-in-place*. This will be the case, even where mediacy is denied in the name of a posited coextensivity between immediacy and the law. A critical engagement with immediacy would take the already present structure of mediacy—thus *being-in-place*—as its point of departure.[13]

The Chorus's closing speech needs to be understood therefore as working within the space opened up by the possibility of mediacy as an original condition. That specific speech takes place within the now present possibility of the suspension of the immediacy of immediacy while confirming both that suspension and the opening of a space. And here it needs to be added, though this addition is consistent with what has just been argued—namely, that part of the theatrical force of Haemon's line is that it is heard as announcing a form of condition-ality.[14] While this gestures towards the evincing of filial respect insofar as the line begins conditionally, more significantly it opens up a space in which what was introduced initially as a type of conditionality takes on the quality of an assertion. What is being asserted is conditionality itself. In other words, dramatic tension is in part constructed and maintained by the range of possibilities opened up by a line whose very conditionality can always point in a number of directions, one of which is that what was initially bounded by forms of conditionality, by the end of the play, will have acquired the status of an assertion. (Again it is essential to note the beginning of Haemon's line: 'if you were not my father . . .'.) What is asserted is, of

---

[13] While it cannot be pursued in this context, what this means is that the basis of critique is not a transcendental conception of the good life. Critique is ground in the ontological status of human being. Not as an abstraction from human being, but as the condition of human being—namely *being-in-place*.

[14] In his commentary Griffith also notes the 'conditional' nature of the opening of the line: (Sophocles 1999: 251).

course, the centrality of τὸ φρονεῖν as opposed to its mere conditional possibility. Assertion is the enacting of conditionality as an actual possibility. The domain of judgement is therefore the domain of the conditional. Their identity is what is being asserted.

(2) Hölderlin's translation of the first line of the Chorus's final speech brings yet another complication into play. The addition is of fundamental importance. Hölderlin translates the line in the following terms.

> *Um vieles das Denken mehr, denn*
> *Glükseeligkeit.*[15]

(Thought is much more than happiness.)

The interpretation of this line, understood as an act of translation, is not governed by questions of accuracy. What matters is the way the relation between τὸ φρονεῖν and εὐδαιμονία is understood within it— an understanding occurring in terms of both the contrastive structure of the line as well as the translation of τὸ φρονεῖν as *das Denken* and *Glükseeligkeit* as the translation of εὐδαιμονία. At work within Hölderlin's translation is the abrupt move away from the primacy of the original relation noted earlier between τὸ φρονεῖν and εὐδαιμονία (a relation that is present even if indeterminate). Given Hölderlin's translation, the possibilities at work in Haemon's juxtaposition of the doubled nature of Creon's law with τὸ φρονεῖν would no longer register. Creon's law is doubled because it is as much the law of the father as it is the law of the *polis*. Hölderlin's translation closes the space in which such a registration could have taken place—namely, the space held open by the necessity of a form of reciprocity between τὸ φρονεῖν and εὐδαιμονία and which subsequently allowed human being to be thought in terms of *being-in-place*. It is perhaps not surprising in this regard that Hölderlin's translation of this moment within the play—namely, the exchange already noted between Creon and Haemon—takes the following form:[16]

---

[15] Hölderlin (2004: x. 212). For a definitive study of Hölderlin on translation as well as a translator, see Louth (1998). While this line is not discussed, George Steiner has provided one of the most sustained engagements with the details of Hölderlin's actual translation. See Steiner (1986: 66–106). See also Rosenfield (1999).

[16] It should be noted that these lines do map directly on to the exchange, as it appears in the original Greek text. As is argued, that is not what matters. What is central is the emphasis of law as opposed to *to phronein*.

CREON. *O schlecht! schlecht! ins Gericht gehn mit dem Vater.*
HAEMON. *Weil ich nicht seh, wie du das Recht anlügest.*[17]
(CREON. O evil, evil, put your father on trial?
HAEMON. I do not see how you lie to the law.)

While it would be essential to work through the lines that follow in order that the force of the exchange appear with more exacting precision, it is nonetheless clear that Hölderlin's concern, as evidenced by this 'translation', is with the law (and therefore it is both the law's unmediated presence as well as the subsequent equation of justice with the immediate act). In other words, not only does Hölderlin position the exchange between Creon and Haemon in terms of the law (*Gericht/Recht*); the possibility of the law's mediation by τὸ φρονεῖν is precluded from the start. Indeed, it is possible to go further and argue that its being precluded is the essential moment in the translation. Thus, it is not surprising that; to the accusation of falsehood and therefore of acting falsely in relation to the law, Creon responds:

Wenn meinem Uranfang' ich treu beistehe, lüg'ich?
(If I remain true to my origin, do I lie?)[18]

What this means is that the hold of law for Creon, as presented by Hölderlin in the translation, cannot be separated from questions of original propriety where propriety is understood as a form of original unity having a necessary singularity. Hölderlin has Creon appeal to an origin that has been separated from a setting in which the evocation of the centrality of τὸ φρονεῖν inscribes the necessity of non-tragic conflict at the centre of human being—a setting stemming from the suspension of the immediacy of immediacy. In other words, Creon resists the possibility announced in Sophocles' *Antigone* by Haemon. However, Haemon within Hölderlin's translation remains caught within the determinations of law. Tragedy occurs therefore at and with the origin's necessary interarticulation with the law and thus where the origin stands as the closure of the space that would have been maintained by the continued presence of mediacy.

[17] Hölderlin (2004: x. 189).
[18] Hölderlin (2004: x. 189). Also, Hölderlin was acutely aware of the problems posed by this line and Haemon's response. It is discussed in the *Anmerkungen zur Antigonä*. See Hölderlin (2004: x. 214).

Despite the problems created by what continues to recur in aspects of Hölderlin's translation of the *Antigone*, it should not be thought that Hölderlin is a straightforward and unequivocal thinker of immediacy. Indeed, his own refusal of immediacy and his recognition of the primacy of mediacy are clear from his commentary on his translation of Pindar Fragment 169a as *Das Höchste* in the *Pindar-Fragmente*.[19] In the case of the Pindar translation, the possibility of an original state holding the law's immediacy in place is refused. In that context he does not offer a translation in which the sovereignty of the king would have been identified with the immediacy of the law, a translation that established the king as an absolute sovereign. (Moreover, it would have been a translation invited by the Fragment's Greek name νόμος βασιλεύς.) Consequently, in his commentary on his own translation Hölderlin's counter-move is clear: 'Die strenge Mittelbarkeit ist aber das Gesez' ('But the strictly mediate is the law').[20] The consequence is that both the Gods and humans will be subject to the law. It will be essential to return to the relation between the position of the original and the attribution of a lawlike quality to mediacy in which law's exigency was located in the necessity of its incorporation of judgement and by extension a concern with life.

At this stage it is vital to remain with the exchange between Creon and Haemon as framed by Hölderlin. To the extent that the law is immediate, there can no space for τὸ φρονεῖν. Such a space is impossible. If, in addition, the immediacy of the law is bound up with origins, then that impossibility is compounded. For Creon the connection is what is there originally and to which he cannot be false or act in a way that a fidelity to the origin is undone. Any other approach allows for the space of mediacy. (Hence the problem of the place of mediacy in the poetic thinking of Hölderlin.) This is the space that Haemon, it has been argued, opens and sustains via his suspension of what has been described as the doubled nature of Creon's law. As has been intimated, what is suspended is the immediacy of immediacy. What that suspension stages is the impossibility of the origin. Or, rather, the impossibility of an origin posited as more original than life—hence the problematic status of Hölderlin's translation. What is precluded by the evocation of an original relation to the law and thus the law having an original presence is the futurity that is inherent

---

[19] See my discussion of Hölderlin's Pindar translations in A. Benjamin (2010).
[20] Hölderlin (2004: xi. 229).

within τὸ φρονεῖν. It inheres within τὸ φρονεῖν because the oscillation between wisdom and judgement opens a domain of activity by yielding a space in which decisions are always to be made, or made decisions are able to be contested (indeed, always able to be contested). Human being is defined by the place where contestable decisions adjudicated by judgement occurs; hence human being as *being-in-place*. That space sustains the future, allowing the future to be lived out. The original, that which would have to be more original than life, becomes therefore an impossibility, or rather that which is possible within the necessary interconnection of law and immediacy. Suspending that interconnection is not an act of infidelity to a naturalized origin; it is the actualization that was always there in the positing of law's immediacy—namely, the impossibility of precluding the counter of immediacy's refusal, which would be the affirmation of the already present possibility of mediacy. The latter is simply judgement as an original condition. The resistance to immediacy is not mere countering. That would be the counter-positing of another form of immediacy. Constructed by such a movement and counter-movement, positing met by counter-positing is the structure of tragedy: a process emerging in the play not just in terms of the way Creon and Antigone respond to each other, but with what they invoke and the difference between what is invoked, in order that their responses have a ground (*albeit* different grounds). As a consequence, the resistance to immediacy is holding open that within which the necessity of the decision can always be encountered and contested (again it needs to be added that encountering and contesting are the work of judgement). Necessity lies, therefore, in the non-tragic conflict to which the decision's exigency gives rise. The decision is an imposed necessity stemming from the original relation of judgement and wisdom.

In Hölderlin's translation not only does τὸ φρονεῖν as *das Denken* have a privileged position; introduced into the line is the necessity of a form of separation insofar as τὸ φρονεῖν and εὐδαιμονία are now held apart—a separation without reciprocity. Hence what is constructed is a position that precludes the possibility of attributing centrality to *eudaimonia* understood as *Glükseeligkeit*. This is, of course, the other eventuality that is inherent in Haemon's admonition (hence its conditional nature). Nonetheless, the question that has to be taken back to Hölderlin's translation of the opening line of the Chorus's final speech concerns not just what is at work in holding *Denken* and *Glükseeligkeit* apart, but why there has been the attribution of greater significance to the former. The setting in which these questions will be addressed is provided by Walter Benjamin's own estimation of Hölderlin's translations in the first instance, and the position of *Glück* and *Glükseeligkeit* within his own philosophical writings in the second.

(3) Towards the end of the introduction that Walter Benjamin provided for his own translation of Baudelaire's *Tableaux Parisiens*— that is, his text 'Die Aufgabe des Übersetzers'—he wrote the following as part of his assessment of Hölderlin's Sophocles translations.

In ihnen stürzt der Sinn von Abgrund zu Abgrund, bis er droht in bodenlosen Sprachtiefen sich zu verlieren.[21]

(In them meaning plunges from abyss to abyss until it threatens to become lost in the bottomless depths of language.)

This abyssal positioning comes to 'a stop' (*ein Halten*) in which 'meaning' (*Sinn*) cedes its place to the work of language. Work has its own formulation. What Benjamin describes as 'die strömende Sprache und die strömende Offenbarung' ('the flow of language and the flow of revelation') is linked to language as a field of activity, which in turn provides the setting where translation becomes a condition of language rather than what would have already been delimited in advance by the concerns of meaning.[22] The move from meaning to language not only underscores the centrality of language by attributing to it its own sense of work; at the same time, it allows for the attribution to texts– *albeit* what he calls 'großen Schriften'—of a quality that inheres 'zwischen den Zeilen' ('between the lines)'.[23] What these texts contain is 'ihre virtuelle Übersetzung' ('their virtual translation'). There is, therefore, an important distinction Benjamin is drawing here between two different senses of presence. There are 'lines' that convey meaning. They contain the words that within the literal act of translation are the ones that come to be translated. There is, however, a form of presence that cannot be reduced to that which is there to be read aloud. Benjamin's names this other presence a 'virtual translation'. Virtuality here needs to be understood in terms of an opening created by the irreducibility of any one actual

---

[21] W. Benjamin (1980: iv.I 21; 1996–2003: i. 253).   [22] Smerick (2009).

[23] In this regards, see the perspicacious discussion both of Walter Benjamin and of Hölderlin's translation by Dennis Schmidt (2001). It forms part of a study of Hölderlin that warrants a detailed study in its own right.

translation to that which is there virtually. What is virtually present is not a translation that is yet-to-be actualized. The supposition here is that the virtual refers to the endlessness of potentiality. Virtual translation is the continual possibility of the translation to come; hence the move from 'meaning' to 'language'. There is an important link, therefore, between what is meant by the term 'virtual translation' and what has already emerged as integral to the distinction between law and judgement (once that distinction is recast in terms of immediacy and mediacy.) Judgement as mediacy is the site of an opening in which deliberation takes place. For Benjamin, in a succinct description of translation, translation is present as a 'form'. Hence he writes:

Übersetzung ist eine Form. Sie als solche zu erfassen, gilt es zurückzugehen auf das Original. Denn in ihm liegt deren Gestez als in dessen Übersetzbarkeit beschlossen.[24]

(Translation is a form. To comprehend it as a form one must go back to the original, for the laws governing the translation lie within the original contained in the issue of translatability.)

'Translatability' (*Übersetzbarkeit*), Benjamin's demanding term, needs to be understood as the quality of language that occasions translations—a quality to be explicated in terms of potentiality and repetition. This will be the case, even though the form of any one translation cannot be predicted. This is, of course, the anti-utopian gesture of refusing the future an image in advance. The future understood as an act of translation will always have language's inherent potentiality as its ground. The question to be addressed concerns the relationship between 'translatability', that which is presupposed or assumed to be at work in Hölderlin's translations and then Hölderlin's actual translation of the opening line of the final speech by the Chorus.

Übersetzbarkeit, understood as the articulation of an abstract philosophical position, becomes the affirmation of potentiality. (Here, of course, that potentiality is a quality of language, named elsewhere by Benjamin as 'reine Sprache'.[25]) The question that endures is more complex than the realization of potentiality.

---

[24] W. Benjamin (1980: iv.1. 9; 1996–2003: i. 254). See also Sallis (2002) and S. Weber (2008).
[25] W. Benjamin (1980: iv.1. 1; 1996–2003: i. 261). On the question of what Benjamin means by 'pure', see Salzani (2010).

Potentiality endures. Actuality involves a form of interruption—the 'expressionless' giving rise to expression—in which there is an-other occurrence. The other occurs. In the celebrated passage from Hölderlin's letter to Böhlendorff, Hölderlin can be understood as writing of the actualization of potentiality. After having argued that it would be wrong to abstract the 'rule of art' (*die Kunstregeln*) from Greek art, he goes on to note:

> *Ich habe lange daran laborirt und weiß nun daß ausser dem, was bei den Griechen und uns das höchste seyn muß, nemlich dem lebendigen Verhältniß und Geschik, wir nicht wohl etwas gleich mit ihnen haben dürfen.*[26]
>
> (I have laboured on this for a long time and now know that, outside what for the Greeks and for us must be the highest—namely, to have a living relation and destiny, we must not have anything similar with them.)

This gives rise to the need for a form of separation. Propriety becomes a mode of relating that is equally a mode of turning apart. Hence there is Hölderlin's concluding claim to the position noted above that 'das eigene muß so gut gelernt seyn, wie das Fremde' ('original propriety must be learnt as well as the foreign').[27] In the strict sense set by Hölderlin's own poetics, productive interruption, the interruption that involves both a form of retention as well as a departure, is thought as a 'caesura'. However, the Hölderlinian caesura is internal to the rhythm of the work (and what is understood by work here are *Die Trauerspiele des Sophokles*) such that what occurs is 'die gegen-rhythmische Unterbrechung', which has the quality of 'das reine Wort' and is present as the condition allowing for representation (*die Vorstellung*) itself.[28] The caesura is a productive interruption within (and as) the work of poetry. The question that has to be addressed here does not pertain either to the interruption or to its presence as productive. Rather the question with greatest acuity will always concern what it is that is interrupted and thus what interruption in such a setting actually means. Here is the point at which, rather than pursue Benjamin's interpretation of Hölderlin as a translator, it is far more appropriate to concentrate on a moment that occurs in his interpretation of two poems by Hölderlin. While

---

[26] Hölderlin (2004: ix. 183).   [27] Hölderlin (2004: ix. 184).
[28] Hölderlin (2004: x. 155).

Benjamin writes of a specific Hölderlinian poetic engagement, it is nonetheless still possible to argue that what he sees as the force of Hölderlin's poetry has greater extension. That force would be its capacity to enact 'einer Verlagerung des Mythologischen' ('a dislocation of the mythic').[29] This accounts for why Philippe Lacoue-Labarthe, writing about Benjamin's engagement with Hölderlin, identifies what he calls 'le courage de la poésie' as the 'courage of quitting mythology, of breaking with it and of deconstructing it' (*courage de quitter le mythologique, de rompre avec lui et de le déconstruire*).[30]

Benjamin identifies the possibility of the displacement of myth. That particular move echoes in the language of 'interruption' (*Unterbrechung*). Moreover, to the extent that commensurability between myth and fate can be maintained, then greater clarity will have been given to the status of what is either interrupted or displaced. The difficulty of using the language of the 'caesura' as though its locus of operation were no more than poetic form is that a commensurability is then assumed between poetic form, on the one hand, and myth and fate, on the other. Such a positioning would misunderstand their presence. For Benjamin, myth and fate are present as naturalized. Hence the undoing of myth and stemming the hold of fate haves to work against their naturalization. (This is an essential preliminary move.) In a sense they have to be denaturalized. That for Lacoue-Labrathe would be the process of 'deconstruction', while for Benjamin it would be the work of what he refers to as 'der destruktive Charakter'. In regards to the work of fate and myth, which would need to be understood as pre-given determinations, destruction involves a form of production that works in a radically different way. Benjamin is clear. 'Dem destruktive Charakter schwebt kein Bild vor' ('The destructive character has no image before him').[31] While not determined in advance, the locus of destruction, thus the possibility of interruption, is positioned in relation to *Schicksal* (fate).

---

[29] W. Benjamin (1980: ii.1. 116). This is a mode of analysis that also informs Benjamin's critique of Gundolf's interpretation of Goethe. For Benjamin, Gundolf was involved in a form of mythologization. Hence Benjamin's own interpretation of Goethe—Goethe's *Wahlverwandschaften* needs to be interpreted as an attempt to break from myth. For a discussion of Benjamin's relation to myth—a discussion that also notes the critical engagement with Gundolf's Goethe—see Mali (1999).
[30] Lacoue-Labarthe (2002: 152).   [31] W. Benjamin (1980: iv.1. 397).

Within the argumentative structure of his 1921 text 'Schicksal und Charakter' Benjamin presents *Schicksal* ('fate') as inextricably bound up with an imposed and then naturalized form of continuity. Historicism, which is an exemplary instance of that continuity, only ever occurs after the event. However, part of its having happened is that it allows that 'event' to have occurred before the process of its incorporation into history as continuity, in order that it then form part of that continuity. This is the process of naturalization. There is an additional element that, in this context, is decisive. Fate also defines the realm of 'guilt' (*Schuld*), a realm in which 'guilt' is imposed on life. The interruption of the work of guilt occurs within a context in which the mistaken confusion of 'justice' (*Gerechtigkeit*) with the 'order of law' (*die Ordnung des Rechts*) has already been identified. The result of the identification of their conflation as mistaken—a mistake in which the politics of justice becomes a politics of revenge—is that it then allows justice to be separated from law, a separation that locates the potential for the interruption of fate in forms of action.[32] That interruption did not occur within law. It distances law in its occurring. Indeed, its location was external to law (or, to be more precise, external to that conception of law that can be differentiated from justice—that is, law as immediacy). In this regard Benjamin writes:

---

[32] The preceding references to potentiality and the reference here to the relationship between potentiality and actions opens another domain of discussion, which, even though it cannot be pursued in detail, still needs to be noted. The discussion by Aristotle in the *Nichomachean Ethics* of the relations between 'habit' and 'virtue' allows for the presence of the latter as a possible action. Hence Aristotle argues that one 'becomes good' (ἀγαθός γίγνεται) (Aristotle, *Nichomachean Ethics* 1106ᵃ24). Hence there are actions that actualize this state of affairs; hence it is present as a potentiality. This is the point of intervention for Agamben, whose reading both of this passage and of Aristotle's presentation of 'potentiality' in the *Metaphysics*, particularly at *Metaphysics* 1046ᵃ30, leads him to argue that there is an accompanying 'potential not to pass into action'. However, it is much more likely that what this alludes to in Aristotle is not a sense of a 'privation' accompanying potentiality but the absence of necessity within potentiality. Were it to be the case that potentiality entailed actuality, then the Megarians would have been right. If they are not right, then there has to be an account of the way in which potentiality is present and yet its actualization is absent. That is not, at the same time, an argument against the centrality of potentiality. Action is an actualization. However, there needs to be a distinction drawn between mere acts (mere habits) and acts that are linked to potentiality where potentiality is actualized within and for life. That actualization will involve a transformation on the level of habit. See, in this regard, Agamben (2013: 91–9).

Nicht das Recht, sondern die Tragödie was es, in der das Haupt des Genius aus dem Nebel der Schuld sich zum ersten Male erhob, denn in der Tragödie wird das dämonische Schicksal durchbrochen.[33]

(It was not in law but in tragedy that the head of genius lifted itself for the first time from the mist of guilt, for in tragedy demonic fate was breached.)

The two significant moments here are the lifting of the head and the presence of a breach. Both need to be understood as figures of interruption. Another name for the staging of this release is *Glück*. In this regard Benjamin is explicit:

Das Glück ist es vielmehr, welches den Glücklichen aus der Verkettung der Schicksale und aus dem Netz des eignen herauslöst.[34]

(Happiness is what releases the fortunate man from the chains of the fates and the nets of his own fate.)

At work here are forms of interruption in which what is interrupted, breached, destroyed, lifted out of, is a repetition—fate, myth—that had taken on the garb of norms. Hence, in this instance, there is a transformation of that setting. In losing the designation of norm they come to be known—and it is fundamental that what is at stake here is knowledge—as fate, myth, and so on. Hence the Hölderlinian caesura, which was limited to prosody and which maintained the setting as it was, is no longer appropriate. The transformation of the setting necessitates a recasting of the caesura in terms of what it will allow. Hence the caesura that was limited to poetic rhythm will now become a caesura of allowing—present therefore as an *arché* without a *telos* occurring for the sake of living. Value has become intrinsic to life.

While more needs to be added, it is possible to conclude by returning to Hölderlin's translation. What is demanded by the Chorus in its final speech is something not monstrous but rather catastrophic.[35] The demand is for an opening that is at the same

---

[33] W. Benjamin (1980: ii.1. 174; 1996–2003: i. 203).

[34] W. Benjamin (1980: ii.1. 174; 1996–2003: i. 203).

[35] Hence what would need to be pursed here is the distinction between the monstrous and the catastrophic. If there is a further limit to Hölderlin's thinking of tragedy, then it lies in the failure to move from one to the other. The monstrous remains.

Die darstellung des Tragischen beruht vorzüglich darauf, daß das Ungeheure, wie der Gott und Mensch sich paart, und granzenlös die Naturmacht und des

time a cessation of the possibility of tragedy. The catastrophe is the interarticulation of τὸ φρονεῖν and εὐδαιμονία. The counter-strophe, which is the caesura of allowing, is the undoing of the possibility that τὸ φρονεῖν could operate in its having separated from the concerns of life. It would be that separation that allows τὸ φρονεῖν as *das Denken*—an existence that was bound up with the law as pure immediacy. The limit of Hölderlin, therefore, was a failure to see that in the caesura's necessity there had to be a transformation of form itself. An opening to that transformation had to be maintained. Maintaining would have demanded the co-presence of *Denken* and *Glükseeligkeit*. It is, of course, precisely that set-up that becomes impossible, and impossibility within thought itself, when the opening line of the Chorus speech is translated as:

> *Um vieles das Denken mehr, denn*
> *Glükseeligkeit.*

Menschens Innerstes im Zorn Eins wird, dadurch sich begreift, daß das granzenlös Eineswerden durch granzenloses Scheiden sich reiniget. (Hölderlin 2004: x. 160)

The presentation of the tragic rests pre-eminently upon this, that the monstrous—how the god and man mate and the power of nature and man's innermost boundlessly unite in wrath—understands itself in such a way that the boundless union purifies itself through boundless separation.

Part II

Tragic Cultures

6

Tragedy with and without Religion:
Hegelian Thoughts

Terry Pinkard

The outlines of Hegel's conception of tragedy are so well known they
need little introduction.[1] Here is the familiar picture. In tragedy, so
Hegel argued, it is not primarily hubris or catharsis that commands
our attention in tragic plays but a contest of right versus right whose
outcome must be the destruction of one or both sides. The paradigm
is Sophocles' *Antigone*, where Antigone is right in performing the
traditional burial rites on her brother in defiance of Creon's orders,
but it is also true that Creon is right to give those orders, Antigone is
wrong in disobeying them, and Creon is justified in punishing her for
such disobedience. Both sides suffer because there is no middle
ground to adjudicate that kind of clash of right versus right. The
impossibility of the amelioration of such a clash leads inexorably to its
tragic conclusion.

As it stands, that much is fine as far as it goes, but it is also, to use a
typical Hegelian expression, rather rigidly one-sided in its presentation. For Hegel, tragedy, like all forms of art (and religion and
ultimately also philosophy), seeks to reconcile us to our place in the
world. However, if indeed both sides are doomed because of the

---

[1] Hegel's discussion of tragedy has its fullest expositions in his lectures on the
philosophy of art, put together on the basis of his lecture notes and his students' notes
after his death in 1831 (see Hegel 1970: xiii–xv, and the fairly good English translation
at Hegel (1975a)—and in his discussion of Greek life in the 1807 *Phenomenology of
Spirit* (see Hegel 1970: iii). There are mentions of tragedy in his other works, but no
extended discussion, except for the very short summary of his views in the lectures on
the philosophy of religion (see Hegel 1970: xvi: 16, 132–5).

inexorability of the clash and the impossibility of its amelioration, it is not clear why viewing such a spectacle would lead to anything like reconciliation. That would lead us to suspect that more is in play in Hegel's conception, and indeed there is. The question Hegel was trying to answer was more like the following: why should or does tragedy matter to us?

We can give an initial, although itself still one-sided, reformulation of Hegel's theory of tragedy as follows. Tragedy occurs when human beings are not in harmony with their world such that their best actions betray them and lead to their suffering or destruction. In this initial formulation, tragedy as a form of art shows us both how we have fallen out of harmony with the world and the shape that the restoration of that harmony would have to assume and why the restoration is reconciliatory. (This short formulation will have to be much qualified and modified later in the light of one of Hegel's other core ideas having to do with harmony with others and oneself.)

What kind of harmony are we talking about? Hegel's initial discussion of this in his 1807 *Phenomenology* had to do with his account of ancient Greek life as a kind of 'ethical life'—*Sittlichkeit*—that held it together. 'Ethical life' holds things together by embodying within itself a set of determinate requirements, which are indexed to the various positions people inhabit within the way of life itself—positions ranging from mother, father, brother, sister, warrior, statesman, artisan, and so on. Such requirements extend over both attitudes and behaviour for those people. What holds ethical life itself together is the shared conviction that, if each carries out the requirements of his or her own position, then the whole produced by those various actions will spontaneously harmonize. Given a more or less Kantian conception of beauty (which in Kant's own particular formulation consists in the spontaneous harmony of intellect and imagination), anything resulting from such spontaneous harmonization will be itself a thing of beauty. A way of life that spontaneously harmonizes itself without there being any kind of plan to guide it will itself therefore be beautiful. What holds ethical life together is, therefore, not that all the actions and the consequences produced by individuals carrying out the requirements of the various social positions can be given a rational structure or put into some clear rational system—it would have no 'concept' guiding it, as Kant would put it. What holds ethical life together is that the whole that is produced is a thing of beauty, something that itself is or at least approaches being a work of art.

In such ethical life, ethical principles are anchored in the lives that people lead. To make a distinction that is crucial for Hegel: in ethical life, people do not encounter obligations, or even rights, so much as they encounter various goods that require certain types of actions that are necessary if those goods are to be realized. 'Moral' obligations as we speak of them in modern times typically hold independently of the offices and stations inhabited by individuals. Likewise, an immoral action cuts across various offices and stations. An ethical action or attitude, on the other hand, attaches to an individual by virtue of the position he or she holds. It is not a stretch to say that in ethical life, under this conception, it is a bit of a falsification to say that people reflectively 'identify' themselves with such principles. Rather, they just *are* those people. There is no gap between themselves and the position that has to be closed by 'identifying' themselves with it.

As such, ethical principles form the first principles of all practical reasoning in ethical life. In such practical reasoning, one reasons not from questions like 'what is required of all people to be moral?', but from questions like 'what is required of me as [brother, warrior, statesman, teacher, etc.] to do what a good [brother, warrior, states-man, teacher, etc.] does?' As Hegel puts it, such principles are the unmoved movers of ethical life.[2] They have us in their grip, not the other way round.

Comprehending what follows from such ethical principles of course demands reflection, deliberation, and conscientiousness. The principles themselves, however, stand outside of such deliberation. They are widely shared and seem to require no justification for themselves. (Or, rather, their 'justification', if it can be called that, lies in how the social whole produced by individuals acting in light of them is beautiful.) They seem to be more natural, to be written into the fabric of things, unlike the man-made laws that are also required if the goods embodied in such ethical principles are to be actually

---

[2] '[Agents] must attain knowledge of the unmoved mover, as Aristotle, calls it, of the unmoved motive force by which all individuals are activated. For this force to become effective, the subject must have developed to a condition of free individuality in which it is fully conscious of the eternally unmoved mover, and each individual subject be must be free and independent in its own right' (*Erst das Wissen der Individuen von ihrem Zwecke ist das wahrhaft Sittliche. Es muß das Unbewegte gewußt werden, der unbewegte Bewegende, wie Aristoteles sagt, der das Bewegende ist in den Individuen. Daß es so das Bewegende sei, dazu gehört, daß das Subjekt für sich zur freien Eigentümlichkeit herausgebildet sei*) (Hegel 1968: 91; 1975b: 77).

realized. That a good warrior exhibits courage is something like a natural fact, even if it requires some reflection or deliberation as to whether courage in any particular case demands withdrawal or advancement. As natural, such 'ethical principles' are a matter of 'substance.' Analogous to natural laws, they are the fixed, immovable principles of life.

The key concept underlying such a conception of ethical life is, as noted, that of spontaneous harmony. What shape could such a harmonious social space take?

Such a community as a whole would, in its very nature, be 'organic' in two senses. First, this organic structure would not be the result of anybody's having designed it. It simply is what it is, and its 'organs' (the various offices, social positions, and stations) are by nature adapted to secure it. Second, if each person (each 'organ') fulfils the requirements of his or her position correctly, then the whole that is produced would spontaneously harmonize with itself. As in an animal organism, its parts do the work they do only in the light of their contribution to the whole organism, and the whole organism is successful only as the parts harmonize with each other.

What distinguishes this as a form of ethical life from that of a tradition-bound way of life is that the individuals in it realize that, although the first principles of such a form of life have to stand outside questioning, what follows from those first principles themselves is a matter of rational deliberation on how best to actualize them. Thus, the way of life must incorporate within itself some conception of the requirements for at least some members of the community to think hard and to think well about how to do what is required and not just simply follow tradition blindly. In Greek ethical life, or so Hegel and many of his fellow Grecophiles at the time thought, that itself required that there be one set of absolute principles placed outside the sphere of reflection and deliberation whose concern was that of the good of the community as a whole. In thinking about the requirements of one's station, one had to think of how actualizing it in one way as opposed to another ultimately best served the good of the community, and the 'spontaneous harmony' at stake could be achieved only if one of the commitments that was at work was that of each citizen putting the community's good in first place among the principles at work in his deliberation. In turn, that required a doctrine of democratic participation among the citizens of each community on how best to actualize the goods at stake. (Hegel makes this point in his lectures on the philosophy of history.[3]) This also required that non-citizens—all women and slaves—had to accept that the good of the community required their exclusion from such deliberation, and this was, so Hegel thought, one of the key reasons for the eventual breakdown of the ancient form of life.

This seemed to commit the ancient Greeks to a view that there were fundamentally no inherent contradictions among the basic goods, although those goods could indeed be actualized in ways that contradicted themselves. Intense reflection and communal deliberation were thus required if such contradictions in actualization were to be avoided.

Greek ethical life therefore required two distinct things to fuse: an unconditional concern on the part of each citizen for the common good and an equally strong sense of one's own individual and idiosyncratic traits and a sense of how best to employ one's talents in the service of such a common good. One was committed to using the full range of one's talents and accomplishments to serve this purpose, and this required that one concern oneself with not being merely a servant of the community but with developing all one's own skills and powers so that one could be such an engaged member of the community. To put it quasi-paradoxically (which means: not really paradoxically), one had to develop one's own individuality to the highest degree in order to actualize the common good.

In the kinds of public deliberations intrinsic to it, the Greek polis thereby had to proceed under the assumption that each person was sincerely taking the good of the community into consideration in making his proposals before the assembly. Otherwise, the deliberations in the polis would fall apart, since each would suspect others of arguing in favour of their own particular interest, even if they disguised it as the common good. Moreover, full political equality had to be presupposed among the citizens, and dissent had to be allowed, although not so far that it become widespread and far-ranging. Each individual agent committed to this regime thus also had to believe that the result would not be a cacophony of different interests but

---

[3] Hegel (1970: xii. 308): 'The democratic constitution is the only one possible here . . . This is the genuine status of the democratic constitution: Its justification and absolute necessity rests on the still immanent objective ethical life' (*Die demokratische Verfassung ist hier die einzig mögliche . . . Dies ist die wahrhafte Stellung der demokratischen Verfassung: ihre Berechtigung und absolute Notwendigkeit beruht auf dieser noch immanenten objektiven Sittlichkeit*).

something more 'organic', such that, if each conscientiously did what was fully required of him, then the result would be a spontaneously harmonious whole. Furthermore, this had to be because nature itself was a spontaneously harmonizing whole that, as Aristotle was later to put it, did nothing in vain. If nature does nothing in vain, then humans acting according to fixed, natural principles can expect that, even where the sense of the action is obscure, it is not in vain.

What then of people who do not carry out what is required of them? Or those who openly defy them or even unwittingly violate them? It cannot be the case that they will just get away with it. The very nature of the world has to be such that justice will be restored. The spontaneous harmony that manifests the beauty of such a form of life also ensures that violators will suffer as a result of their misdeeds, and this itself is also part of the beauty of the whole system, since it involves spontaneously restoring the harmony that had been violated. (Human law partially mirrors this in its own system of punishment.) The function of punishment is to restore the disturbed harmony of things, not, for example, to deter potential violators.

As drama, tragedy takes its standing as an aesthetic presentation— a basic truth about what it means to be a minded creature presented in sensuous form—of how human actions function in the light of an organic world order that naturally restores itself to harmony when it is thrown out of kilter. That world, perhaps it is needless to say, must also be conceived religiously, as having some kind of divine order that has the means to make such restoration.

To the extent that such agents take themselves to be in any way deeply intertwined with that order, they must conceive themselves in the ideal case as possessed of a certain pathos, a current of feeling (such as courage or cunning) strong enough to govern a person's course of action and to explain his actions.[4] Indeed, in the ideal case, an individual's own connection with the ethical principles governing oneself is that of passion, a more or less absolute commitment on the agent's part.[5] The various pathea were expressions within human

---

[4] See Rutter (2011).

[5] 'Laws and principles have no immediate life or validity in themselves. The activity which puts them into operation and endows them with real existence has its source in the needs, impulses, inclinations, and passions of man. If I put something into practice and give it a real existence, I must have some personal interest in doing so; I must be personally involved in it, and hope to obtain satisfaction through its accomplishment' (Hegel 1968: 82; 1975b: 70)

agency of the passions that the different gods could provoke in us. (This was not inconsistent with a conception of human agency as fully deliberative and as capable of acting on reasons. The gods do not pull our strings as if we were their puppets, but they do intervene and sometimes do so precisely by stirring the passions so that we incline to a particular direction.[6]) The conflicts among the passions and the pathea are thus often reflections within us of the conflicts among the different gods. A lack of harmony within ourselves may only be an indication of some deeper divine conflict. If divine conflict cannot be brought into a rational order in which the conflict is removed, then there is also no reason to expect that these conflicts in what could loosely be called 'human nature' could be removed. Since the gods differ among themselves, there will be irreconcilable differences among us and within us because of the divine conflict.[7]

The reconciliatory nature of tragedy has to do with its connection to this divine order. The kind of deep conflict with which tragedy deals is part of the divine order itself, an order that is necessary to the constitution of a beautiful world, although not necessarily of a rationally comprehensible world. It is just and right that people suffer for the wrong they have done, even if the wrong they committed was a component of something they otherwise were required to do

---

[6] This point is argued by B. Williams (1993).

[7] Stephen Houlgate holds that, for Hegel, tragedy is only an aesthetic phenomenon. According to Houlgate, what we get from Greek tragedy is that 'tragic drama teaches us not that tragedy is unavoidable, but that it stems from confusing life with art' (Houlgate 2007: 146–78). This seems wrong to me, both as an account of tragedy and as an account of Hegel's views on it. In making that distinction, Houlgate wishes sharply to separate Hegel's views from those of Aristotle and insists that the feature of tragedy that is crucial for Hegel is simply the contradiction of right versus right. The element of reconciliation is supposed to come from the audience's seeing that justice requires that the protagonists are punished, since, after all, each is not only right but equally wrong. But for what are they punished? For Houlgate, this is only for their refusal to give way, for their own hard-headedness. *Antigone*, he says, 'shows so clearly two tragic characters pursuing justified aims, but destroying themselves through their free and resolute refusal to yield to one another' (Houlgate 2007: 56). That makes tragedy into something like watching some old married couple fight, each yelling, 'No, I'm right, and it's you who's wrong,' all the way to the dissolution of the marriage and of the joint family capital as it is paid out to lawyers in a divorce court. Maybe they did indeed 'have it coming to them' (which is more like poetic justice than real justice), and maybe this is mildly tragic (but only with a little 't'). Houlgate's claim is that, for Hegel, tragedy is perfectly avoidable provided people do not remain so stiff-necked and 'one-sided' in their actions.

as a right action. In the divine order of the world, justified by its spontaneously produced beauty, human action is bound to betray itself, but the world in which such betrayal happens is nonetheless a beautiful world, not because failure and destruction have an aesthetic value in themselves but because they are part of the divine structure of the world. Although the rationale of such a divine order is unintelligible to us—why do the gods do what they do?—a glimpse of the workings of that order is nonetheless reconciliatory when it is comprehended as beautiful, as spontaneously harmonizing itself.

It is not reconciliatory because the sufferings of noble individuals all contribute to anything like a greater good. There simply is no greater or greatest good. There are only the incommensurable, often conflicting goods that the divine order establishes, and the spontaneous harmony of that world as it learns to right itself after disruption is beautiful. The eternal laws of justice, as embedded in the organic order, are themselves necessary to produce that beauty, but there is no reason to expect that these eternal laws, when carried out by humans, will always be consistent with each other. A world of conflicting gods will be a world of tragic human conflict.

How does this play out? Agamemnon takes himself to be compelled to sacrifice his daughter, Iphigenia, in order to get Artemis to provide the winds necessary for the Greeks to sail to Troy. Agamemnon puts on the 'yoke of necessity' to produce the right motivational structure for himself in which he can carry out the sacrifice (the structure being that of a kind of rage), and, after the success of the Trojan expedition, he is murdered by his wife because of his slaughter of the daughter (and some other transgressions). His son in turn avenges himself against the mother for killing the father, and he kills her. He is then doomed to be pursued by the furies. None of those occurrences are particularly beautiful.

On Hegel's view, what is reconciliatory about this story when related in the terms of the tragedians can depend only on a view about the organic nature of the divine world. Things have their purposes, and even such a set of horrifying events—each of which on its own looks as if it has to be on the opposite pole of whatever other pole reconciliation lies on—fit into the divine order. Moreover, it worth also noting the obvious: this divine order is the result not of design but of the necessity that emerges from the various decisions of the different gods themselves, and, in that organic order of things, even the conflicts seem to play a role.[8] They are metaphorically themselves the organs by which this whole spontaneously produces itself.[9] The necessity that produces such a spontaneous harmony is itself beautiful, even if the acts it provokes can be themselves dreadful.

One of the features of such tragedies is that they present a world that looks at cross purposes to human aims, even aimed against them. The gods themselves look rather arbitrary and capricious. From one point of view, even a Greek point of view, Agamemnon is obviously a rather horrendous character. He murders the first husband of his wife, sacrifices his daughter in a kind of self-induced rage, and brings Cassandra as his mistress with him back to Greece and flaunts her to his wife. On the other hand, he organizes the expedition to Troy and in effect stages the great set of events that forms the Greeks as a 'people' (having defined themselves in terms of an 'other', the Trojans, towards whom they were otherwise indifferent). Moreover, it is he who does this, although the gods, knowing him well, lay all the traps. That Agamemnon has brutally to sacrifice his daughter is a matter of indifference to the gods, even if it is a monstrous act to us. Nonetheless, it is wrong, and Agamemnon and his entire household must suffer for it. The punishment may seem unfair, since the accomplices (the gods) are never charged, but that is a human judgement, not a divine concern. The result is a world of beauty, and that should be enough.

---

[8] 'Therefore it is both right and wrong to interpret the gods in general as always either purely external to man or purely powers dwelling in him. For they are both. In Homer, therefore, the action of gods and men goes continually crisscross; the gods seem to bring about what is alien to man and yet actually accomplish only what constitutes the substance of his inner heart . . . This inner interruption of wrath, this check, which is a power foreign to the wrath, the epic poet is fully justified in representing as an external event because Achilles at first appears to be entirely full of wrath alone . . . What in general constitutes the serenity of the Homeric gods and the irony in the worship of them is the fact that their independence and their seriousness is dissolved again just in so far as they evince themselves as the human heart's own powers and therefore leave men alone by themselves in them' (Hegel 1975a: 228).

[9] 'This sort of development is most complete when the individuals who are at variance appear each of them in their concrete existence as a totality, so that in themselves they are in the power of what they are fighting, and therefore they violate what, if they were true to their own nature, they should be honouring . . . So there is immanent in both Antigone and Creon something that in their own way they attack, so that they are gripped and shattered by something intrinsic to their own actual being' (Hegel 1975a: 1217–18).

What Greek tragedy brings out, therefore, is the very issue itself of how deeply committed to a certain view of the world the Greeks had to be, and it presented an aesthetic case for this commitment being absolute, even in the face of such suffering. At the outset, the aesthetic case did not present an argument for this world. It simply laid out beautifully what were the commitments of such a spontaneous harmony. A tragic world made its case for itself in tragic art. It also raised the stakes very high for the Greeks, for behind even the most deeply religious of the tragedies (such as those by Aeschylus) there is the implicit question of whether the view makes any real sense.

Hegel's preference for Sophocles' *Antigone* as the exemplary Greek tragedy has its basis in that. The bones of the play are simple. After Oedipus' death, his family finds itself at odds with itself, and, in the ensuing conflicts over who is entitled to rule, one of the brothers attacks the city. Both brothers are killed, and Creon (an uncle) steps in to rule the city and secure order against a total breakdown. He forbids the standard burial rites for the brother who staged the attack. Antigone resists this, since she claims that she has not a relative but an absolute requirement to carry out such rites. She also knows that she (in particular as a young woman) has an absolute requirement to obey Creon. She is caught and sentenced to death. As a result, Creon's son (Antigone's betrothed) commits suicide, and, in the cave where Antigone has been condemned to die a slow and horrible death, Antigone herself commits suicide.

What is striking about *Antigone* is not merely that there is 'right against right'—Antigone's absolute requirement to perform the rites for her brother, and Creon's requirement to rule the city for the common good and to expect obedience—but that the whole play from a very human point of view seems to hover around the edge of meaninglessness. Creon may be right, but he comes across as a somewhat obsessive tyrant, and Antigone herself, in her principled resistance to Creon, presents herself as a bit of a fanatic. There is a sense that none of this had to happen, that both sides backed themselves into a corner, and that the idea that this is somehow part of the divine order can seem strained, to say the least.

In fact, *Antigone* cannot be just 'right against right', nor just about how two stiff-necked antagonists end up taking each other down. Antigone may have an absolute requirement to perform the burial rites for her brother, and Creon may indeed be absolutely entitled to issue the orders he did and to demand compliance with them, but

Antigone is also under the requirement not to make up her own mind about what she is to do. Requirements are, after all, requirements. What those requirements are is not itself up to us, even though it is up to us about what we do in the light of those requirements. Antigone is thus caught not merely defying Creon (which may well have been right for her to do) but also in making up her own mind about what needed to be done.[10] Antigone is forced into the position where she must do something like 'reflectively' identify with one of the positions she occupies, and this act—which is clearly recognizable to the Greek audience as well as to us (and which thus provokes so many liberal readings of *Antigone* that interpret it as a parable of the struggle of the individual against the state)—is one in which the Greeks could both see themselves and at the same time believe that it is a bad fate she has brought upon herself.[11] However, what this does is in effect to raise the ante: perhaps this world—which is originally conceived as spontaneously harmonizing itself by virtue of some feature of the divine cosmos—itself is indeed senseless. To the extent that this divine order does gradually come to seem senseless, the kind of meaning that the Greeks could find in such suffering itself begins to break down. When what had seemed to make sense (even if only aesthetic sense) begins to stop making sense, we can indeed continue to carry on, doing what we do, but we no longer really understand what we are doing, even when we know fully well what it is that we are doing. At its heart, this is, on Hegel's reading, what *Antigone* means. *Antigone* presented a world in dissolution without yet knowing it was in dissolution.

The Greek political system could maintain its actuality, could really work in the lives of its citizens, only if people assumed, as a matter of course that each citizen, in, for example, Athens, who debated in the public arena, had the good of Athens as his first basic commitment. That in turn required that there be principles (such as the good of Athens) that were beyond deliberation. However, if there is indeed a profound conflict between this condition of the human law and the very nature of the world—if the gods are such that they can induce a situation where the law must be rejected—then the world itself is

---

[10] See also Geiger (2007). Geiger sees *Antigone* as the founding act of a new ethical order. In retrospect, it looks like that, but Hegel sees it more subjunctively—namely, as the last gasp of an older order that will be replaced by another.

[11] Even more disturbing to the Greek audience would have been that they too were being compelled into 'identifying' themselves with Antigone's fate.

contrary to what the human law supposes must be the case. That one might have to choose between the divine law (as Antigone does) and the human law fashioned in the public debates in the polis means that, at the heart of things, people would have to make up their own minds on such key issues. If that were the case, then it could no longer be presumed that, as a matter of course, all citizens of Athens would have the good of Athens as their first principle. Even worse, it means that those people were not merely not in harmony with their world (as tragedy had shown them); they were at odds with each other, and, possibly, greatly at odds with themselves, as Antigone's fate exhibits.

It may well be the case that there is something beyond human comprehension about this. Perhaps the dealings between the gods and men are such that there is a kind of fate to human action that cannot be divined in advance. Perhaps it is our fate that the gods will lead us to such tragic conflicts. That itself is even more unsettling, because, in revealing the unintelligibility of the gods, it points to something that is higher than the gods themselves: fate. This, of course, suggests to the audience what was at first almost impossible for them to comprehend: if we could get a grasp on fate itself, then we frail humans could solve a puzzle that even the gods themselves could not solve. As things turned out, philosophy arose in part as the attempt to solve that puzzle. Rather than 'making sense of things' aesthetically, philosophy offered the alternative of 'making sense of things' as subject to rational enquiry and put into question at least the idea that the basic justifying move in thought about the ethical order had to be about beauty. To use the language of the Romantics, at that point beauty and truth separated. That such and such was the most beautiful story to be told in no way vouched for its being the most truthful story.[12]

---

[12] Christoph Menke argues that tragedy involves a way in which beauty itself (as characterizing the drama) and the tragic (as characterizing the practical actions of people) interrelate. He takes Hegel to have argued that it is the aesthetic pleasure of modern (and ancient) tragedy that overcomes our aversion to the tragic itself. However, this dichotomy (and therefore tension) between the practical and the aesthetic fails to capture the way in which Hegel takes tragic drama to present us with a truth about human self-consciousness that has to do with how the 'whole' is justified for a historical shape of spirit. On Hegel's view, because of the breakdown of the Greek aesthetic ideal of political life, post-Greek (and therefore modern and all post-Christian) tragedy faces a set of problems that are unique to it. For the moderns, it is even more pronounced: tragedy can sustain itself only in the light of an absolute commitment to something like 'freedom' but which itself is possibly undermined

If that is the case, then Greek tragedy was, in Nietzsche's phrase, on the way to committing suicide. It raised issues that ultimately could not be addressed in the aesthetic terms that make tragedy into something that matters and that can reconcile us to those sufferings. The first worm in the apple in classical tragedy is thus the organic conception of the world itself—as a world that naturally rights itself after disruptions to its beautiful order—and what it would mean to think that the world just might not right itself. One would then have conflict without any reassurance that the arc of the world bends towards justice, and the conflict would be simply unintelligible.

The second worm in the apple had to do with the way in which Greek aesthetic democracy rested on slavery to secure the independence of its citizens. The ideal of beauty requires free citizens to harmonize in their actions. However, for that harmony to emerge spontaneously, each citizen had to be free from arbitrary constraint by others, to be independent and not be subject to insidious coercion from other agents. The free citizen had to be an independent citizen. However, such independence could exist only if others did the dirty work of the city. Men ruled their households, and women and slaves did the work that would otherwise have undermined the independence of the citizen.

The vaunted equality of the citizens of the polis thus rested on a profound inequality that also seemed to be natural. Nobody would willingly be a slave, but it was part of the natural order that some people had to be slaves, and thus there were slaves, but each of them had to be coerced into being slaves.[13] (Women did not require that type of coercion for their inequality. As women, they were simply unequal, and they could not cease being women.) Yet, as tragedy continued to throw the idea of a natural order whose arc bends towards justice into question, the very existence of the terms under which the polis could be effective also seemed to be in the process of dissolving—in large part by virtue of the questions the tragedies themselves were raising. The misery of slavery coupled with the belief

precisely because of its sometimes tragic consequences. Indeed, one of the animating questions of the Hegelian philosophy has to do with whether there can be a reconciliation in modern life, given what looks like potentially insurmountably deep tensions within itself. See Menke (2009).

[13] Moses Finley wrote movingly about the ambiguity of slavery in the ancient world and both how it was an object of suspicion and yet deemed absolutely necessary. His own short summary of his views can be found in Finley (1964).

that it was necessary could only be another indication that the populace of Athens were not in harmony with each other or with the world.

The third worm in the apple had to do with the fall of Athens itself. It seemingly repeated in real historical time some of the models of tragedy that were otherwise encountered in myth. After leading the coalition against the Persians, Athens exhibited hubris, as it began to overreach on what it could do. As Thucydides described it, the rise and fall of Athens seemed to embody the close connection between the overreaching of hubris and nemesis (fate). Having done so many things right, Athens, a slave-owning society, could not imagine that it could do things wrong. Possessing great power, the people of Athens began to subordinate principle to self-interest and to conflate the two. Since there was the fatal Greek assumption that the possession of power confers the right to exercise it over the weak—and the existence and necessity of slavery were part of this—Athens could take its overreaching to be part of the natural order. However, especially after the massacre of the people of Delos, Athens stirred fears among its neighbours, and the end result was the defeat and fall of Athens. Rather than being the necessary result of a divine order in which justice is done, that string of events produced only a fanaticism that seemed to know no limit. No real peace could be made, and the result was the dissolution of the social whole, which had been held together by the aesthetic ideal.[14] The picture of a world necessarily righting itself after disruption seemed increasingly to be belied by the facts on the ground and to be put into question by later tragedians such as Euripides and the emerging philosophies of Socrates, Plato, Aristotle, and the Stoics.

Without the idea of the world as an organic whole that naturally rights itself, it is not clear that there is any longer a place for tragedy. What is the story of Agamemnon about if there is no divine order in which the play takes place? Is it simply the story of a bad man who did one great thing?

The marginalization of the Greek world by the Roman Conquest of it showed the apple to be worm-laden all the way through. On Hegel's view, however, the Roman world was fundamentally held together not by anything like a deep conception of beauty but by something

---

[14] See the account of Thucydides in Burrow (2008).

more prosaic: power and the violence necessary to achieve it and to hold it. If Athens at its peaks celebrated itself (as Pericles boasted) as the teacher of Hellas, Rome celebrated itself simply as the most powerful of all the states. It argued for the superiority of its own virtues as being the motivational backbone of its ability to conquer all others. Its very success showed that the gods supported the Romans, not that the whole that was produced was in any way beautiful. Rome was simply willing to use power in a way nobody else had been willing to do. Romans, of course, knew that bad things happened to good people, but that was simply the way the world was, and there was nothing reconciliatory about it. There was no place in the Roman world for tragedy. The real Roman art was satire.[15]

The Christian alternative substituted one god for the many Greek gods. Just as philosophy raised the question as to whether reason could order all the goods and pathea, the idea of the Christian god presumed that the one god arranged the goods of the world in a way that was itself all for the best. This would be a divine order—an order that, even if it did not make sense now, would have its sense one day be revealed to us. How then to understand such conflicts within the framework of guidance from one benevolent, omniscient, and omnipotent god? Since the one god was not at odds with himself, there could be no intrinsic conflict in the various pathae related to the divine order of things.

Where then is the origin of the kinds of deep conflicts that seem to be the stuff of tragedy? It must lie not so much in the very structure of the cosmos but in a limited part of it. It can lie only in human evil, in something like Kant's idea of radical evil as the propensity to put one's self-love (that is, one's own interests) ahead of the moral law.[16]

---

[15] 'Now since what is disclosed in Satire is the dissolution of the Ideal, a dissolution prosaic in its inner content, we have not to look for its actual soil in Greece as the land of beauty. Satire in the form just described belongs properly to the Romans. The spirit of the Roman world is domination by abstraction (i.e. by dead law), the demolition of beauty and joyous customs, the suppression of the family qua immediate natural ethical life, in general the sacrifice of individuality which now surrenders itself to the state and finds its cold-blooded dignity and intellectual satisfaction in obedience to the abstract law' (Hegel 1970: xiv. 514; 1975a: 514).

[16] The other alternative would have been the Manichean outlook, that there are two divinities or at least spiritualities at war with each other and thus inducing us to be at war with ourselves. The power of such an alternative is illustrated by the fact that, despite continuous repression of the Manichean doctrine by a rather powerful church, it has kept on naturally reappearing.

By virtue of being the embodied individuals they are, all people have such a propensity, even if they never exhibit it. Even a very good person has this propensity, which can lead him or her to do evil things while still otherwise leading an exemplary life. (That theme has been the subject of several films by Woody Allen.[17]) The new issue becomes that of 'keeping the faith' with the good in the face of evil in oneself and in others, and it is unclear if tragedy can have any real part to play in such a view. Agamemnon, for example, simply becomes an evil character who has achieved a form of worldly greatness that pales in comparison with the moral law. If Agamemnon is originally about overreaching and the way the gods use us for their own purposes, under the new conception it has to become a tale of how easy it is for bad men to flourish and how evil perhaps only brings more evil in its wake. Clytemnestra's killing of Agamemnon looks more like poetic justice than divine justice, and Orestes' problem with the furies looks more like the terrors of a bad conscience. With the breakdown of the Greek idea of how norms and facts—our aspirations and the way of the world—intertwine, the story of Agamemnon becomes instead something of a cautionary tale more than it is a tragedy.

If so, then it would seem that tragedy would not be about the overreaching on the part of the heroes of tragedy, nor about how the gods' inscrutability and their disputes with each other lead to suffering on our part, but about human sinfulness. However, human sinfulness cannot be an appropriate subject of tragedy. Even though the Christian view of things has a place for sinfulness to be ultimately punished and thus for the world to set aright (although not by itself but by the divine judge), sinfulness is a lack, a failing on the part of individuals, even though all individuals are burdened with it.[18] There

---

[17] In particular, Allen's *Crimes and Misdemeanors* and *Matchpoint* each present a character (a man) whose very important standing, which means so much to him, is in danger of being subverted by a woman with whom he has had or is having an affair. As the plot emerges, it turns out that he comes to believe that the only way to eliminate that threat is to eliminate the person. He kills her (or has her killed), gets away with it, and goes off to resume his life as it had been. The films are character studies of radical evil and of how at a certain point, when the projects at stake seem important enough, it becomes easy enough to let the propensity to substitute one's own set of personal goods for the moral law to take over.

[18] Something like this also begins to appear in late Greek tragedy with the *deus ex machina* arriving at the end to sort out the details and arrange for some kind of justice to be done. This is part of the basis for the well-known antipathy to certain plays by Euripides on the part of people like Nietzsche.

is nothing 'right' about sinfulness, however much a part of the human condition it is supposed to be. It is not tragic that none of us is perfectly good.

Is there a place left for tragedy? There would be if there were something that succeeded the Greek conception of an organic world that naturally righted itself. Now, to the extent that one takes seriously the scientific revolution's impact on our view of nature, there does not seem to be anything like a place for such an organic view of the cosmos. Instead, nature is, as Hegel put it, 'impotent'.[19] It cannot make itself better in any way. Moreover, it makes little sense even to speak of a 'better' ordering of nature. Nature just is what it is.

Nonetheless, even though nature, without creatures like us, cannot comprehend itself as a whole, we (as natural creatures endowed with self-consciousness) can comprehend nature as a whole. As Hegel puts it, 'man is an animal... [but] precisely because he *knows* that he is an animal, he ceases to be an animal and attains knowledge of himself as spirit'.[20] We are, to appropriate a phrase from Charles Taylor, essentially self-interpreting animals. Now, although it requires another long argument to show this, Hegel concludes that any such self-interpretation involves a set of commitments taken to be absolute, unconditional, and what Hegel called a form of life (or alternately a form of spirit) is bounded by such absolute commitments such that, when those commitments break down, the basic form of making sense of things breaks down. Such a breakdown occurs when there are insurmountable contradictions in tensions in the form of life such that it becomes senseless and unlivable. When that happens, we lose our orientation and the meaning of the world dissolves. As it dissolves, that form of life loses its grip on its participants, and its survival becomes uncertain.

For historical and dialectical reasons, the absolute commitments of the modern form of life revolve around an idea—still itself developing—of the absolute character of freedom as having both a certain normative standing and the power to carry out one's commitments. Ultimately, it is the ability to have one's acts be 'up to oneself' and to have those acts make sense.[21] If there are tensions

---

[19] '... die *Ohnmacht* der Natur', in Hegel (1970: ix, §250; 2004: 23).
[20] Hegel (1975a: 80).
[21] Of course, much more needs to be said about that. I have tried to say a bit more in Pinkard (2012).

inherent to an absolute commitment but those tensions make sense, there is the possibility of a reconciliation to those tensions.

Hegel points to Shakespearian tragedies as paradigmatic for the shape of modern tragedy that does without the Greek assumption of a world that bends in an arc towards justice. In Shakespeare, tragedies often occur because of contingency, not because of the gods willing an outcome or laying the traps to provoke a certain result. Our world is such that noble characters can be undone by the world around them, even though there is nothing necessary about the world's doing so. For example, in *Romeo and Juliet*, one has a pure love undone by hatred between families. The two characters, Romeo and Juliet, are each 'love itself'. Their love is so pure that it refuses to yield to this world, and neither of them can endure without the other.[22] The tragedy is that the world is such that these pure lovers cannot prevail, even though it is only an accident that they cannot endure. A world committed to the infinite value of the individual and therefore of his or her whole emotional life will bring in its wake a way of undoing noble people. What makes this tragic is the sense that a set of commitments that are absolute themselves contingently bring the actors to ruin, and the necessity of this commitment is what is reconciliatory.

Hegel himself seemed to be of two minds about this. On the one hand, he thought that the greatness of ancient tragedy would always outweigh that of modern tragedy. Even of Romeo and Juliet, he said, 'but the woe that we feel is only a grievous reconciliation, an unhappy bliss in misfortune'.[23] On the other hand, Shakespeare in particular

---

[22] 'The same is the case in Romeo and Juliet. The soil on which these tender blooms were planted is foreign to them, and we are left with nothing but to bewail the tragic transience of so beautiful a love which is shattered by the crazy calculations of a noble and well-meaning cleverness, just as a tender rose in the vale of this transitory world is withered by rude storms and tempests' (Hegel 1975a: 1232). 'For example, in Shakespeare's *Romeo and Juliet*, Romeo has love as his chief 'pathos'; yet we see him in the most diverse relations to his parents, to friends and his page, in honour-squabbles and his duel with Tybalt, in his piety and trust in the Friar, and, even on the edge of the grave, in talk with the apothecary from whom he buys the deadly poison, and all the time he is dignified and noble and deeply moved. Similarly in Juliet there is comprised a totality of relations to her father, her mother, her nurse, to Count Paris, and the Friar. And yet she is just as deeply sunk in herself as in each of these situations, and her whole character is penetrated and borne by only one feeling, the passion of her love which is as deep and wide and "boundless as the sea", so that she may rightly say "the more I give to thee, the more I have, for both are infinite"' (Hegel 1975a: 239).

[23] Hegel (1975a: 1232).

gives us portrayals of characters who press their own aims and not just the absolute commitments of something like Greek ethical life.[24]

The modern world, not one of immediate ethical life, has actually only one principle at work in it, but that one principle is immensely complex: it is that of freedom, which in turn has historically led to the conclusion that 'all are free', or, to put it negatively, that nobody by nature possesses the authority to rule over anybody else and that all forms of authority are therefore up for grabs and must be rationally defended.[25] (This is in one sense another version of Kant's idea that all people possess a 'dignity' that is beyond all price.[26]) What is noble about the tragic characters in such a world is their unbending commitment to the principle coupled with the knowledge that failure is always a possibility but also no reason to renounce the absoluteness of the principle.[27]

[24] 'It is precisely Shakespeare who gives us, in contrast to this portrayal of vacillating characters inwardly divided against themselves, the finest examples of firm and consistent characters who come to ruin simply because of this decisive adherence to themselves and their aims' (Hegel 1975a: 1229–30).

[25] In Hegel (1991: §29), Hegel expresses the basic character of the idea of freedom in his characteristic way: 'Right is any existence in general which is the existence of the free will. Right is therefore in general freedom, as Idea.' In various other places, he indulges in the mnemonic shorthand he used to give his students (who, as ever, were not always as attentive as professors think they should be) that the movement of history is from the idea that one is free to the idea that some are free and finally to the idea that all are free. (Or to put it in different terms: that, by nature or the gods, one person is entitled to rule, to the idea that some are by nature or the gods entitled to rule, and finally to the idea that nobody is by nature or the gods entitled to rule anybody else.) For example, see Hegel (1975b: 54).

[26] 'The religiosity and ethicality of a restricted sphere of life (for example, that of a shepherd or peasant), in their concentrated inwardness and limitation to a few simple situations of life, have infinite worth; they are just as valuable as those which accompany a high degree of knowledge and a life with a wide range of relationships and actions. This inner centre . . . remains untouched [and protected from] the noisy clamour of world history' (Hegel 1975b: 92).

[27] 'The last important point—the one we now have still to discuss—concerns the tragic denouement to which the modern characters are driven as well as the sort of tragic reconciliation with which this is compatible. In Greek tragedy it is eternal justice which, as the absolute power of fate, saves and maintains the harmony of the substance of the ethical order against the particular powers which were becoming independent and therefore colliding, and because of the inner rationality of its sway we are satisfied when we see individuals coming to ruin. If a similar justice appears in modern tragedy, then, owing to the non-universal nature of aims and characters, it is colder, more like criminal justice, owing to the greater reflectiveness of the wrong and crime into which individuals are forced when they are intent on accomplishing their ends . . . But on the other hand the tragic denouement is also displayed as purely the

Modern tragedy therefore is about the sufferings that contingently follow in the wake of agents seeking to put these modern principles into practice and in their subjective holding-fast to those principles.[28] More colloquially put, such tragedies are about individuals and collectives 'keeping the faith'.[29] Such tragedy is related to, and in one sense grows out of, Christian stories of the martyrs who 'keep the faith' in the face of unbearable tortures and horrors, but the martyrs are not tragic figures. What undoes them is human sinfulness on the part of others, while the martyrs themselves rest assured that a better life awaits them and that their present sufferings are as nothing compared to what is promised them. There may even be something heroic about the martyrs as they subordinate their fears to their faith, but they are not tragic.

Modern tragic figures exemplify Hegel's choicest metaphor for life in the modern world. We must be, he says, 'amphibians' who now live in two worlds: a world of contingency that does not seem to bend in an arc towards justice and a world of absolute commitments and a kind of pledge to the equal worth of all.[30] Aesthetic portrayal of what

effect of unfortunate circumstances and external accidents which might have turned out otherwise and produced a happy ending. In this case the sole spectacle offered to us is that the modern individual with the non-universal nature of his character, his circumstances, and the complications in which he is involved, is necessarily surrendered to the fragility of all that is mundane and must endure the fate of finitude' (Hegel 1975a: 1230–1).

[28] One of the best treatments on the subject of Hegel and modern tragedy is found in two books that are not really about Hegel and modern tragedy but are Hegelian and take up the theme of tragedy in some modern films: Pippin (2010, 2012).

[29] Once again, Hegel takes Shakespeare to be the paradigm: 'Such an independence of character can only occur when the fullest importance is given to what is external to the Divine, i.e. to the particular element in man. Shakespeare's characters especially are of this kind; in them it is precisely this taut firmness and one-sidedness that is supremely admirable. In them there is no question of religious feeling, of an action due to the man's own religious reconciliation, or of morality as such. On the contrary, we have individuals before us, resting independently on themselves alone, with particular ends which are their own, prescribed by their individuality alone, and which they now set themselves to execute with the unshakeable logic of passion, without any accompanying reflection or general principle, solely for their own satisfaction' (Hegel 1975a: 577–8).

[30] 'Spiritual culture, the modern intellect, produces this opposition in man which makes him an amphibious animal, because he now has to live in two worlds which contradict one another. The result is that now consciousness wanders about in this contradiction, and, driven from one side to the other, cannot find satisfaction for itself in either the one or the other. For on the one side we see man imprisoned in the common world of reality and earthly temporality, borne down by need and poverty,

it is like to live such a life and what it might look like plays an essential role in all this (as does philosophy).[31] However, aesthetic portrayal of such figures raises its own problem, the most obvious of which is: how does one satisfactorily portray 'keeping the faith', which is itself intrinsically something inward and not easily available to outward view? (Kierkegaard was later to make much of this dilemma.)

What role does religion play? On the one hand, it seems to play no role at all. Hegel even says this about Shakespeare's greatest characters.[32] These points about modern tragedy can all be stated without any need to have Christianity vouch for their truth. Even though Hegel himself claimed (almost certainly sincerely) to be a Christian, even for him this world does not bend towards justice, even if the Christian god may be presumed to make up for this in his final judgement on people. (Hegel himself rather infamously claimed that the last judgement was that of history, but that is another long story.) Yet, on the other hand, Hegel insisted that his overall view of this was religious.[33] It is no wonder that the contentious nature of

---

hard pressed by nature, enmeshed in matter, sensuous ends and their enjoyment, mastered and carried away by natural impulses and passions. On the other side, he lifts himself to eternal ideas, to a realm of thought and freedom, gives to himself, as *will*, universal laws and prescriptions, strips the world of its enlivened and flowering reality and dissolves it into abstractions, since the spirit now upholds its right and dignity only by mishandling nature and denying its right, and so retaliates on nature the distress and violence which it has suffered from it itself. But for modern culture and its intellect this discordance in life and consciousness involves the demand that such a contradiction be resolved' (Hegel 1975a: 54).

[31] In his rightfully influential book *Tragödie im Sittlichen: Gerechtigkeit und Freiheit nach Hegel*, Christoph Menke claims, roughly put, that the same kind of contradiction that animates *Antigone* (between the absolute duties of familial piety and the necessity of maintaining public order by Creon) appears in modern life as the conflict between freedom and justice and sometimes between personal 'authenticity' and political 'autonomy'. This seems to me to overstate the continuities between ancient and modern tragedy, and it does not adequately take into account the way in which the very meaning of such contradictions changes as the forms of life themselves change. If nothing else, there is the profound shift from seeing the ancient Greek view of principles as self-sufficient to the more psychological nature of modern tragedies, where the believability of such principles is up for grabs and what is at stake comes more and more to be the nature of the commitment the agent undertakes. See Menke (1996).

[32] 'In them there is no question of religious feeling, of an action due to the man's own religious reconciliation, or of morality as such' (Hegel 1975a: 577).

[33] See Pippin (2002). Pippin interprets Hegel's religious views in a way that might be best called a 'heretical' version of Christian religion. His rather deflationary reading of Hegel's religious commitments seems right to me, but it is at the least very controversial as to how close this might be to Hegel considered somehow 'in himself'.

Hegel's putative Christianity formed the earliest basis for the disruptions in his school and has continued ever since to divide interpreters of Hegel. That, together with the status of Hegel's metaphysics (or whether he even had one, remain the most polarizing features of the reception and interpretation of Hegel's philosophy, possibly because the worry about whether religion is still necessary at all is itself such a contentious issue.

Nonetheless, if anything, modern tragedy is about what happens to us after we have had to abandon the organic view of nature and, in Hegel's words, that point in modern life when we find ourselves 'sailing out into the open, with nothing above us and nothing below us, standing alone with only ourselves'.[34] Although that does not sound particularly religious, what role religion would have in it, if any at all, would be a topic for another time. Sailors embarking on the open sea know that, from time to time, through no fault of their own, the sea will swallow them. How much religion is necessary for such modern sailors?

---

[34] Hegel (1970: viii, 31).

7

The (Operatic) Tragedy of Culture: Notes on a Theme in Kierkegaard, Hebbel, and Wagner

Rüdiger Görner

1. PROLOGUE

'Tragedy' stands for the worst case in the human condition. The reception of this, arguably, most challenging of genres demands the spectator in his entirety, meaning the activation of all his faculties.[1] Tragedy illustrates that nothing in life can stay the same. In tragedy man is subject to perpetual change in a downward spiral that points towards catastrophe. Tragedy questions the reliability of values. With Hegel, it illustrates the simultaneity of contradictions inherent in the human existence.

One such contradiction in the period in question in this chapter was the post-Kantian dichotomy between reality and ideality, amplified by the inner disharmony and disillusionment of the German Restoration period (roughly 1815–30). Both Georg Büchner and Christian Dietrich Grabbe gave their voice to what they perceived as a tragic abandonment of interest in politics in favour of idle late-romantic contemplation, mainly in the 1820s and 1830s respectively. Losing faith in one's own capabilities recurred as a feature of the social condition after the failed revolution of 1848–9, mainly among the German bourgeoisie, whereas the formation of the proletariat countered this political apathy by striving towards a distinctly anti-idealistic, concrete positivism in

---

[1] Fuhrmann (1992: 110).

160   *Rüdiger Görner*

terms of social rights and emancipation. This conflict of social interests resulted in political and existential antagonisms, seen certainly by Friedrich Hebbel and Richard Wagner as tragically devisive. However, tragedy is defined by inevitability, while the social movements after 1848 rested on the belief that the social condition could be changed.

Tragedy is mainly about the conflict between Man and fate, or about being at odds with divinity.[2] In classical tragedy the Chorus amplifies this conflict, weighing up plausible and implausible alternatives to what otherwise appears as the inevitable outcome of a (psychological) conflict. In Schiller's terms, the chorus is a living wall in motion. It intrudes into the plot, providing measured commentaries on the way in which fate determines life. In line with a fundamental principle of ancient Greek culture, the *agón*, tragedy presents the individual in competition with his own fate. Tragedy is, therefore, the genre that proves that 'agonizing' over existential issues can have performance qualities. Hölderlin was indeed the first modern philosophical poet who understood the rhythmical qualities of the *stasima* in Greek tragedy, rightly suggesting that the rhythm itself carried meaning. His understanding of rhythm came close to that of post-Homeric poets, like Archilochos, who believed in *rysmós* as the very force that would regulate the course of human affairs. Hölderlin even suggested that it would be possible to reduce the spectrum of diverse tones to a 'basic tone' specific to each 'tragic poem'. In this tone he found 'more disposition for reflection and emotion' than in any other 'poem'.[3] Referring to his own attempt at writing a modern tragedy (*Empedocles*) as a 'tragic ode',[4] Hölderlin underlined the quasi-musical form of his reflections on tragedy, which remained fragmentary and unpublished until the beginning of the twentieth century. They form part of a nexus of conceptions of tragedy and the tragic that include Hölderlin's friends Hegel and Schelling. The latter pioneered a modern understanding of tragedy in the tenth of his *Philosophical Letters on Dogmatism and Criticism* (1795), pointing towards the integration of dialectical thought into the exposition and explanation of tragic situations. Neither Schelling nor Hegel, though, displayed as subtle an understanding for the rhythmical, or indeed

---

[2] For a comprehensive discussion of such fundamentals and their aesthetic history, see the landmark study by Greiner (2012). Greiner investigates the intrinsic interconnection between tragedy and the striving for moral uprightness and integrity.
[3] Hölderlin (2009: 305).   [4] Hölderlin (2009: 258).

musical, structure of Greek tragedy as did Hölderlin. Later on, it was Nietzsche who would (almost intuitively but correctly) declare music, the Dionysian mood, and the dance of the satyrs as the very origin of tragedy.

Interestingly, Schelling in his *Philosophy of Art*, published posthumously in 1859, based on lectures given in Jena in 1802/3 and Würzburg in 1804/5 respectively, referred to his early definition of tragedy, suggesting, however, one major modification: he now claimed that tragedy had *begun* with a 'synthesis', which, in the course of the development of tragedy as a form of drama, disintegrated into a perpetual conflict between individual freedom and fateful necessity.[5] The modern tragic hero, Schelling argued, was torn apart by this very conflict, and yet the ancient Greek dramatists of the classical—that is, Periclean—period, achieved pure artistic beauty in their tragedies. Schelling asked how this was possible.[6] His response sounded less pronounced than Hölderlin's, simply because the latter examined the stylistic and structural means applied by those dramatists, Sophocles in particular. The rhythm of speech, including the caesura, as well as the tonal qualities of the Greek language, provided dramatists with a unique reservoir of effective ways of articulation, which Hölderlin, through his translations of Sophocles, attempted to render in German. The poet's preoccupation with translation (not shared, incidentally, by his friends Schelling and Hegel!) became a feature of his very conception of tragedy, in that he implied a 'curious interrelatedness' of the two.[7] Equally, Hölderlin connected tragedy, and the experience of the tragic, with 'transitions between epochs',[8] suggesting that tragedy had a special role to play in providing such transition. This is of specific interest, because Hölderlin tried to find an explanation for why it is that Greek tragedy continues to be relevant and attract attention. As a dramatic art form, tragedy both looks back and anticipates the future, thus bridging the gap between now and then, here and elsewhere.

Tragedy is unquestionably a constituent of European culture. At times, culture itself has become an object of tragedy, but never more so than during the Shoah. Previous tragedies paled in comparison, and afterwards further experimentation within this form seemed frivolous. What this meant in terms of artistic practice is perhaps

---

[5] Schelling (1976: 341, 345).   [6] Schelling (1976: 340).
[7] Hölderlin (2009: p. xlix).   [8] Hölderlin (2009: p. xlviii).

best illustrated by the blending of tragedy and documentary theatre as exemplified by Peter Weiss's play on the Frankfurt Auschwitz trials, *The Investigation*. It documents tragedy of unprecedented scales and, by the same token, shows the tragic dimension of documenting atrocities. In his play, Weiss used variants of the Greek chorus to provide commentary and judgement on man-made fate. In terms of 'transition', this play—or 'Auschwitz oratorium', as Weiss called it— provides us with an exceptional example of media impact. Its first performance on 19 October 1965 took place at sixteen theatres in the Federal Republic of Germany and the German Democratic Republic, in East and West Berlin at the same time. Almost simultaneously, Peter Brook produced an English version staged in London, and Erwin Piscator's production of the play in West Berlin's *Freie Volksbühne* was broadcast live by German television. The reality of tragedy in the contemporary world was exemplified further when a Rwandan company performed *The Investigation* in 2007 at London's Young Vic theatre, thus examining the connection between Weiss's take on the Auschwitz trials and the Rwandan actors' own experience with their nation's genocide.

Another and very different example of the presence of tragedy after the supposed 'death of tragedy' (George Steiner) illustrates the point that tragedy is intrinsically linked with political developments (in Ancient Greece with the emergence of democracy in the *polis* of Athens). When Susan Sontag staged *Waiting for Godot* in 1993 in besieged Sarajevo, Beckett's play revealed its tragic features but also the resilience of absurd situations and strength than can radiate from the grotesque.

Yet, tragedy in the theatre practice in the modern world is often seen as a provocation with its portrayal of uncomfortable truths about human civilization and seemingly awkward reverberations of ancient myths with their perceived irrationality. Tragedy is indeed an ever-potent reminder of the (hidden) presence of the Other in the shape of uncontrollable forces that impact on our lives.

Tragedy is characterized by the absence of irony, or any form of 'comic relief', in the aforementioned existential conflict between freedom and necessity. And, yet, the proximity of tragedy and comedy is proverbial and, again, an integral part of Schelling's aesthetics. Instead of irony, the dramatist employs pathos. But, if applied inaptly, pathos can turn into something pathetic or insincere and trigger comic situations. In the mid-nineteenth century it was Karl Marx who not only saw this problem with tragedy, but used it for comment on political events of his time. He spoke of the 'great revolution as tragedy'[9] (meaning the French Revolution) that repeated itself as a farce in the failed bourgeois revolutions in the German states and France in 1848–51. This admission implied the continuation of the 'tragedy/comedy' duplicity, rather than its dialectic relationship, as a formative quality in social and cultural development. But Marx also stands for the analysis of the tragedy of social conditions that informed stage work from Richard Wagner's operatic capitalist critique in *Ring of the Nibelung* to the social drama by Friedrich Hebbel and Gerhart Hauptmann.

But, before we turn our attention to the conception of tragedy by Wagner and Hebbel in particular, it is worth pointing out that the underpinning dramatic narrative of this social dimension of tragedy derives, too, from Shakespeare, particularly the connection he suggested between human need and tragedy, most notably in *King Lear*. With reference to this play, Michael Ignatieff in *The Needs of Strangers* points out that 'our education in need is a tragic passage from blindness to sight'.[10] Against this backdrop, *King Lear* can be seen as a 'tragedy of need', with need having a necessity, and therefore uncompromising force, 'which can drive us even to our self destruction'.[11] Lear's need of needs is 'patience', as he says in his exchange with his two deceiving daughters, Goneril and Regan, in the fourth scene of the Act II. But the word 'patience' contains 'pain' and 'suffering', too, and does not only mean 'endurance'. Lear sees himself primarily as victim ('I am a man more sinned against than sinning'[12]), but he is growingly, and grudgingly, aware of his guilt, too, for which he will remorse. It was to take until Eugene O'Neill's trilogy *Mourning becomes Electra* (1932) that guilt would turn into an almost self-sufficient object, or, in Orin's words: 'The only love I can know now is the love of guilt for guilt which breeds more guilt—until you get so deep at the bottom of hell there is no lower you can sink and you rest there in peace!'[13] But the point is that Orin comments on his own words with the 'harsh' laughter of a haunted man. Guilt has become

---

[9] Marx (2000: 19): 'Hegel remarks somewhere that all great [facts] and characters of world history occur twice, so to speak. He forgot to add: the first time as [great] tragedy, the second time as [squalid] farce.'
[10] Ignatieff (1990: 20).   [11] Ignatieff (1990: 50).
[12] Shakespeare, *King Lear*, III.ii.56–7.   [13] O'Neill (2003: 145).

an actor on stage and a protagonist of its own. It performs itself. This, however, is a development that originated in the ambiguity of guilt in Oedipus.[14]

2. REINVENTING ANTIGONE

As George Steiner pointed out, tragedy became alien to cultures that subscribed to monotheistic religions, mainly because the plurality of ancient Greek divinity had generated a mythological richness as a highly differentiated narrative backdrop that supplied fateful motifs and situations. The metaphysically purposeful teleology in monotheism cancelled tragic conflict. And yet it was the cruellest and bitterest of ironies that Judaism was to be exposed to such unprecedented tragedy.

One of the fundamental insights into the mechanisms of modernism contained in Theodor W. Adorno's and Max Horkheimer's *Dialectic of Enlightenment* is the observation that myths and reason simultaneously developed their own distinctly different agendas. And yet, as it happened, they were fatefully intertwined; for any illumination about the workings, or structures, of myths resulted in reason becoming mythlike itself. Both saw guilt as the result of (criminal) action triggered by a curse that was deemed inescapable.[15] According to Adorno and Horkheimer, Odysseus' cunning intelligence broke up this tragic circle; likewise, Oedipus, even though he had to commit atrocities in order to disempower myth, ultimately achieved the same and annulled the authority of the sphinx. Different from Oedipus, Odysseus was spared from any tragic consequences of his actions. He outwitted the Gods, replacing their myth with his own. Oedipus encounters the sphinx-generating myth. Jean-Auguste-Dominique Ingres in his 1808 painting of this moment depicts this encounter as a quasi-erotic one. The painting is charged with sensuality, with death literally lying at Oedipus' feet. The imminent end of the sphinx means that her horrendous prophecy will continue to live instead. Archaic culture is, after all, defined by a chain of curses passed on from generation to generation. This precarious heritage conditions

---

[14] Cf. Scodel (2012).   [15] Horkheimer and Adorno (2004: 66).

and fashions tragedy and may help to explain why Greek tragedy experienced such a pronounced renaissance in literary modernism and, in particular, in post-Second World War Europe—from writers like Jean-Paul Sartre to Sarah Kane, and stage producers like Peter Stein and Christoph Schlingensief. But the major shift from fate as the stage producer of culture, as it were, to personal tragedy, motivated by the protagonist's psychology, had occurred as part of the history of this genre, and most notably in Euripides' *Hippolytus*.

This said, the modernist turn in the reflection of tragedy and its cultural implications came with Søren Kierkegaard's exploration of this subject in his large-scale manifestation of the meaning of existence, *Either-Or* (1843). Interestingly, his discussion of 'The Ancient Tragical Motif as Reflected in the Modern' follows immediately after the exposition of the 'Musical Erotic' as exemplified by the dialectician called A, through Mozart's *Don Giovanni*. Kierkegaard's A takes issue with Aristotle's definition of tragedy for reasons not dissimilar to those for modern criticism of Aristotle's authority: he had perceived tragedy solely as literature, disregarding its theatricality and, with it, performance qualities.[16]

Despite writing, at least initially, under the influence of Schelling's Berlin lectures (1843), and therefore in an anti-Hegelian mood, Kierkegaard was aware of the two most anti-Aristotelian stage works of his time, Goethe's *Faust*, part two in particular, and Christian Dietrich Grabbe's drama *Faust und Don Juan*, with both demonstratively disregarding the unity of space and time. Arguably, Grabbe's Don Juan is 'what this society would be, if it only dared to be itself; he is sensual, selfish and materialistic; but society is less than he, and deserves Don Juan's criticism, for it does not even dare to live according to its true nature'.[17] Faust, on the other hand, has 'despaired of finding in religion and science an approach to the indestructible essence of existence'.[18] He is unable to abandon himself and enjoy a more superficial way of life. Hence Don Juan becomes his role model, whom he can only live up to only by entering a pact—tragically—with the devil. To the discourse on tragedy, Grabbe introduced the conception that the tragic can be triggered by the protagonist detaching himself from his environment. Kierkegaard refers to Grabbe's drama by calling it 'ingenious in some respects'.[19]

[16] Cf. Scodel (2012).   [17] Kaufmann (1940: 89).
[18] Kaufmann (1940: 89).   [19] Kierkegaard (1978: 171; my translation).

Grabbe's tragedy is ingenious for the very reason that it brings together the protagonists of two major *modern* tragedies, with their love for Donna Anna as their common 'interest'. Perhaps more accurately, one should say that Grabbe pitched Faust and Don Juan against each other in a Hegelian sense of the word. After all, and perhaps in a late echo of his friend Hölderlin, Hegel saw the nature of tragedy in 'Entgegensetzung', the pitching of legitimately acting individuals *against* each other.[20] Even though Kierkegaard's knowledge of Hegel remains controversial,[21] it is fair to assume his familiarity with Hegel's reading of *Antigone* in his *Phänomenologie des Geistes* and the second edition of his *Vorlesungen über die Ästhetik*, compiled and published posthumously by his student H. G. Hotho in 1842, the year before Kierkegaard came to Berlin. Hegel's discussion of tragedy in the context of his *Ästhetik* contained a concept that was of equal significance to Kierkegaard in his attempt to examine the 'modernity' of tragedy. It is the concept of 'Weltzustand',[22] whose inner dichotomy Hegel saw as the very basis for any tragic plot. Sharing all his predecessors' interest in the proximity of tragedy and comedy, mainly due to Aristophanes' comedy *The Frogs*, in which the famous tragic playwrights of the time (405 BC) appear as ridiculous figures, Kierkegaard mocks the non-existent sense of responsibility of the farcical politicians of his time. As Steiner quite rightly says, Kierkegaard uncannily anticipated 'the 1848 crisis that, partly at least, originated in the sheer carelessness and indifference of politicians in charge'. Modern tragedy, however, 'is about responsibility, about the acceptance of guilt'.[23]

Against this backdrop, Kierkegaard's philosophical protagonist A suggested the invention of a new Antigone. If, according to Aristotle's *Poetics*, all art was imitation, or mimesis, of human action, then, surely, reinventing Antigone for the sake of explaining the modern version of tragedy was legitimate enough an undertaking.

---

[20] Hegel (1977: 325).

[21] Cf. Fenger (1980), Thulstrup (1980), and Steiner (1986: 54). Fenger and Steiner call Hegel's presence in early Kierkegaard 'pervasive'. Thulstrup is considerably more cautious and emphasizes Kierkegaard's Schelling-inspired critique of Hegel's position on dialectics, tragedy, and the meaning of truth. Thulstrup argues that Kierkegaard was more interested in the characters' attitude towards truth than in their striving towards comprehensive awareness and knowledge as the basis for a successful pursuit of truth.

[22] Hegel (1977: 324).   [23] Steiner (1986: 55).

But the concept of 'reinvention' therefore meant an imitation of the classical Antigone under the auspices of modern times. A's Antigone is conceived as the 'daughter, even the bride of mourning', with pain as her 'dowry'.[24] She is his 'creature' and fictive embodiment of his thoughts. He even imagines having spent a night with her, even though she vanished as quickly as he had invented her. This modern Antigone represents perpetual transformation; her 'reality' is only an 'atmospheric' one. Antigone in the 1843 imagination is proud of, and in love with, her mourning (as if anticipating O'Neill's drama!). What makes her 'modern', however, is her *Angst*. She is driven by anguish; hence restlessness conditions her mourning. The reason for this restlessness is the knowledge of what her father, Oedipus, had done. According to Kierkegaard's A, her memory of him kills her.[25]

One striking feature of this chapter is the complete absence of the Gods in this philosophical 'imagination', or discourse on tragedy. What matters is the nature of mourning then, in the classical era, and now, in 1843. Kierkegaard's A argues that in Greek tragedy mourning was 'deeper', meaning more profound, but pain less pronounced. In modern tragedy it is the other way round: pain is greater and mourning less prominent. But Kierkegaard's A takes his philosophical speculations even further, arguing that there is an erotic relationship between anguish and mourning in modern tragedy. Anguish occupies itself solely with mourning and, in so doing, compensates for the lack of depth in modern mourning.

Aristotle famously argued in point seven of his *Poetics* that, in order for tragedy to be complete or a whole, it required a beginning, middle, and end. Interestingly, Diogenes Laertius was to define divinity as something 'that had neither a beginning nor an end'.[26] This suggests that the very Aristotelian form, if adhered to, stands for aesthetic secularization. Kierkegaard's imagined Antigone confirms this, for his A does not envisage an open-ended scenario but very much a conclusive finale: Memory kills Antigone.

This 'memory' is, according to Kierkegaard, part of Antigone's conscience. Hölderlin had already made this point through his translation of *Antigone*, which pays particular attention to her 'inner voice'. It is a 'counter-voice' to the jargon of power that Creon uses. In Hölderlin's version of the tragedy, Antigone turns into a virtuosa

---

[24] Kierkegaard (1978: 182).   [25] Kierkegaard (1978: 196).
[26] Diogenes Laertius (1999–2002: i. 35).

of conscience whose voice is, as it were, orchestrated by the chorus. Antigone resists convention and, in so doing, invites the spectator to review his own attitude towards given laws and assumed principles. If the spectator refused this 'invitation', he would turn into the unburied Polynices, exposed to blindly accepted custom. Hölderlin and Kierkegaard 'agreed' in calling Antigone's mourning the main protagonist of this tragedy.[27]

3. THE THREE FATES OF MODERNISM

In mid-nineteenth-century tragedy, which in this chapter is perceived as a phase of transition to the modern conception of tragedy, Kierkegaard's Antigone finds that she has two Nordic sisters, Richard Wagner's Brünnhilde, and Friedrich Hebbel's Kriemhild frenzied by revenge for Siegfried's assassination.

As philosophers, dramatists, and musical composers, all three explored the tragic essence of modern culture (the self-defeating conception of progress), and the insufficiency of dialectics as a method of describing cultural processes. The fragility of 'redemption' was the one perceived feature of this tragic essence of modernity; the other was the compensatory function of art and its deceptive production of 'Schein'. This resulted in a 'tragic circle', epitomized by Wagner's *Der Ring des Nibelungen*. As will be shown, his Brünnhilde, together with Hebbel's Kriemhild and Kierkegaard's Antigone, turned into the 'three fates' of modernism.

There was a third dimension to this very transition to the modern conception of tragedy as the essence of modern culture at that time. F. W. Kaufmann, in his early landmark study on *German Dramatists of the 19th Century* (1940), aptly termed the reason for this 'transition' a 'growing disillusionment in idealism',[28] coupled with an increasingly materialistic interpretation of history, and indeed present-day realities. The Aristotelean notion of katharsis had turned into a collective enterprise and an act of *Kulturkritik*, with tragedy

---

[27] Similarly, Martin Walser argued that in tragedy no one but mourning is in the right: Sophocles (1989: 9, 15).
[28] Kaufmann (1940: 89).

becoming the instrument of criticizing the materialistic culture of mid-nineteenth-century Europe.

In all three cases, though, tragedy is also psychologically motivated and therefore stands more in the Euripidean tradition, even though Wagner in particular favoured Aeschylus, also reflected by the Aeschylean tetralogy structure of his *Ring* cycle. Arguably, Wagner's *Tristan und Isolde* was his more genuine contribution to the genre 'operatic tragedy'. The significant point, however, is that with Christoph Willibald Gluck's opera *Alceste* modern tragedy adopted a distinct inter-mediality to its stage realization. But there was more to this development. Melody became an agent in its own right. The orchestral accompaniment interpreted the psychological disposition of the voice and carried additional 'meaning'. Even in the most subtle parts of tonal differentiation, the orchestra amplified the musical quality of emotional situations. Through opera, tragedy has completed a full circle and recuperated its musical origins. No analyst of contemporary culture of that time had recognized this more clearly than (the young) Nietzsche. With Wagner in mind, he could indeed witness the (re-)birth of tragedy from the reality of modern music. This reality was chromatically nuanced and intriguingly balanced when it came to the interplay of, in Wagner's case, musically structured libretti and musical composition with words and verses already tuned, as it were, to challenge musical rendering and interpretation. Music adopted its own narrative with ominous foreshadowing of tragic situations, most prominently developed in the orchestral interludes of Wagner's tragic operas. To name but one example, consider the extended orchestral interlude at the end of the second scene of the first act in *Götterdämmerung*, which enacts an atmospheric transition from the sinister (Hagen's aria 'Hier sitz' ich zur Wacht') to the anguished, caused by the question of whether Brünnhilde should give Siegfried's ring and symbol of their love back to the Rhine maidens in order to avoid further calamities. The music can go off on a tangent but is always bound back to the necessities of the plot and the orchestration of the protagonist's stream of consciousness, or, in Tristan's and Isolde's case, streams of unconsciousness.

Tristan's suffering called for a chromatic depiction in compositional style, but, on the whole, such suffering suggested the tragedy *and* triumph of love, the tragedy of longing *and* the possibility of overcoming it and attaining redemption through transfiguration, as well as the tragedy of subjectivity and its transformation into self-denial. In *Lohengrin* it is but one question—namely, Elsa's enquiring about the knight's identity—that brings about the hero's relapse into tragic solitude and, consequently, the inability to share the life and love of the mortals.

But tragedy operates at more levels in Wagner's *Der Ring des Nibelungen*, with Brünnhilde always being involved in these tragic situations as their agent and victim. Her triumphs are therefore deceiving and short-lived. Once Wotan's favourite daughter and the main Valkyrie, she falls from grace because her will to love gets the better of her. First, she tries to defend and protect the incestuous Siegmund against Wotan's rage; then, she refuses to return the ring of the Nibelung. The hero she lives for, Siegfried, deceives her; and, eventually, she destroys the sacred fortress of the Gods, Valhalla, with the fire of Siegfried's funeral pyre. Whatever she does is unlawful, but, like Antigone, she listens to her inner voice and acts on its command. The only thing she can call into being is, paradoxically, the end of the Gods.

Brünnhilde's farewell aria, inspired by the sight of Siegfried's corpse, tells of the tragedy of knowledge. Now that she knows 'everything' ('Alles! Alles! | Alles weiß ich') she understands that the ring belongs to the Rhine and its maidens, but the ring has first to be 'purified' by the fire that will destroy her before the maidens can reclaim it. She now sees her sorrow 'blooming' ('Lenkt euren Blick | auf mein blühendes Leid'), but she refuses to accept any blame for the tragedy of love and power that has unfolded before everyone's eyes. Different from Kierkegaard's Antigone, Wagner's Brünnhilde is not in love with guilt, sorrow, or mourning. She turns into the bride of destruction. But in this (self-)destruction there is no redeeming feature. The end of the Gods is final, and the process of secularization irreversible. In structural terms, this is the equivalent to Wotan's farewell at the end of *Die Walküre*. In both cases and in the absence of a chorus, any signs of 'hope' are developed by the orchestral reflection on what the respective arias have conveyed. Tragedy now expresses itself in the inevitability of parting and the finality of yearning. Brünnhilde's will to self-realization through love triggers the cataclysm of the Gods to whom she attributes the blame for their collective downfall.

As the first part of the tetralogy demonstrates, material lust has corrupted the Gods. For want of possession, they betray Alberich but, in so doing, draw upon themselves the curse of losing their superiority to the giants. They, in turn, inherit the greed from the Gods, with the consequence that Fafner murders his brother, only to bury the hoard in a cave, where he, in the shape of a dragon, guards the idle metal by sleeping on it. In Kaufmann's words: 'This again is a symbol of the utter senselessness of accumulating a material which in itself has no value whatsoever, and is, at the same time, a condemnation of the greed for materialistic possession in Wagner himself and in his age.'[29] The point in question is that material itself and our attitude to it can cause tragic situations, and that this particular one, gold and greed, was a symptom of Wagner's time. Yet, at the same time, this collective experience can give life to an operatic masterpiece through but *one* artist. The aesthetic morale differs only in degrees from classic principles: even the horrendous and the terrible contain 'beauty', which makes them—in Nietzschean terms—bearable.

The Nibelungen tragedy had attracted public attention since the Swiss scholar Johann Jakob Bodmer rediscovered and edited parts of the saga in 1757. In later life, Goethe drew attention to the potential of this plot, and King Ludwig I of Bavaria commissioned a large-scale mural painting of scenes from the saga for his residence in Munich. In 1834, the dramatist Ernst Raupach published a popular version of the saga as a tragedy (*Der Nibelungenhort*), much performed during the 1840s. Friedrich Hebbel criticized it in 1853 as a form of unacceptable trivialization. In the meantime, the philosopher, aesthetic theorist, and writer Friedrich Theodor Vischer argued that the Nibelungen plot would work only as a large heroic opera. His comments anticipated Wagner's operatic epic, which had been in the making, with notable interruptions, since the late 1840s. Hebbel, however, believed that the Nibelungen tragedy was made for the non-operatic stage, too. He devoted seven years to completing his *Nibelungen* trilogy, which was first performed in May 1861. His trilogy centred on Kriemhild's fate, introducing her as a queen of revenge. In all of Hebbel's tragedies, there is one striking feature that needs to be considered in biographical terms, too: his consciousness of guilt. It appears to have been part of his (non-sentimental) education in the sense that the young Hebbel had found support in the modest home of a Hamburg seamstress, Elise Lensing, who sacrificed literally everything for him: from her hard-earned savings to her social reputation.

[29] Kaufmann (1940: 165).

Hebbel thanked Elise by abandoning her but, in doing so, acquired a sense of guilt that informed his later dramatic work as well as his advocacy of the rights of women.

In line with his principle that in tragedy the hero should 'perish only because of himself', as Hebbel stated in reflections on Schiller's tragedy *Wallenstein*,[30] he constructed a character with Kriemhild, whose rebellion against the cover-up of Siegfried's assassination will lead to unspeakable bloodshed and the destruction of her realm. Hebbel's Kriemhild wants justice for her murdered husband, Siegfried, whose corpse is even desecrated by his murderer, Kriemhild's uncle Hagen of Tronje, while lying in state in the cathedral. The church cannot be a safe haven, and religious belief is at best fickle in an early medieval society that still finds it hard to exchange ancient Germanic mythology for Christian rites. The intensity of Kriemhild's rebellion even surpasses that of Antigone. It makes her seek an alliance with the King of Huns, Etzel, in order to destroy her own people and royal family. As predicated by her mother, Ute, Siegfried's widow turns into a Fury, whose energies are all directed towards creating destruction and the annihilation of an entire culture. By the standards of the 1860s, Kriemhild can be regarded as modern and anti-modern at the same time. Her lust for revenge is archaic but her self-assured political manœuvering and the sheer extent of her emancipation from her social position are clear indications of exceptional self-determination, which she shares with Wagner's Brünnhilde, but only to a far lesser extent with Kierkegaard's Antigone.

Everything points towards death in Hebbel's tragedy, but with no apparent hope for transfiguration. Volker, the court musician, notices that the only music than can be heard on their voyage to Etzel's realm (being, roughly, today's Hungary) is the music of death (Act IV, sc. iii). The boats on which they sail down the Danube are barges of death with dark premonitions as their company, or, in Hagen's words: 'We are caught in the net of death' (Act II, sc. i). Strangely, though, Hagen feels comfortable with this state of being.

Hebbel's tragedy also provides the spectator with a *vir fortis ex machina*, who turns into the *persona prima* of the final phase of the third part of the Nibelungen trilogy. His name is Dietrich von Bern, a moral authority, who will eventually be invited by King Etzel to take

---

[30] Hebbel (1971: iii. 259).

over his realm. Dietrich will do so in 'the name of the crucified', the very phrase with which the tragedy ends.[31] This outcome suggests that the outsider, Dietrich, is likely to establish Christian rule after the purgation of the semi-heathen Nibelungs and Huns.

References to Christian values throughout the drama serve as a substitute for the partial relief from tragic tension in the way music does in Wagner's operas. At the end of Hebbel's trilogy there is no 'Abschied', or farewell, as in Wagner's tetralogy, but a sense of the arrival of a new and more humane order.

4. AN EXCURSION, OR NOTES ON ALCESTE

Experiments with Greek mythology constitute a distinctive feature of modernism in art and thought.[32] A great number of such experiments were conducted on the operatic stage with Euripides' tragedy *Alkestis* as a prime object. In a little-known version, which served Georg Friedrich Händel as the basis for his Alceste-adaptation under the title *Admeto* (1727), based on a libretto by Aurelio Aurelis,[33] Antigone was the former lover of Admetos. When he falls in love with Alkestis, any conflict is resolved by Antigone's voluntarily renouncing her love for Admetos ('Antigona, delusa d'Alceste').

It is, perhaps, consequential that the one document that transformed opera is connected with a tragic subject matter: Ranieri de Calzabigi's and Christoph Willibald Gluck's preface to their opera *Alceste* (first performed in Vienna in 1767, with a fundamentally restructured version in Paris in 1776). The intriguingly 'modern' dimension of Gluck's manifesto includes, most importantly, the plea for overtures that capture the mood of the opera, a much-reduced scope for vocal improvisation and so-called bravura arias, no da capo arias, accompanied rather than *secco* recitatives, and more prominence for the chorus. The latter is interesting, for Gluck defines

---

[31] The original reads: 'Im Namen dessen, der am Kreuz erblich' ('in the name of the one who became pale at the cross') (Hebbel 1971: ii. 325).
[32] This feature in philosophy is discussed in Bubner (1992); in connection with contemporary European poetry, see Grünbein (2005). See also Heaney (1995: 1–16, 38–62).
[33] For a more detailed history of this adaptation and its background, see Heller (2009: 7).

'modern' by (re-)introducing elements of the original Greek drama in a move that one might call retrospective progression.[34]

But it is the Alceste-plot itself that made it attractive for modern experiment. The reinvention of Attic tragedy in opera was originally connected with restraint in musical terms. Gluck avoided any hint of over-expressiveness[35] but supplied an almost gentle interplay of solo aria and chorus (for example, in Alceste's 'Ah malgré moi' in the second act and 'Ah divinités implacables' in the third). One could speak of the drama of gentleness in a tragedy that, ultimately, celebrates marital love. The plot structure is disarmingly simple and, by the standards of the preceding Händel operas, almost subversively so. When Admetos's illness threatens to be fatal, he can continue to live and to reign as king only if someone gives his life for him. His wife, Alceste, sacrifices herself for him and her children. Heracles passes by and is welcomed by Admetos as a guest. He is oblivious to what has just happened, and, when he sees the corpse being carried away, Heracles is of the opinion that a maid has died. When he learns of the real circumstances, he is overwhelmed by the hospitality King Admetos has extended to him regardless of his grief. Heracles, then, vows to challenge death and retrieve Alceste. According to Romain Rolland, Beethoven recognized in Alceste a predecessor of his own operatic heroine, Leonore.[36] But the real significance of this plot, or rather this version of it, for the connection between tragedy and literary modernism is the fact that the 19-year-old poet Hugo von Hofmannsthal produced a paraphrase of Euripides' drama, which served Egon Wellesz as the basis for his opera (1924), which still awaits its revival. Wellesz adds chorus sections to Hofmannsthal's tragic poem; they seem to have come from nowhere but amplify what the composer was really interested in: the clash between cult and barbarism, emotional sophistication and violence. Their Heracles, for example, represents vitality in the face of fate. He strangles death and breaks the all-too-powerful spell of the Gods. But, by recuperating Alceste from death, Heracles undoes her original act of free choice— namely, to die in order to save her husband. Alceste is rescued, yet at the expense of her self-determination.

---

[34] For further reference still of interest, see Einstein (1936).

[35] This was in line with the artistic practices of the time. For further reference, see Ritzer (2012).

[36] Herz (1998).

In Hofmannsthal's text Admet feels overwhelmed, even 'denuded', by Heracles' action, which is about to substitute fate ('Und lautlos wie ein Schleier löst sich ab | Vom nackten Ich das bunte Schicksalskleid'[37]). Hofmannsthal's adaptation suggests in an almost Goethean fashion that the balancing-out of tragic contrasts might be the genuine task left to us when dealing with the legacy of Greek tragedy. But it was the composer Egon Wellesz who implied that the real conflict would occur after the end of classical tragedy—namely, when uncouth heroes like Heracles take fate into their own hands, with their good intentions turning into violations of our free will.

In Hofmannsthal's version, Alceste sacrifices herself on condition that Admet must not take another wife, which he promises to do. This is the reason why, tragically, he hesitates to embrace Alceste when Heracles brings her back from the dead, for he thinks that she is a different person who only resembles his first wife. In his version of *Alcestis*, Ted Hughes makes the chorus suggest to Admetos that from now on 'Necessity' will be his 'new wife', a 'goddess' who 'holds you . . . in her embrace'.[38] This is significant, for it confirms Ignatieff's point, quoted earlier in this brief exploration, that necessities conditioned tragedy,[39] especially those that cannot be met properly.

5. EPILOGUE

But let us finally return to the three cases of exemplary discourses on tragedy in the mid-nineteenth century. They cannot, and should not, be detached from gender considerations, for three male authors investigate the tragedy of the female in their respective cultures. Their mourning (Kierkegaard's Antigone), rebellion (Wagner's Brünnhilde), and raging revenge (Hebbel's Kriemhild) fail to establish anything that could last. These discourses amount to the tragedy of female emancipation before it properly began. Wagner, in particular, pointed to the psychological difficulties in the process of emancipation, as demonstrated by his very last sentence, which he wrote in Venice in February 1883 before suffering a fatal heart attack: 'Gleichwohl geht der Prozeß der Emanzipation des Weibes nur

---

[37] Hofmannsthal (1959: 47).   [38] Hughes (1999: 71).
[39] Ignatieff (1990); see Hölderlin (2009: p. xlviii).

unter ekstatischen Zuckungen vor sich. Liebe—Tragik' ('Even so, the process of the emancipation of woman occurs under ecstatic twitches. Love—tragic').[40] The essay, which contained this phrase, was called 'On the Female in Human Existence' and intended to conclude his study on *Religion and Art*. It was to investigate the identity between female psychology and sexuality and the specificity of the mythical unity of Psyche and Amor in woman. Wagner seemed to have suggested that the desirable social emancipation of women would tragically impact on this unity between their psyche and sexuality. His example was Brünnhilde, who put all her energy into her emancipation from divinity and her ambition to become a properly human being capable of leading a life in love and bearing children.

Incidentally, Nietzsche's famous polemic remark in *Der Fall Wagner* that Wagner's heroines cannot bear children[41] (with the aforementioned notorious exception of Sieglinde as the result of an incestuous relationship with Siegmund in *Die Walküre*) is therefore curiously to the point. Outstanding females, like Wagner's Brünnhilde, but also Hebbel's Kriemhilde and Kierkegaard's reinvented Antigone, tragically fail in their ambition to be just themselves. Cultures, however, that deny women this possibility for mythological, religious, or political reasons are doomed, too.

It appears, though, that the concept 'emancipation' does not sufficiently cover what those three fates of Modernism really represent— namely, the quest for authenticity.[42] The moral implication of authenticity was its terms of reference: religion, the idea of doing good as a precondition for leading a worthwhile existence. Being 'in tune' with the cosmos could be endangered only by the intervention of fate. The main question for Greek tragedy was how Man should react to, and cope with, such fateful intervention. The 'modern' response was for the tragic hero, or heroine, to listen to the inner voice as the very source of proper authenticity and to act in line with this voice's demand(s). In a tragic situation the hero/ine can no longer experience the equanimity of what Rousseau called 'le sentiment de l'existence',[43] the pure experience of being, but is thrown off course by calamitous events. The 'modern' or even 'modernist' aspect comes

---

[40] Wagner (1983: x. 174). For further reference, see Friedrich (2004: 65).
[41] Nietzsche (1980: vi. 34).
[42] I use this concept in line with the definition given by Taylor (1991: 32).
[43] Rousseau (1997: 116).

into play when the hero/ine engages in trying to regain control over his or her own fate. With Charles Taylor, the aim of this engagement can be called 'freedom through self-determination'.[44] Given the withdrawal or absence of the Gods in modern tragedy, such 'self-determination' presupposes utter self-reliance on the 'inner voice' of individual authenticity gaining key significance. But, as all three heroines discussed demonstrate, this self-determination can result in a precarious form of freedom, in the case of Hebbel's Kriemhild at the expense of others. The fact, however, that Antigone, Brünnhilde, and Kriemhild were driven to their extreme expressions of self-determination, from excessive mourning to obsessive revenge, exposes the inner dichotomy of their respective cultures. In that sense they have become iconic figures of the discontent in Modernism with the tragic looming in the background.

---

[44] Taylor (1991: 35).

8

Heidegger's *Antigone*: Ethics and Politics

Katie Fleming

> I am not the one who has decreed that *Antigone* is to be a turning
> point in the field that interests us, namely, ethics. People have
> been aware of that for a long time... Is there anyone who
> doesn't evoke *Antigone* whenever there is a question of a law
> that causes conflict in us even though it is acknowledged by the
> community to be a just law?[1]

In a series of lectures delivered in the mid-1930s, although not published until the early 1950s, and then controversially so for reasons
I will discuss later, Martin Heidegger (once again) addressed and
challenged the Western tradition of so-called metaphysics, which he
would characterize damningly as, in its entirety, forgetfulness of Being.
Rather misleadingly titled (as Dennis Schmidt notes, *Einführung in die
Metaphysik*[2] is 'anything but'[3] an introduction), Heidegger's work
touches on a range of ancient texts and authors. Perhaps predictably,
Sophocles' *Antigone*, and specifically the 'Ode to Man', feature in this
list. Central to Heidegger's reading of the first stasimon is a charged
discussion of its ethical and political import. It is, of course, hardly
surprising that, in the midst of a decade marked by global and national
political turbulence and change, and in the wake of his own political
involvement with Nazism, both as Rector of the University of Freiburg

I thank the audience at the Tragedy and the Idea of Modernity conference, UCL,
and especially my respondent, Martin Ruehl, for their helpful suggestions for this
chapter. My thanks are also due to the editors of this volume.

[1] Lacan (1999: 243).   [2] Heidegger (1953, 2000).
[3] Schmidt (2001: 239).

and as a member of the Party, Heidegger should turn to that tragedy, long the site for political and ethical debate, for his own answers to such questions.[4] No coincidence either that it should be around the question of humanism—'we will attempt . . . to assess who the human being is'[5]—that Heidegger should frame his response; the 'Ode to Man' has prompted many readings of a humanistic kind. But Heidegger was also, as I have discussed elsewhere, intimately involved in the fraught, deeply political, contemporary contest about the name and nature of humanism and its place in intellectual life and the academy in Nazi Germany.[6] Heidegger's confrontation of the humanism question would culminate in his 1947 *Letter on Humanism*, a philosophical document of considerable importance and influence, in which he articulated the concerns that would set the terms for much continental philosophy of the mid-twentieth century:

> Every humanism is either grounded in a metaphysics or is itself made to be the ground of one. Every determination of the essence of the human being that already presupposes an interpretation of beings without asking the truth of being, whether knowingly or not, is metaphysical. The result is that what is peculiar to all metaphysics, specifically with respect to the way the essence of the human being is determined, is that it is 'humanistic'. Accordingly, every humanism remains metaphysical . . . the necessity and proper form of the question concerning the truth of being, forgotten in and through metaphysics, can come to light only if the question 'What is metaphysics?' is posed in the midst of metaphysics' domination.[7]

His interpretation of the choral ode in *Introduction to Metaphysics* in 1935 would seem, therefore, to be a preliminary contribution to this debate and a first shot across the bows. The political focus of his reading also implicates this—otherwise rather abstracted and decontextualized—account of human being intimately and immediately in the politics of

---

[4] Subject to numerous politically charged readings in Germany throughout the 1930s, the play and its heroine would come to be seen as compatible with the doctrines of National Socialism, with Antigone the paradigm of 'germanische Frauengestalt' (Glaser 1938: 105) and the play a dramatization of 'das bindende Gesetz des Blutes' (Joachim 1941: 51).

[5] Heidegger (2000: 158).

[6] See Fleming (2012). Arguably, and not surprisingly, the debate over Sophocles' humanism escalates after the Second World War, in response both to Heidegger himself no doubt, and also to that cataclysmic event. Whitman (1951) makes the case most explicitly, but others, such as Lacan (1999) also pick up the discussion.

[7] Heidegger (1998: 245). Derrida would, of course, critique Heidegger himself for his own humanism, for remaining committed to an 'essentialist' conception of human being, first in 'The Ends of Man' and later, more thoroughly, in *Of Spirit*.

the decade.[8] This chapter, then, will address the intellectual and political significance of Heidegger's turn to the *Antigone* in 1935 to think an authentic ethics and politics for modernity. In this way, it will also cast light on the nature of Heidegger's political engagement—his Nazism—during the 1930s.

In its treatment of the pre-Socratics and Sophocles' *Antigone* (and themes that he would later pointedly revisit in 1942 in *Hölderlin's Hymn 'The Ister'* and in 1947 in *the Letter on Humanism*), *Introduction to Metaphysics* also heralds an important moment in the trajectory of Heideggerian thought more generally, representing, as it does, a kind of bridge between his early and later thought, and exemplifying the famous—or perhaps notorious—'turn'[9] to language (and in particular poetry) to think the truth of Being. In this respect, then, this book is also a critical document (which crucially he sought to publish in 1953, after the war) for determining the political character of Heidegger's later philosophy.[10]

Of course, Heidegger's reading in *Introduction to Metaphysics* of the pre-Socratics and of Sophocles was not an isolated encounter with antiquity. Heidegger's indebtedness to ancient Greece is well known.[11] His encounter with the Greeks can be understood as a grand-narrative mythology of origins, in which the Greek beginning remains the authentic opening, revelation, and locus of Being. Determined to recapture the reflections of the early Greek philosophers on

---

[8] In fact, in *Introduction to Metaphysics* Heidegger quotes from his (now infamous) Rectoral Address (Heidegger 2000: 52), thus placing this book in dialogue with his most explicitly and recognizably political gesture.

[9] Heidegger (1947: 72). See Sheehan (2001) on the *Kehre*.

[10] In this and in what follows, it will become clear that I differ somewhat from, for example, Geiman (2001) in my interpretation of the significance of Heidegger's reading of *Antigone*. Taking both *Introduction to Metaphysics* and *Hölderlin's Hymn 'The Ister'* into account, she argues that, although addressing the same terminology (especially *to deinon*), Heidegger's characterization of human knowing and its relation to being is dramatically transformed between the two texts, from 'the violence of creative founding' to 'the later *Gelassenheit*, the "releasement" towards beings that belongs to meditative thinking and "lets beings be"' (Geiman 2001: 180). While I agree for the most part with Geiman's analysis of the language at stake, I do not follow her in her conclusions about Heidegger's politics. I do not see that his ideas about politics are radically changed, and I would argue that what she identifies as *the* political commitment of the later work, that it let 'politics as the *polos* [sic] come to us' (Geiman 2001: 182), can also be identified in the earlier piece (and is, in both texts, still dangerously associated with other semantically problematic ideas, as I shall suggest in this chapter).

[11] See the thorough treatment of Bambach (2003). See also Beaufret (1973), Zuckert (1996), Schmidt (2001), and Most (2002).

the nature of Being, Heidegger posited his own *Denken* as a deliberate break from the Western philosophical tradition (which until that time, he would argue, had been disastrously dominated by Plato and could be dismissed as 'metaphysics') and insisted that his thought was dependent on, and influenced by, few, if any, of his philosophical predecessors, even Nietzsche; his thought, he argued, was a genuine return to the Greeks.[12]

His radical (in both the revolutionary and reactionary senses of this word) reinterpretation of ancient thought is clear from his re-visioning of that most central philosophical keyword: truth. Central to his 'humanistic' thought of the 1930s and 1940s, and in fact to all his thought, was his insistence on an esoteric or—so he would assert—*truly* pre-Platonic conception of *aletheia*, which he translates within a fertile semantic framework that combines notions of uncoveredness and unhiddenness (he draws attention to the alpha-privative) rather than simply of 'truth'.[13] In revisiting and re-offering pre-Socratic wisdom as the solution to the articulation and comprehension of *(Da)sein*, Heidegger would imply that he had transcended the mistakes of over two millennia of metaphysical error.

It can, unsurprisingly, be shown that Heidegger is more influenced by other philosophers and traditions than he admits,[14] not least because a good deal of his philosophical *œuvre* consists of a meticulous—albeit unorthodox—reading of other thinkers, from Plato to Nietzsche. His resolute return to the Greeks is itself consistent with the most traditional

---

[12] By staging the moment of rupture as originary repetition, Heidegger does indeed break with the dialectical model of history, which graduates towards some *telos*. See, e.g., Roberts (1998).

[13] Paul Friedländer admits there is some ancient support for this etymology of the term. However, he also argues that there is no real evidence that this term was ever understood widely in the manner that Heidegger implies. See Friedländer (1958: 225–6). Friedländer, in fact, is one of the few contemporary scholars of ancient philosophy to take Heidegger's philosophy seriously. No doubt, this is due, in part, to his early interaction with Heidegger: also influenced by Stefan George and Nietzsche, Friedländer thanked the philosopher in the foreword to the first volume of the first edition of *Plato* (1928). Not surprisingly, perhaps, given Friedländer's treatment at the hands of the regime that Heidegger publicly supported, this note of thanks is not to be found in the post-war republication of Friedländer's three-volume study of the ancient philosopher. Indeed, the later edition of this work, initially 'conceived in George Circle terms' (Lane 2001: 123), reveals a certain amount of textual adjustment.

[14] See, e.g., Zuckert (1996) and Bambach (2003). For instance, his return to *Antigone* to pursue an originary ethics is not completely dissimilar to the Hegelian turn to Sophocles.

of occidental philosophical gestures. This Philhellenism can also be read as one with a particularly German history.[15] Such an association was in fact central to Heidegger's own reading of antiquity: he would continue to insist on the special spiritual and linguistic affinity between the Germans and the Greeks.[16] This is, or was, of course, not a Heideggerian invention: species of it—in Fichte, for example[17]—run through German intellectual life for well over a century prior to Heidegger's contributions. Paradoxically, therefore, for the thinker dedicated to the renewal or recovery of the Western intellectual tradition, the most basic of his radical assumptions are rooted in this philosophical and cultural constant. This has long been recognized: in his analysis of the several elements that combined to form the peculiar (and frequently dangerous) picture of German Hellenism held by the scholars of the Weimar and Nazi periods, Momigliano lists this linguistic chauvinism, explicitly linking it to Heidegger:

> *la nozione più o meno esplicita che per capire i Greci bisogna pensare in greco o alternativamente in tedesco. Alla ineffabilità del pensiero greco per coloro che temono di tradurre Paideia, Eunomia, Areté, Hairesis in lingue moderne, fa da contrappeso la sicurezza sulla perfetta traducibilità del greco di Eraclito o di Platone in linguaggio heideggeriano.*

> ([there is] the idea, more or less explicit, that in order to understand the Greeks one needs to think in Greek or alternatively in German. In counterbalance to the ineffability of Greek thought for those who shrink from translating Paideia, Eunomia, Areté, Hairesis into modern languages, stands the certainty of the perfect translatability of the Greek of Heraclitus or of Plato into Heideggerian language.)[18]

This insistence on the privileged intellectual relationship between Greek and by extension German language and thought,[19] coupled with his idiosyncratic and determined translations of certain Greek

---

[15] For discussion of Heidegger's philosophical and political relationship to German Philhellenism, see Lacoue-Labarthe (1987).

[16] See Heidegger (1990: 63).

[17] See Fichte (1978).

[18] Momigliano (1969: 47). His association of Heidegger with a 'colonized' pre-war Hellenism is significant. Heidegger attempted to offer his *Denken* as the solution to the metaphysical tradition that, he believed, resulted in the Second World War (see, e.g., Soffer 1996). Momigliano rejects this philosophical 'novelty'.

[19] This is obviously woven into the debate surrounding the notion of an original or genuine language of thought. See, for instance, Heidegger's notorious remark in the *Spiegel* interview: 'Ich denke an die besondere innere Verwandtschaft der deutschen Sprache mit der Sprache der Griechen und deren Denken. Das bestätigen mir heute

texts, is, then, a marked feature of Heidegger's encounter with the Greeks.[20]

And yet, having argued for the more recognizable or even unoriginal features of Heidegger's Philhellenism, I would not wish to understate its significance. In an article entitled 'Heidegger's Greeks', Glenn Most writes:

> Much of what is typically Greek Heidegger ignores or suppresses or explains away: there is no slavery in Heidegger's ancient Greece, no homosexuality, no heterosexuality, no athletics, no war, no wine, no song, no anger, no laughter, no fear, no superstition. Instead Heidegger focuses on those elements of the ancient Greeks that anticipate the values he would like the Germans to adopt... Insofar as Heidegger's Germans are encouraged to model themselves upon the Greeks, Heidegger's Germans are Greeks in *Lederhosen*; but since Heidegger's Greeks are in fact an idealized projection of specifically German virtues and since all idealizations of the Greeks are ultimately Roman in inspiration, Heidegger's Greeks may be described as being Germans in togas.[21]

The rhetorical (and, it seems to me, syllogistically false) flourish of Most's final sentence undermines the essential truth of his observation. That Heidegger's Greeks are idealized to the point of non-existence is unquestionable. However, to suggest that Heidegger had unwittingly staged a revival of Graeco-Romanitas would seem to ignore Heidegger's own reiterated attempts, whether successful or not, to circumvent that tradition.[22] To undermine the seriousness of Heidegger's interpretation of ancient Greek thought, its degradation, and ultimately its role in the destiny of the West is to misunderstand not only his philosophical innovations, but also their limitations and dangers.

---

immer wieder die Franzosen. Wenn sie zu denken anfangen, sprechen sie deutsch; sie versichern, sie kämen mit ihrer Sprache nicht durch' ('I am thinking of the special inner relationship of the German language with the language of the Greeks and their thinking. The French confirm that for me again today. If they begin to think, they speak German; they assure me that they don't succeed with their language') (Heidegger 1990: 63).

[20] Derrida plays on this very element in Heidegger's own thought. See, e.g., Derrida (1987) on *Geschlecht*.

[21] Most (2002: 95).

[22] Cf. 'Roman thought takes over the Greek words without a corresponding equally authentic experience of what they say, without the Greek word. The rootlessness of Western thought begins with this translation' (Heidegger 1971: 23).

Returning indirectly now to discussion of *Introduction to Meta-phyics* and its treatment of *Antigone*, it is worth framing this reading with another—rather rare—interpretation of the tragic in Heidegger's *œuvre*.[23] For, despite the thoroughgoing nature of Heidegger's engagement with poetic utterance, as a site of and expression of authentic *logos/Sprache* and thus of critical importance to his onto-logical programme whereby language is the home of Being[24] in which *Dasein* ek-sists; and despite his frequent readings of—in particular—the *Antigone* at various points in his work;[25] and indeed despite the 'later' Heidegger's evolution into a philosopher of, one could argue, a kind of spiritualized aesthetics through which, he would insist, his ethical philosophy could be discerned, Heidegger nowhere gives a sustained theory of tragedy. Given the centrality of tragedy to any number of ethical and/or aesthetic discussions in Western thought, not least the young Nietzsche's *The Birth of Tragedy*, this omission could be seen as odd. Not least because, in an essay of 1946, 'The Anaximander Fragment', Heidegger identifies the tragic as a defini-tive characteristic of 'beings in their Being':

> The experience of beings in their Being which here comes to language is neither pessimistic nor nihilistic; nor is it optimistic. It is tragic. That is a presumptuous thing to say. However, we discover a trace of the essence of tragedy, not when we explain it psychologically or aesthetically, but rather only when we consider its essential form, the Being of beings, by thinking the διδόναι δίκην . . . τῆς ἀδικίας.[26]

It is worth pausing to consider this essay in slightly more detail; to do so reveals some important details about Heidegger's profound triangulation here of pre-Socratic thought, the tragic, and (human) being that cast retrospective light on *Introduction to Metaphysics*. The essay begins by quoting the translation of the Anaximander frag-ment—'the oldest fragment of Western thinking'[27]—that Nietzsche gives in his posthumous work, *Philosophy in the Tragic Age of the Greeks*. Composed only a year or so after the publication of *The Birth of Tragedy*, and incomplete, the book repeats—in familiar vocabulary—Nietzsche's insistent demand that ailing (German) modernity should look to ancient Greece for a model of a 'truly healthy culture'.[28] A study

---

[23] See Gall (2003).   [24] Heidegger (1947: 53).
[25] Heidegger (1953: 112–26; 1984: 63 ff., 127 ff.). See Geiman (2001).
[26] Heidegger (1973–4: 611). 'They pay recompense and penalty . . . for their reck-lessness' (Heidegger (1973–4: 577).
[27] Heidegger (1973–4: 576).   [28] Nietzsche (1998: 28).

of the pre-Socratics, the work again celebrates those peculiar cultural and intellectual qualities of Greek culture of which philosophy is the quintessential metonym:

> It seems to me that those ancient wise men, from Thales through Socrates, have touched in their conversation all those things, albeit in their most generalized form, which to our minds constitutes typical Hellenism. In their conversation as in in their personalities they form the great-featured mold of Greek genius whose ghostly print, whose blurred and less expressive copy, is the whole of Greek history. If we could interpret correctly the sum total of Greek culture, all we would find would be the reflection of the image which shines forth brightly from its greatest luminaries.[29]

Given that Heidegger rejects Nietzsche's translation of the fragment as incorrect and his wider readings of the pre-Socratics as 'commonplace',[30] it might initially seem surprising that he should bother to allude to the piece at all.[31] Yet beyond a certain (typically Heideggerian) intellectual posturing and genealogical oneupmanship must lie a more complex explanation for the inclusion of this 'intertext'. For Nietzsche's work, by its very title, signals the privileged interconnectedness of (specifically) pre-Socratic thought and the tragic, an interconnectedness that Heidegger will himself explore in his discussion of the 'true' meaning of the choral ode from *Antigone*. More particularly, Nietzsche's treatise—as the quotation cited suggests—also thinks through the ways in which pre-Socratic philosophy both embodied and created the conditions of possibility for the ancient Greek moment to which both Nietzsche and Heidegger obsessively (re)turn. If we isolate this relationship between philosophy and the tragic and its generation of a ground for authentic becoming, we might see how Heidegger found in this work a precursor to his own project of thinking the truth of Being. Moreover, inasmuch as Nietzsche's book is pervaded by an overwhelming sense of cultural urgency, Heidegger's essay also sets its terms through a series of loaded, apocalyptic questions:

> Do we stand in the very twilight of the most monstrous transformation our planet has ever undergone, the twilight of that epoch in which earth itself hangs suspended? Do we gaze into the evening of a night which

---

[29] Nietzsche (1998: 32).   [30] Heidegger (1973–4: 578).

[31] Immediately after quoting Nietzsche's translation, Heidegger turns to the more 'canonical', and presumably more widely read, version given by Hermann Diels in his seminal *Fragments of the Pre-Socratics*, with which *Philosophy in the Tragic Age of the Greeks* shared the year of publication (1903).

heralds another dawn? Are we to strike off on a journey to this historic region of earth's evening? Is the land of evening only now emerging? Will this land of evening overwhelm Occident and Orient alike, transcending whatever is merely European to become the location of a new but primordially fated history? Are we men of today already 'Western' in a sense that first crystallizes in the course of our passage into the world's night? . . . Are we the latecomers we are?[32]

Echoing here both Nietzsche and Oswald Spengler's *Decline of the West* (1918–23), Heidegger reiterates that *fin de siècle*, also modernist, sensibility that frames modernity in terms of cultural senescence and technological cataclysm. Yet, taking into account the publication date of this essay—1946—Heidegger's reference to 'monstrous transformation' has other connotations that, in the light of his own, deeply fraught, and contested relationship to Nazism and the Shoah, make for uneasy reading.

At the centre of the essay, however, lies a complex discussion of the character of human being. Contained in the Anaximander fragment, Heidegger suggests, is a pre-metaphysical comprehension of beings that acknowledges their transitional nature, their presence as a lingering, emergent from and returning to absence, this latter the concealment that resides behind and runs through every presencing. This presencing is in turn characterized, as the quotation I have given implies, by the διδόναι δίκην . . . τῆς ἀδικίας. At stake here is Heidegger's translation of the central terms *dike* and *adikia*. These he translates not as 'justice' and 'injustice', but as 'Fug' and 'Un-Fug' ('jointure/reck' and 'disorder/without reck'[33]). These co-dependent terms, for Heidegger, describe both the (un)jointedness of beings and Being, but also the relationship between beings. Thus διδόναι δίκην . . . τῆς ἀδικίας encompasses an original ethics: 'If what is present grants order it happens in this manner: as beings linger awhile, they give reck to one another. The surmounting of disorder properly occurs through the letting-belong of reck.'[34] It is being as both jointed and out-of-joint, and that which potentially can give reck to the other, that Heidegger calls 'the essence of tragedy'. A tragic ethics, then, is central to Heidegger's description of (human) being.

---

[32] Heidegger (1973–4: 580–1).
[33] These are the translations that David Farrell Krell gives in his translation of this essay.
[34] Heidegger (1973–4: 614).

This centrality, I believe, should be read into his reading of *Antigone* in *Introduction to Metaphyics*. Characteristically, one might argue, for a philosopher concerned with ontology rather than subjectivity, and who states here 'among the Greeks there were no personalities yet...',[35] individual figures are barely discussed. Antigone herself, long the main attraction, as Steiner's much-referenced study firmly demonstrated, steps aside for a singular reading of Sophocles' 'Ode to Man' (ll. 332–75). As with most of his translations of ancient texts, his rendering of the first stasimon is distinctly decontextualized and somewhat arcane.[36] Heidegger turns the ode emphatically to his own use, envisaging it as a wise document of ancient ontology. Importantly, he rejects the more conventional— indeed 'humanistic'—interpretations of this ode:

> We have already alluded to the fact that this is not a matter of describing and clarifying the domains and behavior of the human, who is one being among many... we have also warded off the other opinion, according to which the ode recounts the development of humanity from a wild huntsman and a traveler by dugout canoe, to a builder of cities and person of culture.[37]

The force of Heidegger's argument hinges on his treatment of the Greek word *deinon*, whose significance the philosopher wishes to reinstate. Against tradition—for instance, Hölderlin and Schadewaldt in their translations of the play give 'ungeheuer'[38]—Heidegger translates this tellingly as 'unheimlich', expressing human *Dasein*'s complex and unsettling relationship to Being and the world: man is 'das Unheimlichste des Unheimlichen'.[39]

> The *deinon* is the terrible in the sense of the overwhelming sway, which induces panicked fear, true anxiety, as well as collected, inwardly reverberating, reticent awe. The violent, the overwhelming is the essential character of the sway itself... But on the other hand, *deinon* means the violent in the sense of one who needs to use violence—and does not just have violence at his disposal but is violence-doing, insofar as using violence is the basic trait not just of his doing but of his Dasein.[40]

---

[35] Heidegger (2000: 159).

[36] Gourgouris, playing on the slippage between the naming of *Antigone* and Antigone, speaks of Heidegger's 'extraordinary violation of the Sophoclean text' (Gourgouris 2003: 147).

[37] Heidegger (2000: 165). [38] Hölderlin (1989: 37); Sophocles (1974: 23).

[39] Heidegger (1953: 114). [40] Heidegger (2000: 159–60).

Terrible, then, *is* human *Da-sein*, and *Dasein*'s relationship to Being itself: this doubling is critical to Heidegger's interpretation of the Ode's expression of human ambiguity and humanity as *deinotaton/* 'das Unheimlichste des Unheimlichen'.

His interpretation of the semantically dense lines 368–71, and in particular line 370, continues this double sense.[41] Content to ignore the specific context of the plot of the play, and its dramatization of the perilous and contradictory necessity of man's being beholden to both human and divine laws, Heidegger instead locates in these terms the sense of an originary community, out of which an authentic politics would become evident, revealing and permitting a transcendent, authentic justice and ethics. His extended extrapolation of *hupsipolis apolis* must be quoted in full:

> The interpretation is completed in the third prominent phrase, verse 370: *hupsipolis apolis*. We find that this phrase is constructed in the same way, and is even situated in the middle of the antistrophe in the same way, as the earlier *pantoporos aporos*. Yet what it says points us towards another dimension of beings. Not *poros* but *polis* is named; not all the routes into the domains of beings are named, but the ground and place of human Dasein itself, the spot where all these routes cross, the *polis*. One translates *polis* as state <*Staat*> and city-state <*Stadtstaat*>; this does not capture the entire sense. Rather, *polis* is the name for the site <*Stätte*>, the Here, within which and as which Being-here is historically. The *polis* is the site of history, the Here, *in* which, *out of* which and *for* which history happens. To this site of history belong the gods, the temples, the priests, the celebrations, the games, the poets, the thinkers, the ruler, the council of elders, the assembly of the people, the armed forces, and the ships. All this does not first belong to the *polis*, is not first political, because it enters into a relation with a statesman and a general and with the affairs of state. Instead, what we have named is political—that is, at the site of history—insofar as, for example, the poets are *only* poets, but then are actually poets, the thinkers are *only* thinkers, but then are actually thinkers, the priests are *only* priests, but then are actually priests, the rulers are only rulers, but then are actually rulers. Are—but this says: use violence as violence-doers and become those who rise high in historical Being as creators, as doers. Rising high in the site of history, they also become *apolis*, without city and site, lonesome, un-canny, with no way out amidst beings as a whole, and at

---

[41] Jebb notes the difficulty in translating adequately *hypsipolis* and *apolis*: Jebb (1891: 77).

the same time without ordinance and limit, without structure and fittingness <*Fug*>, because they *as* creators must first ground all this in each case.[42]

The *polis* then, is the Da, the site in which *Dasein*'s relational web of significance coheres, the mysterious locus of pre-metaphysical existence that enables genuine being, and from which our comprehension of Being might emanate.[43] At first, Heidegger's interpretation here seems obvious to the point of banality: *of course* the *polis* is 'the site of history', no more, and no less, than any historical moment of human existence and being-there. But the chain of thought that Heidegger follows, from his insistence on the authenticity of the different roles within the *polis* ('die Dichter *nur*, aber dann wirklich Dichter . . .'[44]), to their transcendence of their historicity by virtue of their being both 'with no way out amidst beings as a whole, and at the same time without ordinance and limit', suggests something much more significant. If and once identified as such, Heidegger so implies, an originary, authentic community would become (self-)evident, revealing a transcendent, authentic justice and ethics.[45] This pre- or non-metaphysical scene, then, imagines an ethics—that is, a human relationality and civic fullness—not connected to or founded on values

[43] Heidegger's tendency to elide his interpretations of Greek words is also evident here. *Polis* is here equivalent to the Da, yet elsewhere Heidegger will also imply the equivalence of *aletheia, physis*, even *logos*. See, e.g., Fried (2000) for *polemos* as *Dasein*. In this rapidly developing poetic-philosophy Heidegger abandons the 'logical' vocabulary and grammar of philosophy and the search for definition for more mythical pronouncements. For a negative critique of this aspect of *Einführung in die Metaphysik*, see Habermas (1992: 200).

[44] Heidegger (1953: 117).

[45] It is worth asking, although such a question cannot be answered here, whether Heidegger's reading of this ode was influenced by the interpretation of Sophocles given by Wolfgang Schadewaldt (1929). Schadewaldt, another collaborator with Nazism, was instrumental in Heidegger's appointment to the Rectorship of Freiburg, and was later made a dean under his leadership (see Farias and Ott). He was also representative of the movement within classical scholarship that sought to escape the influence of Wilamowitz and articulate a 'new philology' and a 'new' Humanism (see Latacz 2009). It does not seem preposterous, therefore, to imagine that Heidegger would have been familiar with his work. Schadewaldt's book argued that, as a poet of the *polis*, Sophocles depicted a political cosmos that was the human correspondent of a divine cosmos (Schadewaldt 1929: 102–5). Although crucially different in many respects, Heidegger's interpretation, with its insistence on the relational coherence of human being in the Greek *polis*/Da, has faint ties with Schadewaldt's symmetrical universe.

expressed by a false metaphysics, but arising from and characterized by the violent nature of being itself. As he will just over a decade later, Heidegger thinks these ethics through the condition of being itself, the 'Fug' and 'Unfug'. By its very ambivalence, its disjointed relationality to Being and beings, Dasein makes possible an originary ethics.

In his interpretation of this *locus classicus* of the human condition, Heidegger thus reasserted his observation that, in their closeness to Being, unobscured by centuries of metaphysical calcification, the ancient Greeks had recognized both the site of Being and the necessarily and persistently ambiguous relationship of *Dasein* to it. What the 'Ode to Man' captures is both the necessity of the *Da/polis* for *Da-sein*, and *Dasein*'s strange and violent engagement with it[46]—the constant flux of revelation and concealment.

Heidegger's interpretation of the 'Ode to Man' in *Introduction to Metaphysics* is typically complex and contingent.[47] In its movement away from the more 'anthropocentric' *Dasein* of *Sein und Zeit* (1928), towards a more 'poetic' vision of Being,[48] and in its reiteration of his conviction of the morbidity of Western metaphysics and culture, this piece encompasses and anticipates the concerns of later works that seek to establish an ethics of ontology. Heidegger's attempt here to retrieve and articulate an originary ethics during the turbulence of the 1930s, and then, when the work was published in 1953, in the wake of the catastrophes of the Second World War, seems laudable and necessary. His confrontation through his *Denken* of the failures of 'metaphysics' and the rootlessness of the humanistic tradition, yoked as it was to the Platonic fallacy, as he articulated it, signalled the abandonment of the entire Western tradition. Of this dramatic suggestion, Young writes, 'Heidegger's claim that "metaphysics" is the single underlying cause of all of the symptoms of [the] disease [of Western culture] is an extraordinarily ambitious attempt to bring unity out of a seemingly disparate plurality'.[49]

---

[46] Heidegger plays on the movement in meaning between 'das Überwältigende/ überwältig', 'Gewältätigkeit/gewältätig', and 'Walten'.

[47] For a lucid and close reading, see Ardovino (2001).

[48] Heidegger will come to assert that poets are the true 'philosophers' or thinkers. Cf. the development of this idea and the relationship of art to being in his 1935 essay 'The Origin of the Work of Art' (Heidegger 1971: 15–86). See Bambach (2003: 293–7) for an analysis of this and its connection to Heidegger's persistent political and philosophical commitment to autochthony.

[49] Young (2002: 35).

Young's defence of Heidegger here, and elsewhere, is *logically* sound, perhaps, but ethically and politically blind. Much more, it seems to me, is at stake in Heidegger's politics and ethics than this. There are, of course, a variety of—more general—ways in which Heidegger's return to the Greeks might be characterized as politically 'suspect': for instance, his nostalgic regression to an idealized pre-Socratic Greece and his totalizing collapse of Western philosophy with the concurrent rejection of the bases for moral and ethical values are all gestures ultimately compatible with different species of fascism. Moreover, Heidegger's insistence that an originary ethics and politics could emanate from the *polis/Da*, coupled with his equally firm contention (for instance, in the 'Letter on Humanism') that poetry was the voice of authenticity—these factors combining to create a genuine humanism, which borrows its force from Hölderlin's verse 'Voll Verdienst, doch dichterisch wohnet | der Mensch auf dieser Erde'[50]—strays close to the aestheticization of the political common in right-wing and fascist language.[51]

However, *Introduction to Metaphysics* goes further than this, and contains an explicitly damning—and much discussed—sentiment. Towards its conclusion, Heidegger addresses the question of 'values', writing:

> Values as such now become the ground of the ought. But because values stand opposed to the Being of beings, in the sense of facts, they themselves cannot be. So instead one says that they are valid. Values provide the measure for all domain of beings—that is, of what is present at hand. History is nothing but the actualization of values.[52]

This seems a succinct account of his refusal of conventional ethical thinking. But it is the astonishing segue that follows that—for many—condemns the text as a whole:

> All this calls itself philosophy. In particular, what is peddled about nowadays as the philosophy of National Socialism, but which has not the least to do with the inner truth and greatness of this movement [namely, the encounter between global technology and modern humanity], is fishing in these troubled waters of 'values' and 'totalities'.[53]

The intellectual gymnastics required to justify this remark are disingenuous, though of course they have been attempted; the publication

---

[50] Hölderlin (1986: 245).   [51] See Lacoue-Labarthe (1987).
[52] Heidegger (2000: 212).   [53] Heidegger (2000: 213).

of the text in 1953, after Heidegger's own de-Nazification, makes the decision to keep this remark—even to add to it (the line in parentheses was not original to the 1930s lectures)—inexcusable and the significance of it unavoidable.[54] This is not, I hope, to fall into the trap either of condemning Heidegger's philosophy on account of his overt politics of the 1930s (as Rector of Freiburg University) or, conversely, of sanitizing it by distinguishing between the man and his thought. Instead, the essential implications at work in this remark can be read back into the ethical and political programmatics and—crucially— contradictions of his reading of the 'Ode to Man'. For the statement— quite apart from its apparently shocking misrepresentation of Nazi philosophy—makes clear Heidegger's distaste for global technological modernity and its impact on human being and destiny, a distaste at work in his discussion and translation of *techne* in the 'Ode to Man'. He writes:

> *Techne* means neither art nor skill, and its means nothing like technology in the modern sense. We translate *techne* as 'knowing'. But this requires explication. Knowing here does not mean the result of mere observations about something present at hand that was formerly unfamiliar. Such items of information are always just accessory, even if they are indispensable to knowing. Knowing, in the genuine sense of *techne*, means initially and constantly looking out beyond what, in each case, is directly present at hand . . . Knowing is the ability to set Being into work as something that in each case *is* in such and such a way . . . Thus *techne* characterizes the *deinon*, the violence-doing, in its decisive basic trait; for to do violence is to need to use violence against the overwhelming: the knowing struggle to set Being which was formerly closed off, into what appears as beings.[55]

Techne, then (prior to its degradation into technology), as disclosure, is the violent means by which we know Being and beings; but in that disclosure comes the simultaneous realization and recognition that Being holds us, overwhelms us. Tabachnick suggests that Nazi philosophy may somehow represent a *techne* of this sort for Heidegger:

> Heidegger wants us to move away from an emphasis on the permanent and enduring, which is indicative of our technology, towards the feeling and violent character of the *techne* described in *Antigone*. Here, we can see some disturbing implications for Nazi Germany and World War

---

[54] See Rockmore (1992: 239–40).   [55] Heidegger (2000: 169–70).

II. For Heidegger, the massive technological feat of remilitarizing Germany will somehow allow for a return of the essence of the German *ethos* or *Volk* lost in the 'technological frenzy' . . . [56]

Heidegger's uncanny ethics and politics, then, 'without city and site', would appear, on the contrary, to be supported by a distinctly German framework. Authentic being and the politics and ethics that follow it seem—as indeed the chauvinistic association and lionizing of Greek and German thought and language implied—to be dependent on and defined by a profoundly nationalist agenda. This, then, betrays the contradiction inherent in Heidegger's celebration of the pre-Socratic or Sophoclean *polis*. For, even aside from his insistence on the violent nature of being, a violence expressed as being's ambivalence, an ambivalence that persists throughout his thought, analysis of the nature of Heideggerian ethics and politics would suggest that—although he seems at first sight to reject such a position—the very privileging of nearness to Being, and the terrible nature of this nearness for *Dasein*, seem to be predicated on an authenticity[57] and, what is more, a 'home' that undermines the more universal promise of their apparent 'unhomeliness'. And thus Heidegger, far from innovating, merely returns us to that most typical of philosophical positions: intellectual nostalgia, or the longing for an authentic (Greek) home.

[56] Tabachnick (2006: 99). See also Rockmore (1992: 206).
[57] See Capobianco (2001) for a reading of Heidegger's *Antigone* that focuses on the authenticity of the tragic hero.

9

Carl Schmitt: Tragedy and the Intrusion of History

Miriam Leonard

In a recent book, *Theorizing Performance*, Simon Goldhill and Charles Martindale are pitted against one another in a debate about two crucial frameworks for understanding the dynamics of classical reception: the respective models of *Rezeptionsästhetik* and *Rezeptionsgeschichte*.[1] In articulating their different intellectual allegiances, Goldhill and Martindale explore the contentious space between the aesthetic response to the work of ancient art and the demands of careful cultural and historical contextualization of the moment of its reception. It is perhaps no surprise that this debate was staged in a volume dedicated to exploring the reception of Greek drama. Ancient theatre and Greek tragedy, more specifically, have repeatedly been a privileged location for exploring this debate. Indeed, as many of the contributions to this volume show, it was at the close of the eighteenth century in Germany that tragedy became the place where the crucial metaphysical, ethical, and political questions that had preoccupied philosophers also become aesthetic ones. The figure of Kant who is so central to Goldhill and Martindale's debate about history and aesthetics was crucial to this new conceptualization of tragedy. It was in the wake of the publication of Kant's so-called Third Critique that the aesthetic became an inescapable philosophical concept, and this in part explains why aesthetic objects such as tragedy became such important vehicles of philosophical debate. It is perhaps this

[1] Hall and Harrop (2010).

association with Kant, and, in particular, the new philosophical valorization of the aesthetic in the wake of his critiques, which have made the German Idealist reading of tragedy so suspect to historically minded readers of Greek tragedy. For it has often been argued that the universalizing assumptions and abstraction of these philosophical readings have been blind to the historical specificity of Greek tragedy. Yet, from Hegel's engagement with *Antigone* as an exemplification of the historical development of Spirit, to Hölderlin's assertion that 'Greek art is foreign to us', the philosophy of the tragic has looked to tragedy to understand the historical distance as much as the proximity of antiquity.

But, while an awareness of time, I would argue, has always played a crucial role in German Idealism's return to Greek tragedy, it was in the mid-twentieth century that tragedy again became a fertile space for rethinking the conflict between aesthetics and history. Martin Heidegger's return to *Antigone*, as Katie Fleming argues in this volume, is significant for this debate. Both Walter Benjamin and Theodor Adorno, in their different ways, demonstrate the indelible mark of Heidegger's complicity with Nazism on his philosophical discussions of art. But it is perhaps Carl Schmitt, writing out of a similar context to Heidegger, who gives us the most explicit account of the relationship between history and the aesthetic sphere. Schmitt places an exploration of tragedy and the tragic at the heart of his analysis. *Hamlet or Hecuba* provides a different vocabulary for thinking about tragedy and its relationship to history and politics, which, I will argue, can call into question the new and old historicist certainties of much recent scholarship on Greek tragedy. In particular, his essay helps us understand tragedy as an 'intrusion of history' in the continuum of the contemporary.

Carl Schmitt is a highly controversial figure. To an even greater extent than with Heidegger, his works pose the challenge of their participation in a philosophy of Nazism. A documented anti-Semite, Schmitt acquired the sobriquet of the 'crown jurist' of the Third Reich.[2] Despite the fact that Schmitt fell out decisively with the Nazi hierarchy and ended up being investigated by them, he never renounced his association and resolutely refused de-Nazification in the post-war period. Written in 1956, *Hamlet or Hecuba: The*

---

[2] See Gross (2007).

Intrusion of Time into the Play not only looks back on a tragic period of history but also implicitly represents its reflections on history and aesthetics as a reckoning with the aftermath of Nazism.[3] In particular, Schmitt's engagement with literary hermeneutics can be productively contextualized within the broad post-war German academy. He launches his text with the bold affirmation:

> The following pages discuss the taboo of a queen and the figure of the avenger. This discussion leads into the question of the true origins of the tragic action, the question of the source of the tragic, which I can only locate in historical reality. In this way I have attempted to comprehend *Hamlet* from out of its concrete situation.[4]

In stating that he will seek to understand 'the source of the tragic' in 'historical reality' and in a 'concrete situation', Schmitt polemically stakes out his methodology in relation to the dominant models of contemporary literary analysis. Schmitt does not spell out what the alternative to his historical approach might be, but he strongly suggests that others had located the 'the origins of tragic action' elsewhere. By foregrounding the concrete historical situation, Schmitt implies that he was turning his back on analyses that had sought to locate the meaning of the text in the text itself. But, as David Pan argues, there was a political dimension to this gesture, which he disingenuously smooths over: 'Schmitt leaves out of his account, however, that the predominant "text-immanent" criticism was a reaction against the politicization of literature in the Nazi period by a *Germanistik* profession that had "devoted itself in 1933 to National Socialism with more enthusiasm than any other discipline"'.[5] In self-consciously locating the meaning of *Hamlet* in its concrete historical setting, Schmitt was making an appeal for the repoliticization of literary analysis. Where his contemporaries had attempted to avoid

---

[3] *Hamlet or Hecuba* was first published in German in 1956, but, because of Schmitt's compromised position within Germany, it received relatively little attention. During the 1980s, as Schmitt began to achieve a new centrality in political theory, his *Hamlet* text started to attract the attention of scholars from different disciplines. It was translated into Italian in 1983, into French in 1992, and received its first full translation into English only in 2009. On the circumstances of the first Italian translation and the broader reception of this text, see Sitze (2012). Since the English translation the text has produced many fine readings, see Santner (2012), Hammill and Lupton (2012), Critchley and Webster (2013), and the essays in the special volume of *Telos* (2010).

[4] Schmitt (2009: 4).   [5] Pan (2009: 70).

the charge of political complicity by seeking refuge in the realm of pure aesthetics, Schmitt controversially calls for a return to the ideologically inflected hermeneutics of the *Nazizeit*. On the one hand, Schmitt's decision could be seen as a continuation of his conservative political agenda; on the other hand, it could be seen to expose the hypocrisy of former collaborators who were now hiding behind a belief in the autonomy of art.

Pan demonstrates that, despite their radically different political outlooks, Schmitt's insistence on the link between aesthetics and politics shares a great deal with Adorno's. Although Adorno will argue for the potential resistance of the work of art to its ideological situation, he nevertheless insists on the fact that art always participates in broader social and political structures. Even when he is talking about the radical individuality of the *lyric* voice, Adorno argues in a text published almost contemporaneously with *Hamlet or Hecuba* 'that in every lyric poem the historical relationship of the subject to objectivity, of the individual to society, must have found its precipitate in the medium of the subjective spirit thrown back on itself'.[6] Adorno sees the violence that history inflicts on the subject being reflected in the structure of the work of art. Moreover, he sees this incorporation of the 'concrete historical situation' as raising the work of art from the individual to the universal:

> Immersion in what has taken individual form elevates the lyric poem to the status of something universal by making manifest something not distorted, not grasped, not yet subsumed. It thereby anticipates, spiritually, a situation in which no false universality, that is, nothing profoundly particular, continues to fetter what is other than itself, the human.[7]

As Pan concludes: 'Adorno sets up two universalities against each other: ... the false universality of society creates the pathos and isolation of the lyrical subject, and the genuine universality of a projected humanity creates the resistance to society that defines the autonomy of the work of art.'[8] In exploring a dialectic between historical violence and aesthetic autonomy, Adorno's and Schmitt's analyses can both be seen to emerge from the debates of post-war criticism. Although they will give very different evaluations to these components,

---

[6] Adorno (1991: 42).   [7] Adorno (1991: 38).   [8] Pan (2009: 74).

both are reacting to a desire to place literature beyond the realms of history and politics.

While Schmitt's discomfort with post-war literary hermeneutics remains implicit in the text, his distaste for what he calls 'the entrenched views of our German cultural tradition' are manifest.[9] At several points in the argument, Schmitt seeks to differentiate his reading from a 'nineteenth century philosophy of art'.[10] For, in addition to the immediate precedent of the 'text-immanent' criticism of the 1950s, Schmitt saw himself overturning a much longer tradition of post-Kantian aesthetics. In arguing for the priority of history and politics, Schmitt had sought to question the Kantian and 'romantic' investment in the disinterestedness of the aesthetic sphere:

> Philosophers of art and teachers of aesthetics tend to understand the work of art as an autonomous creation, self-contained and unrelated to historical or sociological reality—something to be understood only on its own terms. To relate the work of art to the actual politics of the time in which it was created would presumably obscure its purely aesthetic beauty and debase the intrinsic worth of artistic form. The source of the tragic then lies in the free and sovereign creative power of the poet.[11]

Schmitt associates this belief in the autonomy of art with the 'cult of genius' that 'arose during the German *Sturm und Drang* period of the eighteenth century [...and] has become a credo of the German philosophy of art...The creative freedom of the writer becomes thereby a defense of artistic freedom in general and a stronghold of subjectivity.'[12] Schmitt links the impulse to understand art 'only on its terms' to the rise of individualism and subjectivism in the Romantic age. Schmitt's critique, as Victoria Kahn argues, has a much broader dimension:

> For Schmitt, this idea of the aesthetic is part and parcel of a liberal notion of culture, according to which individuals form themselves just as they artificially create the state. Historically, according to Schmitt, this liberal notion of culture has negated the autonomous realm of politics, which does not involve disinterested contemplation or moral self-fashioning but rather an existential conflict between friend and enemy.[13]

---

[9] Schmitt (2009: 33).   [10] Schmitt (2009: 9).   [11] Schmitt (2009: 32–3).
[12] Schmitt (2009: 33).   [13] Kahn (2003: 69).

For Schmitt, aestheticization is a symptom of romanticism, but it is also a symptom of the wider malaise of modernity. The turn to history constitutes for Schmitt a turning-back of the clock on modernity and its particular understanding of the tragic.

Schmitt's critique of aesthetic autonomy is intrinsically linked to his exploration of the 'source of the tragic'. For immediately after he asks: 'Should historical arguments even be included in the consideration of the work of art?' he continues: 'From where does tragedy derive the tragic action upon which it lives? What is, in a general sense—the source of the tragic?'.[14] Recalling the language of freedom and constraint which permeates the Idealist reading of tragedy, Schmitt first tries to understand the question of the tragic in terms of the 'limits' placed on the 'invention of the writer'.[15] He observes that both the writer and the audience are inhibited by what he calls a common 'public sphere'. The 'concrete presence' of the audience creates an essential context for the play, a context that provides an intelligibility to its action. If the action of the play is met with incomprehension, it is followed by the dissolution of the public sphere, which Schmitt says ends 'in a mere theatrical scandal'.[16] In this way the 'public sphere places a strict limit on the creative freedom of the playwright'.[17]

In Schmitt's analysis, the limit that is placed on Shakespeare's creativity is the immediate historical situation of *Hamlet*'s composition. This constraint makes itself manifest through the very plot of the play. In particular, he is interested in explaining why Shakespeare's tragedy differs from the usual revenge plot structure that one finds in Greek tragedy and Norse legend:

> What should a son do if he wants to avenge his murdered father but in the process comes up against his own mother, now the wife of the murderer? The opening situation contains ... an ancient theme of myth, legend, and tragedy. The equally ancient answer allows for only two possibilities. A son who is caught in this way in a conflict between the duty of vengeance and the bond to the mother has, practically speaking, only two routes open to him. The first route is that of Orestes in Greek legend and the tragedy of Aeschylus: the son kills the murderer as well as his own mother. The other route is followed by the

---

[14] Schmitt (2009: 32).   [15] Schmitt (2009: 35).
[16] Schmitt (2009: 35).   [17] Schmitt (2009: 35).

Amleth of the Nordic legend that Shakespeare knew and used: the son allies himself with his mother, and together they kill the murderer.[18]

As Schmitt sees it, the strangeness of Shakespeare's *Hamlet* is that he refuses both the routes that narrative expectation had prescribed for him. Such opacity arises from Shakespeare's refusal to commit himself to affirming either the guilt or the innocence of the queen. And Shakespeare's refusal has its roots in what Schmitt calls the 'taboo of the queen'. 'I can name this very concrete taboo,' insists Schmitt; 'it concerns Mary Queen of Scots'. The 'unseemly and suspicious haste' with which Mary Stuart married the Earl of Bothwell, the murderer of her former husband, Henry Lord Darnley, father of James I, created a scandal in Elizabethan England. Writing in a period of anxiety surrounding the succession of Elizabeth I, Shakespeare was sensitive to the conflicting politics surrounding James's accession to the throne, and the plot of *Hamlet* is the symptom of this ambivalence. Hamlet is mired in an indecision that mirrors the indecision of Shakespeare. He is blocked from fulfilling his destiny as an avenger by the political sensibilities that preyed on the composition of the play. The very aesthetic fabric of the play is marked by the intervention of a historical 'reality' from which it could not escape. 'A terrible historical reality shimmers through the masks and costumes of the stage play, a reality which remains untouched by any philological, philosophical, or aesthetic interpretation, however subtle it might be.'[19]

Schmitt's historical explanation appears surprisingly mechanistic.[20] There is certainly something flat-footed about Schmitt's confident identification of Gertrude with Mary Queen of Scotts and Hamlet with James I. Parallel approaches to Greek tragedy that sought to match up fictional characters in the plays to specific political and historical figures in a straightforward one-to-one relationship are now largely seen as reductive. As Victoria Kahn and others have noted, however, there is more to Schmitt's 'oddly positivistic' reading than might at first seem to be the case. Schmitt names

---

[18] Schmitt (2009: 12).   [19] Schmitt (2009: 18).

[20] Schmitt appears to base his historical analysis on two works of Shakespearian scholarship: F. G. Fleay, *A Chronicle of the Life and Work of William Shakespeare, Player, Poet, and Playmaker* (London, 1886) and Lilian Winstanley, *Hamlet and the Scottish Succession* (London, 1921; translated into German in 1952). See Schmitt (2009: 26 n. 15).

the 'powerful intrusion [*Einbruch*] of historical reality'[21] onto the play 'Hamletization'. This word describes 'the transformation of the figure of the avenger into a reflective, self-conscious melancholic'.[22] Schmitt seems to suggest that the paralysis of the plot arises from the drama of succession that manifests itself, as it were, as a kind of return of the repressed. The languishing in melancholy rather than the move towards decisive revenge arises from the irruption of the 'public sphere' into the realm of aesthetics.

But, while Schmitt initially seems to argue that this transformation comes about through the specific traumatic circumstances of James I's succession, he later opens his analysis up to a broader historical perspective. As Strathausen argues, 'ultimately what "stands behind" Hamlet's melancholy is not just King James I but the monumental dawn of the entire modern era as such'.[23] In making the transition from Orestes to Hamlet, Shakespeare's protagonist also marks the progress from antiquity to modernity. In other words, when Schmitt asserts that it is the 'intrusion of history' that diverts Hamlet from fulfilling his identity as a classical avenger, he could equally be identifying the very rupture between the ancient and the modern in Hamlet's pathology. Schmitt writes of Hamlet that he 'stands . . . in the middle of the schism of Europe'.[24] In particular, as Schmitt elaborates, he stands at the crossroads between the theological debates of the Middle Ages and the rise of the secular nation state. Hamletization in Schmitt's scheme is a vehicle of modernization. The melancholy paralysis of modernity stands in contrast to the active vengeance of the ancient.

But what is so interesting about Schmitt's analysis is that he insistently maps this discussion of historical change onto a more abstract questioning of the role of historical processes in the creation of literary texts. In the process he identifies three different degrees of 'historical influence':[25] allusion, mirroring, and intrusion. He characterizes allusion as one-to-one correspondences between passages in the text and 'real' historical events such as the veiled reference to a contemporary battle in a mention of the sand dunes of Ostende in Act IV of *Hamlet*. 'Such allusions have something incidental about them; today they are for the most part only significant from a

---

[21] Schmitt (2009: 19).   [22] Schmitt (2009: 19).
[23] Strathausen (2010: 19).   [24] Schmitt (2009: 52).
[25] Schmitt (2009: 22).

literary–historical perspective.'[26] Mirroring consists in the strong influence of a living historical character on the portrayal of a protagonist within the text. Schmitt refers to the much discussed argument that Shakespeare modelled his Hamlet on the Earl of Essex.

> Next to the fleeting allusions and true mirrorings, there is yet a third, highest kind of influence from the historical present. These are structurally determining, genuine *intrusions* [*Einbrüche*]. They cannot be common or ordinary, but their consequences are that much stronger and deeper.[27]

In describing the force of these 'genuine intrusions', Schmitt recalls the discussion of the role of history and aesthetics we found in Adorno. 'Historical reality is stronger than every aesthetic, stronger also than the most ingenious subject.'[28] But, although his formulation calls Adorno to mind, it also seems to anticipate Lacan's conception of the real. Despite explicitly rejecting 'psychologizing' readings of tragedy associated with Freud, from the reference to the taboo to his interest in melancholy to his representation of history as a repressed trauma, Schmitt's text is replete with Freudian vocabulary and thematization. But it is perhaps the Lacanian concept of the 'real' that comes closest to capturing the sense of history's role here. As Strathausen writes: 'It seems clear that critics' interpretative shift from "reality" to the "real" is symptomatic of Schmitt's own underhanded transition from reading *Hamlet* in the situational context of two concrete historical events (i.e., Mary Stuart's marriage and James I's reign as king) to a metaphysical reading of *Hamlet* as a timeless tragedy marked by the absent presence of the real.'[29]

Schmitt's rather crude historical reading of *Hamlet*, then, falls short of the more differentiated analysis of the interaction between the aesthetic and the historical sphere that he delineates in the text at large. But Schmitt's shift in understanding from what Strathausen calls 'concrete historical events' to 'the absent presence of the real' is, in fact, constitutive of his understanding of tragedy. Indeed, Schmitt's definition of the tragic, and his distinction between tragedy and *Trauerspiel*, is constructed around his understanding of these different historical modes.

---

[26] Schmitt (2009: 23).   [27] Schmitt (2009: 25).
[28] Schmitt (2009: 30).   [29] Strathausen (2010: 20).

Schmitt discusses the difficulties he has in approaching this question and, in particular, highlights 'the broadly prevailing philosophy of art and aesthetics',[30] which he later characterizes as the 'entrenched views of our German cultural tradition'.[31] This (post-Kantian) tradition had celebrated the autonomy of art, in general, and had, in particular, located 'the source of the tragic . . . in the free and sovereign creative power of the poet'.[32] Schmitt starts by making a generic distinction between 'lyric' and 'drama'. German aesthetics have been enscorcelled by lyric subjectivity and have failed to understand the distinctive qualities of dramatic art: 'But the freedom to create, which provides the lyric poet with such free play vis-à-vis reality, cannot be conferred upon other types and forms of literary creation.'[33] Drama, Schmitt, argues, through the important limiting role of the audience, grounds the literary production in a concrete historical situation. This is not to argue that theatre does not have its own freedom: 'theatre itself' after all 'is essentially play'.[34] But this is where Schmitt introduces a crucial distinction: 'it is . . . necessary to distinguish between *Trauerspiel* and tragedy to separate them so that the specific quality of the tragic is not lost and the seriousness of a genuine tragedy does not disappear.'[35] Schmitt's discussion of the *Trauerspiel* leads into a detailed analysis of the concept of *Spiel* and its antithetical relationship to tragedy: 'the tragic ends where play begins, even when this play is tearful—a melancholy play for melancholy spectators and a deeply moving *Trauerspiel*. It is with Shakespeare's *Trauerspiel*, whose "play" character also appears in the so-called "tragedies", that we can least afford to ignore the unplayablity [*Unverspielbarkeit*] of the tragic.'[36]

What does Schmitt mean by 'the unplayability of the tragic'? He explains his argument through an analysis of the 'play within the play' in Act III of *Hamlet*. In this connection he quotes Hamlet's conversation with the actors in Act II, a conversation that gives Schmitt the title to his essay:

> Why these Players here draw water from eyes:
> For Hecuba! Why what is Hecuba to him, or he to Hecuba?
> What would he do and if he had my losse?

---

[30] Schmitt (2009: 32).   [31] Schmitt (2009: 33).   [32] Schmitt (2009: 33).
[33] Schmitt (2009: 34).   [34] Schmitt (2009: 37).
[35] Schmitt (2009: 38).   [36] Schmitt (2009: 40).

His father murdered, and a Crowne bereft him.

(Shakespeare, *Hamlet*, II.ii)[37]

In answering the question why does Hamlet not weep for Hecuba, Schmitt uncovers the distinctiveness of tragic action and the true importance of the 'the intrusion of time into the play'. Schmitt observes that, by realizing that, unlike other actors, he is not able to weep for Hecuba, Hamlet is led to recognize the necessity of fulfilling his own vow of vengeance. For Schmitt, Hamlet's proclamation of his inability to weep for Hecuba is programmatic for our own experience of watching the play:

> It is inconceivable that Shakespeare intended no more than to make his Hamlet into a Hecuba, that we are meant to weep for Hamlet as the actor wept for the Trojan queen. We would, however, in point of fact, weep for Hamlet as for Hecuba if we wished to divorce the reality of our present existence from the play on the stage. Our tears would become the tears of actors. We would no longer have any purpose or cause and would have sacrificed both to the aesthetic enjoyment of the play.[38]

To weep for Hamlet would be to sacrifice an understanding of the play's contemporary resonance to a mere aesthetic experience. Schmitt uncovers in the sentimental reaction to Hamlet's fate the ideology of aesthetic autonomy. A real historical reality prevents the audience from seeing Hamlet's predicament as *Spiel*:

> Only a strong core of reality could stand up to the double exposure of the stage upon the stage. It is possible to have a play within a play, but not a tragedy within a tragedy. The play within the play in Act Three of *Hamlet* is thus a consummate test of the hypothesis that a core of historical actuality and presence—the murder of the father of Hamlet–James and the marriage of his mother to the murderer—has the power to intensify the play as a play without destroying the sense of the tragic.[39]

The meta-theatrical device of the play within the play, rather than collapsing the realms of reality and fiction, actually reinforces the distinction. It is because Hamlet refuses to allow his story to descend

---

[37] Schmitt chooses to quote from the text of the First Quarto (1603) because it originated before James I's accession to the throne. He argues that after his accession to the throne the reference to being 'bereft' of the 'Crown' had to be omitted. See Schmitt (2009: 43 n. 31).

[38] Schmitt (2009: 43).   [39] Schmitt (2009: 44).

into *Trauerspiel* that he reaffirms its identity as a tragedy. The disjunction between the actor's reaction to the melodrama of Hecuba and the audience's response to the *tragedy* of Hamlet confirms Schmitt's association of tragedy with a 'core of historical reality'. In associating Hecuba with *Trauerspiel* and Hamlet with tragedy, Schmitt reverses the expected chronology. Hecuba is made to stand in for the debased mourning play of modernity, while it is Hamlet who is accorded the antique grandeur of tragedy. This is all the more paradoxical since it is precisely by locating *Hamlet* in its very specific context of post-Elizabethan England that Schmitt elevates Hamlet's fate to that of a tragic hero.

Rather than eliding the distinction between ancient and modern, between fifth-century Athens and sixteenth-century England, Schmitt's definition of tragedy is predicated on a razor-sharp historical sensibility. Where German Idealism had, to some extent, made the modern condition appear tragic by virtue of its continuity with antiquity, Hamlet's tragic identity results from his distinctively early seventeenth-century dilemma. Schmitt's attempt to understand *Hamlet*'s deviation from the narrative form of the revenge tragedy is predicated on associating the Shakespearian play with a specifically modern predicament. 'Hamletization' is a symptom of modernity. That Hamlet is Hamlet and not Orestes depends on a historical caesura that divides the ancient from the modern. For Schmitt, Hamlet is both indelibly modern and incontrovertibly tragic. And, yet, Schmitt seems simultaneously to argue for the incompatibility of the tragic and the modern. As Katrin Trüstedt writes: 'Schmitt criticizes the lack of seriousness that characterizes the political order of modernity and argues for some type of a re-constitution of the original framework, he devalues the sphere of pure play, of a merely playful theatre that has lost its sense of the tragic and the real.'[40]

Here, as elsewhere, Schmitt is mapping a generic distinction to a political one. 'Hamletization' in Schmitt's lexicon has at least a double meaning. It expresses both the turn to introspective melancholy associated with a certain political impotence and the progression towards a vision of the autonomy of art. In order to understand the nexus of ideas that link tragedy and history, *Trauerspiel* and modernity, it is necessary to bring Schmitt into dialogue with Walter

---

[40] Trüstedt (2010: 102–3).

Benjamin. Schmitt includes an appendix to *Hamlet or Hecuba* that
directly addresses his relationship to Benjamin's *The Origin of German Tragic Drama* (1928). His debt to Benjamin is already evident
from the distinction between tragedy and *Trauerspiel* that he employs
throughout the essay. Benjamin had constructed his analysis of Baroque German theatre around a distinction between *Trauerspiel* and
the classical model of Greek tragedy. He opens his discussion in the
chapter '*Trauerspiel* and Tragedy' with the affirmation: 'The history
of modern German drama has known no period in which the themes
of the ancient tragedians have been less influential.'[41] After discount-
ing the relevance of Aristotle's *Poetics* for understanding the preoccupations of the *Trauerspiel*, Benjamin turns to the very question of
history that so preoccupies Schmitt:

> Historical life, as it was conceived at that time, is its [*Trauerspiel's*]
> content, its true object. In this it is different from tragedy. For the object
> of the latter is not history, but myth, and the tragic structure of the
> *dramatis personae* does not derive from rank—the absolute mon-
> archy—but from the pre-historic epoch of their existence—the past
> age of heroes.[42]

Benjamin's distinction between tragedy and *Trauerspiel*, like Schmitt's,
revolves around the question of the historical content of the drama.
But, where Schmitt sees 'historical life' as the distinguishing mark of
tragedy, Benjamin identifies it as the defining characteristic of
Trauerspiel.

Despite coming to divergent conclusions about the respective
properties of *Trauerspiel* and tragedy, Schmitt and Benjamin are
motivated by a common suspicion of contemporary aesthetics. For,
like Schmitt, Benjamin frames his discussion through a critical
engagement with the nineteenth-century 'philosophy of the tragic':

> The philosophy of tragedy has been developed as a theory of the moral
> order of the world, without any reference to historical content, in a
> system of generalized sentiments, which, it is thought, was logically
> supported by the concepts 'guilt' and 'atonement'. For the sake of the
> naturalist drama, this world-order was, with astonishing naivety,
> approximated to the process of natural causation in the theories of the
> philosophical and literary epigones of the second half of the nineteenth
> century and the tragic fate thereby became a condition 'which is

---

[41] W. Benjamin (1998: 60).   [42] W. Benjamin (1998: 62).

expressed in the interaction of the individual with the naturally ordered environment'.[43]

For Benjamin the philosophy of tragedy developed within German Idealism was a 'thoroughly vain attempt to present the tragic as something universally human'.[44] Representing tragedy as a historicized phenomenon that exceeds the grasp of modernity, Benjamin affirms: 'Nothing is in fact more questionable than the competence of the unguided feelings of "modern men", especially where the judgment of tragedy is concerned.' For Benjamin it is a 'simple fact that the modern theatre has nothing to show which remotely resembles the tragedy of the Greeks'.[45] In this vein Benjamin sees Nietzsche's *Birth of Tragedy* as the culmination of a misguided attempt to understand tragedy outside the 'philosophy of history'.

Benjamin, like Schmitt, links this erasure of history to a championing of aestheticism: 'For Nietzsche . . . tragic myth is a purely aesthetic creation, and the interplay of Apollinian and Dionysian energy remains equally confined to the aesthetic sphere . . . Nietzsche's renunciation of any understanding of the tragic myth in historico-philosophical terms is a high price to pay for his emancipation from the stereotype of a morality in which the tragic occurrence was usually clothed.'[46] Nietzsche may have turned his back on one universalizing reading that had associated tragedy with a transhistorical conception of morality, but his vision of tragedy as a 'purely aesthetic creation' opens onto a new abyss:

> The abyss of aestheticism opens up, and this brilliant intuition was finally to see all its concepts disappear into it, so that the gods and heroes, defiance and suffering, the pillars of the tragic edifice, fall away into nothing. Where art so firmly occupies the centre of existence as to make man one of its manifestations instead of recognizing him above all as its basis . . . then all sane reflection is at an end . . . For what does it matter whether it is the will to life or the will to destroy life which is supposed to inspire every work of art, since the latter, as a product of the absolute will, devalues itself along with the world? The nihilism lodged deep in the depths of the artistic philosophy of Bayreuth nullifies—it

---

[43] W. Benjamin (1998: 101).   [44] W. Benjamin (1998: 101).
[45] W. Benjamin (1998: 101). For a more nuanced and fully developed discussion of Benjamin's 'historicism', see Billings, Chapter 13, this volume.
[46] W. Benjamin (1998: 102).

could do no other—the concept of the hard, historical actuality of Greek tragedy.[47]

Benjamin holds up the 'hard historical actuality of Greek tragedy' as a refutation of Nietzsche's affirmation in the *Birth of Tragedy* that 'only as an *aesthetic phenomenon* is existence and the world eternally *justified*'.[48] Nietzsche's and Wagner's aesthetic nihilism is contrasted to the 'historico-philosophical' understanding of tragedy we find in Benjamin. It is notable that, in his engagement with Nietzsche, Benjamin appears to collapse the distinction between *Trauerspiel* and tragedy that is ostensibly at the basis of his argument. Benjamin's dialogue with Nietzsche, as we saw, emerges from his broader critique of the 'tragic theories of the epigones' on which Nietzsche saw himself turning his back. But, as Benjamin reveals, Nietzsche never refutes their approach to tragedy—his aestheticism is merely the culmination of a tradition that had understood tragedy as an abstract idea and a human universal. Rather than insisting on the earlier distinction he draws between the *mythic* content of tragedy and the *historical* content of *Trauerspiel*, in his repudiation of aestheticism, Benjamin presents both tragedy and *Trauerspiel* as manifestations of a 'hard historical actuality'.

Myth plays an interesting role in this politics of tragedy. Benjamin argues that 'for Nietzsche . . . the tragic myth is a purely aesthetic creation' and is thus associated by Benjamin with the Nietzschean aesthetic abyss. Schmitt, on the other hand, has a different understanding of the relationship between the mythic and the tragic. So he writes:

> In spite of Nietzsche's famous formulation that the birth of tragedy arises out of the spirit of music, it is perfectly clear that music cannot be that which we designate here as the source of tragic action. In another equally famous formulation, Wilamowitz-Moellendorff defines Attic tragedy as a piece of myth or heroic legend. He insists that the origin of tragedy in myth must be consciously incorporated into the definition of tragedy; myth thus becomes the source of the tragic.[49]

But, while Benjamin sees myth as the antithesis to history, Schmitt has a more complex configuration in mind. Despite his previous

---

[47] W. Benjamin (1998: 102).
[48] Nietzsche (1999: 33). See Taxidou (2004: 76).   [49] Schmitt (2009: 45–6).

claims that it is history rather than myth that is at the core of tragic action, he goes on to exonerate Wilamowitz's perspective.

> Nevertheless, the definition remains correct because it perceives myth as part of heroic legend, which is not only a literary source for the writer but living knowledge shared by the writer and his public—a piece of historical reality to which all participants are bound by their historical existence. Attic tragedy is thus no self-contained play. An element of reality flows into the performance from the spectators' actual knowledge of the myth. Tragic figures like Orestes, Oedipus, and Hercules are not imaginary but actually exist as figures from a living myth that are introduced into tragedy from an eternal present.[50]

In Schmitt's recasting, myth does not stand opposed to history but rather represents a shared knowledge that is comparable to the common experience of historical actuality. In other words, within the context of Greek tragedy, the mythic worlds of Orestes, Oedipus, and Hercules have the same uncompromising reality for the spectators as the predicament of James I has to Shakespeare's audience. 'The core of historical reality', he writes,

> is not invented, cannot be invented, and must be respected as given. It enters into tragedy in two ways, and there are thus two sources of tragic action: one is the myth of classical tragedy, which mediates tragic action; the other, as in *Hamlet*, is the immediately available historical reality that encompasses the playwright, the actors, and the audience. While ancient tragedy is simply faced with myth and creates the tragic action from it, in the case of *Hamlet* we encounter the rare (but typically modern) case of a playwright who establishes a myth from the historical reality that he immediately faces.[51]

In his contrast between ancient and modern tragedy, Schmitt sees myth as a form of intensification of history. Shakespeare's achievement was to give *mere* history the reality of myth. Both myth and history are opposed by Schmitt to aestheticism; they both resist mere play. They are what he calls 'the unalterable reality', which he sees as 'the mute rock upon which the play founders, sending the foam of genuine tragedy rushing to the surface'.[52] Rather than seeing Shakespeare's historical content as being at odds with the mythic content of Greek tragedy, Schmitt shows us what they have in common. Indeed,

---

[50] Schmitt (2009: 46).   [51] Schmitt (2009: 48).
[52] Schmitt (2009: 45).

it is by understanding the true function of myth within Attic tragedy that Shakespeare was able to make Hamlet into a real tragedy. So Schmitt concludes:

> His success in grasping the core of a tragedy and achieving myth was the reward for that reserve and respect that honored the taboo and transformed the figure of an avenger into Hamlet. Thus, the myth of Hamlet was born. A *Trauerspiel* rose to the level of tragedy and was able to convey in this form the living reality of a mythical figure to future ages and generations.[53]

Where the ancient tragedians may have translated myth into history, Shakespeare, according to Schmitt, translated history into myth. In posing the question *Hamlet or Hecuba* Schmitt in the end does not ask us to choose between myth or history, antiquity or modernity; he rather shows us how the one is always implicated in the other.

Despite their divergent understandings of myth, Schmitt and Benjamin are united in their suspicion of aestheticism and their attention to the historical core of both ancient and modern theatrical traditions. Nevertheless, the diametrically opposed characteristics they respectively attribute to tragedy and *Trauerspiel* reveal a profound difference in outlook. As Katrin Trüstedt argues:

> Whereas for Benjamin *Hamlet* is a *Trauerspiel*, Schmitt claims *Hamlet* as a modern tragedy that manages to hold fast to the past order represented in and incorporated into this drama. At the foundation of the opposition between *Hamlet* as *Trauerspiel* and *Hamlet* as tragedy, as a play of indecision or as a transposition of tragic action, lie diverging ideas on the nature of the modern turn.[54]

This divergence comes to the fore in their respective discussions of the notion of *Spiel*. As we saw above, Schmitt's conception of 'play' is inextricably linked to his valuation of modernity. It is part and parcel of the turn to aestheticism that he deplores. The realm of pure play that he associates with Hecuba is the negative exemplum that Schmitt holds up in order to highlight the authenticity of the tragic. In Benjamin, by contrast, *Spiel* in its association with modernity is redeemed in its contrast to the mythic austerity of classical tragedy. *Spiel* may be a characteristic of modernity, but Benjamin does not characterize it as pathological. Benjamin rather celebrates the

---

[53] Schmitt (2009: 49).   [54] Trüstedt (2010: 102–3).

theatricality of the modern condition and opposes it to the 'silent' reticence of classical tragedy: 'And in the European *Trauerspiel* as a whole the stage is not strictly fixable, not an actual place, but it too is dialectically split. Bound to the court, it yet remains a travelling theatre; metaphorically its boards represent the earth as the setting created for the enactment of history.'[55] The erosion of the boundaries between the court and the stage, the theatre and its historical setting, is the crowning achievement for Benjamin of European *Trauerspiel*. As Trüstedt phrases it: 'For Schmitt, *Hamlet* demonstrates the way in which the element of "pure play" (*reines Spiel*) of modern *Trauerspiel* is interrupted and disturbed by the tragic core of the real: historical time. Whereas for Benjamin modernity is exemplified by the form of *Trauerspiel*, Schmitt insists that *Hamlet* remains (or renews) tragedy. One must not confuse *Trauerspiel* and tragedy, as Schmitt explicitly emphasizes, "so that the seriousness of a genuine tragedy does not disappear".'[56]

The question of the relationship of history to tragedy has an important political dimension for both Schmitt and Benjamin. While both reject the turn to aestheticism that we witness in Idealism and in Nietzsche's and Heidegger's readings of tragedy, they do so for opposing ideological reasons. For Schmitt, the notion of *Spiel* encapsulates the inauthenticity of modernity. For Benjamin, on the other hand, the *Trauerspiel* represents an attempt in modernity to tie the work of art to its historical and material situation. Schmitt yearns to return to an age of the sovereign state, while Benjamin celebrates the inauthenticity of the *Trauerspiel* as a root to understanding contemporary alienation. Benjamin's book published in 1928 and Schmitt's essay written in 1956 frame the historical period of the rise and the defeat of Nazism. Benjamin's incipient-Marxist and Schmitt's post-fascistic readings are both testimony to the intensity of the debate about the relationship between the historical and the aesthetic spheres during this period. For very different reasons and with starkly divergent consequences, both place tragedy at the heart of this exploration.[57]

---

[55] W. Benjamin (1998: 119).   [56] Trüstedt (2010: 103).
[57] A longer and adapted version of this analysis appears in Leonard (2015).

10

The Tragic Voice of Pascal Quignard

John T. Hamilton

Les philologues ne sont jamais raisonnables.

(Quignard, *Petits Traités*)

Philologists have long been accustomed to interruptions. Queries, suspicions, and doubts, based on erudition or vague intuition or a combination of both, significantly decelerate the pace of reading, suspending the text's discursive drive, imposing a fermata that closes off the text's flow, if only for a brief moment. Time is given for examination or specification, for judging correctness or testing variants, for considering errors or corruptions, for spotting anachronisms, lacunae, or other inconsistencies. Whereas most readers are content with following plots, attending to arguments, or indulging in descriptive observations, the philologist stumbles on the words themselves. Here, method intervenes, turning language itself into a problem. It raises issues, creates difficulties, and thereby hinders complacent, undisturbed reading. It gets stuck on minutiae, lost in details, and thus threatens to obscure the larger picture. It imperils the order of things, thwarting efforts to subordinate a text to a domineering idea or ideology. As Lorenzo Valla and those in his scholarly wake discovered, philology discomforts those authorities bent on promulgating a clear message and preserving their power over doctrinal interpretation. Always ready to break in and overturn dogma, the philologist takes pride in sparking controversies and making everything somehow troublesome and less simple, adducing material that is otherwise lost on the ordinary and well-ordered reader.

It is arguably the love of language, which philology names, that causes the philologist to pause with each word, to relish its particular form, caressing its verbal contours, its morphemic properties, interrogating it to the point where the communicative pulse of the text in which the word occurs comes nearly to a full halt. The one who cherishes or even venerates words hesitates to let them go, to let them be absorbed at once into indisputable ideational content. As a mode of reading, this particular kind of *philia*—the *philia* for *logos*—holds each term back before it departs into imparted meaning, jealously questioning where the word has been, its present whereabouts, and its intended destination. In treating words with loving care before they serve as transparent vehicles of sense, philology breaks off the interpretative process and at times may derail it altogether, for it is loath to let words get away too easily.

Philology upsets smooth reading, even though it aims to provide an ultimately smooth text, even though it freezes the passage with an eye to have it carry on. This is because each word potentially addresses the philologist as a discrete utterance, as a request or even a plea, like a voice that cries out before being sacrificed to the logic of the sentence. And, while a philological interrogation necessarily proceeds by taking the entire passage into consideration, by the sheer act of pausing to question the word, the philologist appears to attend to this intrusive voice before it is silenced—that is to say, before it is perfectly worked into the discourse at hand. If one insists on an opposition between voice and signifier, then reading to track the sense of a text requires great efforts of *devocalization*, of compelling the voice to evanesce into signification, of transforming the mere fact of phonation into a sign.[1] In contrast, philological care tarries with the word that has been charged to dissolve into meaning, listening to it in its solitary cell, administering the last rites, striving to stay the execution of the *vox moritura*, however desperately, however provisionally. And, when the time arrives to move on, to let the words resume their discursive purpose, the philologist humbly stands to the side, willing to assume his or her traditionally ancillary role, a mute witness to the sacrifice of the beloved voice.

In disrupting the text's continuity so as to listen to the word as a discontinuous voice, philology could be said to approximate a

---

[1] On this procedure of semanticization as devocalization, see Cavarero (2005: 33–41).

musical sensibility. Friedrich Nietzsche, the aspiring musician *cum* theorist of tragedy *cum* antichristian, famously takes pause to give pausing its due:

> Philology is namely that venerable art [*jene ehrwürdige Kunst*], which begs of its votaries [*Verehrer*] one thing above all: to go aside, to take time, to become still, to become slow—it is a goldsmith's art and connoisseurship of the *word* which has nothing but delicate, cautious [*vorsichtige*] work to do and achieves nothing if it does not achieve it *lento*. But for precisely this reason it is more necessary than ever today, by precisely this means does it attract and enchant us most strongly, in the midst of an age of 'work', that is to say, of hurry, of indecent and perspiring hastiness [*Eilfertigkeit*], which wants to 'get everything done' [*fertig werden*] at once, including every old or new book:—this art does not so easily get anything done, it teaches to read *well*, that is to say, to read slowly, deeply, looking cautiously before and aft [*rück- und vorsichtig*], with hidden agendas [*Hintergedanken*], with doors left open, with delicate eyes and fingers . . .[2]

Regarding philology as an 'art' and not as a science or discipline allows Nietzsche to redefine its practitioners as devotees prepared to perform the duties expected of them. 'With delicate eyes and fingers,' they attend to the service of words rather than enlist words into the hurried service of communicative meaning. On the basis of productivity, their slowness might be regarded as sluggishness, yet from the perspective of Nietzsche's philology it is clearly a 'good': 'it teaches to read *well* [gut *lesen*].' Proceeding with careful caution—*Vorsicht*—philologists assume the Epimethean and Promethean roles of peering backward and forward—*rück- und vorsichtig*—which render any completion of sense *provisional*, expressing 'hidden agendas' (*Hintergedanken*) that penetrate into the substance of the words that lie 'behind the thoughts'—*hinter den Gedanken*—delving into the substrate of meaning that leaves all work unfinished, incomplete, *unfertig*. 'In the midst of an age of "work"', Nietzsche the philologist proposes a method of idleness, a *désœuvrement* that actively unworks the compulsion to 'get everything done' and close up shop. He does so by leaving doors ajar and keeping his ears open. A critic of the times that are frantically fuelled by instrumental reason, he resets the tempo

---

[2] Nietzsche (1980: iii. 17; 1997: 5; emphases and ellipsis in original; translation modified).

to *lento* in order to rein in the industrial and industrious horsepower that rushes to some definitive goal.

Nietzsche's self-styled philological positions, which persistently inform his moral philosophical escapades, were clearly born, like his idea of tragedy, 'out of the spirit of music'.[3] In an early autobiographical sketch, written while he was still a student in Leipzig, the decision to take up classical philology is explicitly based on a resolution to stifle hopes of becoming a composer:

> From my ninth year I was drawn most strongly to music; in those fortunate circumstances in which one does not yet recognize the limits of one's talents and considers everything that one loves to be attainable, I had written down countless compositions and acquired a more than dilettantish knowledge of music theory. Only in the last period of my life at Pforta, in correctly understanding myself, did I give up all my artistic plans; and from that point on Philology entered into the gap that consequently opened up.[4]

While granting some post-adolescent exaggeration, the passage reveals a quality that persists across Nietzsche's written work. Here, the silencing of music has left a 'gap' or perhaps a gaping wound that only the study of words could patch. It would be, of course, only a partial healing, one that would never entirely remedy what would never cease from festering. The interruption of music, which yields place to classical philology, should be taken as an extended fermata that resounds long after the final chord has been struck.

It is not at all difficult to see how the realm of music continues to exert an intoxicating fascination for the pastor's orphan, particularly after his adoption into Richard Wagner's home, attempting to correct what the philologist comes to characterize as his profession's deafness. Again, musical sensitivity consists in having an ear for the 'break':

> That one must not be in doubt about the rhythmically decisive syllables, that one experiences the break with any excessively severe symmetry as deliberate and attractive, that one lends a subtle and patient ear to every *staccato* and every *rubato*, that one figures out the meaning in the sequence of vowels and diphthongs and how delicately and richly they can be coloured and change colours as they follow each other—who

---

[3] For a comprehensive overview, see Liébert (2004).
[4] Nietzsche (1967–: i. 5. 52–3; my translation).

among book-reading Germans has enough good will to acknowledge such duties and demands and to listen to that much art and purpose in language? In the end, one simply does not 'have the ear for that'.[5]

Throughout his philosophical career, Nietzsche applies his 'third ear' to those verbal breaks in the history of values, to the 'detached notes' and 'robbed time'—'every *staccato* and every *rubato*'—that punctuate and puncture dogmatic systems. It is indeed this musical sensitivity that transforms Nietzsche's idiosyncratic approach to philology into an art of interruption, always ready to give pause, always willing to hearken to the voice behind the words, to the 'vowels and diphthongs' that do not signify in the strict sense but are for this very reason all the more meaningful. Adhering to this pre-semantic yet meaningful phenomenon, Nietzsche is glad to rehearse the polyptoton of his fathers' Redeemer—*qui habet aures audiendi audiat!*—'He that hath ears to hear, let him hear!'[6]

The case of tragedy remains exemplary for Nietzsche, insofar as it proves to be a testing ground for the ear. For, in Nietzsche's well-known view, tragedy stages the conflict between the voice and the word, maintaining the difficult tension between Dionysian music and Apollonian form, between choral song and individualized dialogue, before it is silenced by Platonism, before it is suppressed beneath the demands of a resolving *pax philosophica*. Again, Nietzsche refers to an aspect of persistent, resonant idleness: 'the ecstasy of the Dionysiac state, in which the usual barriers and limits of existence are destroyed, contains, for as long as it lasts, a *lethargic* element in which all personal experiences from the past are submerged.'[7] In other words, Apollonian form, which will eventually give rise to logical schematism, sets the terms that the raving god would break. As Nicole Loraux stresses, Nietzsche's account of the birth of tragedy reveals the 'mourning voice' that resounds as something *interminable*, something repetitive and non-appeasable, a shrill tone that thereby 'diverts, rejects, or threatens . . . the obligations and prohibitions constituting the ideology of the city-state.'[8] For Loraux, whereas civic discourse tends to limit grief, channelling or sublimating lamentation into the persuasive arguments of the funeral oration, tragedy allows the

---

[5] Nietzsche, *Beyond Good and Evil*, §246; Nietzsche (1966: 182; 1980: v. 189).
[6] The reference is to Matthew 11:15. See, e.g., Nietzsche (1974: 213; 1980: iii. 512).
[7] Nietzsche (1980: i. 56; 1999: 40).   [8] Loraux (2002: 26).

wailing to continue to be heard. It recalls what the state works to forget. Concerned precisely for this voice, ever alert to the sufferings of Dionysus, Nietzsche raises philology's resistance to a musical pitch. His work with words unworks the work of mourning, so that the mourning itself never fades off entirely. As an art of breaking free from the precipitous drive of discourse, philology sides with the breaks that tragedy consistently registers. When others gather their things and head for the exit, satisfied with the feeling that everything has been understood, that all the terms have fallen into place, Nietzsche stays put in the theatre, unwilling—like every slow reader—to move on.

There are few writers today who more diligently adhere to this Nietzschean ideal, to the twinned vocation of philology and music, than Pascal Quignard (b. 1948, Verneuil-sur-Avre). With Quignard, as in the case of Nietzsche, philological and musical domains provide a dual orientation that produces the elliptical orbit of an *œuvre* otherwise difficult to classify. To be sure, Quignard's prolific output, like that of his Saxon predecessor, is exceptionally heterogeneous, an intriguing hybrid of genres and styles that would include the novel and the fable, the philosophical essay and the scholarly treatise, aphoristic pronouncements and autobiographical reflections. Although the range of topics and themes covered by his books defiantly resists thematic unity, a deep passion for music tugged by the gravitational pull of texts from Greco-Roman antiquity is discernible across the nearly fifty titles he has published to date.

Neither a professional musician nor an academic, Quignard is nonetheless not simply an amateur. A highly trained cellist, pianist, and organist, he has had opportunities to hold seminars on the ancient novel and medieval literature at the Université de Vincennes and the École Pratique des Hautes Études. Working closely with manuscripts at the Bibliothèque nationale, he engaged in methodical textual criticism to establish texts by Maurice Scève, Dom Deschamps, and the sixteenth-century scholar of Syriac and Aramaic, Guy Le Fèvre de La Boderie. In addition to publishing articles on Heraclitus, Aeschylus, Aristotle, and others, he produced a critical edition and translation of Lycophon's *Alexandra*. Two volumes of his *Petits Traités* appeared in 1984, featuring radically digressive essays on a diverse range of philological matters, which complement his venture in historical fiction of the same year, *Les Tablettes de buis d'Apronenia Avitia*, set on the eve of the Empire's fall and purportedly based on quotidian observations by a learned woman of Roman nobility. With his novel

Albucius (1990), Quignard turns to the fragile Republic of the first century BC, reflecting on the lascivious *Controversiae* of Caius Albucius Silus, which yield a number of key terms that constellate into a densely woven essayistic novel. Meanwhile, since 1988 he has served on the advisory board for the Centre de Musique Baroque and, in 1992, with the support of François Mitterrand, he founded and chaired the Festival d'Opéra Baroque at Versailles. Needless to say, explicitly musical material often comes to be incorporated into the literary work. Sententious comments on audition and the voice illuminate discussions of Latin rhetoric and oratory in *Rhétorique spéculative* (1997). Impassioned remarks on the performance and reception of seventeenth-century music are collated with a revaluation of the ancient sophists. Two important collections of treatises, *La Leçon de musique* (1987) and *La Haine de la musique* (1996), attempt to systematize an overarching phenomenology of musical experience, which is further developed in novels of roughly the same period, for example *Le Salon de Wurtemberg* (1986) and *Tous les matins du monde* (1991), as well as the later novel on musical silence, *Vie secrète* (1998). Most recently, in the five volumes of *Dernier Royaume*, which began to appear in 2002, Quignard continues to commingle meditations on music with recognizably philological concerns, each motivating the other by way of a sustained and fruitful tension.

Quignard repeatedly ascribes his musico-philological inclination to the accidents of his birth. He fondly alludes to his parents, who both taught classical languages and literature, as well as his father's family, who for centuries worked as organists across Europe and the United States.[9] Philology and music would appear, then, to be Quignard's patrimony, a double heritage that navigates his literary ventures between language and sound, between meaning and articulation, between the word and the voice. All the same, questions remain. Is it justified to include Quignard among the ranks of philologists? Does his work contribute in any relevant or rigorous way to this well-established discipline? Or does he simply exploit scholarly resources to enhance his own creative inclinations? How, in fact, should we distinguish literary art from a science of words? And would such a distinction be helpful or even valid? What if Nietzsche was correct?

---

[9] See, e.g., 'Pascal Quignard par lui-même', in Marchetti (2000: 191).

What if philology is neither a discipline nor a science but rather 'a venerable art'?

With Quignard, music and philology are perfectly complementary insofar as both pursuits are based on an ear for the break. Among his many childhood recollections, the writer singles out dinners with his maternal grandfather, Charles Bruneau, the historical linguist who co-authored the magisterial *Histoire de la langue française*, published in 1905.

> At my grandfather's house, not a meal went by that he did not get up to leaf through [*fouiller*] Bloch and Wartburg, Godefroy, Littré, Chantraine, Ernout-Meillet, in order to assure himself of the etymology of such or such a word that he just employed... My mother, his eldest daughter, was made from exactly the same strange wood of the Ardennes, precise to the point of obsession, stubborn [*têtu*].[10]

This account not only identifies the source of Quignard's later obsession with the etymological latencies of verbal language, but also calls attention to that key aspect, noted above, of philology as the technique of interrupting consumption. Rising from the table to reach for the lexica and etymological dictionaries, breaking off the conversation to dispute semantics, charting a word's derivation—all bring the continuous flow of communication to a decisive halt. Words are wrested free from their context. In his novel *Albucius*, Quignard again refers to his maternal grandfather in particularly telling terms: 'My grandfather listened only to the form of what was being said. Human language never had any sense.'[11] Rather than employ language as a transparent vehicle of sense, these arresting acts problematize each word, turning every term into a hindrance or an obstacle, an object thrown onto the path of rational discourse. Quignard's dual concern for music and philology expresses this distrust in the viability of a language that all too readily consumes words in the service of broader signification.

In particular, Quignard's stubbornness slows down the process of devocalization, hoping to hold on to the voice before it passes into its signifying function. A telling illustration is given in his own theory of the birth of tragedy, which bears many Nietzschean traits, insofar as it hinges on notions of listening, the break, and the voice's ultimate sacrifice. Accordingly, Quignard proposes what might be described as

---

[10] Interview in Lepeyre-Desmaison (2001: 77).   [11] Quignard (1990: 41).

a non-Aristotelian account of tragedy, one that refuses to subordinate the song to the plot. However, in an altogether provocative move, Quignard evades the *Poetics* by looking elsewhere in Aristotle's work, marshalling the Philosopher's anthropological musings from the opening of the seventh book of the *Historia animalium*:

φέρειν δὲ σπέρμα πρῶτον ἄρχεται τὸ ἄρρεν, ὡς ἐπὶ τὸ πολύ, ἐν τοῖς ἔτεσι τοῖς δὶς ἑπτὰ τετελεσμένοις · ἅμα δὲ καὶ τρίχωσις τῆς ἥβης ἄρχεται. καθάπερ καὶ τὰ φυτὰ μέλλοντα σπέρμα φέρειν ἀνθεῖν, πρῶτον Ἀλκμαίων φησὶν ὁ Κροτωνιάτης. Περὶ δὲ τὸν αὐτὸν χρόνον τοῦτον ἥ τε φωνὴ μεταβάλλειν ἄρχεται ἐπὶ τὸ τραχύτερον καὶ ἀνωμαλέστερον, οὔτ' ἔτι ὀξεῖα οὖσα, οὔτε πω βαρεῖα, οὔτε πᾶσα ὁμαλή, ἀλλ' ὁμοία φαινομένη ταῖς παρανενεθπρισμέναις καὶ τραχείας χορδαῖς · ὃ καλοῦσι τραγίζειν.

(The male begins to bear seed, in most cases, when he reaches the age of twice seven years; and at the same time hair begins to appear upon the pubes, just as plants about to blossom bear seed, as Alcmaeon of Croton was first to remark. About the same time, the voice begins to alter, getting harsher and more uneven, neither shrill as formerly nor deep as afterward, nor yet of any even tone, but rather like an instrument whose strings are frayed and out of tune; and it is called the bleat of the billy-goat.)[12]

Here, it is the final verb, *tragizein*, that intrudes upon the narrative and causes the writer and reader to falter. Two definitions of the verb, together with a parenthetical explication, are provided: 'puer comme un bouc et muer de voix (chanter comme un bouc ou comme celui qui en rappelle l'odeur)'—'to stink like a goat and to break the voice (to sing like a goat or like someone who recalls its odour).'[13] Aristotle's description of male pubescence and its vocal effects is therefore summoned to reveal something fundamental at work in the conception of Greek tragedy, for Quignard explicitly aligns the verb *tragizein* with the definition of *tragōidia* as 'goat-song'. Quignard will keep his notion of tragedy in close relation to the odoriferous goat, to the animal that, according to Aristotle, may have a 'voice' (*phōnē*) without possessing, like humans, *logos*. For Quignard, the tragedy heard in *tragizein* is the fatal disappearance of the child's voice, of the voice that connects the self to prepubescent childhood. Thus, Quignard regards the ancient dramatic art in general anthropological terms as

---

[12] Aristotle, *Historia animalium* 7.1: 581ᵃ. My translation.
[13] Quignard (2002a: 83).

the sacrifice of the child, of one's former self. In sum, tragedy is the record of a lost voice.

The passage from the *Historia animalium* is cited in *La Leçon de musique*, in an essay entitled 'A young Macedonian debarks at the port of Piraeus', which is loosely framed around the life of Aristotle. Quignard's *Leçon* is composed of three distinct parts, each consisting of strikingly terse aphorisms, which readily recall Nietzsche's late style. Moreover, just as Nietzsche's genealogical method insisted on relating philosophies to the philosophers' lives, all three of Quignard's essays are structured by biographical details: the first based on the life of the French composer and violist Marin Marais (1656–1728) and the last on ancient Chinese legends surrounding the figure of the musician Tch'eng Lien. The theme of music's role in diverse experiences of change, loss, and mourning constitutes the guiding thread that connects the poetic reflections and etymological associations that course through each section. Quignard thus puts into play a network of motifs, which ultimately formulate a sweeping theory of the voice, one that, although grounded in historical and cultural specificity, nonetheless transcends these particular coordinates so as to speak to the human condition in general.

The central piece on Aristotle opens in 366 BCE with a brief description of the philosopher as an 18-year-old, as he arrives in Athens to attend Plato's Academy. An oblique reference is made to Paul-Bernard Grenet, who, in his biography of the renowned Stagirite included in his *Histoire de la philosophie ancienne* (1960), affirms that when Aristotle first spoke to Plato the younger man's voice was 'low and hoarse' (*basse et rauque*).[14] It is thereby suggested that Aristotle undertakes his studies after having suffered the break in his voice. In Quignard's reading, the pursuit of philosophy follows upon the loss of a prior voice and the acquisition of one that is new, adult, or productive. Philosophy is subsequent to tragedy.

By relating tragedy directly to the child's voice and its loss, Quignard appears to elaborate a key Nietzschean idea. At the conclusion of *The Gay Science*, the final aphorism (§342) introduces the figure of Zarathustra in a passage that is repeated almost perfectly verbatim at the head of Nietzsche's next book, *Also sprach Zarathustra*. The aphorism is entitled 'Incipit tragoedia', as if Zarathustra's

---

[14] Quignard (2002a: 82).

gospel should function as a demonstration of a voice otherwise lost in conventional philosophy.[15] With his own 'incipit philosophia', Quignard gestures back precisely to that loss denoted by the word *tragedy*, a gesture that illustrates what he elsewhere designates as a decidedly 'antiphilosophical' tradition.[16]

As Quignard's essay continues, the breaking of the voice, understood as marking a young man's initiation into adulthood, is made discernible in many aspects related to the ancient festival, which served as the original context for tragic performance:

> It was at the very beginning of spring. The *tragōidia* is the goat song. The entire village, during the grand procession, sang. The reed-flutes accompanied the song. Some large simulacra of the erect male sex were carried forth. Back then Aeschylus or Sophocles led the chorus. On the first day the bull was sacrificed. Before the competition (that which is choral, that which is danced, that which is theatrical were not yet dissociated), the suckling pig was sacrificed upon the altar. What one called dances were the procession of wine jars, the parade of armor. They danced, which is to say: they stamped their feet. Finally the trumpets sounded.[17]

With these straightforward, concise declarations Quignard creates a scene of spring awakening, replete with ritual sacrifice, the collective celebration of virility, and the musical accompaniment of the 'reed-flutes' or *auloi*. The description recalls Aristotle's comparison of pubescence with blossoming, as well as likening the young man's voice to an instrument producing uneven tones. Etymological clues further propel Quignard's meditation. For example, the sound of the *auloi* is soon described as 'the great quavering'—'le grand chevrotement'—a word that instantly recalls the bleating of the she-goat (*chèvre*).[18] In conjuring the Great Dionysia as the origin of tragic performance, Quignard insists on keeping the goat (*tragos*) in direct view.

With quick strokes, Quignard relates the eventual emergence of the tragic spectacle, wherein the audience is detached from the masked performers, while showing how the primal ritualistic context persisted across the centuries. In this regard, his intention differs little from many

---

[15] Nietzsche (1974: 274–5; 1980: iii. 571); cf. *Also Sprach Zarathustra* (Nietzsche 1980: iv. 11).

[16] Quignard (1995: 11).   [17] Quignard (2002a: 84).

[18] Quignard (2002a: 85).

classicists before him who attempted to spell out tragedy's provenance in archaic ritual. What distinguishes Quignard's approach is a pronounced (and highly selective, if not altogether tendentious) attendance to etymological undertones and networks, to what otherwise remains latent in the cultural vocabulary. Throughout, he characterizes this attentiveness as a particularly musical sensitivity. Other scholars have noted how Quignard engages a quasi-musical approach to accumulate etymologically driven motifs. Claude Coste, for example, refers to the writer's 'search for the original music in words' and the 'obsessive presence of music' in his books.[19] Similarly, Gilles Dupuis describes 'the harmonic secrets of Quignard's style, the small notes that sound out in the void'.[20] As already suggested, this kind of investigation, this kind of exploration into the resonant vestiges of the lexicon, is undertaken by means of breaking with the narrative conveyed, by listening to the voice silenced in the word.

For Quignard, then, Attic tragedy is a historically situated musical performance that rehearses a universal, anthropological drama concerning the human subject's relation to language and the voice, a relation that is essentially one of loss or sacrifice. That is to say, tragedy signifies what must be forfeited in order that signification may take place. Cultural gains—everything that is beneficial and useful to life—are purchased with a loss of the useless.

To designate these transformative losses, Quignard consistently employs the polyvalent term *mue*. Derived from the Latin *mutare*, *la mue* may denote not only the breaking of the pubescent male's voice, but also the sloughing of a snake's outer skin, the moulting of a bird's feathers, or the shedding of hair. In addition to these usages, *la mue* evokes the notion of silencing represented by the adjective *muet*—from the Latin *mutus*, originally designating creatures that can only pronounce *mu*. Accordingly, the voice muted in meaning points to a trace of animal, non-verbal life in human being. What Quignard hears in *la mue* is the phonation that has evanesced into the semantic sign. In addition, the visual rhyme with *musique* and the association with the *mysteries* and the *mustoi* remain in play throughout.

On an anthropological level, the first loss or *mue* is birth itself, insofar as the infant is torn from the auditory, self-contained realm of

[19] Coste (2003: 125–6).   [20] Dupuis (2000: 121–2).

fetal existence.[21] Earlier in *La Leçon de musique*, Quignard makes frequent reference to embryology, which claims that the ears are the first organs to develop in the womb: 'The human ear is pre-terrestrial and pre-atmospheric. Even before breath, before the cry which it gives forth [*déclenche*], two ears bathe for two or three seasons in the amniotic sac, in the womb's resonator.'[22] Situated in an airless space ('préatmosphérique') and removed from the ground for encountering others ('préterrestre'), the womb resounds without engaging with any exteriority, without breaking the circuit of the burgeoning self, which, at this point, is not divorced from its nourishing envelope. Quignard stresses the musicality of this pre-natal site, which he elsewhere describes as 'the maternal sonata'.[23] Birth into the world's atmosphere, where the voice can be borne off away from the self, marks the end of this primal concert. It is an entrance into time itself.

The second *mue* occurs with the acquisition of verbal language, whereby the infant's phonation is transformed into a system of conventional signs. This loss is closely analogous to what Jacques Lacan has identified as 'the second death', as an inscription into the structures and strictures of the so-called Symbolic register. According to Lacan, when the voice is redirected along the guidelines of signification, the pure pleasure in sound—useless *jouissance*—is rejected or at least rendered dispensable or unnecessary, emphatically *insignificant*. Quignard, who has occasionally expressed his indebtedness to Lacan, would no doubt corroborate the psychoanalyst's assessment:

> The coming into operation of the symbolic function in its most radical, absolute usage ends up abolishing the action of the individual so completely that by the same token it eliminates his tragic relation to the world... At the heart of the flow of events, the functioning of reason, the subject from the first move finds himself to be no more than a pawn, forced inside this system, and excluded from any truly dramatic, and consequently tragic, participation in the realization of truth.[24]

In Lacan's view, the subject of the signifier is hardly a master of the words he or she employs but rather nearly an automaton, limited by

---

[21] Jean-Louis Pautrot (2004) clearly locates the series of breaks that organize Quignard's reflections on music, language, and cultural phenomena.
[22] Quignard (2002a: 52).   [23] Quignard (2002b:109).
[24] Lacan (1988: 168).

an external system. The subject is the one subjected and thereby eliminated from a 'tragic relation to the world', from a 'tragic participation in the realization of truth'. Quignard rehearses a similar argument, yet he would postpone the 'tragedy'—the point at which the subject emerges—to the pubescent stage, when the *mue* closes the subject off from the child's life.

For it is the third loss, the *mue de voix*, that exclusively concerns male adolescents, that Quignard identifies as 'the tragedy' on the basis of Aristotle's use of *tragizein*. Whereas birth robs the infant of gapless affect and language acquisition destroys the inarticulate purity of immediate phonation, the breaking of the voice separates the young man from his past: a threshold experience, coloured by the odour of puberty and leading to the imposition of sexual difference.

> A child loses his voice, this is a male event. This voice—its identity, the very expression of his identity, the voice which linked this body to the mother tongue, the voice which linked this mouth, these ears, these sonorous memories to the mother's voice, which did not appear to recognize a break [*mue*]—this voice is forever broken. It is lost forever.[25]

In the section devoted to tragedy, Quignard characterizes this 'event' specifically as a 'sacrifice': 'During the *mue* of the boys, in ancient Greece, it is the bleating of the goat that betrays the defining sacrifice of the species.'[26] The break is therefore heard as a symptom of differentiation and discrimination—of the 'sacrifice définitoire'.

Is this, then, all that we can expect from the philologist's attentiveness: an acknowledgement of loss, a consignment to silence? Or does something positive emerge from the evanescence of these voices?

The three privative 'events' eradicate some aspect of auditory experience—the uterine, the infantile, and the prepubescent. The link to the directly preceding period is for ever silenced. Yet, although the past is dispatched to the stillness of the no longer or the never again, it does not cease to resonate. Indeed, for Quignard, it resounds precisely as silence. In Quignard's view, cultural activity and especially musical performance, including tragedy, are modes of reparation, attempts to address the series of alterations and deprivations that occur in the course of human life.[27] Quignard's brand of

---

[25] Quignard (2002a: 33).   [26] Quignard (2002a: 89).
[27] Cf. Coste (2003: 125–46).

philological reading, which engages in ceaseless interruptions, is motivated by an insistence on listening. 'To obey the voice unto death. To listen all the way to the destination of its fate. To listen to the voice until the voice goes silent.'[28] Reading in this sense has little to do with receiving information and instead adheres to the evanescent voice. Creative writing proceeds according to the same desire: 'To write is to hear the lost voice . . . It is to search for language in the language lost.'[29] Accordingly, *La Leçon de musique* aspires to be 'a work of music hailing a lost voice or devising a voice that has become impossible'.[30] The centre point of art is the irretrievable.

Quignard's philology may be highly unconventional and perhaps even unrecognizable as philology in the general sense of the term, yet his understanding of Greek tragedy, tied to his notion of the 'tragedy' of the lost voice, is not altogether remote from more straightforward exercises in philological practice. Walter Burkert, for example, also interrupts his reading of Attic tragedy by attending to the word *tragōidia*, which he finds troublesome. Why, Burkert asks, is 'tragedy called τραγῳδία—a word which seems to impose the animal on the development of high human civilization, the primitive and grotesque on sublime literary creations'.[31] Just as Quignard conjures an archaic scene of spring ritual and sacrifice, Burkert feels compelled to return 'to the religious basis of tragedy and indeed to Greek cult in general'.[32] He methodically adduces the various attempts to understand the word's denotation, as meaning a 'song of goats', where dancers dressed as goats (Welcker, Wilamowitz), as referring to the goat that was the original prize in the tragedy competition (Reisch), and as commemorating a goat sacrifice at the height of the festival (Nilsson).[33] Like Quignard, he eventually posits 'sacrifice' as the crucial event that motivated tragic performance, alluding to Aeschylus' *Agamemnon*, Sophocles' *Trachiniae*, Euripides' *Medea* as illustrative examples of plays that hinge on sacrificial victims. Yet, whereas Burkert regards Attic tragedy as an artistic sublimation of this ritualized violence, Quignard hears a document in loss. The human relationship to animal existence is not a problem to be resolved but rather an anthropological fact to be respected.

---

[28] Quignard (1997: 376).   [29] Quignard (2002c: 94).
[30] Quignard (2002a: 74). On this point, see Bogliolo (2000: 109–17).
[31] Burkert (1966: 88).   [32] Burkert (1966: 88).
[33] See Burkert's useful résumé with complete bibliography: Burkert (1966: 88 n. 2).

Quignard's thesis on the birth of tragedy corresponds in many ways with well-known theories grounded in French Structuralism, particularly the insistence, central to the work of Claude Lévi-Strauss, that culture is continuous with or an extension of nature. His assessment, therefore, shares much with the analyses formulated by Jean-Pierre Vernant, Marcel Detienne, and others. Moreover, in construing the tragic break of the adolescent's voice as the establishment of sexual difference, Quignard implicitly alludes to René Girard's theory of originary violence and non-differentiation, which is subsequently quelled by the imposition of culture based on a scapegoat's sacrifice.[34] However, where structuralism has generally opposed conventional 'philological' readings, Quignard redefines philology in such a way that it can contribute to and enhance typical structuralist interpretations. Much of this redefinition involves a profound interest in the archaic, which instigates a philology that renounces its traditionally ancillary role in the service of philosophical understanding. Here, Quignard's explicitly 'antiphilosophical' intent is closely allied to Nietzsche's critique of Euripides and Socrates.[35] Tellingly, Nicole Loraux's own reading of Nietzsche's text leads her to describe tragedy as 'antipolitical', alluding to the way tragic performance is at odds with civic discourse.[36]

What is specifically philological about Quignard's approach is that he demonstrates fundamental continuities between nature and culture by way of interruption—that is, by bringing communicative, significant, rational language to a halt in order to hear the voice silenced by the word, by tearing through the veil of culture that covers over loss in order to expose the loss itself. This kind of disruption, in Quignard's view, lies at the core of tragic performance. In a reading of Euripides' *Bacchae,* he is particularly explicit:

> Dionysus, the god of the tragic sacrifice of the goat, the god who maddens the spectators with his animal masks, the god who causes spinning in dance and delirium in wine, is the god who interrupts language. He short-circuits all sublimation. He refuses the mediation of conflicts. He tears off every piece of clothing to the original nudity.[37]

---

[34] For a comprehensive analysis of Quignard's indebtedness to structuralism and to the work of Lévi-Strauss and René Girard in particular, see Alvares (2012).

[35] See, e.g., Nietzsche's remarks in *The Birth of Tragedy*, §§12–13; Nietzsche (1999: 59–67).

[36] Loraux (2002: 26–9).   [37] Quignard (2007: 327).

Defined emphatically as the 'god who interrupts language', Dionysus oversees the break that is fully staged in Euripides' drama. '*Omophagia*: the mother devours her son raw and thus makes him return, by means of blood, back into the body of her who expelled him. This is the bloody ecstasy that founds human societies.'[38] Although clearly discontent with civilization, Quignard's reading of the *Bacchae* significantly qualifies uterine existence, which he previously described with some perverse nostalgia as 'the maternal sonata'. Retrospectively, the breaks that humanity suffers may be felt to deprive us of some past pleasure, but we should be relieved that the irretrievable remains so. The loss of the voice preserves us in time and saves our lives from violent dissolution, until the final break, the ultimate *mue*, which is death itself.

> Aristotle dies. But it is the realist, the zoologist who dies. Meticulously [*minutieusement*] he abandons the day, the odor, the voice, himself. Even the broken voice [*la voix muée*], he leaves behind. The broken voice breaks [*mue*] into something less hoarse and less unequal. The last cloak he leaves behind is life.[39]

In the end, Quignard's idiosyncratic philology, his auditory attention to the minutiae of language broken off from language, is nothing other than the tragedy of tragedy.

---

[38] Quignard (2007: 326).   [39] Quignard (2002a: 95).

Part III

Tragic Canons

11

The Ends of Tragedy: Schelling, Hegel, and Oedipus

Simon Goldhill

In 1795 or thereabouts, the familiar story runs, 'the tragic' was invented, and, with it, German Idealism's construction of tragedy became the dominant critical model for the nineteenth century; tragedy thus became an integral model for philosophy; and Oedipus, the searcher, became the figure of the philosopher, a paradigmatic figure for philosophy itself. This story has been told and retold with considerable sophistication as a key narrative of the intellectual history of German Idealism and, indeed, the history of the nineteenth century's legacy in modernism.[1] This chapter will suggest, however, that a crucial aspect of such a history has been consistently unrecognized, and that this failure of recognition reveals a deep-seated and continuing ideological complicity with a specifically Christian religious strand of Idealist thinking.

The phrase 'the ends of tragedy', my theme, should be understood at several interrelated levels. First, it refers to how tragic dramas reach closure, how their narratives end. Second, it implies a question about how tragedies reflect on and debate the notion of closure, finality, death, both from an aesthetic perspective as a question of formal structure, and from a moral perspective, which, since Aristotle, has been formulated as an issue of whether a man's suffering is a just,

Especial thanks to Miriam Leonard and Joshua Billings for extremely insightful discussion of these issues over recent years. A version of this chapter appeared in PMLA 129.4 (2014) 634–48.

[1] Lacoue-Labarthe (1989, 1998); Schmidt (2001); Szondi (2002); Eagleton (2003); Goldhill (2012: 137–263); Billings (2014).

motivated theodicy. Third, it alludes not just to Nietzsche's celebrated claim that the introduction of philosophical or specifically Socratic thinking into tragedy destroyed the embracing integrity of the Dionysiac experience of the *Gesamtkunstwerk*, but also, and more importantly to the Idealist argument, that the privileged genre of tragedy offers a fundamental insight into the ends of man—the purpose of humanity in the dark light of death, and the potential for transcendence. What is at stake in the ends of tragedy for Idealist thinking is nothing less than the teleology of the aesthetic in relation to *Sittlichkeit*, the subject's ethical self-positioning.

I shall argue in this chapter that the readings of Oedipus developed by Schelling and Hegel in particular, which are the most instrumental in establishing Oedipus as the figure of philosophy, require and construct a notion of the end of Oedipus that not only violently distorts the plays of Sophocles on which their arguments rely, but also does so from a specific Christianizing position. But before we can embark on this analysis, three crucial elements of background need outlining.

The first concerns the Idealist commitment to tragedy as a genre. Recent criticism has spent a good deal of effort in expounding the tyranny of Greece over the nineteenth-century German imagination, the unique place of tragedy within this philhellenic turn to the classical past, and the 'Sophocles complex', which sets Sophocles' plays as the pinnacle within this idealized view of ancient Greece.[2] This is not the place for a full doxography of this work. But there are several elements of it that will prove especially significant for what follows, and need at least lapidary expression here.

One corollary of the emphasis on the tragic (as opposed to tragedies) is a generalizing bent within Idealist accounts of the genre of tragedy and the dramas themselves. So, as I have discussed at length elsewhere, generalizing about tragedy has the effect of downplaying any particular tragedy's specific political interests—to the extent that Matthew Arnold, in Germanizing mode, can dismiss even Sophocles' *Antigone*, Hegel's icon of the tragic, from the elite canon of the truly tragic, on the grounds that the play's local argument about the specific legal issue of the burial of the body of a traitor cannot be interesting.[3]

---

[2] E. Butler (1935); Silk and Stern (1981); Kain (1982); Steiner (1986); Schmidt (2001); Lambropoulos (2006); Goldhill (2012: 137–263); all with further bibliography.

[3] Goldhill (2012: 137–65); on Arnold's intellectual engagement with German/ Greek thought, see Faverty (1951); Anderson (1965); de Laura (1969); Carroll (1982); Gossman (1994); and especially Leonard (2012); more general background in Collini (1994) with Collini (1991).

This search for the truly tragic has a lasting effect on the canon of plays out of which the image of the genre is formed. Most significantly, however, the abstract, normative idea of the tragic results in tragedy becoming the site where aesthetics, politics, and history are most intimately intertwined. So, for Hegel, building on Schelling's work, tragedy is 'a testing ground and validation for main tenets of [his] historicism, for the dialectical scenario of his logic, and for the central notion of consciousness in progressive conflict'.[4] In Hegel's project, tragedy is a prime route into challenging Kant, and developing his own sense of the historicity of ethics and its relation to what could be called 'collective' normative values, and the compulsions under which a human subject works—a process that goes to the heart of Hegel's sense of a human self-consciousness divided against itself, and yet in progress through this division and its transcendence. So closely interconnected are the structure of tragedy and the structure of Hegel's thinking that critics have declared that *The Phenomenology of Spirit* 'is a tragic text'; it has 'a tragic conception of truth'; its dialectic is 'structurally tragic'.[5] Now, within his historicizing teleology Hegel strives to construct a universalizing view of *the* family and of *the* state as abstract and general principles, but it is through his insistence on conflict as the essence of tragedy that Hegel's model continues to have a profound effect on contemporary criticism, not just in the clash of systems of belief or commitments, but in the internal conflicts of the ethical agent in historical context. For Hegel, tragedy is a doorway to rethinking Kant's notion of the subject.

The power of the response of German Idealism to Kant, then, is that 'tragedy and the tragic' become a way of exploring central questions of human freedom, political autonomy, self-consciousness, and ethical action, which repeatedly integrates the tragic into a philosophical regime. Generalizing about the tragic takes tragedy from the sphere of literary genre and establishes it as a means to comprehend the self as a political, psychological, and religious subject. Tragedy is a route to the self-definition of modernity.

Inherent in this construction of the tragic is a heightened focus on the individual subject as a locus of tragedy—the heroic individual (a notion that can always find a genealogy in Aristotle or

---

[4] Steiner (1986: 21).
[5] Eagleton (2003: 41); de Beistegui (2000: 28). See also George (2006).

Aristotelianism[6])—or, as I have just expressed it, the internal conflicts of the ethical agent in historical context. Schelling is exemplary of this focus on the individual. For Schelling, the 'innermost spirit of Greek tragedy'[7] is located in the struggle and fate of the hero. It is in the heroic individual that we perceive the tension between inner freedom and the external necessity that sums up why tragedy is such a powerful representation of the *Sittlichkeit* of humans. That Oedipus freely bears the punishment that an inscrutable but necessary fate has decreed for him constitutes him as the archetypal tragic hero. The Idealist drive towards the general absorbs the focus on the individual by making the individual archetypal: 'The individuals in the high tragedy of the Greeks . . . do likewise have individual aims, but the substantial thing, the "pathos" which, as the essence of their action, drives them on, has absolute justification, and for that very reason has in itself a universal interest.'[8] So, in lines we will return to: 'This is the most sublime idea and the greatest victory of freedom: voluntarily to bear the punishment for an unavoidable transgression in order to manifest his freedom precisely in the loss of that very same freedom, and to perish amid a declaration of free will.'[9] For Schelling, the individual hero is the *only* location of such moral sublimity: 'This is also the only genuinely *tragic* element in tragedy.'[10] The hero achieves his sublime state by calmly bearing the disasters fate sends him, and it must be *necessity* and not mere bad luck or misfortune that faces him:

> The hero of tragedy, one who nonetheless calmly bears all the severity and capriciousness of fate heaped upon his head, represents for just that reason that particular *essential nature* or unconditioned and absolute in his person . . . It is essential that the hero be victorious only through that which is not an effect of nature or chance, and hence only through inner character or disposition, as is always the case with Sophocles.[11]

Hegel too establishes 'essentially free individuality', the 'self-sufficiency of the citizen',[12] at the centre of his vision of tragedy, though his idea of the individual is developed in far more complex ways than Schelling, and with a far more involved sense of what 'self-consciousness' might entail, for a historical subject. 'The feeling accordingly of

[6] See Gellrich (1988).   [7] Schelling (1989: 254).
[8] Hegel (1975a: i. 568).   [9] Schelling (1989: 254).
[10] Schelling (1989: 254). For the background here, see Barth (1991).
[11] Schelling (1989: 89).   [12] Paolucci and Paolucci (1962: 165–7).

subjective self-consciousness in relation to necessity is this sense of repose which abides in the region of calm, in this freedom, which is, however, still an abstract freedom . . . Whoever has this consciousness of independence may be indeed outwardly worsted, but he is not conquered or overcome.'[13] The sense of independence and necessity is basic, for Hegel as for Schelling, to understanding the tragic hero: 'Those individuals are in a special way in subjection to necessity and have a tragic interest attaching to them, who raise themselves above the ordinary moral conditions, and who seek to accomplish something special for themselves.'[14] Although Hegel has a far more developed sense of what the community and its wisdom might be, and even locates ethical conduct within the community—for Schelling the individual is starkly 'the negation of the larger group'[15]—it is in the individual where the questions of *Sittlichkeit* are focused.

When we turn to look in detail at how the ends of Oedipus are conceptualized by Schelling and Hegel, it will be within this framework of generalizing about the tragic and the crisis of *Sittlichkeit* located in the suffering individual hero.

The second element of necessary background concerns Greek tragedy's sense of an ending.[16] Sophocles remained obsessed with Aeschylus' *Oresteia* throughout his writing career. The *Oresteia* is not merely a trilogy whose journey towards the reconciliations of the law court is articulated in a series of teleologically charged systems of imagery (from dark to light, from corrupt sacrifice to civic ritual, from purple tapestries as progression towards death to purple robes in a progression to the Acropolis); the trilogy also repeatedly signals the multifaceted and fissured language of ending and fulfilment throughout its journey. *Telos* can mean end, fulfilment, consummation, sacrificial rite, death, tax, and, at turning points of the trilogy's narrative, these multiple senses are part of the punning crisis of language that is so much a force in Aeschylus' drama.[17] So, in a celebrated and paradigmatic demonstration of her manipulative power over language and its multiple meanings, Clytemnestra ushers her husband, Agamemnon, towards the house and his death with the

---

[13] Paolucci and Paolucci (1962: 323).   [14] Paolucci and Paolucci (1962: 323).
[15] Schelling (1989: 69). See Schulte (1992).
[16] See Dunn (1996); Segal (1996); Dunn, Roberts, and Fowler (1997); Segal (2001: 108–22); Rehm (2002: 221–35); Wilson (2004: esp. ch. 1); Budelmann (2006).
[17] Zeitlin (1965); Lebeck (1971); Goldhill (1984a, b).

prayer (*Aga.* 973–4): 'Zeus, Zeus, the fulfiller [*teleie*], fulfil [*telei*] my prayers; may you take care to fulfil what you intend to fulfil [*telein*].' *Zeus teleios*, 'Zeus the fulfiller', is a common cult title in the Greek world, but the triple repetition and punning on the language of *telos* releases the semantic richness of the term. This is also a sacrifice, the corrupt sacrifice of regicide, the reversal of the rite (*telos*) of marriage between husband and wife. *Telein* announces the death (*telos*), the end of the king; just as his murder is conceptualized as paying back, the 'tax' (*telos*) of revenge. For Clytemnestra, this murder is also a consummation devoutly desired, as it is the end point of a narrative foretold. The *Oresteia* made the language and process of ending fully part of the tragic agenda, and both Sophocles and Euripides repeatedly and in the most deep-rooted manner continue to explore the ends of tragedy.

So, in Sophocles' *Ajax*, for example, a play that does not sit comfortably with either Hegel's or Schelling's account of the ideal tragedy, the hero Ajax commits suicide halfway through the play, after discussing why his life is not worth living. His disastrous situation is as much self-motivated as it is external; he scarcely bears his fate calmly; his end is not the end of the drama.[18] Indeed, the second part of the play proceeds to discuss how Ajax's end is to be conceptualized, and how some form of closure can be reached. Ritual—the burial of Ajax—provides formal closure to the plot of the drama. But, even here, Teucer, Ajax's brother, feels compelled to exclude Odysseus from the rite, even though Odysseus has been the prime facilitating agent in reaching the political compromises that enabled the burial. That Odysseus has been a deadly enemy of Ajax cannot be forgotten, at the end, even though such flexibility of judgement has been crucial to reaching the ritual closure.[19] Sophocles—and this is typical of his dramaturgy—opens a broad and disturbing semantic vista at the very moment of apparent ending. The *Ajax* has a lengthy and explicit discussion by Ajax and then his supporters and enemies about his end, and dramatizes vividly the difficulties of reaching a political, moral and ritual closure. The sense of an ending is fully thematized in the play.

In a similar way, *Electra* manipulates its theatrical and mythic heritage to provoke a reflection about ending.[20] The last word of

---

[18] See, on *Ajax*, Segal (1981: 109–56); Goldhill (1986: s.v *Ajax*); Whitlock Blundell (1989: 60–105); Hesk (2003); Nooter (2012: 31–55); each with further bibliography.

[19] See Burian (1972); Goldhill (1986: 85–8); Henrichs (1993); Hesk (2003: 124–30).

[20] On *Electra* and specifically the ending, see Goldhill (2012: 201–30, with further bibliography).

play with classic self-reflexivity is 'ended'—*teleôthen*. Yet, at this announcement of consummation, not only has Aegisthus not yet been killed, but also the audience is left uncertain whether Orestes will be pursued by the Furies, as in Aeschylus, or whether he will be exonerated in the Athenian court. The final conversation of Aegisthus and Orestes hints at a narrative to come—that Sophoclean opening of a vista, again—but, rather than the torch-lit procession to the religious centre of the city with which the *Oresteia* closes, the *Electra* ends with an uncomfortable return of the son and his victim to the darkened heart of the house. The moral uncertainties, which the ending of this play provokes, are in striking discontinuity with the formal closure of exit. If a woman's end within the patriarchal ideology of representation is marriage or death, Electra herself is left without the release for which she has prayed. In Aeschylus, Electra is sent inside to await marriage; in Euripides, she is promised a marriage to Pylades; in Sophocles, Electra has no marriage; and her silence— after so much out-of-place ranting—leaves the audience with a final question about the end of revenge.

The *Philoctetes*, in turn, has a double ending, as the human characters' decision to leave for Greece is redirected towards Troy by Heracles' appearance *ex machina*—an ending that has inevitably become a critical crux.[21] The *Trachiniae* too, with its deep anxiety about the foretold end of Heracles, looks uncertainly forward, like the *Electra*, from its own closure to a narrative to come. The word *telos* is repeatedly used for the fulfilment of the prophecies given to Heracles, but, with the clarity that comes to a dying hero at the end, he realizes that he has long misunderstood what *telos* means: 'The prophecy said that, at the present and now living time, release from the toils laid upon me would be fulfilled [*teleisthai*]. I thought that meant a happy future. I now realize that it meant nothing else than my death.'[22] He rereads the *telos* of fulfilment as the *telos* of death. Yet, ironically enough, there are many hints in the play of the well-known story of Heracles' transformation into a divinity on Olympus, achieved traditionally by being burnt on a pyre, precisely as he is here commanding

---

[21] Most studies discuss this. See, for representative accounts of the debate, Rose (1976); Easterling (1978); Segal (1981: 292–361); Falkner (1998); Lada-Richards (1998); Schein (2005).

[22] Sophocles, *Trachiniae* 1169–72.

his child to enact. As Heracles spells out that he had not before understood what his prophesied *telos* meant, he is ironically misunderstanding again what his consummation is to be.[23]

In Sophocles, in short, there is a sophisticated, self-aware, manipulation of the lineaments of narrative closure, integrally intertwined with the dramatization of the failures and misprisions of self-knowledge, and, above all, the ironic complicities of human hopes and fears of consummation, fulfilment, and release. When we turn to the endings of Oedipus, it must also be within the framework of this complex and self-implicating discourse of closure.

The third contextualization, the modern critical tradition from which we are looking back at how tragic ends have become so charged, can be expressed even more succinctly, at least in outline. Although Aristotle's *Poetics* determined that the end of a hero is a crucial matrix for discussing the effects of tragedy, and although Nietzsche's proclaimed end of tragedy linked aesthetic and philosophical crisis, George Steiner, followed by Bernard Williams, has argued influentially that a Christian teleology fundamentally changes how tragedy's end can be conceptualized.[24] The hope of Christianity threatens the tragedy of the tragic end. Suffering is reconstrued as a challenge to faith to be transcended in the promise of eternal life. Steiner's *Death of Tragedy* makes Christianity an angel of death for the truth of tragic despair. In tracing Schelling's and Hegel's Christianization of ending, my argument contributes to this debate about tragedy in relation to modern religious commitments, and specifically about the nineteenth-century Sophocles' 'piety' conceived as 'an education into Christ'.[25]

Now, Christianity proclaims the certainty of its end. Modern criticism, however, especially the criticism of tragedy, has made 'tension and ambiguity' its watchwords. Although there have been ideologically loaded attempts to rediscover a certainty of ending for tragedy, most coherently perhaps in the survival of the collective of the city in the form of the chorus over the destruction of the elite individual, or, from a counter-position, in the values of the elite families for contemporary politics, nonetheless a contemporary critical expectation of the openness of closure is the flip-side of resistance

---

[23] On *Trachiniae* and the ending, see Easterling (1981); Goldhill (2012: 159–62).

[24] Steiner (1961); Williams (1993).

[25] See Goldhill (2012: 201–30); the quotation is from Plumptre (1865: p. xcviii).

to any Christianization of tragedy's ends.[26] The privileging of ambiguity and the resistance to Christianization together mark contemporary criticism's reaction against its nineteenth-century philological, institutional heritage—and it is within such a framework that the following argument is self-consciously placed.

Schelling's account of Oedipus is central to his account of tragedy. As we have already seen, the innermost truth of tragedy is to be found in the clash between freedom in the subject and external necessity, 'a conflict that does not end such that one or the other succumbs, but rather such that both are manifested in perfect indifference as simultaneously victorious and vanquished'.[27] The *end* of tragedy is part of its very definition. Schelling goes on to explore this generalization via Aristotle's sense of the different forms of an end that a suffering hero experiences, and concludes with the celebrated assertion that I have already quoted: 'This is the most sublime idea and the greatest victory of freedom: voluntarily to bear the punishment for an unavoidable transgression in order to manifest his freedom precisely in the loss of that very same freedom, and to perish amid a declaration of free will.'[28] Hence, for Schelling, Oedipus becomes the paradigm of the tragic, since the hero 'brings down upon himself other consequences of his unmerited guilt' because he 'cannot rest until he himself has disclosed the entire, terrible entanglement and that entire, frightful fate itself'.[29] Schelling goes on, however, to gloss the ending of tragedy in a fascinating way. First, he dismisses the too easy theology of calling on God: 'it would be ruinous for the whole essence of tragedy to call on the gods for help for the sake of ending the tragedy externally'—so, for Schelling, there can be no *deus ex machina* in a true tragedy, because it provides only a formal, external closure, but leaves the action 'internally inconclusive'. Rather, what is needed— and this is Schelling's conclusion to his discussion of endings—is 'that the action must not be merely externally but rather internally self-enclosed, in the disposition of the character himself, just as it is an internal rebellion that the tragic element actually provokes'.[30] Tragedy is a drama of the internal self, the subject, and thus needs an ending at this level. 'Only from this *inner* reconciliation does that harmony emerge that is required for completion.'[31] Reconciliation

---

[26] See Seaford (1995); Griffith (2011).   [27] Schelling (1989: 251).
[28] Schelling (1989: 254).   [29] Schelling (1989: 254).
[30] Schelling (1989: 258).   [31] Schelling (1989: 258).

requires 'the greatness, free acceptance and elevation of inner disposition'.[32] And, for this process, adds Schelling with explicit emphasis, the primary motive of reconciliation is religion. Thus Oedipus in the *Oedipus Coloneus*, because of his ritual transformation in that play, is to be seen as the paradigm of the closure in internal reconciliation. Oedipus is called by God to his ending: 'the highest transfiguration occurs when the God calls.'[33]

Schelling's argument depends, first of all, on a particular and remarkably distorted retelling of Sophocles' two plays. He starts by recapitulating Oedipus' story, but this first summary of the myth strikingly stops *before* the action of the play itself: 'He marries his mother and begets with her that unfortunate line of sons and daughters.'[34] Later, he returns (as we saw above) to Oedipus' search to reveal 'the entire, terrible entanglement', which expresses the central sections of the *Oedipus Tyrannus* in barest outline. But at no point does Schelling actually mention, let alone discuss, the end of the *Oedipus Tyrannus* as a play. Why does this matter? Because the end of Sophocles' drama provides a fundamental challenge to Schelling's argument, a challenge that he never faces.

There are two crucial aspects of the ending of the *Oedipus Tyrannus*, which together form the dominant critical questions for contemporary criticism. First, as Peter Burian has articulated with greatest clarity, *Oedipus Tyrannus* embodies a profoundly shocking structural surprise.[35] From the opening declaration of the king that he will pursue the killer of Laius, the punishment of destruction or exile has been promised, and the build-up of expectation has been intense. Teiresias, the unfailingly true prophet, has foretold Oedipus' exile on Cithairon, where he will bewail his fate as he wanders. Oedipus himself in his anguish has demanded that he be cast out to where no one will be able to see him, and demands that he should be allowed to wander, blind, on the mountain where he should have died before the shepherd's mercy preserved him for his terrible fate. In the very last scene, Oedipus again enforces this demand. He begs Creon (l. 1436): 'Cast me out with all speed from this land.' But Creon precisely rejects hasty action, and declares he will ask the god at Delphi for advice. Consequently, not only is Oedipus left on stage for nearly another 100 lines addressing his daughters and Creon, but also his final exit is

---

[32] Schelling (1989: 258).   [33] Schelling (1989: 258).
[34] Schelling (1989: 253).   [35] Burian (2009). See also the works cited in n. 16.

not via the *parodos* to Cithairon, but back through the central door inside the darkened house, to await the word of god, which the play will leave silenced. The self-conscious, momentary opening of a vista of future narrative, coupled with a silenced question, is, as we have seen, the exemplary Sophoclean twisting of dramatic closure.

For Jean-Pierre Vernant, in one of the most influential of modern readings of Sophocles' *Oedipus Tyrannus*, the structural expectation of exile goes to the very heart of the mythic and ritual models through which Oedipus is represented.[36] For Vernant, Sophocles remains a riddle because he combines the models of *turannos* [king] and *pharmakos* [scapegoat] in one figure—both the royal figure who leads the state and the polluted figure who needs to be expelled ritually to preserve the integrity of the state. Both are liminal figures, and Vernant argues that the play traces in Oedipus' fall a transformation from exalted ruler, almost like a god, to the polluted pariah who needs expulsion. 'The union in one man of these two figures, one the inversion of the other, constitutes [Oedipus] as a riddle, an enigma that oscillates between the furthest poles of human possibility.'[37] So strongly does Vernant feel this sense of the play's structural articulation that he can write: 'at the end of the tragedy, Oedipus is hounded from Thebes just as the *homo piacularis* is expelled to remove the defilement.'[38] As Pierro Pucci drolly notes: 'It might seem narrow-minded and literal to object that in this play Oedipus is not expelled, and does not even leave Thebes or his palace.'[39]

Yet Vernant is exemplary of the way many modern readers have struggled to negotiate this violent change of expectation at the end of the play. With the shocking wildness that only the most austere textual scholarship can countenance, Roger Dawe proposes that the whole last scene should be deleted as an interpolation.[40] Taplin follows his friend and teacher Colin Macleod in suggesting that the Sophoclean ending brings us 'something far more realistic, down-to-earth and painful' than 'the grand suicidal gesture'—a continuation of

---

[36] Vernant and Vidal Naquet (1972: 101–31; 1981: 87–119). See also Girard (1977); Gellie (1986); Pucci (1992).

[37] Burian (2009: 104).   [38] Vernant and Vidal-Naquet (1972: 117; 1981: 100).

[39] Pucci (1992: 171).

[40] Dawe (2006). See also Dawe (2001). He was preceded by Mueller (1996). Finglass (2009) points out that his own cogent refutation might not even be necessary, as no scholar has agreed with Dawe.

humiliation and guilt in his own home.[41] Here is the second great question provoked by the ending. What is to be made of Oedipus' demands and Creon's refusal? What does it tell us of the *Sittlichkeit* of the hero? So, by way of contrast with Taplin and Macleod, Bernard Knox sees the ending of the play producing a 'renewed insistence on the heroic nature' of Oedipus, a continuing strength and determination of purpose.[42] For Helene Foley, however, the end of the play contrasts the 'the leadership of Oedipus, who is still trying to exercise his old mastery in a characteristic way, and the new leadership of Creon'.[43] And there are many other nuances of interpretation that focus on the place of *kratos* ('power', 'authority') at the close of the drama. Modern readings of the *Oedipus Tyrannus* are compelled to face the play's ending as a dramatic, structural surprise, which opens a series of difficult semantic issues about the hero's figuration—the ends of Oedipus.

It is striking, then, that in his retelling of the Oedipus story Schelling moves from the discovery of the familial horror of incest and parricide, to exile, to the 'internal reconciliation' of the hero's transfiguration at Colonus. The ending of the *Oedipus Tyrannus*, with its refusal of exile and its subsequent questioning of the *Sittlichkeit* of the hero, is simply and significantly silenced. Yet, even with the *Oedipus Coloneus*, a play that seems so clearly to thematize ending— Sophocles' last play, the death and transfiguration of Oedipus, Oedipus' retrospective accounting of his own life—the drama's closure is drastically under-read by Schelling. Oedipus curses his own sons to mutual slaughter, and at the end of *Oedipus Coloneus* Antigone declares she will return to Thebes to attempt to block the enacting of this curse. As she exits on the opposite *parodos* from Theseus and the others, who are returning to Athens, her solitary, doomed departure invests the final scene with a presentiment of the violent tragedy of family violence to come. It is only by ignoring this ending that Schelling can maintain his view of the 'high morality and absolute purity of the Sophoclean works',[44] dependent as it is on the soul's harmonious integrity and lack of division: 'The effect on the soul is to cleanse it from passion instead of arousing it, and to round it off and make it inwardly whole rather than wresting it out and dividing it.'[45]

---

[41] Taplin (1978: 46).   [42] Knox (1957: 194).   [43] Foley (1993: 536).
[44] Schelling (1989: 262).   [45] Schelling (1989: 262).

The calm lack of division that Schelling finds in Sophocles depends on him not facing the ending of either tragedy.

Hegel takes his start from his friend Schelling's work, and expands and deepens his argument.[46] Yet his understanding of Sophocles is equally dependent on an extraordinary comprehension of the ends of Oedipus. There can be no doubting the importance of Oedipus to Hegel's account of the subject's emergence into ethical consciousness, that prime moment in the history of philosophy and the philosophy of history. Central to Hegel's account of how 'ethical consciousness must acknowledge its opposite as its own actuality; it must acknowledge its guilt'[47] is the revelation of how 'actual reality . . . keeps concealed within itself this other aspect alien to clear knowledge, and does not show itself to consciousness as it truly and fully is [*an und für sich*]'. This process is exemplified by Oedipus, whose story is glossed with this remarkable passage:

> In this way, a hidden power shunning the light of day, waylays the ethical self-consciousness, a power which bursts forth only after the deed is done, and seizes the doer in the act. For the completed deed is the removal of the opposition between the knowing self and the reality over against it. The ethical consciousness cannot disclaim the crime and its guilt. The deed consists in setting in motion what was unmoved, and in bringing out what in the first instance lay shut up as a mere possibility, and thereby linking on the unconscious to the conscious, the non-existent to the existent. In this truth, therefore, the deed comes to light:—it is something in which a conscious element is bound up with what is unconscious, what is peculiarly one's own with what is alien and external:—it is an essential reality divided in sunder, whose other aspect consciousness experiences and finds to be its own aspect, but as a power violated by its doing, and roused to hostility against it.[48]

Through this revelatory waylaying of the ethical self-consciousness Oedipus becomes the figure for philosophy—a figure where a dynamic process of division, hostility, and violation seem to stand against Schelling's too easy proclamation of a lack of 'wresting . . . and

---

[46] As Billings (2013b, 2014) points out, the relationship with Hölderlin is also highly significant. See also Pippin (1988), Schulte (1992), and the general background in Beiser (2002); Pinkard (2002).

[47] Hegel (1967: 491).

[48] Hegel (1967: 490). 'All the parallels between Freud and Hegel come to a head in this passage' (Rudnytsky 1987: 162).

dividing'. Yet Hegel's description of Oedipus' ending, written some twenty-five years later, in particular both picks up Schelling's readings and reveals even more tellingly an underlying religious agenda (although it is sometimes asserted that Hegel's commitments to a religious agenda weakened over the years). Here is the crucial passage of Hegel's argument, which warrants extensive quotation and analysis:

> More beautiful finally than this more external way of conclusion is the inner reconciliation, which because of its subjectivity already borders on the modern. We have the most perfect ancient example of this before us in the eternally marvellous *Oedipus at Colonus*. He has unknowingly killed his father, mounted the throne of Thebes and the bed of his own mother; these unconscious crimes do not make him unhappy. But the old riddle-solver forces the knowledge of his own dark fate out and acquires the terrible consciousness that he has become this in himself. With this solving of the riddle of himself he has, like Adam when he came to consciousness of good and evil, lost his happiness. Now he, the seer, makes himself blind, now he expels himself from the throne and departs from Thebes, as Adam and Eve were driven from paradise, and wanders away, a helpless old man. But he, sorely afflicted, who in Colonus instead of obeying his son's desire that he return, invoked on him his own Furies, expunges all division in himself and purifies himself in himself, a god calls him to him; his blind eye becomes transfigured and clear, his bones become a saviour and safety for the city which received him freely as a guest. This transfiguration in death is his own and our reconciliation appearing in his individuality and personality itself.[49]

Like Schelling, Hegel finds 'inner reconciliation' more aesthetically and ethically satisfying than external forms of closure—it 'borders on the modern', which here, as often in German Idealist thought, is a positive sign of a linkage between the antique past and the possibilities of the future. The perfect example of this nearly modern form of ending is antiquity's *Oedipus Coloneus*. The mention of the play cues Hegel's retelling of the Oedipus story. The *Oedipus Tyrannus* is seen as the 'old riddle-solver . . . solving the riddle of himself'—a 'terrible consciousness' of his own act. This is immediately likened to Adam in the Old Testament (and, as we will see, it is precisely the 'Old Testament' rather than the 'Hebrew Bible' that matters here). So, he continues, Oedipus 'expels himself from the throne and departs from

---

[49] Hegel (1975a: ii. 1219).

Thebes, as Adam and Eve were driven from paradise'. Once again, we can notice that the actual end of the *Oedipus Tyrannus* is silenced and becomes self-expulsion and departure—a quite different sense of agency from Sophocles' play. Yet the analogy between Adam and Oedipus is far from straightforward. In Hegel's own terms, Oedipus is asserting his own agency, while Adam are Eve are driven out. Adam and Eve have disobeyed God, wilfully; Oedipus has unwittingly transgressed, and fulfilled what a God has predicted for him. Oedipus knows that parricide and incest are wrong and seeks to avoid the crime; Adam and Eve gain knowledge of good and evil only after transgressing. The shakiness of the analogy should alert us to the ideologically charged work it is doing in the argument. For the expulsion leads to a remarkable description of Oedipus' end. As in Schelling, Oedipus is transfigured, and, as in Schelling, this end is described as an internal reconciliation. What is more, and despite Hegel's description of the divisions of ethical self-consciousness, Oedipus 'expunges all division in himself', a sort of self-purification and achievement of clarity, as God calls to him. This is a triumph of his 'individuality and personality itself'. Like a saint, his bones become a saviour. Indeed, 'this transfiguration in death' is described as '*his own and our* reconciliation' (emphasis added). Oedipus' final death is a reconciliation for us as much as for him. Oedipus dies for us. The analogy with Adam now makes more sense. In Christian theology, Adam is a figure for Jesus, who died for us. As Hegel himself says about Adam in Genesis, he 'is to be understood as representing the second Adam, namely, Christ'.[50] Called by God—and the God of Oedipus is always singular, as if within a monotheistic world— Oedipus allows each of us to reach a transcendent, integrated self-purification.

Now, Hegel is also fully aware that Oedipus cannot be simply Christianized: 'Attempts have been made to find a Christian tone here: the vision of a sinner whom God pardons and a fate endured in life but compensated with bliss in death.'[51] He immediately moves into what is a standard opposition for him: on the one hand, the Christian dispensation means 'religious reconciliation is a transfiguration of the soul, which bathed in the spring of eternal salvation, is lifted above its deeds and existence in the real world...and now

---

[50] Hegel (1944: 103). On Hegel's Christology, see Shanks (1991).
[51] Hegel (1975a: ii. 1219).

holds itself secure against those imputations [of earthly guilt] in the certainty of its own eternal and purely spiritual bliss';[52] on the other hand, 'the transfiguration of Oedipus always still remains the Greek transfer of consciousness from the strife of ethical powers, and the violations involved, into the unity and harmony of the entire ethical order itself'.[53] Hegel's thinking is, of course, deeply rooted in a teleological movement towards the Christian and, specifically, Protestant dispensation. Yet, in this thinking, the Greek ethical past is a crucial grounding, and here the simile 'like Adam', which cues the second Adam, works to close the gap between the Greek past and the Christian present, between Oedipus' and our reconciliation.

It is clear why there can be no place in Hegel's account for the curse of Oedipus to find dramatic embodiment in the doom-laden exit of Antigone, nor for Creon's refusal of exile to Oedipus at the end of the *Oedipus Tyrannus*. As Oedipus' defeat of the Sphinx can be seen as a symbol or myth of the triumph of the West over the East as the rise of civilization[54]—as Bachofen writes startlingly, 'Oedipus marks the advance to a higher stage of existence'[55]—so Oedipus here becomes a figure not just of philosophy but of the supersessionist potential of Christian transfiguration.

We can draw three significant conclusions from this brief discussion. First, German Idealist arguments about Oedipus set an agenda for later criticism with their fascination with the question of ending and how tragedy is integrally and inherently a question of how to end. It is a remarkable factor in the history of criticism that, from the 1820s onwards, not only is German Idealism the dominant critical framework for approaching tragedy, but also criticism progresses as if there were no history *before* German Idealism. The history of tragic criticism would certainly want to start for us even before Plato, and would certainly want to recognize the importance of the Renaissance,

---

[52] Hegel (1975a: ii. 1219).   [53] Hegel (1975a: ii. 1219–20).

[54] 'Wonderfully, then, must the Greek legend surprise us, which relates that the Sphinx—the great Egyptian symbol—appeared in Thebes, uttering the words: "What is that which in the morning goes on four legs, at midday, on two, and in the evening on three?". Oedipus, giving the solution, *Man*, precipitated the Sphinx from the rock' (Hegel 1975a: ii. 1214); see also Rudnytsky (1987: 220), and, more generally, Leonard (2012: 177–216). Hegel writes in terms to delight the psychoanalysts that the Sphinx 'is at it were the symbol of the symbolic' (Hegel 1975a: ii. 1214).

[55] Bachofen (1967: 181).

when opera starts as a form of tragic revivalism, and the eighteenth century, when forms of neo-classicism in opera and theatre are crucial and much debated as theoretical enterprises as much as practices. Yet, this more recent history finds few layerings or traces in the nineteenth-century criticism, especially in the more popular handbooks, where Schlegel is so often the touchstone. For the remainder of the nineteenth century and much of the twentieth it is as if the French and Italian writers of these earlier periods had nothing to say. German Idealism is a form of conscious forgetting or silencing as well as the development of a new theoretical apparatus. So, the 'happy ending' of Gluck's tragic operas, for example, in the eighteenth century can be a subject of focused contemporary discussion in theoretical and practical terms, in a way quite closed to the nineteenth century's sense of true tragedy.[56] Rather, for the nineteenth and indeed most of the twentieth centuries, ending is conceived according to a German Idealist agenda, as a search for internal reconciliation and external formal closure, where happiness, say, is replaced by an ideal of transcendent suffering, and where the future vistas and open questions of Sophoclean dramaturgy are fully repressed. It is a strange irony that Vernant, who did so much to re-evaluate the influence of German Idealism, not least in his seminal article on the will in tragedy, should echo their reading of the end of *Oedipus Tyrannus* in his declaration that the play sends Oedipus into exile. It might even be said that Vernant's fertile privileging of tension and ambiguity rather than escaping the terms of German Idealism's sense of closure merely inverts it.

Second, the German Idealist discourse demotes the importance of the so-called external ending—that is, the formal, aesthetic, narrative sense of a dramatic ending—in favour of an internal reconciliation, both for the figure of the hero and for the spectators. This internal reconciliation depends on at least three interlinked elements: first, a focus on the individual as the privileged site of tragedy, a crucial plank of Idealist critical thinking on tragedy, which has deep and continuing implications for how politics and the collective are to be conceived within tragedy; second, a specific modern psychology of internal division and harmonization, understood as modern, and deeply implicated with notions of alienation, ethical self-consciousness,

---

[56] See Goldhill (2011: 87–124).

and the necessity of human suffering;[57] and, third, and perhaps most importantly, a willingness to see the process of reconciliation as led by religion, framed by religion. This speaks directly to Schelling's and Hegel's investment in a specifically Christian teleology.[58] Schelling, paradigmatically, argues that Caldéron is greater than Shakespeare, because, unlike in Shakespeare, 'the primary feature and the foundation of the entire edifice of his art Caldéron has, of course, received from the Catholic religion, whose view of the universe and of the divine order of things requires that there be *sin* and sinners', and thus, because of the 'general necessity of sin', the 'entire element of fate develops out of a kind of divine providence'.[59] Therefore, 'these are absolute relationships, it is the absolute world itself', a 'more genuine element of fate', and thus his tragedy is 'more pure'—'comparable only with Sophocles'[60]: the inevitable forced linkage between Sophocles' tragedies and Caldéron's commitment to the Catholic Church is telling. Unlike Steiner's questioning of whether tragedy can be Christian, for Schelling the most pure tragedy is informed by a Christian and Catholic teleology. German Idealism is located fully within nineteenth-century theological concerns. Yet it is striking that so much current scholarship that engages with Hegel's Antigone or the suffering self in tragedy ignores any self-implication with this Christian teleology and its German Idealist construction.

My third conclusion is that, in order to reach this sense of reconciliation and internal transformation, it is essential for Schelling and Hegel to add the *Oedipus Coloneus* to the *Oedipus Tyrannus*, as if there were one unbroken story of Oedipus. As Joshua Billings has noted, the importance of the *Oedipus Coloneus* to German Idealism has all too often been unrecognized in the fascination with Oedipus the riddle-solver as a figure for philosophy.[61] What is more, this melding of the two plays requires that the endings of both plays are systematically misrepresented. That is, the lack of exile, the lack of control of Oedipus, and the lack of psychological transformation or harmony at the end of the *Oedipus Tyrannus* have to be recuperated

---

[57] For a seminal discussion of nineteenth-century psychology, see Shuttleworth (1996); with Taylor and Shuttleworth (1998).

[58] See Shanks (1991, 2011); Krell (2005); Hodgson (2012), each with further bibliography.

[59] Schelling (1989: 273).　　　[60] Schelling (1989: 275, 274, 276).

[61] Billings (2013c).

in a reading of the end of the *Oedipus Coloneus*, which in turn forgets about Antigone's miserable anticipation of continuing disaster, with which the play actually ends—her return to Thebes, which may parallel Oedipus' return into the polluted house at the end of the *Oedipus Tyrannus*. The Idealist sense of an ending depends on a radical redrafting of the endings of Sophocles' dramas.

Modern criticism of tragedy is still necessarily embroiled with the gravitational pull of Hegel and German Idealism. It is not merely that Vernant's influential turn away from models of reconciliation seems to reverse the terms of Hegel's and Schelling's agenda rather than rethink them, but rather that the most engaged political readings of tragedy continue explicitly to read with a set of questions formed within German Idealism. So, there is a flourishing feminist debate, led by Judith Butler and Bonnie Honig, focused on the *Antigone*, which is explicit in its return to Hegel for its starting point, in the hope of rethinking family relations and the modern state.[62] Similarly, the Marxian analysis of Szondi or Eagleton, with the fascination for the ideas and ideals of community explored in tragedy and its criticism, follow not just the political inheritance of German Idealism but also the theatrical tradition formed in response to it.[63] So, too, critics seeking for a philosophical reading of tragedy—Martha Nussbaum, say, or Bernard Williams—also buttress their work with references to the masters of German Idealism.[64] Yet the full weight of the specific Idealist construction of a sense of an ending within a Christian teleology has not been adequately appreciated even within these debates (let alone with the less self-conscious inheritance of Idealist categories in contemporary literary criticism). It is testimony to the power and influence of the Idealist agenda for tragedy that their model of the transcendent suffering of the heroic individual remains so pervasive a critical horizon of expectation, especially in the case of critics who would vigorously reject a Christian teleology as an intellectual agenda for criticism of Greek tragedy. Is it possible to work with the Idealist notion of the suffering yet transcendent subject without complicity with its teleological models? Is this model of the

---

[62] See Butler (2000); Honig (2013); both with extensive bibliography. See also in particular Chanter (1995); Mills (1996a); Benhabib (1996); and, more generally on the issue of agency and tragedy in Hegel, Speight (2001). I have had my go at this issue in Goldhill (2012: 231–48).

[63] Szondi (2002); Eagleton (2003).   [64] Nussbaum (1986); Williams (1993).

heroic individual not to be seen as a worrying model for contemporary analysis? Perhaps the most pressing task for the criticism of tragedy is to explore a model of tragedy that can not merely articulate the genealogy of modernism in German Idealist thought, but also traverse its insistent inheritance.

12

The Tragedy of Misrecognition: The Desire
for a Catholic Shakespeare
and Hegel's *Hamlet*

Simon Critchley

One version of the post-Kantian settlement in philosophy is that the critical dismantling of the claims of dogmatic metaphysics in the *Critique of Pure Reason* has the consequence that questions concerning the ultimate value of human life pass from the domain of religion to that of art. Kant's critique of metaphysics achieves the remarkable feat of showing both the cognitive meaninglessness of the claims of traditional philosophy to know the supersensible, while establishing the *moral* necessity for the primacy of practical reason—that is, freedom. Yet, the question that this raises is how can freedom take hold or manifest itself in the world of nature, if that world is governed by causality and mechanistically determined by scientifically established natural laws? Does not Kant leave human beings in what Hegel would call the *amphibious* position of being both freely subject to the moral law and determined by an objective world of nature that has been stripped of any value and that stands over against me as a world of alienation?

The philosophical task after Kant was how to achieve a reconciliation of the dualisms of nature and freedom or pure and practical reason. The view that is adumbrated in Kant's account of aesthetic judgement, and announced with increasing conviction in Schiller's *Letters on the Aesthetic Education of Man* and incipient romantic and idealist trends in the Germanophone 1790s, is that the artwork is the vehicle for such reconciliation. The artwork provides *a sensuous image of freedom* and brings into harmony the domains of pure and practical reason. In the breathtaking 1796 single folio fragment 'The Oldest System-Programme of German Idealism', the authors (the text is variously attributed to the erstwhile college chums Hegel, Hölderlin, and Schelling, although it usually thought to represent best the ideas of the latter, who was in his early 20s at the time) write: 'The highest act of reason, which embraces all ideas, is an aesthetic act, and that *truth and goodness* are brothers *only in beauty.*'[1] As Schelling declares in 1800, 'art is the organon of philosophy' or 'the keystone in the entire arch'[2] that will span the regions of nature and freedom that Kant had divorced.

But what is meant by 'art' here? For Schelling, the highest exemplar of art is drama and the highest manifestation of drama is *tragedy*, in particular Sophoclean tragedy. As Peter Szondi has convincingly shown, what begins with Schelling is a philosophy of *the tragic* (*das Tragische*), which has an almost uncanny persistence in the Germanophone intellectual tradition. In his 1802–3 lectures, *Philosophy of Art*, Schelling writes, and the Kantian echoes in this formulation resound:

> The essence of *tragedy* is thus an actual and objective conflict between freedom in the subject on the one hand and necessity on the other, a conflict that does not end such that one or the other succumbs, but rather such that both are manifested in perfect indifference as simultaneously victorious and vanquished.[3]

For Schelling, it was precisely this sort of equilibrium between freedom and necessity that the Greeks—by which he means Sophocles' *Oedipus the King*, where this play weirdly but not untypically figures as a synecdoche for an entire culture—achieved in tragedy.

> The Greeks sought in their tragedies *this* kind of equilibrium between justice and humanity, necessity and freedom, a balance without which they could not satisfy their moral sensibility, just as the highest morality itself is expressed in this balance. Precisely this equilibrium is the ultimate concern of tragedy. It is not tragic that a premeditated, free transgression is punished. That a guiltless person unavoidably becomes increasingly guilty through fate itself, as remarked earlier, is the greatest conceivable misfortune. But that this guiltless guilty person [*dieser*

---

[1] Hegel (1970: i. 235).   [2] Schelling (1978: 231).
[3] Schelling (1989: 251).

schuldloser Schuldige] accepts punishment voluntarily—this is the *sub-limity* of tragedy [*das* **Erhabene** *in der Tragödie*]; thereby alone does freedom transfigure itself into the highest identity with necessity.[4]

Tragedy is the keystone in the arch that unites freedom and necessity, practical reason and pure reason. In other words, the tragic is the completion of philosophy after Kant. And it is philosophy's completion in a *sublime* act. Namely, that Schelling's claim is that what the Greeks sought in their tragedies was an equilibrium between 'justice and humanity, freedom and necessity', and this equilibrium is what finds expression in tragedy. The sublimity of tragedy is the free acceptance of punishment by this guiltless guilty one.

If art is the completion of philosophy and tragedy is the pinnacle of art, as the identity of freedom and necessity, and if this was somehow the case for the tragic Greeks, then the vast question that this raises, and that Schelling spends the remaining pages of *The Philosophy of Art* groping towards, is to what extent tragedy is realizable in modernity. The problem here can be framed by Schelling's assertion that 'modernity lacks fate'—namely, that it has no sense of the movement of necessity as that against which the activity of the free subject collides.[5] Otherwise said, modernity is the experience of contingency. Ancient tragedy is defined by an experience of fate that imposes an error, or what Aristotle called *hamartia*, in the subject. This is not possible in the modern world. Schelling writes that 'the element of character takes the place formerly occupied by fate'.

1. WE NEED A SOPHOCLES OF THE DIFFERENTIATED WORLD

This is where we can turn to Shakespeare and *Hamlet*. Schelling compares English commentators on Shakespeare to a bunch of drunken farmers quarrelling in front of a country pub wholly ignorant of the beautiful theatrical landscape that surrounds them. In other words, Shakespeare requires a more sober and systematic Germanic interpretation. This is the key to Schelling's interpretation of Shakespeare, and I quote at length:

---

[4] Schelling (1989: 255).   [5] Schelling (1989: 257).

If we now summarize our findings and express succinctly Shakespeare's relationship to the sublimity of the tragedy of antiquity, we must call him the greatest creator of *character*. He cannot portray that sublime, purified and transfigured beauty that proves itself in the face of fate, a beauty that coincides with moral goodness...He *knows* that highest beauty only as individual character. He was not able to subordinate everything to it, because as a modern—as one who comprehends the eternal not within limitation, but rather within boundlessness—he is too widely involved in universality. Antiquity possessed a concentrated universality, and viewed allness [*die Allheit*] not in multiplicity but rather in unity.

There is *nothing* human that Shakespeare did not touch upon; yet he touches it only individually, whereas antiquity touched it in totality. The elements of human nature from the lowest to the highest lie dispersed within him. He knows it *all*, every passion, every disposition, youth as well as age, the king and the shepherd. If our world were ever lost, one could recreate it from the series of his works. Whereas that ancient lyre enticed the whole world with *four* strings, the new instrument has a thousand strings; it splits the harmony of the universe in order to create it, and for that reason it is always less calming for the soul. That austere, all-soothing beauty can exist only in simplicity.[6]

If Shakespeare's genius lies in his creation of character, then the freedom of character plays itself out in a world without fate, a world where the four-stringed ancient lyre has been replaced with a thousand-stringed beast. That is to say, with the emergence of the differentiated world of modernity, what disappears is the possibility of tragic sublimity. Schelling's seemingly hopeful question—the question with which *The Philosophy of Art* ends, or, rather, fades out—is whether there can be a modern Sophocles. Or, as he puts it: 'We must, however, be allowed to hope for a Sophocles of the differentiated world...'.[7] As the long quotation makes clear, despite his genius, this new Sophocles *cannot* be Shakespeare. He was, in the final analysis, too *Protestant* to allow for this possibility. Schelling writes: 'Shakespeare was a Protestant, and for him this [i.e. the *Fatum* of antiquity] was not a possibility.'[8]

What, or rather who, is required in order to recover the sublimity of ancient tragedy is a 'southern, perhaps Catholic, Shakespeare'.[9]

---

[6] Schelling (1989: 270–1).   [7] Schelling (1989: 273).
[8] Schelling (1989: 269).   [9] Schelling (1989: 273).

That is to say, someone who can allow for the public, institutional reconciliation between the fact of error or, in Christianity, *sin*, and the possibility of redemptive grace. This leads Schelling to a closing, and rather desperate, reading of Calderón, where Schelling discusses just one play by the Spanish dramatist, read in A. W. Schlegel's German translation. Regardless of the undoubted virtues of Calderón, what interests us here is the desperation on Schelling's part to discover a Catholic Shakespeare, a Sophocles of modernity. I think it is the same desperation that leads the young Nietzsche initially towards the possibility of a rebirth of tragedy through the music or more properly the opera of Wagner, and which leads the later Nietzsche in his last writings on music towards Bizet's *Carmen*. In *The Case of Wagner*, a very late text, after seeing *Carmen* for the twentieth time, Nietzsche writes:

> So patient do I become, so happy, so Indian, so settled—To sit five hours: the first stage of holiness.[10]

And again:

> This music is cheerful, but not in a French or German way. Its cheerfulness is African; fate hangs over it ... *il faut méditerraniser la musique*.[11]

So deep is the Wagnerian sickness in Nietzsche that he will accept anything—Mediterranean, Indian, African—that might allow him to recover his health. Sadly, it did not work.

Schelling's *Philosophy of Art* concludes with a quasi-Nietzschean pathos of mourning at the passing of great art in modernity. The final words of the lectures read like a premonition of the later arguments of *The Birth of Tragedy*:

> I will remark only that the most perfect composition of all the arts, the unification of poesy [*Poesie*] and music through song, of poesy and painting through dance, both in turn synthesized together, is the most complex theater manifestation, such as was the drama of antiquity. Only a caricature has remained for us: the *opera*, which, in a higher and nobler style both from the side of poesy as well as from that of the other competing arts, might sooner guide us back to the performance that ancient drama combined with music and song.

---

[10] Nietzsche (1967: 157).   [11] Nietzsche (1967: 158–9).

Music, song and dance, as well as all the various types of drama, live only in public life [*öffentlichen Leben*], and form an alliance in such life. Wherever public life disappears, instead of that real, external drama in which, in all its forms, an entire people participates as a political and moral totality, only an *inward*, ideal drama can unite the people. This ideal drama is the worship service [*Gottesdienst*], the only kind of *truly* public action that has remained for the contemporary age, and even so only in an extremely diminished and reduced form.[12]

With the disappearance of public life in modernity—what Hegel would call *Sittlichkeit*, ethical life—the possibility of tragic sublimity, understood as a genuinely political artwork—that is, an artwork that legislates for the community, has evaporated. We are left with a caricature of ancient tragedy in the form of the opera, on the one hand, and the empty, idealized ritual of the church service, on the other hand. Modern art, on this view, is nothing else but the expression of the absence of the public realm. It is with this nostalgic northern longing for a southern Catholicism that Schelling's *Philosophy of Art* ends.

2. UNBEARABLE CONTINGENCY: HEGEL'S *HAMLET*

It is here, as an antidote to the desire for a Catholic Shakespeare, that I would like to turn to Hegel. For us, Hegel is *the* philosopher of the tragic. He is the philosopher with the deepest understanding of the nature of tragedy: its internal movement, contradictions, and collisions, indeed what we might call the *collisional* character of tragedy. If that manner of conceiving experience that Hegel calls 'dialectics' can be understood as thinking in movement, then it is arguable that dialectics has its genesis in tragedy, or at least in a certain understanding of tragedy. Although it might be said that Schelling also sees tragedy dialectically in terms of the collision between freedom and necessity, the vital difference between them turns on the question of *history*. Schelling, like so many literary critics that follow him, offers a philosophical idealization of tragedy that lacks a historical understanding of art's unfolding. As Benjamin notes, what he calls 'the

[12] Nietzsche (1967: 280).

philosophy of tragedy' is 'a theory of the moral order of the world, without any reference to historical content, in a system of generalized sentiments'.[13] What is misguided in the multiple iterations of 'the philosophy of tragedy' from Romanticism onwards is its universalistic a-historicism usually based on a series of metaphysical assumptions about a purported human nature.[14]

For Hegel, and this is already clear from his reading of the *Antigone* in *The Phenomenology of Spirit* onwards, tragedy is the aesthetic articulation of the historical disintegration of ethical life or *Sittlichkeit* through the strife of civil war and the life and death struggle between the essential elements of the political life of the city state. In tragedy, the substance of ethical life divides against itself, dissolving in war and splitting into a multitude of separate individual atoms. This passes over into the impotent Stoicism of the solitary self in a world defined by law—that is, Rome—and the experience of modern self-alienation that Hegel associates with the word *Kultur*. History must form an essential part of any account of tragedy. This is where we can shed some light on the Danish gloom of *Hamlet*.

Moving (not unproblematically, it must be acknowledged) from the early Hegel of the *Phenomenology* to the late Hegel of the *Aesthetics*—and indeed the 1,237 pages of the *Aesthetics* conclude and culminate with a stunning interpretation of *Hamlet*—in modern tragedy individuals do not act for the sake of the substance of ethical life. What presses for satisfaction, rather, is the subjectivity of their private character. In ancient tragedy, the conflict at the heart of the substance of ethical life finds expression in opposed but equally justified characters, each of whom embodies a clear 'pathos': Antigone *versus* Creon, or Orestes *versus* Clytaemnestra. However, if conflict in ancient tragedy finds articulation in the externality of substance, then in modern tragedy the conflict is internal to subjectivity.

Hegel and Schelling seem initially very similar on this point. Hegel asserts that in the portrayal of individual characters Shakespeare stands 'at an almost unapproachable height', making his creations 'free artists of their own selves'.[15] As such, Shakespeare's tragic characters are 'real, directly living, extremely varied' and possessing a 'sublimity and striking power of expression'.[16] Yet—and here comes

---

[13] W. Benjamin (1998: 101).   [14] See R. Williams (1979).
[15] Hegel (1975a: 1217–28).   [16] Hegel (1975a: 1228).

the dialectical underside of this claim—creatures like Hamlet lack any resolution and capacity for decision. They are dithering figures in the grip of 'a twofold passion which drives them from one decision or one deed to another simultaneously'.[17] In other words, thinking of Carl Schmitt, they are Hamletized, vacillating characters inwardly divided against themselves. Upheld only by the force of their conflicted subjectivity, characters such as Hamlet or Lear either plunge blindly onwards or allow themselves to be lured to their avenging deed by external circumstances, led along, that is, by contingency.

In the vast sweep of an ancient dramatic trilogy, like the *Oresteia*, what is at stake in the *agon* or dramatic conflict is eternal justice shaped by the power of fate, which saves the substance of the ethical life of the city against individuals, such as Orestes and Clytaemnestra, who were becoming too independent and colliding violently with each other. Hegel insists, and I think he is right, that if a similar justice appears in modern tragedy, then it is more like *criminal* justice, where—as with Macbeth or with Lear's daughters—a wrong has been committed and the protagonists deserve the nasty demise that is coming to them. Tragic denouement in Shakespearian tragedy is not the rigorous working-out of fate, but 'purely the effect of unfortunate circumstances and external accidents which might have turned out otherwise and produced a happy ending'.[18] Hegel enjoyed a happy ending, as we will see presently, but the point is that the modern individual must endure the contingency and fragility of 'all that is mundane and must endure the fate of finitude'.

Yet—and this is where Hegel's remarks on *Hamlet* begin to cut much deeper—the problem is that we cannot *bear* this contingency. Hegel argues: 'We feel a pressing demand for a necessary correspondence between the external circumstances and what the inner nature of those fine characters really is.'[19] Thus, we want Hamlet's death not simply to be the effect of chance, owing to the accidental switch of poisoned rapiers. *The Tragicall Historie of Hamlet, Prince of Denmarke* affects its audience profoundly, and it seems that there is a deep need—at once aesthetic and moral—for something greater than mere accident. It is as if there is something unbearable about the contingency of life that finds articulation in *Hamlet* and elsewhere in Shakespeare. This is what leads, I think, to the longing for a Catholic

---

[17] Hegel (1975a:1228).   [18] Hegel (1975a: 1231).
[19] Hegel (1975a: 1231).

Shakespeare in Schelling, to Benjamin's claim that *Hamlet* is a Christian tragedy of Providence or indeed the nostalgic memory of that Christian longing in Schmitt. It is the yearning for a redemptive artwork that would both reveal our modern, alienated condition and heal it. It is a nostalgic yearning for reconciliation between the individual and the cosmic order that one finds all over Shakespeare criticism.

Such nostalgia is indeed one way of interpreting the character of Hamlet, bound by a longing that is his very paralysis. From his warped idealization of his father as a lost hyperion who offers one assurance of a man, to his dream of a perfected act that does not overstep the modesty of nature and strikes at the exactly right time, to his overblown rage centred on the thought of multifarious villains—'O villain, villain, smiling, damned villain!' 'That one may smile, and smile, and be a villain'[20]—Hamlet might be seen as a conservative rebellion against the contingency and atomized *anomie* of the new social order. And, not to belabour the Freudian points, his chief complaints centre on the figures of his Oedipal triangle—himself, his mother, and Claudius—with the dead father propped up as all that is right in a world gone to hell. Perhaps it is this yearning for a Catholic Shakespeare that must be given up in order to see *Hamlet* aright and see ourselves in its light. Perhaps we will have to dispense with the Ghost's Purgatorial prayer for an unadulterated life, for Catholic absolution, for an absolute. In a deep sense, *Hamlet* is a tragi-comic melodrama, at times a farce.

3. HEGEL LIKES A HAPPY ENDING

Hegel does not put it as strongly as this, and, in any case, he has a dialectical trump card up his sleeve: tragedy is overcome by comedy and both are overcome by philosophy. The failure of aesthetic reconciliation leads to the requirement for philosophical reconciliation. From a Hegelian perspective, Schelling is wrong because his philosophical idealization of tragedy lacks a historical understanding of

---

[20] I.v.109. *Hamlet* citations refer to the text in *The Oxford Shakespeare*.

art's unfolding. For Schelling, the structure of art in its highest expression—that is, drama—is deduced from tragedy. The history of art since Greek tragedy is a falling-away from that ideal. For Hegel, by contrast, not without some nostalgia for the loss of Greek ethical life and his deep admiration for Sophocles, comedy supplants tragedy, and comedy is the very element in which art dissolves and prepares the passage for conceptual elaboration—namely, philosophy. Comedy—and one thinks both of Aristophanes, whom Hegel constantly praises, as well as of Shakespeare's comedies and also of Hegel's wonderful reading of Diderot's *Rameau's Nephew* in *The Phenomenology of Spirit*—is the raising of art to the level of cognition where it then dissolves. Hegel's system is a comedy and has to be a comedy, insofar as history culminates with the institutional expression of freedom in the form of the modern state. Funny. This is where we could begin a meta-critique of Hegel, along the lines one can find in the very young Marx.[21] But the aesthetic point is that perhaps Hegel will always have the last laugh, that comedy stands higher than tragedy, and that the true *comédie humaine* is philosophy.

This is why Hegel likes a happy ending. He makes the brilliant remark, which might echo in the ears of contemporary partisans of trauma, loss, and generalized aesthetic miserabilism:

> I must admit that for my part a happy denouement is to be preferred. And why not? To prefer misfortune just because it is misfortune, instead of a happy resolution, has no other basis but a superior sentimentality which indulges in grief and suffering and finds more interest in them than in the painless situations that it regards as commonplace.[22]

The tragedy of suffering, such as we find in Sophocles, is ethically justified only when it serves some higher outlook, such as fate, otherwise it is simply an Eeyore-esque wallowing in misery (which, incidentally, makes Hegel closer to Winnie the Pooh). A happy ending would be better. If art—and Hegel is thinking in particular of Greek statuary—is the unity of the idea and appearance in sensuous ideality, then comedy can present this unity only as self-

---

[21] I am thinking of Marx's 'Critique of Hegel's Doctrine of the State', from 1843, when Marx was in his mid-twenties.
[22] Hegel (1975a: 1232).

destruction. For Hegel, the absolute can no longer be contained within aesthetic form. Comedy is art's dissolution and its passage beyond itself. This is why comedy is the entrance into philosophy.

And, of course, the turn from comedy towards philosophy out from one's being-as-misery-guts is already foreshadowed by Hamlet. After the encounter with the Ghost, Hamlet cautions Horatio: 'There are more things in heaven and earth, Horatio, | Than are dreamt of in your philosophy', and then promptly (and weirdly, one might add) tells him that his plan is to put on an antic disposition.[23] The next time we hear from Hamlet, he is the clownish provocateur in the fishmonger scene with Polonius, followed by the Hamlet of satirical philosophical sparring with Rosencrantz and Guildenstern. The oscillation between tragi-comedy and philosophy, is an imbroglio best summed up by Hamlet himself as he hurtles towards the limits of rationality:

HAMLET.   O God, I could be bounded in a nut shell and count myself a king of infinite space, were it not that I have bad dreams.

GUILDENSTERN.   Which dreams indeed are ambition, for the very substance of the ambitious is merely the shadow of a dream.

HAMLET.   A dream itself is but a shadow.

ROSENCRANTZ.   Truly, and I hold ambition of so airy and light a quality that it is but a shadow's shadow.

HAMLET.   Then are our beggars bodies and our monarchs and outstretched heroes but the beggars' shadows—Shall we to court? For, by my fay, I cannot reason.[24]

Who else other than Hegel could follow Hamlet's reasoning here, where substance dialectically reverses into shadow, infinite space is a bad dream, ambition is a ghost that takes flight in sleep, and a monarch is found only in the shade of a beggar's body. Hamlet's self-consciousness is the Hegelian prowess of the tautological infinity of a nutshell—an identity that is its own undoing. What aesthetic reconciliation can there be? Perhaps this helps explain T. S. Eliot's statement that Hamlet is an artistic failure, along with his scathing critique that the longing for creative power in the mind of a critic has led to a particular weakness where instead of studying a work of art they find only their semblable. Goethe sees Hamlet as Goethe and Coleridge sees Hamlet as Coleridge.

---

[23] I.v.175–6.   [24] II.ii.252–63.

4. HAMLET IS A LOST MAN

What finds expression in Schelling and the shoals of philosophers and literary critics who swim in his wake, beginning with Coleridge, is an *aesthetic absolutism*. This is the conviction that the antinomies of modernity can be reconciled in a dramatic total artwork that would restore the substantiality of ethical life in a tragically sublime act. Having seen the old order dissolve into suspicion, surveillance, and political violence, we get it all back in a new and reconciled form with God in his heaven and a true king on his throne. Against this, what I think Hegel's reading of *Hamlet* adumbrates is that reconciliation in modern tragedy is a fake reconciliation. It shows how the desire for an absolute unravels into an experience of self-dissolution and non-identity. The final scene of *Hamlet*, like the final scene of *King Lear*, is not the triumph of some Christian idea of providence nor is it any rebirth of Attic tragedy. It is simply a stage full of corpses, what Adorno perspicuously sees as a crowd of puppets on a string, and which James Joyce describes, in an eerily prophetic remark: 'The bloodboltered shambles in act five is a forecast of the concentration camp'.[25] In other words, *Hamlet* is a *Trauerspiel* whose force is tragicomic and whose macabre ending verges on the melodramatic. As Melville writes of Hamlet in *Pierre: or, The Ambiguities*, he falls 'dabbling in the vomit of his loathed identity'.[26]

But there is one further and fascinating twist in the tail of Hegel's reading of *Hamlet*. Looked at from the outside, Hamlet's death might seem to have been accidentally caused by the unfortunate switcheroo of swords. But, on two occasions, Hegel advances a brief but perspicuous psychological profile of the Danish prince. What he finds inside Hamlet is morbidity, melancholy, worry, weakness, and, most of all, in a word repeated three times in these passages, *disgust*. Hegel writes:

> But death lay from the beginning in the background of Hamlet's mind. The sands of time do not content him. In his melancholy and weakness, his worry, his disgust at all the affairs of life, we sense from the start that in all his terrible surroundings he is a lost man, almost consumed by inner disgust before death comes to him from outside.[27]

---

[25] Joyce (1986: 154).   [26] Melville (1852: 232).   [27] Hegel (1975a: 1231).

Hamlet is a lost man. He is the wrong man. He should never have been commanded by the Ghost to avenge his murder. His disgust with the world induces not action but *acedia*, a slothful lethargy. Hamlet just lacks the energy. As Hegel writes:

> His noble soul was not made for this kind of energetic activity; and, full of disgust with the world and life what with decision, proof, arrangements for carrying out his resolve, and being bandied from pillar to post, he eventually perishes owing to his own hesitation and a complication of external circumstances.[28]

It is my contention, which will be elaborated, that what is caught sight of by Hegel is a *Hamlet Doctrine* that turns on the corrosive dialectic of knowledge and action, where the former disables the latter and insight into the truth induces a disgust with existence. Rubbernecking the chaos and wreckage of the world that surrounds him while chattering and punning endlessly, he finally finds himself fatally struck and strikes out impetuously, asking Horatio to sing him a lullaby.[29] Do we even *like* Hamlet? Is he a nice guy? I do not think so.

5. HAMLET'S MULTIPLE MISRECOGNITIONS

Let me conclude with some remarks on the tragedy of misrecognition in *Hamlet*. The melancholic Danish prince misrecognizes Polonius for the King when he kills the former thinking it was the latter. He misrecognizes Ophelia for his mother, saying to her all the nasty things he wanted to say to Gertrude: 'Go thy ways to a nunnery', 'God gave you one face and you make yourselves another',[30] and so on. Hamlet calls Ophelia the whore that he suspects his mother to be. Hamlet confuses Gertrude with Claudius and Claudius with Gertrude. In one amazing moment, he even calls Claudius his mother. When the King protests, Hamlet's reasoning is as follows: 'Father and mother is man and wife. Man and wife is one flesh—and so: my mother.'[31]

---

[28] Hegel (1975a: 1226).
[29] Some of these formulations are borrowed from Elizabeth Bryant.
[30] III.i.122, 144.   [31] IV.iii.54.

Hamlet cannot strike out at the one he hates—namely, Claudius—and whom he cannot kill. He can kill only the one he idealizes—namely, Laertes, who is a kind of double for Hamlet. He says of Laertes: 'By the image of my cause I see | The portraiture of his.'[32] Laertes is a mirror that Hamlet holds up to himself and, as we have known since Lacan, all that we experience in the mirror is misrecognition or *méconnaissance*, not ourselves but some imaginary other that fascinates us and holds us in thrall to our self-deception. It is not myself that I see in the mirror, but some sickly, captivating reflection that I am not.

But Hamlet's most fundamental misrecognition is in his relation to his own desire. He cannot recognize his own desire because he always lives through the desire of the other, doing the other's bidding. Even if they share the same name (which was an innovation that, somewhat mysteriously, Shakespeare added to the source texts for the *Hamlet* story), the desire to revenge his father's murder is the Ghost's desire, not his own. Hamlet Senior commands Hamlet Junior. He is also in lockstep with his mother's desire throughout the play. It is not a question of Hamlet's own desire that perplexes and punishes him. It is the enigma of *her* desire. What *does* Gertrude want? *Was will das Weib?*

At either end of the play, when Hamlet suspends his wish to return to Wittenberg (good old protestant Lutherstadt), it is the desire of Claudius. Similarly, the whole conceit that leads up to the final, fatal, foil fight is not Hamlet's plan; it is Claudius's. Hamlet dies wearing his enemy's colours. Hamlet does not live in his own time or at his own hour, but at the time and hour of the other.

Hamlet's desire is deeply inhibited and inhibition turns inward into a narcissistic melancholy that is unable to sustain any love for the living. Hamlet loves only what is dead: his idealized ghostly phallic father; the old court fool whose skull he idly toys with, Yorick; and poor Ophelia. His narcissistic desire is unleashed only in relation to the other qua dead—that is, qua impossibility. It is only when Ophelia is dead that Hamlet can declare his love for her, screaming in the grave in a life and death struggle with his double, Laertes:

> I loved Ophelia. Forty thousand brothers
> Could not, with all their quantity of love,
> Make up my sum.[33]

---

[32] V.ii.78–9.   [33] V.i.259–61.

Hamlet's dazzling linguistic brilliance—his ceaseless punning, antic disposition, and manic ratiocination—flows directly from his narcissistic inhibition of desire. Dostoevsky famously wrote in *The Brothers Karamazov* that hell is the incapacity to love. The Ghost of his father might well spend his days in painful, purgatorial fire, but Hamlet is in hell. This is why Denmark is a prison. This is why the world is a prison.

To make things even worse, Hamlet is a very bad Aristotelian. He undergoes no reversal or *peripeteia*, nor does he experience any recognition or *anagnoreisis*. This is why Hegel is right to insist that Hamlet is a lost man. Furthermore, in my view, *Hamlet*—the play, not the persona—permits no *katharsis*, no release or sublimation or purification of desire (however we understand that fuzzy and hard-to-define Aristotelian concept). Hamlet—the persona and not the play—exhibits a relentless intelligence, a melancholy inwardness that occasionally flips over into manic energy and exuberance. But we feel no release at the end of the play, which, of course, is Shakespeare's longest (Hamlet in its entirety sometimes feels like Hamlet in its eternity). From beginning to end, the sheer violence and percussive power of Shakespeare's language have us rolling around on the floor or biting the carpet. And nor should *Hamlet* permit us any *katharsis*. If *Hamlet* is the quintessentially modern tragedy, this is because it enacts the tragedy of modernity, which also allows us no relief, release, or the satisfaction of desire. *Hamlet* is a wonderful, proto-Beckettian tragi-comedy, a *Trauerspiel* without redemption, a mournful, melancholic, and melodramatic farce.

And so is our world.

13

Margins of Genre: Walter Benjamin and the Idea of Tragedy

Joshua Billings

Walter Benjamin appears only in passing in Peter Szondi's 1961 *Versuch über das Tragische* (*An Essay on the Tragic*). After surveying theories of 'the tragic' from Schelling to Scheler, Szondi turns to Benjamin briefly in his 'Transition' from discussions of philosophy in the first part to analyses of tragedy in the second. Benjamin's liminal position in Szondi's book is appropriate to his place in the larger question of the tragic that has preoccupied German thinkers since around 1800. At first glance, Benjamin might seem to lie outside the tradition altogether. His 1928 *Ursprung des deutschen Trauerspiels* (*Origin of the German Mourning Play*) opposes the hypostasization and moralism of the concept of the tragic adumbrated by German Idealism and its epigones, and seeks to replace a unified, transhistorical understanding of the genre of tragedy with a historically differentiated one.[1] Against attempts to find an essential tragic content operative equally in antiquity and modernity, Benjamin argues that Greek tragedy and modern works called tragedies are fundamentally opposed in their content. Though Benjamin is not the first to struggle with the question of tragedy's generic continuity, he is radical in his rejection of any common ground. He recognizes, according to Szondi, 'that there is no such thing as *the* tragic'.[2]

Benjamin's ostensible subject in the book is the body of German serious drama of the seventeenth century written by figures such as

---

[1] The *Origin* essay is cited with translations modified from W. Benjamin (1998).
[2] Szondi (2002: 49).

Lohenstein, Gryphius, and Opitz. He calls these works *Trauerspiel*, in contrast to the ancient Greek genre *Tragödie*.[3] In defining the early modern genre of *Trauerspiel*, Benjamin consistently opposes the ancient and modern forms, and argues for their irreconcilability. This rejection of the tragic might seem to leave Szondi—and philosophical criticism generally—in aporia. Philosophical discussions of tragedy in the Idealist tradition have regularly posited a conceptual core to Greek tragedy and then sought to mobilize such a concept for concerns of aesthetics, ethics, politics, metaphysics, and historical thought (among others). Doing without such a core would seem to threaten any attempt to make ancient tragedy philosophically purposeful and to render Greek tragedy radically alien to modernity. Limited rigorously to the empirical, interpretation would seem to forgo any aesthetic claims.

Benjamin, though, shifts the terrain of philosophical investigation from the concept of the tragic to the category of genre itself, and seeks to elaborate a way of making historical particularity philosophically meaningful. 'Benjamin does not replace the philosophy of the tragic with poetics,' Szondi writes, 'but rather with the philosophy of the history of tragedy'.[4] Of course, this is not in itself a novel project, but Benjamin finds the most powerful and widespread model for reconciling history and theory, the Hegelian dialectic, inadequate because of its teleological assumptions. Instead of a perspective that attempts to rationalize diachrony, Benjamin seeks in effect to rationalize synchrony—or to elaborate a form synchrony outside of temporality. For Benjamin, there exists a more profound temporality than that experienced in becoming and passing away, and it is in this other realm of history that he locates his theoretical project.

The effort is laid out in famously obscure fashion in the 'Knowledge-Critical Preface' ('Erkenntniskritische Vorrede'), but enacted throughout the discussion of the *Trauerspiel*. Benjamin describes his project as 'historical–philosophical' (*Geschichtsphilosophisch*), a crucial word that marks his proclaimed difference from previous critics of tragedy.[5] It might be understood as characterizing an investigation that brings out the singularity of moments of the past, but in a way that makes them philosophically fruitful beyond their historical

---

[3] Hence the translation in W. Benjamin (1998) of the title as *The Origin of German Tragic Drama* is misleading.
[4] Szondi (2002: 49).   [5] See S. Weber (2008: 143–4).

moment. Later in the book, Benjamin defines the task of philosophical criticism as demonstrating the 'philosophical truth-contents' that lie buried in the 'historical matter-contents' of an artistic form.[6] Benjamin's discussion follows this imperative, in general terms, by seeking out the elements of German *Trauerspiel* that have a meaning beyond their local historical context, and placing them in dialogue with works external to the genre. Juxtaposing these internal and external histories of the genre, Benjamin finds durable truth-contents emerging.

Benjamin's search for the truth-contents of German *Trauerspiel* leads him to consideration of a number of forms and works that lie outside of the strict historical and linguistic boundaries of his study. Most significantly, he discusses Greek tragedy at some length, contrasting it with the *Trauerspiel* in one of the book's two major divisions ('*Trauerspiel* and Tragedy'). Benjamin draws on the dramas of Shakespeare and Calderón, the engravings of Dürer, and the form of the Platonic dialogue, among others, to illustrate significant differences between the baroque and the ancient forms. Much of the image of the *Trauerspiel* is in fact constructed through such contrasts and polarities, and it is surprisingly rare to find generalizing statements about the form (this is a contrast to Benjamin's discussion of tragedy, which proceeds in much more categorical terms). *Trauerspiel* itself can be elusive in the essay, as it is glimpsed so often from its margins and opposites. Yet this interplay between centre and periphery is crucial to Benjamin's effort to find a more authentic form of generic history. The margins of *Trauerspiel* are essential to Benjamin's discussion as the points at which the idea of the genre becomes visible.

1. IDEAS OF TRAGEDY

Benjamin understands genre as a historical rather than a theoretical category in the first instance, and he accordingly rejects the application of concepts gained from Greek tragedy to German *Trauerspiel*. Yet outlining the essence of the ancient form and formulating its relation to the modern is a crucial aspect of his project. An

---

[6] W. Benjamin (1974: 358; 1998: 182).

engagement with Nietzsche establishes the framework for Benjamin's discussion of the continuity between Greek tragedy and German *Trauerspiel*.[7] For Benjamin, Nietzsche's work opened an 'abyss of aestheticism',[8] in its understanding of the Apollonian and Dionysian principles as fundamental and apparently atemporal drives. Nietzsche sees the Greeks as having an originary (and therefore privileged) relation to the tragic—but one that could, in the right circumstances, be revived through the advent of a 'music-making Socrates' (§15).[9] Though Benjamin broadly approves of Nietzsche's differentiation of the ancient tragic spirit and rejection of the moralizing readings of his predecessors, the notion of a possible rebirth of tragedy is antithetical to Benjamin's historical understanding. Nietzsche's dream of a re-creation of Greek tragedy in Wagnerian music drama leads to his 'renunciation of any understanding of the tragic myth in historical–philosophical terms'.[10] Nietzsche's method seems antithetical to Benjamin's own 'historical–philosophical' project, because of its tendency to dissolve the historical particularity of a work in an undifferentiated aesthetic realm.

Nothing could be further from Nietzsche's understanding of Greek tragedy than the definition of the genre Benjamin actually quotes, by Nietzsche's one-time antagonist, the Hellenist Ulrich von Wilamo-witz-Möllendorff: ' "an Attic tragedy is a self-contained piece of heroic legend, poetically adapted in elevated style for presentation by a chorus of Attic citizens and two or three actors, and intended for performance as part of the public worship at the shrine of Dio-nysus." '[11] Throughout his discussion Wilamowitz employs formal and historically specific terms, concentrating not on tragedy *tout court* or even 'Greek tragedy', but on *Attic* tragedy, describing the means and occasion of performance, and, most of all, emphasizing the foundation of tragedy in 'heroic legend' (*Heldensage*). This last point proves crucial for Benjamin, whose central distinction between tragedy and *Trauerspiel* contrasts tragedy's basis in myth with *Trauerspiel*'s basis in history (*Geschichte*). The 'matter-contents' of the two genres seem to be fundamentally opposed: tragedy depicts mythical stories from the remote past, whereas *Trauerspiel*, despite

---

[7] On Benjamin's reading of Nietzsche, see McFarland (2013: 74–82).
[8] W. Benjamin (1974: 281; 1998: 103).　　[9] Nietzsche (1980: 1, 102).
[10] W. Benjamin (1974: 281; 1998: 102).
[11] W. Benjamin (1974: 284–5; 1998: 106); Wilamowitz-Möllendorff (1889: 107).

often being set in far-flung places and times, concerns the political circumstances of historical life.

Benjamin's description of Greek tragedy delves further into the content of tragic myth than Wilamowitz did, bringing out the 'truth-contents' of the form as the way that it instantiates a particular relation to divinity. Benjamin's discussion of Greek tragedy is heavily indebted both to his friend Florens Christian Rang, and to his reading of Franz Rosenzweig's *Der Stern der Erlösung* (*The Star of Redemption* (1921)). Relying mainly on the writings of Rang, Benjamin sees the centre of tragedy as the *Opfer*, 'sacrifice' or 'victim'—the dual valences of the word marking the protagonist both as a victim of the gods and, simultaneously, as a sacrifice for the good of the community.[12] From the materials of myth, tragedy creates a 'tendentious reforming of the tradition', which makes the events of the heroic past into a force for cohesion and creation in the present:

> Tragic poetry is based on the idea of sacrifice [*Opferidee*]. The tragic sacrifice [*Opfer*], however, is distinguished from any other sacrifice in its object—the hero—who is a first and last sacrifice at once. Last in the sense of an atoning sacrifice [*Sühnenopfer*], which falls to the gods who are upholding an ancient right. First in the sense of an action that takes the place of another [*stellvertretenden Handlung*], in which new contents [*Inhalte*] of the life of the people announce themselves.[13]

Tragedy for Benjamin looks backward to myth, in which the gods seem arbitrarily to impose suffering on humans, and forward to a future politico-religious community that is capable of governing itself and regulating its own system of crime and punishment. Aeschylus' *Oresteia* might be exemplary: in the progress from the cycle of retribution depicted in the *Agamemnon* and *Libation Bearers* to the civic justice of the *Eumenides*, Benjamin (via Rang) sees the invalidation of the ancient rights of the god and the establishment of a new order. Orestes, though not actually killed, suffers for obeying the command of the god, but his suffering at the same time forms the basis for the Attic community in which justice is a civic matter and the old rights of retribution are neutralized. Greek tragedy, for Benjamin, is animated by a prophetic consciousness, as the hero looks

---

[12] See S. Weber (2004: 163–7) on Benjamin's disagreement with and reformulation of Rang on the details of this description.
[13] W. Benjamin (1974: 285; 1998: 106–7).

forward to a future in which humanity gains a form of ascendancy over the divine.

In his description of the prophetic quality of the tragic hero, Benjamin seems to be drawing primarily on Rosenzweig. *The Star of Redemption* had described silence (*Schweigen*) as the distinguishing feature of the tragic hero, a species of 'meta-ethical man', and Benjamin reproduces a crucial passage: '"In his silence the hero burns the bridges connecting him to god and the world, elevates himself above the realm of personality, which defines itself against others and individualizes itself in speech, and so enters the icy loneliness of the self."[14] Combining Rosenzweig's tragic silence with Rang's progressive description of the sacrifice, Benjamin reads the heroism of the protagonist as a silent protest against the mythological world around him. The tragic hero's advanced consciousness looks forward to a more moral order than exists in myth, to the *polis* in which tragedy is performed. The silence of the hero 'neither looks for nor finds any justification, and therefore throws suspicion back on his persecutors'. Tragedy's reformulation of legendary stories translates the 'demonic' question of human justification in the eyes of the gods into the cosmological question of divine justice. Tragedy reformulates the ambiguity (*Zweideutigkeit*, literally 'double meaning' but perhaps better as 'duplicity') of myth—the way it makes innocent humans guilty before the gods—as paradox, as the guilt and innocence of gods and humans alike.[15] Seeing paradox as the essential content of tragedy brings Benjamin close to Hölderlin's fragment that begins 'The meaning of tragedies is most easily grasped through paradox' (*Die Bedeutung der Tragödien ist am leichtesten aus dem Paradoxon zu begreifen*).[16] As an enthusiastic reader and critic of Hölderlin, Benjamin would have known the fragment's identification of tragedy as a representation of the coincidence of absolute fullness and absolute emptiness, and Hölderlin's reading of tragedy as a confrontation of god and man.[17] The paradox of Benjamin's reading is located in the way that the injustice of divinity and the justice of the hero coincide,

---

[14] W. Benjamin (1974: 286–7; 1998: 108); Rosenzweig (2005: 85–6).

[15] 'The tragic is to the demonic as paradox is to duplicity. In all the paradoxes of tragedy—in the sacrifice, which, in complying with ancient statutes, creates new ones, in death, which is an act of atonement but which sweeps away only the self, in the tragic ending, which grants victory to man, but also to god—duplicity, the stigma of the daimons, is in decline' (W. Benjamin 1974: 288; 1998: 109).

[16] Hölderlin (1992: ii. 174).   [17] See Balfour, Chapter 3, this volume.

and so 'in tragedy pagan man realizes that he is better than his gods'.[18]

A consequence of this reading is that, despite the earlier praise of Nietzsche for rejecting moralizing readings of tragedy, Benjamin places Greek tragedy in an emphatically ethical sphere. What distinguishes Benjamin's reading from the idealist theories he dismisses, though, is the assumption that the moral content of Greek tragedy is one with that of modern works. In contrast to Nietzsche, who denies any relation of aesthetics to morality, Benjamin sees tragedy and *Trauerspiel* alike as expressions of a broadly ethical outlook, in which aesthetic form is inextricable from moral and theological contents. There is something quite Hegelian about this project, and Benjamin's silence concerning Hegel's theory of tragedy is surprising. The 'Religion' chapter of the *Phänomenologie des Geistes* similarly sees tragedy as proleptic within Greek culture, accounting for the form of tragedy through a distinction between the archaic chorus and the more ethically developed protagonists.[19] Benjamin would certainly not endorse the teleology operative in Hegel's account, but he might have learned from its reading of Greek tragedy as bound up in the process history, and the attribution of substantive though temporally limited concerns to the genre.

2. MARGINS OF *TRAUERSPIEL*

Trauerspiel is distinguished from tragedy most of all in its vision of the moral world. Because of the influence of a neo-Aristotelian theory of drama, *Trauerspiel*'s formal constitution can be deceptively similar to that of ancient tragedy. Benjamin's fundamental task is to formulate differences in content that lie below apparent similarity, and to pinpoint the moment of rupture. Yet, as Samuel Weber has shown, the rupture is not absolute: there are important moments of continuity from Benjamin's understandings of tragedy to his theory of *Trauerspiel*, which can be seen as an almost parodic reformulation of Greek tragedy.[20] The bridge between the two forms is the death of

---

[18] W. Benjamin (1974: 288; 1998: 109–10).
[19] Szondi (2002: 51–2) notes this affinity.
[20] See S. Weber (2008), and Weber, Chapter 4, this volume.

Socrates, which for Benjamin establishes the pattern of the martyr drama that will be the fundamental story of *Trauerspiel.* The martyr- dom of Socrates, a death that takes place in history rather than myth, in speech rather than silence, entirely lacks the prophetic element of tragedy. It points forward to no emerging order, establishes no relation of human existence to divinity. Yet the form of the dialogue restores the performative quality of Greek drama by investing its figures with 'purely dramatic language, before the dialectic of tragic and comic. This purely dramatic quality restores the mystery that had gradually become secularized in the forms of Greek drama: its speech is that of the new drama and at once that of the *Trauerspiel.*'[21] The Socratic dialogue forms an immanent counterpart to tragedy's tran- scendent content, emptying drama of its prophetic consciousness and grounding it in the present time. Like Nietzsche (and Hegel), Benja- min sees Socrates as an anti-tragic, prosaic figure, but Benjamin's more nuanced generic thought finds in the Platonic dialogue a new dramatic model, which transforms the tragic hero from a prophet who points the collective forward in time to a martyr whose death forms the basis for communal memory and commemoration.

The lack of any vision of the future might seem radically to differentiate the death of Socrates from the death of the Christ (which might be a more obvious template for Christian martyr drama). Where the Crucifixion has an obvious prophetic element, the death of Socrates turns out to be closer to the world of the *Trauerspiel* in having no redemptive quality. This is typical of Benja- min's understanding of baroque religion. As Benjamin presents it, the effect of Luther's teaching was to erect a barrier between the worldly and the spiritual through the rejection of good works as a way to salvation. With divine grace removed from the earthly sphere of sin and atonement, a sense of meaninglessness pervades historical life:

> In that [Lutheranism] denied [good works] any particular miraculous spiritual effect, referred the soul to the grace of faith, and made the secular–political sphere a testing ground for a life that was only indir- ectly religious, created for the demonstration of civic virtues, [Luther- anism] did, it is true, instil into the people a strict sense of obedience to duty, but in its great men it produced sorrow.[22]

---

[21] W. Benjamin (1974: 297; 1998: 118).
[22] W. Benjamin (1974: 317; 1998: 138).

Earthly existence does not look forward to any form of redemption, or see itself as the preparation for a new life. This seems characteristic of both Catholic and Protestant baroques, though Benjamin will distinguish implicitly between their responses to the *Trauer* of the period. Where the Renaissance had discovered an affinity with antiquity in its anticipation of new life, the baroque exists in a state more akin to the Middle Ages, in which divinity seemed distant and the salvation of the individual obscure. This absence of a future order on earth is definitive for the world of *Trauerspiel*, which finds itself in a world in which earthly actions are devoid of transcendent meaning. 'Something new arose: an empty world.'[23]

Trauerspiel plays out in this empty world, and its mourning is directed at this loss of meaning—indeed, in part at the loss of tragedy's (and renaissance Christianity's) prophetic element.[24] *Trauerspiel*'s mourning is not inert or elegiac, however: in it, mourning (*Trauer*) finds expression in play (*Spiel*). 'Mourning is the state of mind [Gesinnung]', Benjamin writes, 'in which feeling revives the emptied world as a mask [maskenhaft], in order to derive an enigmatic satisfaction in contemplating it'.[25] The playful quality of *Trauerspiel* forms a consolation (*Trost*) for the fundamental lack of seriousness that the baroque finds in earthly existence.[26] Concretely, this manifests itself in a strong tendency to artifice: complex plots, striking visual displays, rhetorical fireworks. The trope of the world as stage belongs to this impulse, as does the character of the intriguer, a central feature of these dramas, who 'choreographs' the actions of the play with a 'demonic' subtlety.[27] The stage-world appears as radically contingent, empty of greater significance, and subject to an inscrutable fate; the only thing to be done while waiting for this fate to become manifest in death is to play.

Yet the playful tendencies of German *Trauerspiel* are incompletely realized. What they lack is the capacity for self-reflection, which would allow German works to attain a distanced perspective on their own fate, rather than returning—as Benjamin finds that they

---

[23] W. Benjamin (1974: 317; 1998: 139).

[24] S. Weber (2008: 156): 'What does the German baroque mourning play mourn? According to our previous interpretation, the answer that imposes itself is: the death of tragedy.'

[25] W. Benjamin (1974: 318; 1998: 139).

[26] W. Benjamin (1974: 260–1; 1998: 81–2).

[27] W. Benjamin (1974: 273–7; 1998: 95–8).

do—to the gloomy necessity of death. The capacity for genuine play is demonstrated most of all by the dramas of Calderón, which are able to turn the artificiality of baroque drama on itself in a playful and potentially infinite process of reflection. Calderón's dramas present heroes with a virtuosic capacity for reflection, which allows them 'to turn the order of fate around like a ball in their hands, and contemplate it now from one side, now from the other'.[28] This is a particular characteristic of the sovereign, whose reflection is defined by the ironic juxtaposition of his power over men with his powerlessness before the 'order of fate'. As a semi-transcendent figure, the king in Calderón's dramas is able to comprehend the whole of existence as mere play, but to fill this playful space with an intensity of reflection that compensates for the emptiness of action.

Not so the German baroque, which could not create a sovereign figure to match the kings of Calderón. The rulers in German *Trauerspiel* are hardly masters of themselves, let alone of their human worlds. They appear radically 'creaturely' in their appearances on the stage of life, and, when not portrayed as depraved, venal tyrants, the kings of *Trauerspiel* appear weak and indecisive. German *Trauerspiel* returns again and again to the 'antithesis between the power of the ruler and his capacity to rule'.[29] Again, it is Calderón who depicts the more aesthetically complete form of creatureliness. In his dramas, the animalistic quality of the sovereign is redeemed by a sense of honour that offers a means of rising above the creaturely. Adherence to a worldly code of honour offers individuals a higher purpose than their own animal desires—and a more dramatically viable motivation than the dull virtue of martyrs. The sense of honour fills the space previously occupied by the certainty of divine justice, and provides a standard of earthly action that would otherwise be lacking. The presence of an immanent ideal for conduct compensates, in Calderón's works, for the creaturely subjection of humanity: 'In Spanish drama the creaturely exposure of the person, through an unparalleled dialectic of the concept of honour, becomes capable as nowhere else of a superior, indeed a reconciliatory presentation.'[30]

Given the extent to which Benjamin sees all baroque drama as theological, there is an irony to using a Catholic dramatist to

---

[28] W. Benjamin (1974: 263; 1998: 84).
[29] W. Benjamin (1974: 250; 1998: 70–1).
[30] W. Benjamin (1974: 266; 1998: 87).

exemplify the basically Protestant form of *Trauerspiel*. 'Nowhere but in Calderón could the perfect form of the baroque *Trauerspiel* be studied. The very precision with which the "mourning" and the "play" can harmonize with one another gives it this exemplary validity—the validity of the word and of the object alike.'[31] Calderón's dramas represent the perfected form of *Trauerspiel*, and are paradoxically marginal and central to Benjamin's discussion: they stand outside the genre, but provide a kind of ideal that allows Benjamin to decode the unrealized tendencies of the *Trauerspiel*. One might wonder whether Calderón could attain this aesthetic perfection precisely because he was a Catholic, and therefore not subject to the same ethic of immanence that so oppressed German Lutherans. Yet Benjamin sees the sense of meaninglessness as characteristic of all the baroque, Catholic and Protestant, even as his analysis uncovers substantial differences between the works produced by different confessions. Whatever the reason, Calderón's dramas define a formal teleology for the German *Trauerspiel*, which constantly seeks—though inevitably fails—to transcend its mourning through play.

The German *Trauerspiel*'s capacity for play remains irretrievably earthbound, and leads only further into self-absorption, creating what for Benjamin is the paradigmatic condition of the baroque: melancholy. 'The theory of mourning . . . can only be developed in the description of that world which is revealed under the gaze of the melancholy man.'[32] Melancholy is characteristic of the rulers of *Trauerspiel*, and seems to come from a consciousness of their creaturely state, their vulnerability to the shocks that *Trauerspiel* inevitably portrays. Baroque melancholy is importantly undialectical: it is the pure, unredeemed experience of immanence (connected to the deadly sin of *acedia*, 'sloth'). Benjamin contrasts this state, which he locates in the Middle Ages as well, with the classical and renaissance dialectic of melancholy, which sees melancholy as a madness linked to creative genius.[33] The medieval/baroque conception, Benjamin insists, does not recognize any compensation for the state of melancholy, even as it inherits elements from the more optimistic notions of the renaissance, such as the prophetic and poetic abilities of the melancholic. The medieval/baroque 'demonic' understanding of

---

[31] W. Benjamin (1974: 260; 1998: 81).
[32] W. Benjamin (1974: 318; 1998: 139).
[33] W. Benjamin (1974: 325; 1998: 147).

melancholy and the ancient/renaissance dialectical conception form the poles of Benjamin's discussion, but they are importantly interwoven. The interpretation of Dürer's 1514 *Melencolia I* mediates between these poles, recognizing both the dialectical resonances of the figure of Saturn and the demonic image of the stone, which Benjamin interprets as a symbol of *acedia*. The latter, baroque element is Benjamin's main addition to the discussions of Warburg and Panofsky, and allows him to bring Dürer's work into the baroque— where, chronologically, it does not belong.

In Dürer, Benjamin finds a more complete presentation of the polarities of baroque melancholy than in any *Trauerspiel*. With one exception:

> With the characteristic attitude of the reaction of the Counter-Reformation, the creation of types in German *Trauerspiel* follows the mediaeval scholastic image of melancholy. But still the complete form of this drama is fundamentally different from this type: its style and language are inconceivable without that bold twist with which Renaissance speculation discerned in the features of crying contemplation the reflection of a distant light, which shined back to it out of the ground of self-absorption. At least once the age succeeded in conjuring the human figure that corresponded to the dichotomy of the neo-antique and the medieval light in which the baroque saw the melancholic. But Germany was not the country able to do so. It is Hamlet.[34]

Though the introduction of Shakespeare is not a complete surprise at this juncture in the work, it is highly dramatic.[35] Hamlet appears as the theatrical counterpoint to Dürer's engraving, a figure that incorporates the complexity of baroque melancholy, divided between the deadly sin of *acedia* and the dialectic of madness and inspiration. Hamlet seems to transcend this dual character of melancholy: 'His life, as the exemplary object of his mourning, points before its expiry to the Christian providence in whose womb his mournful images are transformed into blessed existence.'[36] Benjamin seems to be referring to Hamlet's final speech, which issues a prophecy:

---

[34] W. Benjamin (1974: 334; 1998: 157).

[35] Hamlet has come up in the discussion of the tragedy of fate that concluded the previous part: W. Benjamin (1974: 312–16; 1998: 133–8). His speech beginning 'What is a man' is then picked up at the opening of the next chapter, which begins the discussion of melancholy. Shakespearian characters were also used to demonstrate the figure of the intriguer: W. Benjamin (1974: 304–7; 1998: 125–8).

[36] W. Benjamin (1974: 335; 1998: 158).

I do prophesy th' election lights
On Fortinbras. He has my dying voice.
So tell him, with th' occurrents, more and less,
Which have solicited. The rest is silence.[37]

Hamlet's address to the future recognizes the sorrowful 'occurrents' that have brought about his death, but also foresees order restored in Denmark, a consolation for the arbitrariness of fate.[38] In viewing the events that caused his doom as providential, 'Hamlet alone is a spectator of the graces of God [*Zuschauer von Gottes Gnaden*]'.[39] He attains the distance necessary to become a 'spectator' of the play of his own life, dissolving the medieval melancholy of self-absorption into the Renaissance melancholy of prophecy.

Benjamin's discussion of Hamlet, even more so than the discussion of Calderón, has a curious position within the generic understanding of *Trauerspiel*. There is, first of all, an uncertainty as to the actual object of discussion—the play *Hamlet* or the character Hamlet— which is significant in so far as the conclusion of the work might be interpreted differently if one were to read beyond Hamlet's death.[40] The focus on the character Hamlet is surprising in Benjamin's discussion, which otherwise is quite conscious of the difference between presentation and representation. But here it is not the representation of melancholy in *Hamlet* that is at issue, but Hamlet's own melancholy (intepreted almost as a symptom of a real person). Moreover, far from sharpening the particularity of baroque melancholy, Benjamin ends by assimilating Hamlet and *Hamlet* to the ancient/Renaissance model. Hamlet, of course, remains a baroque hero: speech, rather than silence, is his characteristic mode, and his death is the result of a confrontation not with divine necessity, but with historical circumstance.[41] Yet, like the ancient tragic hero, Hamlet's death looks

---

[37] Shakespeare, *Hamlet*, V.ii.307.

[38] Newman (2011:150–4) investigates the roots of Benjamin's interpretation of Hamlet in Rochus von Liliencron's 1877 novella 'Die siebente Todsünde'.

[39] W. Benjamin (1974: 335; 1998: 158).

[40] The ambiguity might be reflected in the strange locution with which Benjamin introduces the discussion: 'Es ist der Hamlet' (W. Benjamin 1974: 334; 1998: 157).

[41] This is emphasized in the earlier descriptions of Hamlet: 'Hamlet, as is clear from his conversation with Osric, wants to breathe in the fate-heavy air [*shicksalsschwere Luft*] like oxygen in one deep breath. He wants to die by chance [*Zufall*]' (W. Benjamin 1974: 315; 1998: 137).

forward to a new age in its prophetic element. The first division of the book, '*Trauerspiel* and Tragedy', ends with the paragraph on Hamlet, coming full circle to antiquity—but antiquity as reformulated by the Christian Renaissance. Hamlet's melancholy does not just define the baroque, but seems to transcend it.

Once again, understanding the German *Trauerspiel* seems to necessitate looking beyond it, to the works in which the impulses of the form are more coherently displayed. Indeed, the boundaries of what is relevant to the baroque can seem rather arbitrary, taking in as they do Calderón and Shakespeare, but excluding (apparently) Corneille and Racine, who lived contemporaneously and would be obvious points of comparison.[42] Benjamin defines the baroque less in chronological terms than in stylistic and even philosophical ones. The major oppositional categories are, of course, the classical and the Renaissance, but with his description of the death of Socrates as the creation of the language of the *Trauerspiel* and of Dürer's engraving as an anticipation of baroque melancholy, Benjamin extends the baroque well beyond any meaningful periodization. The baroque seems to invade every historical moment Benjamin discusses.

3. ORIGIN AND CONSTELLATION

What, then, could be the origin of German *Trauerspiel*? Benjamin never tells us outright. In fact, it is difficult to discern what kind of answer the question of the origin expects: it does not seem to refer to an invention or evolution. One cannot point to a single originary moment of German *Trauerspiel*. Though Benjamin insists that origin is a historical category, it is not localizable within temporality. Here is Benjamin in the 'Preface':

> Origin [*Ursprung*], though a wholly historical category, has nothing in common with emergence [*Entstehung*]. In origin is not meant the becoming of what has emerged but rather that which is emerging from becoming and passing-away [*Im Ursprung wird kein Werden des Entsprungenen, vielmehr dem Werden und Vergehen Entspringendes*

---

[42] A new issue of Yale French Studies investigates Benjamin's mooted but never pursued companion to the *Trauerspiel* book, on French drama: Bjornstad and Ibbett (2014).

gemeint]. The origin stands in the river of becoming as a whirlpool [*Strudel*] and draws in its rhythm the emergence-material [*Entstehungs-material*] into itself.[43]

Ursprung (origin) does not concern when and how a form actually originated in history—this is the content of *Entstehung* (emergence)—but rather, the way a form is manifested through history. Though its parameters are defined by becoming and passing -away, an originary phenomenon is not limited by its temporal existence; as 'that which is emerging from becoming and passing-away', its life is located outside historical processes. Origin draws in 'emergence-materials' in the process of becoming, but, as a whirlpool, interrupts their flow and removes them from their temporal context.[44] The history in which the origin is recognized is not a single extent of time, but the 'fore- and after-history' (*Vor- und Nachgeschichte*) of a form, in which possibility is created, realized, and transformed.[45] There is thus a virtual quality to the origin's existence—it describes the way a form is present in history as an idea, not as a concrete reality. And this can be recognized only retrospectively: the authenticity of an origin, Benjamin writes, must be proven from a standpoint in which the originary phenomenon 'appears completed, in the totality of its history'.[46] The significance of an origin is only revealed retrospectively, when a multiplicity of elements are recognized as having an ideal coherence that emerges from history but ultimately stands outside of temporality.

The origin of German *Trauerspiel*, then, would not be a single moment. Rather, it would be a configuration of elements, each with its own distinct historical location. In seeing these elements as part of an originary phenomenon, one would understand them as 'restoration, re-establishment on one hand, and therefore as uncompleted, unfulfilled on the other'.[47] Each element of the origin would repeat an essential content while creating new possibilities for this content. This 'dual insight' of the origin might equally describe the way that genre

---

[43] W. Benjamin (1974: 226; 1998: 45).

[44] On the whirlpool and metaphors of flow in W. Benjamin, see Friedlander (2012: 60–2).

[45] 'Origin does not, therefore, raise itself out of actual findings, but relates to their fore- and after-history' (W. Benjamin 1974: 226; 1998: 46).

[46] W. Benjamin (1974: 226; 1998: 44–5).

[47] W. Benjamin (1974: 226; 1998: 45).

exists in time, as a notional essence that is manifested in different ways, each manifestation creating new possibilities for the future. Though Benjamin locates *Trauerspiel* in time, understanding it adequately requires looking beyond its moment of flourishing to grasp what is essential and what is contingent in any individual instance.[48] The life of baroque *Trauerspiel* can therefore repeat Socratic and medieval *Trauerspiele*, be foreshadowed by Dürer and Shakespeare, be parallel to Calderón's works, and in turn be repeated by the romantic *Schicksalstragödie*. These are all to be understood as elements of the origin of *Trauerspiel*.

Though Benjamin's category of origin can seem to shade into the typological, it is rigorously distinguished from understandings of baroque style as a possibility of any time and place (usually opposed to 'classical' periods of various kinds).[49] The stylistic understanding of the baroque is essentializing: it sees a single quality as manifested in different ways, but as nevertheless traceable to a single logical origin. Benjamin's understanding of origin, by contrast, refers to a kind of ideal history, which is formed by multiplicity: the origin of the baroque is not to be sought in a single time, but is nevertheless recognized as the configuration of distinct moments. The *Trauerspiel* without its fore-history in the Platonic dialogue and after-history in Romanticism would be a different phenomenon. Emerging from a different set of temporal instances, it would represent a different virtual configuration of elements. Benjamin's theory of origin opposes the ahistorical notion of 'baroque style' in favour of a conception rooted in actual historical instances.

An 'originary phenomenon' is one in which the coherence of disparate historical moments is recognized virtually and from a distance. It thus has an affinity with Benjamin's spatial image of the constellation.[50] Both are used to define genre as an 'idea', a term Benjamin uses in idiosyncratic fashion, to mean 'the objective inter-pretation [of phenomena]'.[51] The relationship between phenomena and idea is not one of incorporation—the idea is not the sum or

---

[48] The origin has some affinity with the Nietzschean concept of 'eternal return', but is distinguished by its rejection of a form of super-historical causality, such as the will. Another figure for this conception of history as repetition is 'natural history': W. Benjamin (1974: 227; 1998: 47). See Hanssen (1998: 40–8).

[49] See Newman (2011: 64–76) on contemporary debates concerning baroque style (though I see Benjamin's notion of the origin more as a reaction against such debates).

[50] Friedlander (2012: 60).   [51] W. Benjamin (1974: 214; 1998: 34).

average of the phenomena it interprets, nor is it the larger whole
to which they contribute—but rather one of 'representation' (*Reprä-
sentation*, eschewing the standard terms of German philosophy *Vorstellung* and *Darstellung*).[52] 'Ideas relate to things as star-maps
[*Sternbilder*] to stars.' Benjamin will often use the word 'constellation'
(*Konstellation*) to refer to this relationship, but the choice of 'star-
map' is significant here, as it points to the imaginary quality of the
lines drawn between stars (where 'constellation' might suggest an
intentional organization). A star-map or constellation is a series of
virtual connections between stars that gives them form. The form,
importantly, is not evident until it is recognized; even then, it remains
heuristic, guiding meaning as an interpretation of configuration. The
idea recognizes a formal coherence of disparate phenomena, and
therefore re-presents their empirical existence in the realm of truth
(as the origin incorporates historical materials into a unity that
transcends history).[53] Interpreting phenomena, the idea transforms
them from discrete points into a meaningful image. This process of
transformation, for Benjamin, brings about the 'salvation [*Rettung*] of
phenomena and the presentation [*Darstellung*] of the ideas'.[54]

The consequences of Benjamin's doctrine of ideas for understanding genre are profound. Genre, for Benjamin, is an idea in which a
variety of discrete works are given form as a virtual arrangement. It is
irrelevant whether the idea was apparent to the practitioners of the
form, as the form is of a different order from the works it encompasses. The works retain their individuality and specificity even in
being recognized as belonging to an idea. Indeed, the individual
work's uniqueness is heightened by the creation of a constellation;
where previously it had been part of a vast, undifferentiated mass of
stars, it now obtains a definitive place as one point of a form's outline.
Since each point exists on the edge of the figure it circumscribes, the
unique, idiosyncratic elements of an idea are particularly important
to its form: 'The idea is explained [*umgeschrieben*, equally "circumscribed"] as the figuration [*Gestaltung*] of the coherence in which the
singular-extreme stands with its equals.'[55] The idea is given shape by

---

[52] This is contrasted with the *Begriff* ('concept'), which does seem to be a kind of
abstraction from individual to general, but which nevertheless allows for ideas to
represent phenomena.

[53] See Jennings (1987: 199–201).   [54] W. Benjamin (1974: 215; 1998: 35).

[55] W. Benjamin (1974: 215; 1998: 35).

its most extreme phenomena. In terms of genre, this means that especially successful works—such as *Hamlet* or the dramas of Calderón—contribute to the idea of genre more than workmanlike productions (like those of the German *Trauerspiel*). The margins of Benjamin's discusion are thus formative in their marginality. 'An important work—either it founds its genre or destroys it, and in perfect works both are united' (*Ein bedeutendes Werk—entweder gründet es die Gattung oder hebt sie auf und in den vollkommenen vereinigt sich beides*).[56]

With this theory, Benjamin denies the validity of both the deductive understanding of genre, which posits a single essence and applies this essence to various works, and the inductive understanding, which reasons from the various works to a single essence. Genre for Benjamin is fundamentally an interpretation, and can therefore not pre-exist phenomena, nor, since it belongs to a different order from phenomena, can it be abstracted from them. Most of all, genre is not an essence but an idea—virtual and perhaps provisional, but coherent. Genre makes sense of its phenomena in one way, but does not preclude other senses being made of them, as the phenomena are shown in a different coherence. Benjamin's understanding of genre has a certain dynamism to it. Returning to the temporal model, it could be said that each element of an origin, as it emerges from becoming and passing away, forms a point on a constellation. It is the task of the critic to recognize how elements emerge from 'historical matter-contents' and, in the origin or constellation, become 'philosophical truth-contents'.

Benjamin's approach to genre through its margins offers a response to the problem of thinking tragedy as a coherent genre, ancient and modern. It rejects the uncritical application of concepts gained from one to the other, but retains the possibility of a rich philosophical understanding of genre in history. Grasping an artistic form requires looking beyond its historical existence and immediate theoretical context to the marginal phenomena that create and circumscribe its possibility. Philosophical criticism seeks to understand the possibilities—already realized, being realized, and to-be-realized—of a form. Though tragedy and *Trauerspiel* transcend any single moment, they do not stand outside of history, but are

---

[56] W. Benjamin (1974: 225; 1998: 44).

recognized as ideas offered by the sum of their histories. History becomes theory through the objective interpretation of the philosophical critic, who must recognize the virtual coherence of a multiplicity of disparate and apparently unrelated phenomena.

Despite its ambition and challenge, Benjamin's description of the task of the critic has a surprising modesty, in so far as it describes the aim of philosophical criticism as the re-presenting of a coherence that is itself already legible:

> It is the object of philosophical criticism to prove that the function of artistic form is this: to make historical matter-contents [*historiche Sachgehalte*], such as lie at the basis of every meaningful work, into philosophical truth-contents [*philosophische Wahrheitsgehalten*]. This transformation of material-content into truth-content makes the loss of effectiveness, in which from decade to decade the attractiveness of earlier charms diminishes, into the basis of a new birth, in which all ephemeral beauty wholly falls away and the work presents itself as a ruin.[57]

This credo has a certain redundancy to it, since it sees criticism as simply 'proving' the function of artistic works. But it is a redemptive redundancy, which finds 'a new birth' in the ruins of a form—the origin Benjamin finds in the ruins of *Trauerspiel*. Criticism is the act of witnessing the transformation of historical matter into the truth-contents inherent in an originary phenomenon. Benjamin's language for this moment of recognition borders on the mystical: truth (*Wahrheit*) must be given through contemplation, and not discovered through seeking or questioning.[58] Contemplation discerns the idea as constellation by allowing the coherence of disparate elements to emerge in new and surprising ways. Benajmin directs philosophical criticism towards a moment of recognition, as the image formed by a constellation becomes apparent. This truth is not found whole at any single point, but distributed through the extremes of the form. Presenting the origin of German *Trauerspiel*, then, requires an immersion in the margins of the genre, and a criticism that seeks to make these peripheral elements central: 'Method is detour [*Methode ist Umweg*]'.[59]

---

[57] W. Benjamin (1974: 358; 1998: 182).

[58] For example: 'Die Wahrheit ist ein aus Ideen gebildetes intentionsloses Sein' (W. Benjamin 1974:216; 1998: 36).

[59] W. Benjamin (1974: 228; 1998: 28).

14

Williams on Nietzsche on the Greeks

Robert B. Pippin

1

In his 1993 Sather lectures *Shame and Necessity*, Bernard Williams made clear what many had long surmised: his debt to the thought of Nietzsche and especially his debt to Nietzsche's views on the pre-philosophic or 'tragic' Greeks. There are many specific references to Nietzsche in Williams's book, and he clearly viewed Nietzsche as his most important ally in attacking the institution he held in such low regard that he associated it with slavery, using the same epithet, 'the peculiar institution', that had been prominent in discussions of slavery. But the institution that both Williams and Nietzsche seemed to consider not just wrong-headed but pernicious and completely unworthy of human allegiance was 'morality'. Neither of them, of course, meant thereby to be championing complete amoralism, or a complete indifference to considerations about how human life might best be lived.[1] Their target was the Christian inheritance and its legacy (most apparent in the modern moral philosophy of Kant), with its notions of duty, self-sacrifice, and its asceticism and its fixation on motivational purity. So for both, a pre-Christian culture in which an alternative picture of human life and human ideals could be found,

I am grateful to Mark Jenkins, Glenn Most, and Candace Vogler for conversations about the topics in this chapter.

[1] In the sense, for both, of how '*I* might best live', not how 'anyone at all, at any time, might best live'.

one that nevertheless maintained some great claim on the Western—that is, our—imaginary, was very important.[2]

Moreover, neither was all that impressed with the results for ethical life of the turn to philosophy accomplished by Socrates, and Plato. (Williams's position on Aristotle is more complicated because he so admires Aristotle's attention to moral luck. But Williams still rejects a 'teleological ethics'.[3]) Nietzsche seemed to hold Socrates and philosophy responsible for the end of the superior ethical perspective of 'Greek tragic culture', and, together with Nietzsche, Williams thought it one of the greatest 'con jobs' in history that Socrates convinced courageous, prudent people that, because they could not tell him what courage or prudence was, they did not know what they were doing, and so could not have really been courageous or prudent. One of Williams's most famous and controversial thoughts is a Nietzschean one: that 'self-consciousness kills ethics', or 'reflection can destroy [ethical] knowledge'.[4] In one of the most important conclusions of *Ethics and the Limits of Philosophy*,[5] Williams makes clear that he means by such claims *philosophical* reflection, as if what ethical life needs is a theory, a rational grounding. It does not. Within ethical life there, is of course, reflective deliberation, but its content is much more psychologically interrogatory for Williams, just as it is in Nietzsche. What do I really want? What are my motives? What is it actually that I am doing? What would this action mean to another? And, without signing on to Nietzsche's nihilism diagnosis, Williams makes the Nietzschean point that what modern ethical life needs is a kind of 'confidence', not something that can be achieved by philosophy, and something that the 'pervasive presence' of reflection in our age can promote if it is undertaken 'from strength' and not 'from weakness of self-deception and dogmatism'. That 'strength', 'weakness', 'self-deception', and 'dogmatism' are meant in a Nietzschean voice is confirmed by the next sentence. 'Confidence is not the same as optimism; it could rest on what Nietzsche called the pessimism of

---

[2] 'It is not a paradox that in these very new circumstances very old philosophies may have more to offer than moderately new ones, and a historical story could be told to show why this is so' (B. Williams 1993: 198).

[3] B. Williams (1993: 74).

[4] B. Williams (1993: 148); see p. 155 on 'more ethical knowledge' in the 'less reflective past'.

[5] B. Williams (1986).

strength.'[6] This is, of course, a term Nietzsche uses for the tragic culture of the Greeks.

Now Williams did not agree with Nietzsche on the supposed 'innocence' of the Greeks or their tragic poets, their status as child to our adult, and he did not agree that they displayed openly a kind of brutality or realism about power self-deceptively and pathologically continued but disguised in the Christian moral tradition. But he says that Nietzsche offered us 'more than this line of thought', and that it is a deeper set of Nietzschean ideas that he wants to take up—namely, 'joining in a radical way the questions of how we understand the Greeks and how we understand ourselves'.[7] The substance that emerges from this joining is very clear. It amounts to Williams's withering attack on the 'progressivists' such as Snell and Adkins who are out to show that the epic and tragic poets either completely lacked or grasped only very primitively the notions of agentive causation, intention, responsibility, and interiority that we now realize we need for an adequate account of agency and responsibility.[8] On the contrary, Williams argues, the epic and tragic poets had all the concepts they needed to make the relevant distinctions. What we have and they do not is simply a body of bad philosophy, the philosophy necessary to support the morality institution. By seeing ourselves in the Greek poets and not just in the Greek philosophers, we can start to free ourselves from the morality delusions. Williams argues for this relevance by pointing out often that, if the progressivists were right, then our experience of such literature would be of some strange, heartless, cruel, barely intelligible foreign tribe, almost unrecognizable as 'one of us', objects of study, rather than of engagement. But we *are* gripped and moved in ways that belie the distance the progressivists want to create. In a paradoxical but telling phrase, he notes that there is a difference between 'what we [actually] think' and 'what we merely think we think'[9] about normative matters, and the experience of Greek literature can make this distinction vividly clear.

---

[6] B. Williams (1993: 171).   [7] B. Williams (1993: 10).

[8] Not being a classicist, I am unsure of the status of Williams's targets in his attack. I am told that it is widely accepted that this scholarship is dated and has been superseded, and I am even told that Williams is going beyond beating dead horses. He is digging them up to beat them again. I have no view on the matter.

[9] B. Williams (1993: 7).

But perhaps the deepest level of sympathy between Nietzsche and Williams arises out of his common cause with Nietzsche on our current historical fate in late modernity, what we have to face now, what we cannot avoid. The proper study of Greek literature can help us understand and face such a fate, just as Nietzsche insisted, especially at the beginning of his career in *The Birth of Tragedy*. Nietzsche's name is not mentioned in the following passage, one of the most stirring and sweeping in *Shame and Necessity*, but there is no mistaking his profound influence. It is such a fine broadside that I will permit myself to quote it in full.

> We are in an ethical condition that lies not only beyond Christianity but beyond its Kantian and Hegelian legacies. We have an ambivalent sense of what human beings have achieved, and have hopes for how they might live (in particular, in the form of a still powerful ideal that they should live without lies). We know that the world was not made for us, or we for the world, that our history tells no purposive story, and that there is no position outside the world or outside history from which we might hope to authenticate our activities. We have to acknowledge the hideous costs of many human achievements that we value, including this reflective sense itself, and recognize that there is no redemptive Hegelian history or universal Leibnizean cost–benefit analysis to show that it will all come out well enough in the end. In important ways, we are, in our ethical situation, more like human beings in antiquity than any other Western people have been in the meantime. More particularly, we are like those who, from the fifth century and earlier, have left us traces of a consciousness that had not yet been touched by Plato's and Aristotle's attempts to make our ethical relations to the world fully intelligible.[10]

Indeed the passage is *so* redolent of Nietzschean sensibilities that it prompts the same sort of prudent, understandable recoil that many have had to Nietzsche on such topics as 'nihilism'. One rarely finds contemporary philosophers making such startling pronouncements, with this 'Nietzschean' language of whole historical epochs closing or opening. Can we really be said to be *beyond* the Christian era? To be beyond the Kantian and Hegelian legacies? What could that mean? Just *who* is beyond *what*? Nor do we hear such confident finality of judgement. History tells *no* purposive story whatsoever? Claims like Hegel's about the progressive realization of human freedom are

---

[10] B. Williams (1993: 166).

wholly worthless? Such heterodox suggestions about the founders of our philosophical tradition are also rare: that, from the start, Plato and Aristotle muddied waters that had been not only clearer but more humanly nourishing.

2

But the fact that the two philosophers had the same institution in their critical sights, that the rhetoric of their criticism went well beyond standard philosophical disagreement, and that their sense of the fate of late modernity in the Western, Northern industrialized world invoked the same epochal, grand gestures of failure and radical revaluation, also disguises some sharp differences between them, differences that are actually quite important and that, when understood, help make clearer that the final import of the critique of morality in Williams's two most important books, *Ethics and the Limits of Philosophy* and *Shame and Necessity*, is actually (and surprisingly, given the rhetoric) quite limited, quite a bit more limited than Nietzsche's. This difference between them will then help explain some differences in their respective appeals to epic and tragic Greek poets. At least that is what I will try to argue.

There is, first of all, a difference of emphasis in their respective accounts of 'post-Greek' styles of thought about normative matters, influenced so massively as it is by 'morality'. For both, the Socratic question is the unavoidable and paramount one: how ought one to live? For Nietzsche this seems to be primarily a calling of oneself to accounts, a self-evaluation that has a prominent psychological dimension, one especially urgent given the modern prevalence of self-deceit. What do I really want, love? What really motivates me? What am I willing to do in the light of such aspirations? How much under the shadow of *what others want me to want* do I stand? An insistence on a kind of existential authenticity is very prominent, one possible by virtue of one's having achieved a great degree of independence from others. The process of self-fashioning is just that, an individual's *self*-fashioning. As Phillippa Foot and Jürgen Habermas and Tracy Strong and Alexander Nehamas have all argued in influential commentaries, there is an unmistakable aesthetic dimension to such an attempt, one that can often look uncomfortably indifferent to the effects of one's attempts on others. (I say this seems to be what Nietzsche means, because we still do not have an authoritative interpretation—or even standard disagreements about what the interpretative options are—of the very strange but obviously crucial text where the nature and limits of human dependence and independence is worked out in some way: *Thus Spoke Zarathustra*. The central drama in that story revolves around Zarathustra's changing and complex relation to his public and his disciples, or, one could say, Zarathustra's rhetorical 'politics'.[11])

On the other hand, Williams takes for granted that questions about how one should live, as the central ethical questions, immediately and unavoidably raise questions about the effects of whatever I propose doing *on others*. Counting such considerations as possible reasons to do or forebear from doing something simply constitutes ethical thought, even for positions like ethical egoism.[12] No question about how one ought to live can get very far without conceding that any human life must be a social existence and so that at some significant level the question of how I ought to live is inseparable from the question of how *we* ought to live, in what ways we are bound to each other, and how we ought to acknowledge this fact.[13] So he states clearly this difference from Nietzsche at the beginning of *Shame and Necessity*, claiming it a great limitation of Nietzsche's thought that 'he did not move to any view that offered a coherent politics'[14] and just thereby his relevance for contemporary societies is limited.

And there are other differences that are even more important. Williams has essentially two main complaints against the morality institution, two problems he wants to use Greek literature to counter. The first concerns its model of moral agency and human responsibility. That is, morality tries to *limit* human responsibility, by which Williams mostly means culpability, to what is done *intentionally*, and the strictness of this limitation comes with a correspondingly harsh emphasis on a kind of absolute blame as the appropriate reactive attitude. (If the individual is responsible at all

---

[11] See the discussion in Pippin (2006).   [12] B. Williams (1986: 12–13).

[13] See Williams's extensive defence of the appropriateness of a concern with shame in ethical matters, or on the opinions of others: B. Williams (1993: 82 ff.). Also relevant: his interesting speculation about book two of Plato's *Republic* and his suspicion that the man described there, so well known for injustice but believing himself to be just, might very well be a 'deluded crank' (B. Williams 1993: 99).

[14] B. Williams (1993: 10).

only because he could always have done otherwise, then he and he alone as a distinct individual causing a unique set of bodily movements is *absolutely* responsible.) Accordingly, the proper mode of agent regret is guilt, a kind of self-punishment that is potentially unending, it being for ever unclear when any such self-punishing attitude is 'enough'.

Williams's genealogy of such a moral self-understanding is interestingly different from Nietzsche's. For Nietzsche, it is understandable that those suffering under near complete domination by others— Jews and later Christians under the power of Roman masters, for example—would devise a framework under which the masters' egoism was intentional, caused by those masters alone, and which could have been otherwise but for their selfish decisions, and so wholly attributable to them, blamable, just as the slaves' own failure to revolt was likewise a decision, an intentional indifference to suffering in this world for the sake of heavenly reward and moral rectitude. This also involves for Nietzsche a pathetic self-inflation of the volitional powers of individual, all as a compensatory strategy for really being of such weak or slavish character or nature.

Williams, however, in an analysis that involves some of his most important ideas, notes that the effect of the adoption of the moral notion of responsibility, while it can seem like the self-inflation described by Nietzsche,[15] is actually a way of greatly *limiting* the responsibility of the agent, or *protecting* the agent's self-image from the effects of chance or luck. If I am responsible for what I intentionally do, then I am responsible *only* for what I *intentionally* do, and not for what I bring about but unintentionally. The harm I inadvertently do (except in cases like negligence) has nothing to do with me, and I may, in effect, walk away 'untainted' by such ill effects. Accordingly, I can profess bewilderment at what Oedipus puts himself through, all that suffering. He did not, after all, intentionally kill his father, but the haughty stranger on the road to Locris. For Williams, if we try to understand why we do *not* react with such bewilderment to Oedipus (or to Agamemnon or to Ajax) but understandably and

---

[15] This is a thesis Williams wants to reject, holding instead that the social roles we simply happen to occupy (such as son, or brother, or American) can provide reasons for our actions without our having 'chosen' such roles. Williams sounds this note whenever he is criticizing the morality system's stress on the voluntary, its insistence that I am bound only by what I bind myself to.

sympathetically, we will begin to understand that what we think we think about the burden of moral luck is not actually what we think.

The moral picture of agency also involves a sweeping denigration of any self-interested or desire-based human motives (at least it does according to Williams), in favour of a rationalistic criterion, one that adopts a universal point of view. This is Williams's second major concern, what he calls morality's insistence on aspiration for motivational 'purity'.[16] Since Williams famously argued that there could be only 'internal reasons' for action, considerations related to my 'motivational set', such a standard for worthiness in acting was a mere fantasy, and conceding that did not at all mean that, therefore, all human action was basely self-regarding, outside anything that could be called 'the ethical'.

Nietzsche also had such a concern, but his worry about morality's picture of agency is much more radical than Williams's, and that will lead us to the real substance of their differences and from there to differences in their treatment of the Greeks. But it is also relevant to note first that Nietzsche also had far more substantive concerns with the morality institution than did Williams. While the agreement just noted explains their common suspicions about individual responsibility and about asceticism and self-denial, one never finds in Williams Nietzsche's unremitting denigration of the actual Christian virtues and their secular counterparts: humility, pity, brotherly love, forgiveness of enemies, peaceableness, charity, tolerance, gratitude, benevolence, altruism, selflessness. All such traits are for Nietzsche expressive of a slavish cast of mind and all make the achievement of anything truly worthwhile much less likely. Most importantly, Nietzsche's criticisms culminate in what he thinks all such character defects ultimately require: an egalitarianism that is not merely political (although Nietzsche certainly expressed himself clearly about that political dimension) but that supported the notion of the absolute moral equality or moral worth of every individual just as such. Williams, on the other hand, was clearly some version of an egalitarian liberal democrat. ('Some version', because his preference was not for a liberalism of rights or a liberalism of self-realization but what he called a 'liberalism of fear'.[17])

---

[16] B. Williams (1986: 175).
[17] As in his collection, B. Williams (2005). See my discussion in Pippin (2007).

3

I said before that what Williams wanted out of his contrast between Greek literature and the morality system (and sometimes between Greek literature and philosophical theory itself) was limited, or at least much more limited than Nietzsche's contrast. What I meant, aside from the fact that Williams was an egalitarian liberal democrat, was this. Williams thinks there would be something inhumanly cold about an indifference to the effects of what I did, even if I did not act intentionally, and so, he argues, Greek literature can help us see something that we have been using the morality system to try to forget: that we bear the burden of what we have done and its consequences, even if we did not act intentionally. Morality cannot shield us from the burdens of moral luck. Oedipus is, of course, the prominent example. But Williams clearly does not think Oedipus is to be held accountable *in the same way* as a man who meant to kill his father and so intentionally killed his father. (Oedipus certainly does not think so, and his last long speech in *Oedipus at Colonus* would suggest that the phrase Williams likes—'I suffered those deeds more than I did them'—could be interpreted to mean 'I simply suffered them, I *did not do* them, and what suffering I bear because of them, all of it, is a great cosmic injustice'.) The phrase that sums up Williams's whole position is 'we know that in the story of one's life there is an authority exercised by what one has done, and not merely by what one has intentionally done'.[18] But this 'authority' is *not* the authority of what one has intentionally done and the mark of the difference is what response others are entitled to have. In the non-intentional case, blame by others is not appropriate, for example, and the audience certainly does not react as they would if they had seen a parricide. Here is Williams's formulation.

> But one thing it [tragedy] expresses is that the significance of someone's life and its relation to society may be such that someone needs to recognize and express his responsibility for actions when no one else would have the right to make a claim for damages, or be in a position to.[19]

But if this is so, then Williams must be using the term 'responsibility' ambiguously, in one sense for intentional actions and in another sense for unintentional. One commentator has suggested we

[18] B. Williams (1993: 69).   [19] B. Williams (1993: 74).

distinguish simple 'accountability' from 'culpability', and that is a good suggestion.[20] But if *this* is so, then no great frontal assault on the model of agency in the morality system is being mounted. Its central link between the intentional and the fully culpable is maintained, not challenged by Williams, and a kind of qualification or footnote is added: unintentional effects nonetheless can hugely alter a life, and their burden must be borne, regret is appropriate, even if not in the way blameworthy actions and results must be borne. If we are able to show that an agent's ignorance was culpable or the product of reckless indifference, then we are able to qualify the notion again, distinguish strict unintentionality from a culpable form, and again preserve the central intuition. Williams is quite right to show that all these distinctions and an appreciation of their importance is alive and well in epic and tragic poetry, contra the progressivists, but the philosophical pay-off is not high.

It is a little higher with Williams's attack on the notions of unconditionality, obligation, the denigration of the role of desire in action, and the strict link between purity of motivation and praiseworthiness. His neo-Humean account is made at great length and with much subtlety in *Ethics and the Limits of Philosophy*. But a major element of the critique—the denial that obligations are always and everywhere all-trumping considerations in ethical deliberation—is not an argument that relies on any deep alteration in the underlying issue at stake in Williams's attack: the right way to understand the connection between an agent and her deed, what she must bear, what she owes, from having acted, rather than because of what happened to her. Moreover, a good deal of what morality wants to encourage and criticize is preserved in Williams's own voice, something Stephen Darwall pointed out.

> Williams himself believes we should recognize obligations (he refuses to call them 'moral') and correlative rights 'that one cannot ignore without blame'. Like almost any moralist, he says that obligation 'is grounded in the basic issue of what people should be able to rely on'. And he includes under this rubric the traditional negative obligations and obligations to aid when the need is 'immediate'. How does this differ in substance from the status that moral obligations are ordinarily thought to have?[21]

[20] Witt (2005).
[21] Darwall (1987: 82). This passage is quoted in a valuable article by Clark (2001: 114).

So Williams does not deny that one is obligated to do what one promised to do, and is obviously willing to countenance some universal absolute proscriptions (it is never permissible to torture children for one's amusement). He wants only to abandon appeals to strict unconditionality, to deny that all obligations derive from higher obligations, and that only another obligation can override an obligation. But, given that the Kantian metaphysics needed to support these claims is worth discarding anyway, again the pay-off for our understanding of morality and agency (as opposed to seeing what is wrong with Kant or Hare or Smart) is not high.

4

This is the context in which I would like to discuss the central question raised above. That question was how to understand the relation between an agent and her deeds, and therewith how to hold such an agent 'to accounts' for what she has done. We have already seen that, compared with Nietzsche, Williams's embrace of ' "the tragic culture of the Greeks" versus Christian morality' is quite limited in scope, not terribly substantive, consistent with a liberal egalitarianism, and concerned mostly with how we should understand the burden of unintended consequences. In *Ethics and the Limits of Philosophy*, he prosecutes his case mostly against the arguments of several philosophers, as if these arguments amounted to something like the 'essence' of the morality institution. In *Shame and Necessity*, he deals mostly with the 'progressivists', as if refuting them with his sensitive, and often brilliant, interpretations of Greek texts would clear the air and allow us to see something close to the fact that Christianity is mostly 'the longest and most painful route from paganism back to paganism'.[22] The question for Williams now is whether he is right that, in effect, we can 'see' in epic and tragic poetry *everything* we need to do justice to relatively unproblematic intuitions about this relation. I do not think we can; I think Nietzsche

---

[22] B. Williams (1993: 12). This is a variation of the well-known Polish joke that communism is the longest road from capitalism back to capitalism. Williams says, of course, that this is *not* what he is saying about Christianity, but he is clearly quite taken with the thought. I think it fair to say that it is what he is *tempted* to say.

knew that too, and that this is related to some of the differences between Nietzsche and Williams.

The first thing to note is that Williams's approach to this issue is naturalist and broadly compatibilist but not very ambitious metaphysically. He is happy to admit that human beings are 'metaphysically free', but he insists 'this news is less exciting than it might sound'.[23] His full formulation of the issue is the following.

> Human beings are metaphysically free in the negative sense that there is nothing in the structure of the universe that denies their power to intend, to decide, to act, indeed to take and receive responsibility in the fundamental and intelligible sense that we found... already in Homer.[24]

He goes on to say that 'the real obstacles to our freedom... are not metaphysical but psychological, social, and political'.[25] Despite the recent flurry of attention to the putative metaphysical underpinnings of Nietzsche's project, I think that this is basically a Nietzschean thought too, with the emphasis on the 'psychological' limits to freedom.

The only notion of a causal relation between agent and deeds that Williams thinks he needs (rightly, I believe) is what we might call a forensic notion of causality; the relation relevant to the law, for example. Assigning legal responsibility does not require metaphysics. When the law seeks to determine 'who *did* it?', it does not mean to ask whether a noumenal subject or neurological processes or the closed set of the physical events in the history of the universe should be said to have ultimately caused the movement. The law wants to know whether it was the butler or the mistress who shot Jones, and it needs to establish that whoever did it was not coerced, mistakenly shot Jones, thinking he was an intruder, or was crazy. All the deliberative faculties required for such a forensic notion are fully on view in Greek literature, Williams shows, as is the distinction between intentional and unintentional (as in the case of Telemachus at the end of the *Odyssey*, a case Williams dwells on to make this point). But this is a very standard picture of a singular agent with the mental capacity to reflect before acting, deliberate, form intentions, and bring about bodily movements.

---

[23] B. Williams (1993: 152). [24] B. Williams (1993: 152).
[25] B. Williams (1993: 152).

Nietzsche's picture is quite different, and the difference indicates how much farther away from the so-called Christian picture he wants us to be, compared to Williams. The canonical formulation is, quite typically, couched in a figurative language that makes restatement in traditional philosophic terms risky. I will have time to stress only one salient aspect. Here is the formulation, from *On the Genealogy of Morals*.

> And just as the common people separate lightning from its flash, and take the latter to be a deed, something performed by a subject, which is called lightning, popular morality separates strength from the manifestation of strength, as though there were an indifferent substratum behind the strong person which had the freedom to manifest strength or not. But there is no such substratum; there is no 'being' behind the deed, its effect and what becomes of it; the 'doer' is invented as an afterthought,—the deed is everything.[26]

Williams is aware of this passage and notes correctly that, despite appearances, given so much of what Nietzsche says about human actions, motivation, the kinds of creatures we have 'made' ourselves into, self-deceit, and so forth, it cannot make what Williams calls the 'uninviting' claim that 'we never really do anything, that no events are actions'.[27] But he says little about how to interpret the position positively.

What is interesting about the passage is that, even though Nietzsche is denying that there is any doer, or substratum-agent, *separable* from the deed, he does not say that there are only bodily movements, that there is no difference between my raising my arm and my arm going up.[28] He says instead that, in effect, the doer is *in* the deed, or, as the tradition inspired by Herder and stretching through Hegel to Wittgenstein would put it, the doer is 'expressed' in the deed. Agents can *ex ante* formulate all sorts of intentions and commitments, even sincerely, but, when it comes time to act, they find, by what they are actually willing to do, that they are in reality not committed or not as strongly committed, to the action as they would have *ex ante* insisted. And Nietzsche shows no inclination to explain such occurrences by appeal to 'weakness of the will'. Like Williams, he thinks that such a notion of the will, as understood by Christianity—a

---

[26] Nietzsche (2006: 26).   [27] B. Williams (1994: 241).
[28] I argue for this interpretation in Pippin (2010b: ch. 4).

volitional 'engine' needed, distinct from the passions and the intellect, in order to explain, as in St Paul, that 'I do the very thing I hate'—is a moralized faculty, that is, one that is created in the service of some moral picture of the soul, one that would not be necessary but for these moral purposes. When we do not do what we avowed we would do, we do not weakly fail to follow through; we simply discover what we are actually committed to. This does in fact entail quite a counter-intuitive claim: that we only can properly ascribe intentions to ourselves *post hoc*, after actually acting. But that is exactly what Nietzsche means by insisting that 'the deed is everything' (*Das Thun ist alles*).

Of course, in nearly all instances, what we do properly corresponds to what we avow, but the 'failed' cases reveal, for Nietzsche, something of the general picture of the soul needed. And that picture is an expressivist one (or one might say an 'actualization' one, where the intention is coming to be realized, at work, in the doing), not one in which discrete mental states like intentions cause bodily movements. The picture is much more like an author or sculptor who finds only *in the attempt* to express a provisional idea what in fact the idea could be, as externalized or expressed. Such provisionality in our avowals is crucial to the picture, otherwise we would fall back into the lightning-flash, or doer-deed model in another way. *Ex ante* intentions or ideas 'then' get expressed in deeds or objects, and we would have made no progress beyond the standard picture. But, as just indicated, while actions require such *ex ante* avowals (Nietzsche never denies this; we must be able to say what we are doing), they are always provisional, contradictable, or underminable by what we are actually willing to do or say.

Ultimately this different model for action means that our whole picture of self-knowledge must be very different from the intuitively powerful one: a 'turn inward' and an inner reflection in a search for true motives, a relation between a self and some sort of object, an inner self. And there are many other things to be worked out for this expressivist picture to be plausible, but there are two points of relevance to Williams that I would like to stress.

First, although he does not draw out explicitly any of the above implications from the *Genealogy* passage, it is very clear that he has some (but not all) of the same suspicions about *akrasia* theories, and even some of the same willingness to reject *ex ante* models of intentional action. I mean his example in the second chapter of *Shame and Necessity* about a man having an affair, who ends the affair, but finds himself wavering, finding occasions still to meet the lover. Williams notes that, in effect, what settles what he really intended to do is with whom he ends up. (Or: 'Das Thun ist alles.')

> But if in the end, if he and his wife separate and he goes on to live with his lover, it may be that those episodes will count not as *akrasia*, but rather as intimations of what were going to prove his truly stronger reasons. It is an illusion to suppose that there had to be at the time of those episodes a particular kind of psychological event that occurred if things turned out in one of those ways, and not if they turned out in the other; yet *akrasia*, to the extent that it offers a psychological explanation, is supposed to explain an event. We have reason to say that *akrasia* is not so much a psychological concept as (in the broad sense) an ethical one, an element that serves to provide an ethically significant narrative.[29]

But there is an implication of this way of looking at things that Williams also accepts, but this implication will return us to the general question of whether we can find everything in Greek epic and tragic poetry that we need in order to account for it. The issue comes out most clearly in Nietzsche's remarks on the issue so crucial to Williams's analysis in *Shame and Necessity* of agent regret and the variety of forms it can take. The passage is again from *On the Genealogy of Morals*, in the second section, paragraph 15. Nietzsche refers to a passage in Spinoza, where Spinoza is himself, having also rejected the picture of a separable causal centre of agency, wondering what to say about the *morsus conscientiae*, the bite of conscience, or agent regret. If I, being I, could not have acted otherwise, whence such regret? Nietzsche notes that Spinoza had in effect 'reinvented' this conscience and had not abandoned it.

> 'The opposite of *gaudium*,' he finally said to himself,—'a sadness accompanied by the recollection of the past event which turned out contrary to expectation'... 'something has gone unexpectedly wrong here', not 'I ought not to have done that'.[30]

Finding out that I was not actually who I had taken myself to be, and the sadness that accompanied this, is the right way to understand such regret. Now, in the Socratic pre-emptive objections to what would be the Aristotelian notion of *akrasia*, Socrates also treats the deeds as the measure of what a person truly believes to be good for

---

[29] B. Williams (1993: 45).   [30] Nietzsche (2006: 56).

him, no matter what he avows. But a disconnect between the avowal and the deed is taken to be a sign of ignorance. If someone does not do what he avows to be good for him, then he does not truly believe the rejected action or end would have been good, and he obviously mistakenly pursues something else, and, in this, he is simply wrong.

Given this picture, Nietzsche, though, is much less interested in figuring out how to hold people to account, at least as compared to Williams. Nietzsche wants to expose the 'falseness' in human self-avowals and ascriptions, not so much blame them, shame them, or even justify a way to find them accountable, and his framework for correctly explaining why people actually act the way they do is so much larger than the individual agent, that, apart from his discussing of the social institution of how we hold people to their promises and thereby train each other to hold ourselves to our promises, he is not much interested in how we assign such accountability, treats the issue always as a matter of varying practices, given various, contingent general needs at a time, and does not seek any foundation for such practices. Indeed, so little interested is he that one might say that, from a Nietzschean perspective, Williams seems more interested in *expanding* the essentially Christian notion of individual responsibility, *insisting that we must also bear the burdens as individuals of what we unintentionally do!*

But the implications of the passages we have been looking at— and this is massively borne out by Nietzsche's entire critique of Christianity—is that we need a different and more complicated picture of the soul to account for what Nietzsche is after and what Williams wants to follow—the contested phenomenon of self-deceit, genuinely knowing something about oneself, but finding a way—however hard it has always been for philosophers to account for it—of 'hiding' it from oneself, or, in Sartre's famous image, 'fleeing myself', something always deeply paradoxical (I am always still there, wherever I flee to). When I find out that I am not who I took myself to be, it is not as if I discover I am something like a different person. For me to have been motivated to do what I actually did, I have to be in some sense aware of what end I am trying to accomplish, but 'aware' of it in a self-deceived way. Nietzsche's whole account of Christianity is based on a claim that the motivation of Christians to be Christians is actually what he calls *ressentiment* against the powerful, not a genuine commitment to humility and charitableness. The latter may be what they tell themselves, but what they do and say (especially their depiction of

the suffering of the damned, for example) reveals their true motivations, motivations that could only motivate if some intentional in-
order-to structure were in place, but 'self-hidden in some way'. And, as
noted before, Williams is certainly no sceptic about self-deceit. It is
profoundly central to his own project as well. Just recall, from that
florid, long passage about the end of the Christian era that I quoted
earlier, that Williams's greatest aspiration or 'hope' was that human
beings could live *without lies* (not without insecurity, or in peace or
even with justice), and he makes clear in many places, particularly in
his attack on Christianity and in his last book on truthfulness, that
he does not just mean the lies we tell each other, but more importantly
the lies we tell ourselves. (This is particularly clear in one of Williams's
finest pieces of writing, chapter eight of *Truth and Truthfulness*, his
Trillingesque account, 'From Sincerity to Authenticity'.[31] More on that
in a moment.)

5

The point of this brief, inadequate summary of Nietzsche's attack on
conventional post-Christian models of agency was to note the centrality of self-deceit in that expressivist account, and how supremely
difficult it is to avoid self-deceit. Now, an extremely interesting
question, but one far too large to address here, is just when in the
Western tradition did self-deceit become an identifiable problem?
For our purposes, though, the question is a bit smaller but no less
contestable: is it a phenomenon, a way of explaining a character, an
account of the structure of the soul, that one can find in the Greek
literature Williams is defending? One thing one can say at least: it is
not a phenomenon Williams himself ever identifies as such or even
indirectly in the Greek literature he considers. In fact, there is a kind
of gaping disconnect between the way he treats the historical progressivists in *Shame and Necessity*, where he writes as if he thinks that
all claims that the pre-philosophical Greeks are missing some understanding of ourselves crucial to an adequate account are based on the
'distortions' of the morality system, and the way he treats them in his

---

[31] B. Williams (2004: 172–205).

last book, *Truth and Truthfulness*, where he is much friendlier to exactly that notion of something lacking, although he does not draw out any implications from this for his earlier account.

In some sense the contrast in question is routine, conventional. In Aeschylus' *Oresteia*, Orestes is faced with equally horrific alternatives—either to avenge his father's murder by murdering his mother, or not to do so and so directly disobey the command of Apollo—but it certainly never occurs to Orestes to question his own motives, to ask himself whether his own surface explanation of his motives is true, and never to wonder whether what he thinks he is commanded by a god to do might be his own motivated projection. It is often rightly said that the classical tragedies assume a kind of necessary ignorance on the part of tragic heroes, an ignorance made all the more painful for the audience in their knowledge of what the hero cannot know, in what is intimated by the Chorus and by the inevitable prophet or soothsayer, who is never, perhaps can never, be believed. But the point at issue is that the relevant state in question is ignorance; a result of hybris or finitude or whatever, but ignorance. The contrast between Orestes and the Orestes-like Hamlet is thus profound. Hamlet is for ever wondering about all these things, and even about the status of his father's supposed 'ghost'. (So the Hegelian contrast between ancient and modern tragedy seems confirmed: Orestes knows what he must do and why, but those requirements are 'objectively' incompatible; but Hamlet's tragedy is that he is in doubt about what is actually required and especially in doubt, subjectively, about himself.) But what is surprising is that, when Williams treats such issues in chapter eight of *Truth and Truthfulness*, he admits (with a qualification, as if he realizes how important is the concession) *that such an issue could not have arisen without Christianity* and the anxiety generated by Christian morality's insistence on honesty about oneself, on the pervasiveness of self-deceit, on the threat of falseness in one's sense of one's own rectitude, and so on the necessity of a lifelong and very difficult project of self-enquiry new to the Western tradition. (Socrates' understanding of the oracle's command, 'know thyself', had little to do with Hamlet's problem, but rather had to do with the requirement to know what it is to be a human being and so how best to live, best for anyone, anywhere, and anytime.) Consider how he describes his sense of the problem of understanding the ideals of sincerity and authenticity in modernity.

The history in question certainly has something to do with Christian traditions of self-inquiry, and it is tempting to speculate that the rise of authenticity—besides its connection with the weakening of fixed social identities . . . —was shaped by the Protestant rejection of auricular confession. The priest could absolve me on the basis of what he took to be my best efforts at sincerity, and reassure me that I had done enough. When I was alone before a silent God, it might well seem that only an absolute sincerity would do, a total confrontation with myself.[32]

Aside from an overemphasis on Protestantism (the issue in question is also a burning one for Augustine, say, or Pascal), this seems to me exactly the right intimation, that the whole notion of interiority itself and our access to our very selves had become a very different issue in the philosophy and literature of the West because of both the altered historical world ('the weakening of fixed social identities') and the influence of Christianity and its requirements of its adherents. Williams is right to insist on the fact that the emphasis on sincerity and authenticity, and the potential failure of attempts at both, is an 'invention' that requires a historical genealogy, not a philosophical assessment. But, in *Shame and Necessity*, such a sentiment is not prominent, and he uniformly treats the morality institution as something like a philosophical and hermeneutic *mistake*, one we have fortunately grown out of, and not as a response, in the way Hegel would understand, to inadequate and incomplete forms of self-understanding, inadequacies visible in tragedies like Antigone. And Williams treats the 'progressivist' classicists by rightly attacking the shallowness of their interpretations and the philosophical crudity of their concepts of agency and reflection, but he does not note that, for all of that, they were onto *something* in their general sense that the classical understanding of the *soul's relation to itself* 'lacked' something, something other than moralized and so unnecessary notions.

In his own account of the origin and fate of sincerity as an ideal in Rousseau, Williams begins with an episode, probably *the* pivotal episode, in Rousseau's *Confessions*, and it is clear from his descriptions that it is hardly an episode that could conceivably have appeared in a Homeric epic. Rousseau reports that he stole a ribbon, and, when the theft was detected, immediately accused a fellow employee, Marianne, of having taken it. He is believed, and she is dismissed without a

---

[32] B. Williams (2004: 301 n. 1).

reference. Rousseau reports that he was haunted by this episode his whole life, and is clearly especially haunted by his being unable to give a clear explanation of why he did this. (Marianne had been a good friend to Jean-Jacques.) At times he tries to use a more 'classical' or traditional explanation, that he was overcome by shame and fear of being found out, a way of saying in effect that he did not, in any robust sense, fully 'do' the deed; something, his passions, interrupted and clouded his normal reasoning. But he is not satisfied with this and in an amazing confession tries to argue that he acted *because* of his friendship with Marianne. He had intended all along to give the ribbon to her, and for that reason her name was the first that sprang to his lips. Williams rightly calls Rousseau's bizarre appeal to his benevolence a 'touching achievement of self-deceit'.[33]

And in going on to discuss Diderot, Williams draws very wide conclusions from his analysis, and again it is striking how historicist his perspective is. He argues that Rameau in *Rameau's Nephew* could be seen as an 'extreme enactment of what modern culture involves, a self-consciousness which can no longer feel unreflectively at home in its social environment'.[34] And later he notes that any attempt to place such a high value on sincerity, such as Rousseau's, will lead, in our world, the new world of modern self-understanding, 'inevitably to self-deception'.[35]

6

Two brief concluding remarks. First, the more Hegelian sentiments of *Truth and Truthfulness* actually correspond more with the more consistently genealogical approach taken by Nietzsche when considering both the relation of the Christian self-understanding to the ancient, and the achievements and limitations of such a revolution. For example: 'The history of mankind would be far too stupid a thing if it had not had the spirit of the powerless injected into it.'[36] And:

> It was on the foundation of this *essentially dangerous* form of human existence, the priestly form, that man first became an *interesting animal*

---

[33] B. Williams (2004: 176).
[35] B. Williams (2004: 199).
[34] B. Williams (2004: 190).
[36] Nietzsche (2006: 17).

and that the human soul first acquired *depth* in a higher sense and became *evil*—and these are the two basic forms of man's superiority, hitherto, over other beasts.[37]

Second, there is perhaps some irony in the fact that, if Williams had lived to follow through the more historical–genealogical approach— that is, what is clearly the Hegelian approach he had adopted in *Truth and Truthfulness*—and in its light had reviewed and revised *Shame and Necessity*'s language of mistakes, distortions, evasions, in favour of his later appreciation of what is *gained* with the Christian distrust of putative self-knowledge, his results would have been considerably more Nietzschean than they already are.

[37] Nietzsche (2006: 16).

Epilogue: Tragedy and Modernity, Closing Thoughts

Michael Silk

The editors of this volume have invited me to offer some closing thoughts on tragedy and the idea of modernity. They will, I trust, take it as a compliment to themselves, and an acknowledgement of the importance of their endeavour, if I take their introduction, rather than the more specifically focused essays that follow, as my point of departure. What I wish to do is draw attention to some of their formulations and emphases and suggest certain qualifications. In offering these thoughts, considerations of brevity mean that, in several cases, I can do no more than gesture towards arguments that would call for much fuller discussion to be properly convincing. I hope it will not be thought unduly narcissistic if I refer to some such fuller discussions in publications with which my own name is associated.

The volume, and the editorial introduction in particular, confronts the rich engagements of (largely) German thinkers with (largely) Greek tragedy, along with the new category of 'the tragic' that arises from these engagements in the Romantic age. I am delighted to see, as also to be associated with, this project, but at the same time I would query the terms in which the editors make the case for its significance. At the outset, they declare: 'The tradition of philosophical appropriations of Greek tragedy encompasses many of the most important thinkers of the nineteenth, twentieth, and twenty-first centuries, including Hegel, Kierkegaard, Nietzsche, Freud, and Heidegger.'[1]

---

[1] Introduction, this volume.

The slippage from 'philosophical' to 'thinkers' is noteworthy here (is Freud a *philosopher*?), but more immediately the terms of the claim are provocative: *many* and *most*? It is easy enough to cite counter-examples ('important thinkers' who have not significantly, or not at all, 'appropriated' Greek tragedy) within the traditions of German thought (from Kant to Wittgenstein), let alone beyond: Mill and Darwin, Croce and Eco, Tolstoy and Bakhtin, Bergson, Saussure, Merleau-Ponty, Foucault—and plenty more besides. A headcount of 'thinkers' isn't called for, indeed, but it would surely be to the point, not simply to focus on appropriators (as the editors and then the contributors largely do), but also to assess the strength and currency of this appropriative tendency against others. That would be challenging, no doubt. In some kinds of history, relative assessment is standard practice; but in the history of ideas, it mostly isn't. It can be done, though, even if only summarily,[2] and as the editors' effective claim is that tragedy and the tragic have proved to be special, even very special, it would be appropriate here for the claim to be amplified in some such way. Not just 'look at *my* shop-window: it's special', then, but 'look at mine: it's *more* special than hers, or his, or theirs, *because* . . . '. *How* special is it, in fact?

In any case, on the editors' own terms, 'appropriation' leaves it unclear how significant, or otherwise, the role of tragedy proves to be within the thought of individual thinkers. 'Hegel's engagement with tragedy determines not merely the content, but also the form, of his philosophy', say the editors.[3] Here, indeed, we are on firm ground (though I for one would see 'helps to direct' as more circumspect than 'determines'), and a comparable claim—that is, a claim comparable in weight—must be made for Nietzsche. But for Kierkegaard (whose specific interest in tragedy is surely outweighed by his engagements with humour and irony)? For Heidegger? And for Freud? Later in the Introduction, the editors invoke 'the tragic philosophy of Freud': a nice but slippery formula that seems designed to bring together Freud's 'reading of Sophocles' *Oedipus Tyrannus*' and his latter-day cultural pessimism, whether explicitly connected to tragedy or not.[4]

---

[2] For a summary example, with reference to the scope of 'the classical tradition' within overall Western experience, see Silk, Gildenhard, and Barrow (2014: 241–8). A celebrated and less summary example, centred on the Romantic age itself, is Abrams (1953).

[3] Introduction, this volume.   [4] Introduction, this volume.

But anyone who inspects (say) Freud's impressive treatise on jokes (*Der Witz*, 1905) would not think to credit its author with a definitive preoccupation with tragedy (the example, it will become clear, is not chosen at random). Then again: 'Marx... placed tragedy at the heart of [his] explorations of... revolution...'.[5] At the *heart*? Marx's interest in Greece and things Greek (tragedy included) is real enough, but even without reference to (let alone *with* reference to) his ultimate millennial-optimistic goals, tragedy can hardly claim the kind of centrality within his 'explorations' that it does for Hegel or for Nietzsche.

In this context, the impressive claim that tragedy has 'created a certain modernity'[6] seems to me to lose, rather than gain, force. *That* claim, though larger than all the others, is surely more defensible, as well as more consequential, than some of the specific claims just noted. Yet here, too, the issue of relative currency surfaces. *Demonstration* of such a claim would require a wider consideration of diffuse currents of thought and response than those attachable to specific 'appropriators'. At this juncture, the editors' comments on the Romantic generation's significant linkage between the concepts of the tragic and the sublime are very much to the point[7]—but, I would want to add, the two concepts arguably belong to a larger set within which the significance (or sometimes even the presence) of any one member is easy to mistake. The concepts in question are not all new, but all are classically derived, and if not new, are at least (in this endlessly inventive Romantic age) newly reinterpreted. What they are reinterpreted *as* is a set of distinctive realities pitched somewhere between qualities of art (or even life) and modes of experience: the tragic, the sublime, and, along with them, irony, pathos, and humour. In the intellectual frameworks of some thinkers (Kierkegaard, for one) the whole set figures—though I am not aware that the set, as a set, has received any definitive discussion. However, consideration of any one member (including the tragic) would profit from such a discussion; and, given the classical origins of these concepts, classicists should not be shy about contributing to it.[8]

---

[5] Introduction, this volume.   [6] Introduction, this volume.

[7] Introduction, this volume. Whereas the editors tend to stress the centrality of German Idealist philosophy to their concerns, is it not Romanticism that more broadly defines the age?

[8] Cf., then, the discussion of the sublime in Silk, Gildenhard, and Barrow (2014: 364–74), and my own comments on pathos in Silk (1988). In this general connection, I welcome the prominent treatment of irony in this volume.

Implicit here is a larger point: diffusion of ideas cannot be limited to philosophical appropriators, and ideas cannot be limited to philosophy. Consider the modern German tradition of literature, and thought, that J. P. Stern has subsumed under the heading of 'the dear purchase'.[9] The phrase points to a cluster of existential responses represented by such formulae as 'the harder the task, the greater its value' and 'the supreme value of intensity and sacrifice'.[10] On one level, these responses can be read as 'the secularized version of the Christian idea of sacrifice';[11] on another, though, they assume, mediate, and diffuse the now embedded notion of the tragic. Stern himself does not foreground this particular relationship, but it is implicit in his whole presentation of the distinctively German 'concern with ideology and metaphysical speculation as explanations for social and political phenomena',[12] along with his insistence on the continuity of German thought, from Herder and Hamann at the end of the eighteenth century to the twentieth-century modernisms of Rilke and Thomas Mann—but also, more disturbingly, the continuity between some of the preoccupations of those impressive achievers and the ideology of the Third Reich. For if (Stern argues) Mann's *Doctor Faustus* (published in 1947) represents the final decisive expression of that Germany, 'the monstrosity of National Socialism was [its] final though not disconnected degradation'.[13] And, across the spectrum of the twentieth-century instantiations of the ideas in question, the influence, or use, or misuse, of *the* 'tragic philosopher', Nietzsche,[14] is pervasive. Nietzsche's 'morality of strenuousness' represents 'the "dear purchase" in its purest form';[15] and, as the poet Gottfried Benn 'confessed' in a letter of 1949, 'what else have we done these last fifty years but trot out and vulgarize his gigantic thoughts and sufferings?'[16] In the Germany, then, whose terminus is marked by this 'confession' by Benn and that famously intellectual novel by Mann, but equally and dismally by the 'degradations' of Nazism, the influence of 'tragic philosophy' is both diffuse and (though, no doubt, open to alternative estimations) still profound. And, in a large cultural perspective, such an influence on the workings and unworkings of modern 'thought' surely counts for more—*even* more—than the specific influence of tragedy itself on important individual thinkers.

---

[9] Stern (1995).   [10] Stern (1995: 10–11).   [11] Stern (1995: 11).
[12] Stern (1995: 368).   [13] Stern (1995: 368).   [14] Stern (1995: 16).
[15] Stern (1995: 346).   [16] Stern (1995: 12–13).

'Thought'—to invoke the editors' own slippage—exceeds 'philosophy', both in scope and in wider cultural signficance.

But, if the editors are inclined, perhaps, to overemphasize philosophies and the direct impact of tragedy on their formation, they seem
to me to understate the value of some of the philosophies in question,
and in particular the capacity of German philosophical theories of
tragedy to illuminate tragedy itself. 'An understanding of German
Idealism and its aftermath . . . is central to getting to grips with both
the generalities and the detail of tragic criticism'; 'these chapters show
the continuing value of a serious confrontation with Idealism—if only
to reject it'.[17] Yes, but—'serious confrontation' with the theories of
Hegel and Nietzsche, in particular, can only inform and enhance a
response to tragedy, and far beyond the capacity of their only established rival, Aristotle's *Poetics*. Whereas Aristotle's categories and
analyses have had an unmatched historical importance, Hegel's
model of tragic conflict and Nietzsche's Dionysiac/Apolline dialectic
have the continuing power to inspire and (in the best sense) provoke
response.[18] The editors properly acknowledge that 'addressing the
shortcomings of the philosophical tradition requires also an appreciation of its merits for reading tragedy';[19] and their informed understanding of the need to challenge the still fashionable reading habits
of classical scholarship, in particular, is wholly admirable—but one
might well wish the case to be made yet more strongly.

As far as Nietzsche is concerned, I would say that the editors'
reference to 'the interplay between . . . reflection and . . . irrationalism'
in Greek tragedy significantly underplays the power of his dialectic to
illuminate tragic drama; and here it is perhaps symptomatic that at
one point they (like many others) are content to simplify his 'tragic
philosophy' with the phrase 'Nietzschean aestheticism'.[20] At several
points in his career, Nietzsche does, of course, make great play with
'the aesthetic', and never more so than in his first book, *The Birth of
Tragedy* (1872). But Nietzsche—even, visibly, in that first book—is
setting forth on a path that will make him one of the founding fathers
of existential thought; and one can hardly allude to his 'aestheticism'
without acknowledging the existential quality of his 'aesthetic'. 'Only
as an *aesthetic phenomenon* can existence and the world be eternally

justified': this, in *The Birth of Tragedy* itself (ch. 5),[21] and elusive though the formulation is, and elusively related though it is to comparable Nietzschean formulations here and elsewhere, it sufficiently indicates that whatever the tragic philosopher is upholding, it is not 'aestheticism' as commonly understood.[22] The Nietzsche of the early 1870s who publicly demanded that the spectators of 'musical tragedy' be 'true aesthetic spectators' (*The Birth of Tragedy*, ch. 24) also knew that 'the spectator of Aeschylean tragedy [responded] as whole man, not aesthetic man'[23]—with the seeming contradiction aptly reflecting the gap between Kantian and his own post-Kantian usage.

It is not only Attic tragedy, but Shakespearian drama on which the great German theories cast their light. The Shakespearian presence in so much modern theorizing of tragedy is, of course, something that the editors (and several of their contributors) are actively aware of— but its implications, and complications, are, from their point of view, awkward. Widening the canon in *this* way opens it up in *others*. 'Should Greek works be differentiated from other traditions of tragic writing?':[24] the editors rightly point to the issue, but hardly acknowledge its scope. Once one lets Shakespeare in, as one must, two large literary–theoretical questions (and/or aesthetic–existential questions . . .) come to the fore: where should we draw the limits of 'tragedy, pure and simple' (George Steiner's phrase)?[25] and, given that many, like Samuel Johnson,[26] have seen Shakespeare's genius as not 'purely' tragic, but as tragicomic, should the quest initiated by the philosophers of the tragic, and properly foregrounded by the editors, be widened to a comparative assessment of contrasting world views, tragic, tragicomic, and comic too?

The first of these questions (on 'tragedy, pure and simple') points at once to the towering tragic drama of Racine in the French seventeenth century—the 'elephant in the room' as far as German 'tragic philosophy' is concerned (and conspicuous by its absence from this volume, too). 'The list of tragedies "pure and simple" is very short,'

---

[21] 'nur als *ästhetisches Phänomen* ist das Dasein und die Welt ewig *gerechtfertigt*' (emphases in original).
[22] *Pace*, e.g., Walter Benjamin's thoughts on the subject, discussed by both editors in their respective chapters in this volume. 'Comparable formulations': Silk and Stern (1981: 294–6).
[23] A note of 1871: Nietzsche (1967–: 3. 3. 285).
[24] Introduction, this volume.   [25] Steiner (1996).
[26] *Preface to Shakespeare* (1765).

says Steiner—but he has no hesitation in identifying 'the three or four supreme plays of Racine' as prime specimens.[27] And, not unrelatedly, Steiner's discussion addresses the second question as well: 'why does human sensibility, in its creative and analytic motions, find the tragic to be more elevated, more fascinating, more conducive to major aesthetic forms and metaphysical suggestion, than it does the comic?'[28] Steiner's pointed (and as yet unanswered) question bears decisively on both of mine, as it does on the preoccupations of the editors and their contributors. I make no claim to have any ready answer myself, but would at least suggest that pointers towards a possible answer are to be found in the painfully constructed thoughts of Kierkegaard[29] and the rather more butterfly reflections of Jean Paul[30]—and add that it is certainly no coincidence that both of *these* thinkers belong, however eccentrically, to the Germanic tradition from which the notion of 'the tragic' itself arises.[31]

In fact, an exploration of wider continuities and deeper contrasts is called for—and, with it, a willingness to commit to categories and questions that espouse the universal. Here, the editors again deserve great credit for challenging fashion (and not only classical–scholarly fashion), though they seem also, perhaps, to hesitate. 'Ever since Aristotle,' they note, 'tragedy has been seen to have a . . . privileged relation to universalism'.[32] Well, yes—though it should be said that, until the eighteenth century and the rise of historicism, virtually *all* artistic or literary categories enjoyed the same privilege: 'tragedy' is one of the categories that managed to survive the damaging perspectives of historical relativizing, which is what, all too often, historicism has turned out to mean. As Hesiod might have put it, there are actually two kinds

---

[27] Steiner (1996: 542).   [28] Steiner (1996: 534).

[29] Esp. those in the *Concluding Scientific Postscript* (*Afsluttende uvidenskabelig Efterskrift*, 1846).

[30] *Vorschule der Ästhetik*, 1804.

[31] The long history of tragicomic experiments and the not-quite-so-long history of readings of works of all sorts as 'tragicomic' also deserve particular attention in this connection, and not least because of the common *modern* perception that tragicomedy is itself distinctively *modern*: Silk (2000: 71–2). 'Modern art', said Mann in 1926, 'sees life as tragicomedy' (preface to Freissler's translation of Conrad's *The Secret Agent* as *Der Geheimagent*); and a century earlier, we already hear it said that 'the drama . . . which in the same breath moulds . . . tragedy and comedy is the salient characteristic . . . of today's literature' (Victor Hugo, preface to *Cromwell*, 1827). This and other examples in Silk (2000: 71–2).

[32] Introduction, this volume.

of historicism: good and bad. The good kind seeks to place the language, the idiom, the conventions of (say) a Greek tragedy against the wider ('contextual') realities of the Greek language, the Greek theatre, and Greek culture; the bad pretends that no other treatment of a Greek tragedy has any interpretative status, and that, in particular, any attempt to draw conclusions from the tragic experience (or whatever) of one culture, or period, and then relate them to the experience of another can only mislead and should only be discouraged.

The editors' remarks about 'universalism' and 'privilege' clearly imply a certain tolerance: 'the historicism of recent years' (they refer to the influential school of Vernant) 'can be as unreflective as the universalism it supplanted'.[33] Once again: yes, but... Universalizing can be done badly and inadequately—but historicizing of the second kind is, almost by definition, unreflective *per se*. The editors go on to suggest that 'the pitfalls of an uncritical application of modern concepts to ancient texts are all too obvious'.[34] The pitfalls of *anything* 'uncritical' are obvious, surely; and 'application' is suspect in itself, if it means, as it often does, the denial of open, sensitive, integrated response (this being the ideal) in favour of the arbitrary imposition of intellectual formulae or categories, from whatever source. Imposition of Aristotelian categories on Greek tragedy, for instance, is no less suspect than any other.

I commend the editors' call for specialist scholars (and not just specialist classicists) to respond and speak up beyond their specialism. In this endeavour, though, as the editors say, 'classicists have a distinctive voice'—but not just in 'thinking about what it means to read the ancients'.[35] If the relationship of tragedy to 'modernity' is to be appreciated 'as a phenomenon of classical reception'[36] (or, as I would much prefer to say, of *the classical tradition*),[37] classicists are assuredly, in principle, well placed to take a lead in the necessary dialogue.[38] The endeavour—the editors' endeavour—is indeed as admirable as it is important, and my qualifications are not meant to suggest otherwise.

---

[33] Introduction, this volume.

[34] Introduction, this volume. Vernantian 'concepts' are themselves in one sense 'modern' (structuralist), but this is hardly the time and place to argue the point.

[35] Introduction, this volume. [36] Introduction, this volume.

[37] On the difference between classical reception and the classical tradition, see Silk, Gildenhard, and Barrow (2014: 3–9). The relevance of Shakespearian tragedy to the project makes it apparent, from the start, why the more inclusive 'tradition' is at issue.

[38] Cf. Silk (2001: 44–5).

APPENDIX

Jacob Bernays, 'Outlines of Aristotle's Lost Work on the Effects of Tragedy', sect. IV

Translated by James I. Porter

Translator's Note: The following is a translation of the fourth and final section of Bernays's essay *Grundzüge der verlorenen Abhandlung des Aristoteles über Wirkung der Tragödie* (Bernays (1970 [1857])), the section that contains the most striking of Bernays's arguments about catharsis. Owing to its unavailability in translation and to its departure from the more narrowly philological method of the early parts of the essay, section IV is the least well represented in the literature on Bernays's theory of catharsis, both in Classics and elsewhere. Bernays's preamble and sections I–II exist in an English translation by Jennifer Barnes (Bernays 2006). A complete rendering of the article would have to include section III and the several pages of appendices that pass for 'Notes'. Bernays writes a formidable German that is at once quaintly old-fashioned and devilishly baroque. I have done my best to make him readable in English while respecting his style and logic. Page numbers given in brackets are to the 1970 reprint followed by the 1857 original. All notes are my own. I am grateful to Constanze Güthenke for her careful comments on my translation. Any errors that remain are naturally my own.

[40/171] IV

From this understanding of catharsis [as elaborated in the first three sections of this essay[1]] we gain, first and foremost, the following positive result, and it is hardly trivial: the cathartic effect of Greek and of every true tragedy no longer needs to be established by analysing individual dramas. As long as a moral reform of the passions was sought for and found in catharsis, such an analysis was indispensable, for the simple reason that it does not require the unimpeachable instincts of genius of the sort that protected Goethe or Plato

---

[1] These included a polemical preamble against Lessing and his following; a section on the medical analogy to the pathological processes of catharsis (I); a section on pity and fear (II); and a section on the evidence for Aristotle's theory of *katharsis* in the writings of Iamblichus, Porphyry, and Proclus (III).

[from error],[2] but only ordinary candour to acknowledge that a moral effect of tragedy like this cannot be *immediately* felt, and all the less so the better a tragedy is. As Goethe rightly emphasizes (see p. 5/137), the [tragic] effect would have to be immediate if it were to be accorded so permanent and venerable a place in the definition of tragedy. If Lessing, in the haste that spurred him on in his *Dramaturgie*, had not considered himself released from the obligation to make such a demonstration [of the moral function of catharsis] through an analysis [of individual plays] [40/172]—if, say, he had attempted the demonstration, realized its inevitable failure, and then reconciled himself to this insight—in that case he might well have given up his assumption that abstracting the possibility of moral catharsis from Greek tragedy could be justified by appealing to Aristotle, though doubtless not his view about the moralizing function of theatre. That was a given for the century in which he lived and which had not yet been emancipated by Goethe.

To be sure, Lessing's successors, less hasty than he, took up with renewed zeal the analysis that he left unfinished—with what degree of success others may decide as they wish, if they can bear the sight of such a procrustean catechism, conditioned as it was by the moral compendium of the eighteenth and nineteenth centuries being imposed upon the powerful Muse of Aeschylus, who towers over all such morality, the gentler Muse of Sophocles, who disregards all such morality, and the impassioned Muse of Euripides, who overwhelms all such morality. Aristotle was completely freed from so distressing an affair, which requires hauling the great tragic triumvirate in for moral interrogation, and so are we in Aristotle's wake.

Aristotle's postulate of catharsis requires of tragedy nothing more than that it should provide the spectator with a subject matter capable of releasing in him the twin emotions of pity and fear. *How* the poet should go about structuring his work to this end is something for which Aristotle furnished the most rigorous and seminal guidelines imaginable in chapters 13 and 14 [of the *Poetics*], backed up with abundant references to the repertoire of the Greek stage, some commendatory, others critical. On the other hand, the fact *that* tragically effective plays achieve this pathological effect is something he most certainly did not seek to establish by adducing literary historical evidence, not even once he reached the now lost portion [of the *Poetics*]. Indeed, if anyone had asked him for such evidence, he would have answered as he does in a similar circumstance elsewhere in his works (for in such cases

---

[2] Bernays knows that Plato and Goethe reached the same conclusion on different grounds: Plato felt that tragedy was not a locus of moral value or any value (it was in fact morally dangerous), hence it could offer no moral benefit (though he nowhere discusses catharsis *per se*); Goethe had other, enlightened reasons, and Bernays returns to these at the end of section IV.

he tends to become rather brusque): 'that is to ask for proofs in matters where our feelings are too reliable to be in need of any further substantiation' (ζητεῖν λόγον ὧν βέλτιον ἔχομεν ἢ λόγου δεῖσθαι).[3] Only once does he apply the yardstick of the general theory of catharsis—not to individual model dramas, but to the tragic power of the model poets. And the result, which has caused so many readers to throw up their hands in astonished disbelief, runs like this: 'however much Euripides may falter in matters of dramatic [41/173] organization, he manifestly is and remains the most tragic of the poets' (καὶ ὁ Εὐριπίδης, εἰ καὶ τὰ ἄλλα μὴ εὖ οἰκονομεῖ, ἀλλὰ τραγικώτατός γε τῶν ποιητῶν φαίνεται).[4]

A judgement like this would be utterly inexplicable if Aristotle had required of catharsis that it bring about a moral improvement or even only an immediate quieting of the passions. For, however removed one may be from the puerile and cavalier misprision that the Romantics outrageously committed against Euripides, one will look in vain for either ethical or artistic quiet and harmony in the poet or his plays. Instead, what one finds there is a revelling in things being torn apart and in the act of disruption itself, an ecstatic despair, and groans of compassion (*Mitleid*), fetched from the very depths of the understanding and the heart, for the old world on the brink of collapse, and a delicious fear (*Furcht*) and shuddering (*Schaudern*) at the prospect of a fast-approaching new age. These are the feelings that flow from the personality of Euripides into his dramas and then ravish the spectator in turn, carrying him away in similar orgies of pity and fear. But it is for these very reasons—because Euripides has an impact like this, because he so powerfully elicits these emotions and gives their flood so deep and broad a channel into which it can disgorge itself—that he is the most cathartic of the poets. And, because the most immediate effect of tragedy consists in this cathartic disturbance and discharge, Aristotle can rebuke Euripides for his other poetic deficiencies while in the same breath affirming that he is the 'most tragic of the poets'—and what is more, that he is 'manifestly' (*phainetai*) this. The unanimous opinion of Greek audiences confirms this judgement about Euripides, just as their opinion attests to the fact that *all* good tragedies satisfy the requirement of a pathological catharsis, some to a greater and others to a lesser degree. Indeed, Aristotle's judgement can be explained in no other way.

A correct understanding of catharsis not only makes reconciling the ancient poets and Aristotle unnecessary; it also produces a welcome agreement with the fundamental perspectives of Goethe, which (there is no denying it) have shaped the hearts and minds of all true progeny of our

---

[3] Aristotle, *Physics* 8.3, 254ª31. More literally, 'to seek an explanation in a case where we are too well off to require argument' (trans. R. P. Hardie and R. K. Gaye).

[4] Aristotle, *Poetics* 13, 1453ª29.

century. As Goethe saw it, the offensive aspect of Lessing's moral explanation lay less in the fact that it incorporated the effect [of tragedy] into the definition [of tragedy] [42/174] than in the fact that this effect was now supposed to be as indirect and accidental as a moral effect can only ever be. Goethe found it incredible that Aristotle should have had in mind not merely an effect, 'but what is more, a *remote* effect that a tragedy might *possibly* have on the spectator'.[5] Goethe's attitude here is the same as in natural science, where he cannot abide the idea of a capricious and gratuitous teleology that foists a purpose onto natural objects and that, to borrow a piece of British wit, allows fire to exist in the world so that the smoker may light his cigar with it. For the same reason he will not brook this *transcendental* teleology in art either, not even in Aristotle, who—as Goethe knew as well as anyone— made final causes one of the four pillars of his own method of causal explanation.

In the diagnosis of natural objects, and especially of natural organisms, Goethe had no objection to appealing to the kind of effect that designates either what follows by necessity from an object's nature alone or the inalienable definition of an individual entity in its particularity alone, or even the outwardly turned aspect of its innermost properties alone—that is, the kind of account that permits one to say about fire that it ignites, about plants that they are fragrant, or about man that he masters the world with his thoughts. And Goethe would have taken just as little offence at this notion of an *immanent* teleology in the definition of an 'organism' of art. Indeed, the catharsis of tragedy, correctly understood, designates nothing other than an effect that is indissolubly linked to intrinsic purposiveness. Just as fire ignites if a combustible material approaches it, so must a tragic action that is composed of sad and frightful events induce an outbreak of pity and fear in anyone who is capable of being moved to these affections—that is, any spectator who is endowed with a natural constitution. If only Goethe had been able to carry out his well-known resolution, which he sadly made only when it was too late, to learn decent Greek and, no less, to do so by reading Aristotle! His aesthetic principles, combined with sound linguistic proficiency, would have led him to a correct view of the final clause of the definition [of tragedy in *Poetics*, ch. 6]. And, on the other hand, he would have realized that his requirement of a 'rounding off [of the action] through its resolution',[6] which appears to him to be imperative and which [43/175] he wants to impose on that final clause (at the cost of horrific violence to the text), is of course recognized as valid by Aristotle. But it is also given its rightful due in an earlier clause in the same definition, which requires that

---

[5] Goethe, *Nachlese zu Aristoteles' 'Poetik'*, in Goethe (1999 [1827]: 336); Bernays's emphasis.
[6] Goethe (1999 [1827]: 336).

tragedy should represent a 'complete action' (τελείας πράξεως)—an action that, as Aristotle himself says, 'has a beginning, middle, and *end*' (τὸ ἔχον ἀρχὴν καὶ μέσον καὶ τελευτήν).[7]

From this point on, the more clearly catharsis emerges as a broadly conceived universal, one that is congenial to both ancient and modern poetry, the more essential it will be to demonstrate what normative force catharsis has in its full and principal meaning for poets and audiences alike. The quickest and surest way to achieve this is to allow the universality of catharsis to emerge from Aristotle's thoughts along the genetic route that he himself favoured. The majority of its conceptual factors have been encountered by us already, albeit in a scattered fashion, as is only to be expected from an enquiry that proceeds by zigzags along a heuristic and critical path. The order of these thoughts in their inner coherence will surface only at the conclusion of our enquiry, where they will also serve as a recapitulation of the individual steps taken along the way.

As is almost always the case wherever Aristotle puts forward his signature claims, so too here: he grounds his argument in empirical fact. The fact in this case lies in the realm of ecstatic behaviour, which in Oriental and Greek antiquity occurred all that much more frequently the more deeply such a welling-up and overflowing of the entire psychic apparatus must have stimulated the lively excitability of those peoples, and the more their self-consciousness (a function that had not yet consolidated its sovereignty) gave in, unresistingly, to self-renouncing rapture. Where the human spirit had not yet made itself at home within, the state of ecstasy was considered to be holy and divine: accordingly, public cults took orgiastic frenzy under their consecrating wing and ordained for it fixed forms of assuagement. Among these priestly means of quieting ecstasy was a procedure that stilled motion through motion and boisterousness within through boisterous song.

This procedure, above all else, must have attracted the attention of a philosopher like Aristotle, who is never more eager to pursue reality's traces than when they appear to lead in the opposite direction of abstract logic. In order [44/176] to be able to grasp this phenomenon philosophically, which was there for all to see but incomprehensible to the masses and for that reason taken to be holy and an object of marvel, he connected it to comparable medical experiences. Like cathartic instruments that heal the body by extruding the diseased matter out into the open, the frenzied songs of Olympus work on the ecstatic element within, drawing it forth: the ecstatic element bubbles up against the fetters of consciousness without being able to loosen them on its own. This relentless agitation would bring down the protective foundations of the mind unless the mind could find a support in the power of song, in whose train it is now carried away: enraptured, it rushes

---

[7] Aristotle, *Poetics* 7, 1450[b]26.

headlong forward and gives itself over to the pleasure that comes with bursting free of all the constraints of the self; once this pleasure has been atoned for, the mind reverts to the calm composure of its regulated condition.

In both the ordinary somatic and the ecstatic forms of catharsis, equilibrium is restored after it has been [momentarily] lost through a solicitation of the disturbing matter;[8] only, the ecstatic catharsis is distinguished by the fact that it is capable of generating merely temporary but never lasting relief, and by the fact that it is always accompanied by the feeling of pleasure, as is consistent with the nature of ecstasy. In this differentiated form, the phenomenon observed in ecstatic catharsis proves to be susceptible of a generalization that takes in every kind of affection in the soul. And here the generalization is not arrived at by way of a string of analogies, any more than is the case elsewhere in Aristotle. Instead, the fact in question is grasped at its conceptual centre and is then, as it were, given room so that it can expand outward into a circle in which the related facts will effortlessly fall into place. For, all forms of *pathos* [affection] are essentially ecstatic; in all of them a person is put *outside of himself*. And in ecstasies in the proper sense, which is what Aristotle and the Greeks meant by 'enthusiasm', we find the most violent ecstatic manifestations of all, because here ecstasy lacks an object: it ignites itself and feeds on its own flame. That is precisely why the symptoms and the effects of the healing process can be observed here in their purest form. And what obtains in ecstasy—that is, the primary form of *pathos* [Urpathos], which is bound up with *no* object at all—must be able to be successfully transferred onto a *pathos* that is kindled by determinate objects. This transference must take place if the circumstances entailed by the involvement with any given object [45/177] are to receive due attention, and if we bear in mind that generic, pathological catharsis, like its specific paradigm ecstatic catharsis, merely exercises a temporary effect and that it is always accompanied by a feeling of pleasure.

It must have been precisely these two corollaries,[9] both of which are demanded by logic, that tempted Aristotle to develop his theory of catharsis even further, especially given the way they so seamlessly meshed with his most cherished psychological and ethical principles. For he held it neither possible nor desirable to suffocate entirely the part of the soul that is inhabited by the emotions (τὸ παθητικόν). In a lost treatise, he clearly stated that 'the emotions, if they are correctly used, become weapons of virtue',

---

[8] By 'solicitation' (*Solicitation*), Bernays understands a stirring-up or agitation (κίνησις) of the affections in the soul, following Aristotle (e.g. Aristotle, *Politics* 8.7, 1342ᵃ8). See Bernays (1970 [1857]: 30/162, 32/164, 47/165, 41–2/173–4).

[9] I.e., the last two stipulations named: the temporariness of the effect and its component of pleasure.

much to the astonishment of Seneca, who was enamoured with the concept of Stoic indifference (ἀπαθία).[10] And he was unwilling to allow reason to govern that part of the soul that is affect-laden the way a lord governs his slaves; rather, it should issue commands only 'as a public official or constitutional king commands its lawful citizens'.[11]

In other words, the less that Aristotle expected healing to result from the deadening radical cures of the emotions, the greater must have been the trust he placed in the discharging effects of pathological catharsis, precisely because of the sporadic and temporary nature of their palliation. And he must have embraced the hedonic nature of these effects as doubly welcome, both practically and theoretically. For, as far as praxis is concerned, every reader of his *Ethics* knows that Aristotle did not regard pleasure (ἡδονή) with either the solemn contempt of Plato or the fierce loathing of the Stoics. Even in those cases where he feels he has to warn against the power of pleasure to distort judgement, he confesses to knowing the feeling that stole over the Trojan elders when they saw Helen approaching: they found it quite understandable that Trojans and Greeks alike should endure so many sufferings on account of this woman whose very aspect was like that of an immortal goddess, but they were nevertheless prepared to send her away, 'lovely though she was',[12] lest further 'woes' should befall themselves and their children (ὅπερ οὖν οἱ δημογέροντες ἔπαθον πρὸς τὴν Ἑλένην, τοῦτο δεῖ παθεῖν καὶ ἡμᾶς πρὸς τὴν ἡδονήν, καὶ ἐν πᾶσι τὴν ἐκείνων ἐπιλέγειν φωνήν).[13]

Given this attitude, Aristotle could hardly dispute the general applicability of the cathartic process, whose healing powers are amply demonstrated in the case of ecstasy, simply because [46/178] this process is at the same time necessarily hedonic. On the contrary, he will have gladly seized on the even greater opportunity to bring to light, now as a theoretical consideration, a component of all forms of *pathos* that was hedonic and that could facilitate catharsis. I have already noted in a related context[14] how among poets and in popular lore it was a familiar notion from time immemorial that even the darkest emotions were mingled with pleasure. There I also made reference to Aristotle's attempts in his *Rhetoric*, in keeping with the popular slant of that work, to make philosophical deductions about some of the emotions that display striking mixtures of the same sort—for instance, the 'sweetness' of anger and the 'joyfulness' of sadness.

---

[10] Seneca, *On Anger* 1.17 = fr. 80 Rose.
[11] Aristotle, *Politics* 1.5, 1254^{b}5. [12] Homer, *Iliad* 3.158.
[13] 'We ought, then, to feel towards pleasure as the elders of the people felt towards Helen, and in all circumstances repeat their saying' (Aristotle, *Nicomachean Ethics* 2.9, 1109^{b}9–10; trans. W. D. Ross).
[14] 'Ergänzung zu Aristoteles' *Poetik*', in *Rheinisches Museum für Philologie*, NS 8 (1853), 567 = Bernays (1880 [1853]: 143).

Aristotle was able to reserve a deeper and more coherent justification of these scattered hints for the section on catharsis in his *Poetics*,[15] where the sequence of ideas made it imperative and also significantly easier to do so. There, ecstasy was the culmination of the entire argument. And in order to expose the hedonic element in every affection, Aristotle needed only to remind his readers again first of the fact that every affection, inasmuch as it places a person outside himself, is ecstatic (p. 44/176), and then of his definition of pleasure (ἡδονή) from the *Rhetoric*, according to which pleasure depends upon a sudden disturbance and restoration of psychic equilibrium (κίνησις τῆς ψυχῆς καὶ κατάστασις ἀθρόα καὶ αἰσθητὴ εἰς τὴν ὑπάρχουσαν φύσιν),[16] in other words, that pleasure too depends upon an ecstatic process. Consequently, every affection, because it contains an ecstatic element, also contains a hedonic element, however painful the object that elicits it may appear to be. And a solicitation of the affection will 'relieve' the affected person 'under the accompaniment of a feeling of pleasure' (κουφίζεσθαι μεθ᾽ ἡδονῆς, p. 11/143),[17] that is, will afford him a catharsis, if it presents its object in such a way that the ecstatic pleasure, expanding the individual and bursting it apart from within, prevails over the power of the object—a power that as it were compresses the individual from without and is for that reason the source of unpleasure (λύπη).

And yet not all the affections prove to be equally worthy of attention: the catharsis that corresponds to their specific nature will not in every case merit closer evaluation by ethical philosophers or introduction into life and custom by practical ethicists (in ancient parlance: [47/179] lawgivers). The more unique the object stimulating the emotion is and the more its stimulation depends upon the particular character and the changing vicissitudes of the individual, the less philosophers and lawgivers will want to attend to this affection. Their concern is directed at those emotions that repeatedly flare up around the most diverse objects, and therefore are present in every normal human nature as *affections* (cf. p. 17/149),[18] and that are ready to erupt at any time, simply because they belong to the constitution of human beings generally. And just as such *universal* emotions have a justifiable claim to a catharsis that caters for them alone, so too will this claim be best satisfied by those emotions.[19] Through the sheer abundance of their objects these emotions nearly attain the objectlessness of pure ecstasy, which renders them more readily prone to cathartic treatment. And, as in pure ecstasy, where all that is required is that the lively power of movement in the universe at large should be channelled into an ecstatic nature [i.e., person] by means of intoxicating song, so too in the case of universal emotion one does not

---

[15] A section that is now lost, according to Bernays.
[16] Aristotle, *Rhetoric* 1.11, 1369ᵇ33–5, *inter alia*.
[17] Aristotle, *Politics* 8.6, 1342ᵃ14–15.   [18] 'Affectionen'.   [19] 'Affecten'.

have to look far and wide for objects that can prompt a catharsis: social life, with its never-ending reversals, offers an all too ready supply.

Now, long before a philosopher first came up with aesthetic theories, the spirit of the Greek race, which found its voice in the poets, developed a genre of poetry to celebrate and honour God, a God that put individuals into a genuine state of rapture when they first approached him and for whom, accordingly, orgiastic ceremonies remained for ever sacred. This genre of poetry simultaneously preserved and ennobled the original Bacchic ecstasy while adapting it to now altered social circumstances: it did so by substituting an enthusiastic frenzy that was directed at no object in particular with a representation of universal and human destiny that was designed to excite universal human emotions in an ecstatic form. It was not only the poet who was acutely conscious of *which* emotions it was that tragic drama gave rise to whenever he reflected on what he had produced in an inspired state, but also the ordinary spectator in the audience endowed with the simple capacity to feel.

Of particular significance in this regard is the way Plato, when he is discussing the organic unity of the poetic work of art in the *Phaedrus*, describes the bungling poetaster. This aspiring poet draws himself up next to Sophocles and Euripides and fancies that [48/180] he has sufficiently shown himself to be their equal in the department of poetry simply by stating 'that he knows how to produce pity-inducing tirades at one moment and fearful and frightening ones at another, as he pleases' (ὡς ἐπίσταται ῥήσεις ποιεῖν ὅταν τε βούληται οἰκτράς, καὶ τοὐναντίον αὖ φοβερὰς καὶ ἀπειλητικάς).[20] Clearly, even the poetaster recognizes that tragedy is directed at pity and fear. What proves his illegitimacy as a poet is the fact that he wants to reach this goal by means of 'tirades' and that he views the two emotions as opposites (τοὐναντίον) that merely follow each other sequentially in time. What Plato's own view of the matter is, and how differently he would himself cast the relationship of fear to pity, is impossible to determine with any certainty based on this one remark above. But on the various other occasions when he discusses tragedy in the later dialogues, the word 'fear' is completely absent and only 'pity' is singled out as a tragic emotion, possibly because Plato, older now and disaffected with poetry, has no interest in delving any deeper into the theory of tragedy. Be that as it may, precisely because it expresses not Plato's own thoughts but the sentiments of the greater masses, the passage from the *Phaedrus* testifies all the more reliably to the fact that even the most ordinary spectator could be as deeply moved by fear as by pity. Yet, it fell not to Plato or to any other philosopher, but to Aristotle alone to deduce from this palpable fact the secret of the tragic art

---

[20] Plato, *Phaedrus* 268d. Bernays has slightly abridged the quotation.

and, to the extent that mysteries like this can enter into the public domain, to make it accessible to rational thought through definitions and principles. This was Aristotle's unique and lasting contribution.

Acquiring this secret was facilitated in the first instance by the direction he took in his reflections on catharsis, but above all by the insight he had gained, independently of aesthetic theory, into the nature and reciprocal relationship of these two emotions. From the outset these can only have appeared to him to be both supremely universal and ecstatic–hedonic[21] emotions—in other words, they must have appeared to be as worthy as they were capable of producing a specific catharsis. For, given that he considered self-sufficiency and self-satisfaction ($α\mathring{v}τάρκεια$) to be the highest form of perfection, one that God alone possessed while mankind for ever strove to attain it, Aristotle must have recognized in pity and fear, beyond all other emotions, the two doors that are flung wide open and through which the external world [49/181] invades the human psyche. It is through these openings that the irrepressible force of the affective element of the mind wells up and hurls itself against the balanced coherence within in order to suffer along with others who experience the same feelings and to tremble before the tumultuous chaos of strange and threatening things. However, it was not this recognition by itself that enabled Aristotle to discover the mechanisms by which pity and fear are aroused, but rather its connection to the much deeper insight that he develops in his *Rhetoric*—namely, the notion that pity and fear are constitutively bound up with each other, and that one has pity for another only on account of what one fears for oneself. It was this insight into the mutual implication of pity and fear that finally permitted Aristotle to map out the means by which pity and fear are aroused in the case of genuine catharsis and thereby to expose the inner economy of tragedy, as he does in chapters 13 and 14 of the *Poetics*.

The principles spelled out there have a single goal—namely, to ensure that nothing in the course of the action or in the nature of the characters should weaken this intertwining of pity and fear. No matter how sharply marked his or her individuality may be and no matter how singular his or her lot may be, the person who excites pity must remain sufficiently close to the primary form (*Urform*) of the universal human character, and his or her destiny must originate plainly enough from the urn that contains the fates of the whole of humankind, so that the spectator can see himself in the mirror of another who is like himself ($\acute{o}\,\acute{o}μοιος$), and so that the pity he feels for the suffering that is depicted on stage can be returned to him as a reflex of the fear he harbours within himself. Pity, in other words, is safeguarded from singularity

---

[21] *Ekstatisch hedonisch*, lit. 'ecstatically hedonic'—i.e. hedonic in an ecstatic way. Presumably not all pleasures are ecstatic, or rather palpably ecstatic.

through its association with fear. And fear, on the other hand, can never be aroused directly or through a [lifeless] thing—for example, through the mad deeds of a moral monster (μιαρός), which would have to be reckoned the horrific activity of an insensible thing and not the expression of a conscious individual's will. For fear should never impinge on the spectator with such disabling power that it robs him altogether of the mental freedom that is required for fellow feeling. Fear should never expel pity (ἐκκρουστικὸν τοῦ ἐλέου).[22] Rather, the tragic poet should elicit objective fear only in the refracted form of subjective pity, and only as a premonition that reflects the suffering of the tragic hero onto the spectator. And, if the poet steadily draws tight the bond that constitutively links the two emotions from within, his work will [50/182] automatically precipitate its cathartic—that is, ecstatically hedonic—excitement.

For, if pity becomes so universalized that the spectator becomes one with the tragic hero, then the pain that the bare fact of suffering (αὐτὸ τὸ πάθος)[23] can cause on its own, quite independently of the compassion that it causes, will vanish before the rapture that accompanies this stepping outside of one's self—not least because the awareness one has of the [theatrical] illusion, an awareness that is never entirely dormant, already serves to mitigate this empirical pain. By contrast, an object of fear that is directly represented would remain an unabated source of overwhelming pain even given the most prescient awareness of the [theatrical] illusion, simply because fear is anything but a rational emotion. Instead of dissolving in ecstasy and pleasure, the spectator's self, if it were faced with such terrors, would double up in a cringing mass within. Only if objective fear is mediated through personal pity can the purely cathartic process unfold in the spectator's mind. And it does so in such a way that the spectator's self, through its experience of fellow-feeling,[24] expands and merges into the self of the whole of humanity. At this point it stands face to face with the frightfully sublime laws of the universe and its incomprehensible powers, powers that encompass the whole of humanity, and it allows itself to be pierced by a fear that, although it is an ecstatic shuddering in the face of the universe, is at the same time a source of unrivalled and unadulterated pleasure. For, as Aristotle states clearly, it is not an overwhelming fear (φοβεῖσθαι) that tragic fear will exercise, but rather a shuddering (φρίττειν),[25] that is, the kind of loosening jolt[26] that runs through a person whenever he experiences any intense physical or mental pleasure whatsoever.

---

[22] Aristotle, *Rhetoric* 2.8, 1386ª22.   [23] Aristotle, *Poetics* 14, 1453ᵇ18.

[24] *Mitleid*: either 'pity' or 'fellow-feeling'. In its components (*mit + Leiden*), the German word conveys two senses: compassionate awareness and sharing in another's sufferings.

[25] Aristotle, *Poetics* 14, 1453ᵇ5.   [26] Or 'shock' (*Erschütterung*).

Given the light that the theory of catharsis sheds on the principles of *Poetics* chapters 13 and 14 and above all on the idea of tragic fear, it is now possible to address properly the question that has received so much attention of late—namely, how Aristotle could pass over in silence the idea of fate in tragedy. The more reasonably minded among those who put the question do so in order to abolish the notion of a blind and capricious fate, which is nothing but the aberration of a misguided Romanticism: it is an idea that nowhere arises in genuine works of poetry, nor is it one that will ever provoke theoretical reflection in a philosopher. One only wonders how it happened that Aristotle failed to mention even once the relationship of the tragic heroes to the general law that presides over the universe, a relationship that in every tragedy is instrumental to the progress of the action and to the decisions taken by the characters [51/183], above all in Greek tragedy. Yet, even if 'fate' or a similar word does not occur in the *Poetics*, this does not mean that Aristotle overlooked the *thing*, to the extent that fate has a bearing on the construction of tragedy. The more powerfully the non-philosophical Greek world, down to the last hour of its collapse, felt itself to be governed by the inscrutable powers of fate, and the more resignedly it lent all its clarity and beauty to this high shadow screen, the more determined was Greek philosophy to eliminate *fate* from its vocabulary, along with other like terms that are mere stammering attempts to name the essence of everything that exceeds comprehension. And so, from the time when Democritus and Anaxagoras first devoted themselves to the explanation of individual phenomena and Socrates did the same through the instrument of dialectic, philosophers sought to replace fate with the clearest and most sharply defined equivalents that they could produce within their respective conceptual systems. Not even in his *Ethics* does Aristotle make any allowances for fate, although this is where one would most expect him to do so. It was only in the Stoa, which was no longer a purely Greek school, that the concept of providence (πρόνοια) first became visible—a concept that, like so many other notions in this school, was imported from the Orient. As the philosophy evolved the need arose to make use of the counterpart of providence—namely, fate (εἱμαρμένη). And it was only in later philosophical systems that were built on and against the Bible, which was itself brightly illumined by the concept of providence, that questions about fate and related concepts managed to attain the high degree of significance that they eventually enjoyed in the history of modern thought.

In order to establish a counterweight to the unstable nature of tragic material, it was precisely in his *Poetics* that Aristotle took it upon himself, more rigorously than he does in his other writings, to found his principles only on the simplest and clearest of concepts. Fate has no place among these, not then and not today. As a result, the principles employed by Aristotle have an empirical appearance, and, for many of his readers who are accustomed to the spicy flavour of the modern speculative idiom, perhaps a certain blandness. And yet anyone who appreciates the innocent simplicity of the ancient thinkers will quickly notice that, in Solger's apt phrase, all these empirical principles were drawn up under the '*quiet* assumption of a "higher reason"'.[27] And it would be difficult to say that [52/184] relentlessly and noisily harping on this higher reason, the way modern aesthetics does, is any real improvement. If nothing else, we can expect the endless treatments of tragic fate to bear no other fruit worth mentioning beyond the recognition that the tragic hero need not be an evil creature, but he must be destroyed through an ethical failing. And no one has stated this very principle more rigorously and clearly than Aristotle (μεταβάλλειν ἐξ εὐτυχίας εἰς δυστυχίαν μὴ διὰ μοχθηρίαν ἀλλὰ δι᾽ ἁμαρτίαν τινά).[28]

He developed it at first out of his concept of fear: this could be aroused in the spectator only through suffering that afflicts someone whom he views not as an aberrant individual but as an equal (ὁ φόβος περὶ τὸν ὅμοιον).[29] For Aristotle, every genuine interest in fate springs from what he calls fear. Consequently, by tragic fear he understands the thrilling sensation that runs through a person whenever he envisions his place in the universe and its mysterious laws dictating punishments and rewards—an awareness that comes neither by observing individual actions nor through conceptual understanding but from intuition alone. Tragedy and the ultimate end towards which all of its elements aims—namely, tragic fear fuelled by pity—appeared to Aristotle to be neither capable of nor intended for moral improvement or intellectual enlightenment. For such purposes he felt that other means should be mobilized. He would have agreed with every word of what an artist like Goethe (above p. 5/137) was candid enough to admit: 'No art can have any impact on morality; only philosophy and religion can do this.'[30] Instead, Aristotle allotted to tragedy a by no means inferior task: that of representing to man his relationship to the universe in such a way that the oppressive feeling that stems from this relationship—a feeling that leaves the masses groping their way forward aimlessly and numbed, while nobler spirits strive to hold their own against it by resorting, precisely, to religion and philosophy—erupts for brief moments in pleasurable shuddering. As a philosopher, Aristotle can attribute no lasting improving power to a surge of ecstasy like this. But he does consider the experience to be morally harmless (χαρὰ ἀβλαβής ['a harmless joy']).[31] He would also have agreed

---

[27] Solger (1826: ii. 524.).
[28] 'To pass from good fortune to bad fortune, not because of wickedness, but because of a mistake' (Aristotle, *Poetics* 13, 1453ª15). Bernays has abridged the quotation and added τινά.
[29] 'Fear for someone like oneself' (Aristotle, *Poetics* 13, 1453ª5–6).
[30] Goethe (1999 [1827]: 337).   [31] Aristotle, *Politics* 8.7, 3142.16.

with another sentiment of Goethe's, save for its poetic superlative: 'I do not seek my well-being in the fixity of a stone. Shuddering is the best part of mankind.'[32]

---

[32] Goethe, *Faust* II, Act I, 6272. *Schaudern* ('shuddering') can also mean 'awe', but Bernays's preference for the former is evident from his essay. Cf. n. 25.

References

Abel, L. (1963). *Metatheatre: A New View of Dramatic Form*. New York.

Abrams, M. H. (1953). *The Mirror and the Lamp: Romantic Theory and the Critical Tradition*. New York.

Adorno, T. W. (1991). *Notes to Literature*, i, ed. R. Tiedemann, trans. S. Weber. New York.

Agamben, G. (2013). *Opus Dei: An Archaeology of Duty*, trans. A. Kotsko. Stanford.

Alt, P.-A. (2000). *Schiller: Leben-Werk-Zeit*. Munich.

Alt, P.-A. (2008). *Klassische Endspiel: das Theater Goethes und Schillers*. Munich.

Alvares, C. (2012). 'Prédation et violence fondatrice: La Chasse dans la réinterpretation par Pascal Quignard de la théorie mimétique-sacrificielle', *L'Esprit Créateur*, 52: 35–47.

Anderson, W. D. (1965). *Matthew Arnold and the Classical Tradition*. Ann Arbor.

Ardovino, A. (2001). 'L'Antigone di Heidegger', in Montani (2001), 149–98.

Armstrong, R. (2005). *Freud and the Ancient World: A Compulsion for Antiquity*. Ithaca, NY.

Ashfield, A., and De Bolla, P. (1996) (eds). *The Sublime: A Reader in British Eighteenth-Century Aesthetic Theory*. Cambridge.

Bachofen, J. J. (1967). *Myth, Religion and Mother Right: Selected Writings of J. J. Bachofen*, trans. R. Manheim. Princeton.

Balfour, I. (2002). *The Rhetoric of Romantic Prophecy*. Stanford.

Balfour, I. (2006). 'Torso: (The) Sublime Sex, Beautiful Bodies, and the Matter of the Text', *Eighteenth-Century Studies*, 3: 323–36.

Bambach, C. (2003). *Heidegger's Roots: Nietzsche, National Socialism, and the Greeks*. Ithaca, NY.

Barnes, J., Schofield, M., and Sorabji, R. (1975) (eds). *Articles on Aristotle*. London.

Barone, P. (2004). *Schiller und die Tradition der Erhabenen*. Berlin.

Barth, B. (1991). *Schellings Philosophie der Kunst: Göttliche Imagination und ästhetische Einbildungskraft*. Freiburg.

Baumgart, H. (1875). 'Der Begriff der tragischen Katharsis', *Jahrbücher für classische Philologie*, 2/1: 81–118.

Beaufret, J. (1973). *Dialogue avec Heidegger: Philosophie Grecque, vol. 1*. Paris.

Behler, E. (1986). 'A. W. Schlegel and the Nineteenth-Century *Damnatio* of Euripides', *Greek, Roman and Byzantine Studies*, 27: 335–67.

Beiser, F. (2002). *German Idealism: The Struggle against Subjectivism, 1781–1801.* Cambridge, MA.

Beiser, F. (2005). *Schiller as Philosopher.* Oxford.

Belfiore, E. S. (1992). *Tragic Pleasures: Aristotle on Plot and Emotion.* Princeton.

Benhabib, S. (1996). 'On Hegel, Women and Irony', in Mills (1996b), 25–44.

Benjamin, A. (2010). *Place, Commonality and Judgment: Continental Philosophy and the Ancient Greeks.* London.

Benjamin, A. (2014). *Working with Walter Benjamin: Recovering a Political Philosophy.* Edinburgh.

Benjamin, W. (1974). *Ursprung des deutschen Trauerspiels,* in *Gesammelte Schriften,* ed. R. Tiedemann and H. Schweppenhäuser. 7 vols. Frankfurt (1972–91), i. 203–430.

Benjamin, W. (1980). *Gesammelte Schriften,* ed. R. Tiedemann and H. Schweppenhäuser. 4 vols. Frankfurt.

Benjamin, W. (1996–2003). *Selected Writings,* ed. M. Bullock and M. Jennings. 4 vols. Cambridge, MA.

Benjamin, W. (1998). *The Origin of German Tragic Drama.* London.

Bernays, J. (1880 [1853]). 'Ergänzung zu Aristoteles' Poetik', in J. Bernays, *Zwei Abhandlungen über die aristotelische Theorie des Drama.* Berlin, 134–86. (First published *Rheinisches Museum,* 8 (1853).)

Bernays, J. (1880 [1859]). 'Ein Brief an Leonhard Spengel über die tragische Katharsis bei Aristoteles', in J. Bernays, *Zwei Abhandlungen über die aristotelische Theorie des Drama.* Berlin, 119–32. (First published *Rheinisches Museum,* 14 (1859).)

Bernays, J. (1885). *Gesammelte Abhandlungen,* ed. H. Usener. Berlin.

Bernays, J. (1970 [1857]). *Grundzüge der verlorenen Abhandlung des Aristoteles über Wirkung der Tragödie.* Breslau; repr. Hildesheim and New York, with an introduction by K. Gründer.

Bernays, J. (2006). 'Aristotle on the Effect of Tragedy', in *Oxford Readings in Ancient Literary Criticism,* ed. A. Laird, trans. J. Barnes. Oxford, 158–75.

Biale, D. (2011). *Not in the Heavens: The Tradition of Jewish Secular Thought.* Princeton.

Billings, J. (2011). 'Greek Tragedy and *vaterländische* Dichtung', in Kortländer and Singh (2011), 9–22.

Billings, J. (2013a). '"An Alien Body?": Choral Autonomy around 1800', in Billings, Budelmann, and Macintosh (2013), 133–50.

Billings, J. (2013b). 'Choral Dialectics: Hölderlin and Hegel', in Gagné and Hopman (2013), 317–39.

Billings, J. (2013c). 'The Ends of Tragedy: The *Oedipus at Colonus* and German Idealism', *Arion,* 21: 111–29.

Billings, J. (2014). *Genealogy of the Tragic: Greek Tragedy and German Philosophy.* Princeton.

Billings, J., Budelman, F., and Macintosh, F. (2013) (eds), *Choruses, Ancient and Modern*. Oxford.

Birnbaum, A. (2008). *Bonheur Justice. Walter Benjamin*. Paris.

Bjornstad, H., and Ibbett, K. (2014) (eds). *Walter Benjamin's Hypothetical French Trauerspiel*. Yale French Studies 124. New Haven.

Blumenthal-Barby, M. (2009). 'Pernicious Bastardizations: Benjamin's Ethics of Pure Violence', *Modern Language Notes*, 124/3: 728–51.

Bogliolo, G. (2000). 'Musique et silence', in Marchetti (2000), 109–17.

Bowlby, R. (2007). *Freudian Mythologies: Greek Tragedy and Modern Identities*. Oxford.

Brandis, C. A. (1860). *Handbuch der Geschichte der Griechisch-romischen Philosophie*. Berlin, v.1.

Broadie, S. (1991). *Ethics with Aristotle*. New York.

Bubner, R. (1992). *Antike Themen und ihre moderne Verwandlung*. Frankfurt am Main.

Budelmann, F. (2006). 'The Mediated Ending of Sophocles' *Oedipus Tyrannus*', *Materiali e discussioni per l'analisi dei testi classici*, 57: 43–61.

Burian, P. (1972). 'Supplication and Hero Cult in Sophocles' *Ajax*', *Greek, Roman and Byzantine Studies*, 13: 151–6.

Burian, P. (2009). 'Inconclusive Conclusion: The Ending(s) of *Oedipus Tyrannus*', in Goldhill and Hall (2009), 99–118.

Burian, P. (2010) 'Gender and the City: *Antigone* from Hegel to Butler and back' in K. Bassi and P. Euben (eds), *When Worlds Elide: Classics, Politics, Culture*. Lanham, 255–99.

Burke, E. (1958 [1756]). *A Philosophical Enquiry into the Origins of our Ideas of the Sublime and the Beautiful*. Repr. edn. London.

Burkert, W. (1966). 'Greek Tragedy and Sacrificial Ritual', *Greek, Roman and Byzantine Studies*, 7/2: 87–121.

Burrow, J. (2008). *A History of Histories: Epics, Chronicles, Romances, and Inquiries from Herodotus and Thucydides to the Twentieth Century*. New York.

Butler, E. M. (1935). *The Tyranny of Greece over the German Imagination*. Cambridge.

Butler, J. (2000). *Antigone's Claim: Kinship between Life and Death*. New York.

Bywater, I. (1900). 'Milton and the Aristotelian Definition of Tragedy', *Journal of Philology*, 27/54 (1900): 267–75.

Calder, W. M., and Günther, T. (2010 (eds). *'Du, von dem ich lebe!': Briefe an Paul Heyse*. Göttingen.

Capobianco, R. (2001). 'Limit and Transgression: Heidegger and Lacan on Sophocles' *Antigone*', *Review of Existential Psychology and Psychiatry*, 26/1: 17–26.

Carroll, J. (1982). *The Cultural Theory of Matthew Arnold*. Berkeley and Los Angeles.

Carter, D. (2011) (ed.). *Why Athens? A Reappraisal of Tragic Politics.* Oxford.

Cavarero, A. (2005). *For More than One Voice: Toward a Philosophy of Vocal Expression*, trans. P. A. Kottman. Stanford.

Cavell, S. (1976). 'The Avoidance of Love: A Reading of *King Lear*', in *Must We Mean What We Say?* Cambridge, 267–353.

Chanter, T. (1995). *Ethics of Eros: Irigaray's Rewriting of the Philosophers.* New York.

Chase, C. (2012). 'The Half-Life of a Stumbling Block', *diacritics*, 40/1: 80–115.

Clark, M. (2001). 'On the Rejection of Morality: Bernard Williams's Debt to Nietzsche', in R. Schacht (ed.), *Nietzsche's Postmoralism: Essays on Nietzsche's Prelude to Philosophy's Future.* Cambridge, 100–22.

Collini, S. (1991). *Public Moralists: Political Thought and Intellectual Life in Britain 1850–1930.* Oxford.

Collini, S. (1994). *Matthew Arnold: A Critical Portrait.* Oxford.

Coste, C. (2003). *Les Malheurs d'Orphée: Musique et littérature au XXème siècle.* Paris.

Couturier-Heinrich, C. (2011). 'Gottfried Hermann, un philologue kantien', *Revue germanique internationale*, 14: 73–90.

Critchley, S., and Webster, J. (2013). *Stay Illusion! The Hamlet Doctrine.* New York.

Darwall, S. (1987). 'Abolishing Morality', *Synthese*, 72: 71–89.

Dawe, R. (2001). 'On Interpolations in the Two Oedipus Plays of Sophocles', *Rheinisches Museum*, 144: 1–21.

Dawe, R. (2006). *Sophocles: Oedipus Rex.* Rev. edn. Cambridge.

de Beistegui, M. (2000). 'Hegel: or the Tragedy of Thinking', in de Beistegui and Sparks (2000), 11–37.

de Beistegui, M., and Sparks, S. (2000) (eds). *Philosophy and Tragedy.* London.

de Laura, D. (1969). *Hebrew and Hellene in Victorian Britain.* Austin.

de Man, P. (1996). *Aesthetic Ideology.* Minneapolis.

de Man, P. (2012). 'Hölderlin and the Romantic Tradition', *diacritics*, 40/1: 100–29.

Derrida, J. (1987). 'Geschlecht: Heidegger's Hand', in J. Sallis (ed.), *Deconstruction and Philosophy: The Texts of Jacques Derrida.* Chicago, 161–96.

Derrida, J. (1987). *De l'esprit: Heidegger et la question.* Paris.

Destrée, P. (2013). 'La Catharsis tragique à l'épreuve de Philodème et des Néoplatoniciens', in D. Iozzia (ed.), *Philosophy and Art in Late Antiquity: Proceedings on the International Seminar of Catania, 8–9 November 2012.* Acireale, 91–113.

Diogenes Laertius (1999–2002). *Diogenis Laertii Vitae philosophorum*, ed. M. Markovitch. Stuttgart.

Dreyfus, H., and Hall, H. (1992) (eds). *Heidegger: A Critical Reader.* Oxford.

Duden (1989). *Das Herkunftswörterbuch.* Mannheim, Vienna, and Zurich.

Dunn, F. (1996). *Tragedy's End: Closure and Innovation in Euripidean Drama.* Oxford.

Dunn, F., Roberts, D., and Fowler, D. (1997) (eds). *Classical Closure: Reading the End in Greek and Latin Literature.* Princeton.

Dupuis, G. (2000). 'Une leçon d'écriture: Le Style et l'harmonie chez Pascal Quignard', in Marchetti (2000), 121–30.

Eagleton, T. (2003). *Sweet Violence: The Idea of the Tragic.* Oxford.

Easterling, P. (1978). '*Philoctetes* and Modern Criticism', *Illinois Classics Studies*, 3: 27–39.

Easterling, P. (1981). 'The End of the *Trachiniae*', *Illinois Classics Studies*, 6: 56–74.

Egger, J. (1883). *Katharsis-Studien.* Vienna.

Einstein, A. (1936). *Gluck*, trans. Eric Blom. London.

Falkner, T. (1998). 'Containing Tragedy: Rhetoric and Self-Representation in Sophocles' *Philoctetes*', *Classical Antiquity*, 17: 25–58.

Farias, V. (1989). *Heidegger and Nazism*, ed. with a foreword by J. Margolis and T. Rockmore, French materials trans. P. Burrell, with the advice of D. Di Bernardi, German materials trans. G. R. Ricci. Philadelphia.

Faverty, F. (1951). *Matthew Arnold, The Ethnologist.* Illinois.

Fenger, H. (1980). 'Hegel, Kierkegaard, and Niels Thulstrup', in H. Fenger, *Kierkegaard: The Myths and their Origins*, trans. G. C. Schoolfield. New Haven.

Ferris, D. (2000). *Romantic Hellenism.* Stanford.

Fichte, J. G. (1968 [1807–8]). *Addresses to the German Nation*, ed. G. A. Kelly, trans. R. F. Jones and G. H. Turnbull. New York.

Fichte, J. G. (1978 [1807–8]). *Reden an die deutsche Nation.* Hamburg.

Finglass, P. (2009). 'The Ending of Sophocles' *Oedipus Rex*', *Philologus*, 153: 42–62.

Finley, M. I. (1964). 'Between Slavery and Freedom', *Comparative Studies in Society and History* 6/3: 233–49.

Fleming, K. (2012). 'Heidegger, Jaeger, Plato: The Politics of Humanism', *International Journal of the Classical Tradition*, 19: 82–106.

Foley, H. (1993). 'Oedipus as *Pharmakos*', in Rosen and Farrell (1993), 525–38.

Foley, H. (2001). *Female Acts in Greek Tragedy.* Princeton.

Foley, H. (2003). 'Choral Identity in Greek Tragedy', *Classical Philology*, 98/1: 1–30.

Foley, H. (2012). *Reimagining Greek Tragedy on the American Stage.* Berkeley and Los Angeles.

Freud, S. (1953–74 [1905–6]). 'Psychopathic Characters on the Stage', in *The Standard Edition of the Complete Psychological Works of Sigmund Freud*, ed. J. Strachey. London, xviii. 304–10. (Written 1905–6; first published 1942.)

Fried, G. (2000). *Heidegger's Polemos: From Being to Politics*. New Haven.

Friedlander, E. (2012). *Walter Benjamin: A Philosophical Portrait*. Cambridge, MA.

Friedländer, P. (1928). *Platon. Eidos. Paideia. Dialogos*. Berlin and Leipzig.

Friedländer, P. (1958). *Plato 1. An Introduction*, trans. H. Meyerhoff. London.

Friedrich, S. (2004). *Richard Wagner: Deutung und Wirkung*. Würzburg.

Fuhrmann, M. (1992). *Dichtungstheorie der Antike: Aristoteles, Horaz, Longin*. Darmstadt.

Gagné, R., and Hopman, M. (2013) (eds). *Choral Mediations in Greek Tragedy*. Cambridge.

Gall, R. (2003). 'Interrupting Speculation: The Thinking of Heidegger and Greek Tragedy', *Continental Philosophy Review*, 36: 177–94.

Geary, J. (2006). 'Reinventing the Past: Mendelssohn's *Antigone* and the Creation of an Ancient Greek Musical Language', *Journal of Musicology*, 23/2: 187–226.

Geiger, I. (2007). *The Founding Act of Modern Ethical Life: Hegel's Critique of Kant's Moral and Political Philosophy*. Stanford.

Geiman, C. P. (2001). 'Heidegger's Antigone's', in Polt and Fried (2001), 161–82.

Gellie, G. (1986). 'The Last Scene of the *Oedipus Tyrannus*', *Ramus*, 15: 35–42.

Gellrich, M. (1988). *Tragedy and Theory: The Problem of Conflict since Aristotle*. Princeton.

George, T. (2006). *Tragedies of Spirit: Tracing Finitude in Hegel's Phenomenology*. Albany.

Georgopoulos, N. (1993) (ed.). *Tragedy and Philosophy*. Houndsmill.

Girard, R. (1977). *Violence and the Sacred*. Baltimore.

Glaser, K. (1938). 'Blutsbande und Staatsgewalt in der "Antigone" des Sophokles', *Die Alten Sprachen*, 3: 105–12.

Gödde, S. (2009). 'Therapeutik und Ästhetik—Verbindungen zwischen Breuers und Freuds kathartischer Therapie und der Katharsis-Konzeption von Jacob Bernays', in M. Vöhler and D. Linck (eds), *Grenzen der Katharsis in den modernen Künsten: Transformationen des aristotelischen Modells seit Bernays, Nietzsche und Freud*. Berlin, 63–91.

Goethe, J. W. v. (1887). *Goethes Werke [Weimarer Ausgabe]*, ed. J. L. G. v. Loeper, E. Schmidt, H. F. Grimm, W. Scherer, B. Seuffert, and B. L. Suphan. 143 vols. Weimar.

Goethe, J. W. v. (1999 [1827]). 'Nachlese zu Aristoteles' Poetik', in *Sämtliche Werke, Briefe, Tagebücher und Gespräche, vierzig Bände*, ed. H. Birus, A. Schöne, and H. Reinhardt, xii. *Ästhetische Schriften 1824–1832: Über Kunst und Altertum*. Frankfurt am Main, v–vi. 335–8. (First published in *Kunst und Altertum*, 6/1.)

Goff, B. (1995) (ed.). *History, Tragedy, Theory: Dialogues on Athenian Drama*. Austin.

Goldhill, S. (1984a). *Language, Sexuality, Narrative: The Oresteia*. Cambridge.

Goldhill, S. (1984b). 'Two Notes on *telos* and Related Words in the *Oresteia*', *Journal of Hellenic Studies*, 104: 169–76.

Goldhill, S. (1986). *Reading Greek Tragedy*. Cambridge.

Goldhill, S. (2008). 'Generalizing about Tragedy,' in R. Felski (ed.), *Rethinking Tragedy*. Baltimore, 45–65.

Goldhill, S. (2010). 'Cultural History and Aesthetics: Why Kant is No Place to Start Reception Studies', in Hall and Harrop (2010), 56–70.

Goldhill, S. (2011). *Victorian Culture and Classical Antiquity: Art, Opera, Fiction and the Proclamation of Modernity*. Princeton.

Goldhill, S. (2012). *Sophocles and the Language of Tragedy*. Oxford.

Goldhill, S., and Hall, E. (2009) (eds). *Sophocles and the Greek Tragic Tradition*. Cambridge.

Gomperz, T. (1897). *Aristoteles' Poetik übersetzt und eingeleitet von Theodor Gomperz. Mit einer Abhandlung: Wahrheit und Irrtum in der Katharsistheorie des Aristoteles, von Alfred Freiherrn von Berger*. Leipzig.

Gossman, L. (1994). 'Philhellenism and Anti-Semitism: Matthew Arnold and his German Models', *Comparative Literature*, 46: 1–39.

Gourgouris, S. (2003). *Does Literature Think? Literature as Theory for an Antimythical Era*. Stanford.

Goux, J.-J. (1993). *Oedipus, Philosopher*. Stanford.

Greiner, B. (2012). *Die Tragödie: Eine Literaturgeschichte des aufrechten Ganges. Grundlagen und Interpretationen*. Stuttgart.

Griffith, M. (1999). *Sophocles' Antigone*. Cambridge.

Griffith, M. (2011). 'Twelve Principles for Reading Greek Tragedy', in Carter (2011), 1–7.

Grillparzer, F. (1964 [1820]). 'Über das Wesen des Dramas', in *Sämtliche Werke: Ausgewählte Briefe, Gespräche, Berichte. Dritter Band, Satiren, Fabeln und Parabeln, Erzählungen und Prosafragmente, Studien und Aufsätze*, ed. P. Frank and K. Pörnbacher. Munich, 301–7. (Written 1820; first published 1872.)

Gross, R. (2007). *Carl Schmitt and the Jews: The 'Jewish Question', the Holocaust and German Legal Theory*, trans. J. Golb. Madison.

Grünbein, D. (2005). *Antike Dispositionen: Aufsätze*. Frankfurt am Main.

Gründer, K. (1991). 'Bernays und der Streit um Katharsis', in *Die aristotelische Katharsis: Dokumente ihrer Deutung im 19. und 20. Jahrhundert*, ed. M. Luserke. Hildesheim, 352–85.

Habermas, J. (1992). 'Work and Weltanschauung: The Heidegger Controversy from a German Perspective', in Dreyfus and Hall (1992), 186–208.

Hall, E., and Harrop, S. (2010) (eds). *Theorising Performance: Greek Drama, Cultural History and Critical Practice*. London.

Hall, E., and Macintosh, F. (2005). *Greek Tragedy and British Theatre 1660–1914*. Oxford.

Hall, E., Macintosh, F., and Wrigley, A. (2004) (eds). *Dionysus since 69: Greek Tragedy at the Dawn of the Third Millennium*. Oxford.

Halliwell, S. (1986). *Aristotle's Poetics*. Chapel Hill, NC.

Halliwell, S. (2003). 'La Psychologie morale de la catharsis: Un essai de reconstruction', *Études philosophiques*, 4: 499–517.

Halliwell, S. (2012). *Between Ecstasy and Truth: Interpretations of Greek Poetics from Homer to Longinus*. Oxford.

Hamlin, C. (2006–7). 'Hölderlin's Hellenism: Tyranny or Transformation', in *Hölderlin-Jahrbuch* 2006–7, 252–311.

Hammill, G., and Lupton, J. R. (2012) (eds). *Political Theology and Early Modernity*. Chicago.

Handke, P. (1969). *Die Innenwelt der Außenwelt der Innenwelt*. Frankfurt am Main.

Hanssen, B. (1998). *Walter Benjamin's Other History: Of Stones, Animals, Human Beings, and Angels*. Berkeley and Los Angeles.

Heaney, S. (1995). *The Redress of Poetry: Oxford Lectures*. London.

Hebbel, F. (1971). *Werke in drei Bänden*, ed. J. Müller, 4th edn. Berlin.

Hegel, G. W. F. (1944). *Lectures on the Philosophy of Religion*, trans. J. Sibree. 3 vols. New York.

Hegel, G. W. F. (1967). *The Phenomenology of Spirit*, trans. J. Baillie, intro. G. Lichtheim. New York.

Hegel, G. W. F. (1968). *Vorlesungen über die Philosophie der Weltgeschichte*, ed. J. Hoffmeister. Hamburg.

Hegel, G. W. F. (1970). *Werke in zwanzig Bänden*, ed. E. Moldenhauer and K. M. Michel. Frankfurt.

Hegel, G. W. F. (1975a). *Aesthetics: Lectures on Fine Art*, trans. T. M. Knox. 2 vols. Oxford.

Hegel, G. W. F. (1975b). *Lectures on the Philosophy of World History: Introduction, Reason in History*. Cambridge.

Hegel, G. W. F. (1977). *Vorlesungen über die Ästhetik. Teil III: Die Poesie*, ed. R. Bubner. Stuttgart.

Hegel, G. W. F. (1991). *Elements of the Philosophy of Right*. Cambridge.

Hegel, G. W. F. (2004). *Hegel's Philosophy Of Nature: Being Part Two of the Encyclopedia of the Philosophical Sciences (1830), Translated from Nicolin and Pöggeler's Edition (1959), and from the Zusätze in Michelet's Text (1847)*, trans. A. V. Miller. Oxford.

Heidegger, M. (1947). *Platons Lehre von der Wahrheit mit einem Brief über den Humanismus*. Frankfurt.

Heidegger, M. (1953). *Einführung in die Metaphysik*. Tübingen.

Heidegger, M. (1971). *Poetry, Language, Thought*. New York.

Heidegger, M. (1973-4). 'The Anaximander Fragment', trans. D. Krell, *Arion*, 1/4: 576-626.

Heidegger, M. (1984). *Hölderlins Hymne 'Der Ister'*. Gesamtausgabe 53. Frankfurt.

Heidegger, M. (1990). 'Spiegel Interview with Martin Heidegger', in Neske and Kettering (1990), 41-66.

Heidegger, M. (1998). *Pathmarks*, ed. W. McNeill. Cambridge.

Heidegger, M. (2000). *Introduction to Metaphysics*, trans. G. Fried and R. Polt. New Haven.

Heller, W. (2009). 'Admeto, Re di Tessaglia', in *The Cambridge Handel Encyclopedia*, ed. A. Landgraf and D. Vickers. Cambridge, 7-9.

Henrichs, A. (1993). 'The Tomb of Ajax and the Prospect of Hero Cult', *Classical Antiquity*, 12: 165-80.

Hermann, G. (1802) (ed.). *Aristotelis de arte poetica liber cum commentariis*. Leipzig.

Herz, J. (1998). 'Der Mythos als Zeitspiegel: Der Alkestis-Stoff auf der Musikbühne', *Neue Zürcher Zeitung*, 21-22 March, 53-4.

Hesk, J. (2003). *Sophocles: Ajax*. London.

Hinderer, W. (2005). 'Schiller's Philosophical Aesthetics in Anthropological Perspective', in Steven Martenson (ed.), *A Companion to the Works of Friedrich Schiller*. Rochester, NY, 27-46.

Hodgson, P. (2012). *Shapes of Freedom: Hegel's Philosophy of World History in Theological Perspective*. Oxford.

Hofmannsthal, H. (1959). *Alkestis: Ein Trauerspiel*. Wiesbaden.

Hölderlin, F. (1943-85). *Grosse Stuttgarte Ausgabe*, ed. F. Beissner, A. Beck, et al. 7 vols. Stuttgart.

Hölderlin, F. (1986). *Selected Verse*, ed. and trans. Michael Hamburger. London.

Hölderlin, F. (1988). *Essays and Letters on Theory*, ed. and trans. Thomas Pfau. Albany, NY.

Hölderlin, F. (1989). *Sophokles Antigone*, ed. M. Waber and E. Selge. Frankfurt.

Hölderlin, F. (1992). *Sämtliche Werke und Briefe*, ed. M. Knaupp. 3 vols. Munich.

Hölderlin, F. (2004). *Sämtliche Werke*, ed. D. E. Sattler. Munich.

Hölderlin, F. (2009). *Essays and Letters*, ed. J. Adler and C. Louth. London.

Honig, B. (2013). *Antigone Interrupted*. Cambridge.

Horkheimer, M., and Adorno, T. W. (2004). *Dialektik der Aufklärung: Philosophische Fragmente*, 15th edn. Frankfurt.

Houlgate, S. (2007). 'Hegel's Theory of Tragedy', in S. Houlgate (ed.), *Hegel and the Arts*. Evanston, 146-78.

Hug, A. (1872). 'Der doppelsinn in Sophokles Oedipus König', *Philologus*, 31: 66-84.

Hughes, T. (1999). *Alcestis*. London.

Ignatieff, M. (1990). *The Needs of Strangers*. London.

Janko, R. (1992). 'From Catharsis to the Aristotelian Mean', in A. I. Rorty (ed.), *Essays on Aristotle's Poetics*. Princeton, 341–58.

Jebb, R. C. (1891). *Sophocles. The Plays and Fragments. Part III: The Antigone*. Cambridge.

Jennings, M. W. (1987). *Dialectical Images: Walter Benjamin's Theory of Literary Criticism*. Ithaca, NY.

Joachim, F. (1941). 'Der nordische Blutgedanke in der "Antigone" des Sophokles', *Die Alten Sprachen*, 6: 51–5.

Joyce, J. (1986). *Ulysses*, ed. H. W. Gabler. New York.

Judet de la Combe, P. (2010). *Les Tragédies grecques sont-elles tragiques? Théâtre et théorie*. Montrouge.

Kahn, V. (2003). 'Hamlet or Hecuba: Carl Schmitt's Decision', *Representations*, 83/1: 67–96.

Kain, P. (1982). *Schiller, Hegel and Marx: Society and the Aesthetic Ideal of Ancient Greece*. Kingston and Montreal.

Kant, I. (2011). *Observations on the Feeling of Beautiful and the Sublime and other Writings*, trans. P. Frierson, ed. P. Frierson and P. Guyer. Cambridge.

Kaufmann, F. W. (1940). *German Dramatists of the 19th Century*. Los Angeles.

Kessler, H. L., and Nirenberg, D. (2011) (eds). *Judaism and Christian Art: Aesthetic Anxieties from the Catacombs to Colonialism*. Philadelphia.

Kierkegaard, S. (1978). *Entweder-Oder*, ed. H. Diem, W. Rest, and N. Thulstrup. 2nd edn. Munich.

Kitzinger, M. R. (2008). *The Choruses of Sophokles' Antigone and Philoktetes: A Dance of Words*. Mnemosyne Supplementa 292. Leiden and Boston.

Knox, B. (1957). *Oedipus at Thebes*. New Haven.

Knox, B. (1964). *The Heroic Temper: Studies in Sophoclean Tragedy*. Berkeley and Los Angeles.

Kommerell, M. (1957). *Lessing und Aristoteles: Untersuchung über die Theorie der Tragödie*. Frankfurt am Main.

Kortländer, B., and Singh, S. (2011) (eds). *'Das Fremde im Eigensten': Die Funktion von Übersetzungen im Prozess der deutschen Nationbildung*. Tübingen.

Krell, D. (2005). *The Tragic Absolute: German Idealism and the Languishing of God*. Bloomington.

Kristeva, J. (1980). *Pouvoirs de l'horreur: Essai sur l'abjection*. Paris.

Lacan, J. (1988). *Seminar II: The Ego in Freud's Theory and in the Technique of Psychoanalysis, 1954–55*, ed. J.-A. Miller, trans. S. Tomaselli. New York.

Lacan, J. (1999). *The Ethics of Psychoanalysis, 1959–60: The Seminar of Jacques Lacan. Book VII*, ed. J.-A. Miller, trans. D. Porter. New York.

Lacoue-Labarthe, P. (1987). *La Fiction du politique*. Mesnil-sur-l'Estrée.

Lacoue-Labarthe, P. (1989). 'The Caesura of the Speculative', in *Typography, Mimesis, Philosophy, Politics*, ed. C. Fynsk. Cambridge, MA, 208–35.

Lacoue-Labarthe, P. (1998). *Metaphrasis: Suivi de la théâtre d'Hölderlin*. Paris.

Lacoue-Labarthe, P. (2002). *Heidegger: La Politique du poème*. Paris.

Lada-Richards, I. (1998). 'Staging the *Ephebeia*: Theatrical Role Playing and Ritual Transition in Sophocles' *Philoctetes*', *Ramus*, 27: 1–26.

Lambropoulos, V. (2006). *The Tragic Idea*. London.

Lane, M. (2001). *Plato's Progeny: How Plato and Socrates Still Capture the Modern Mind*. London.

Laplanche, J. (1961). *Hölderlin et la question du père*. Paris.

Laplanche, J. (2007). *Hölderlin and the Question of the Father*, trans. L. Carson. Victoria, BC.

Latacz, J. (2009). 'C. Modern Philology (from 1800). 4. 1920–1945: The Return to the Singular ("Inner Form", "Shape", "Idea")', in M. Landfester (ed.), *Brill's New Pauly. Encyclopedia of the Ancient World. Classical Tradition Volume IV Oly-Rul*. Leiden/Boston, 417–20.

Lear, J. (1992). 'Katharsis', in A. Rorty (ed.), *Essays on Aristotle's Poetics*. Princeton, 315–40.

Lebeck, A. (1971). *The Oresteia: A Study in Language and Structure*. Washington.

Leonard, M. (2005). *Athens in Paris: Ancient Greece and the Political in Postwar French Thought*. Oxford.

Leonard, M. (2012). *Socrates and the Jews: Hellenism and Hebraism from Moses Mendelssohn to Sigmund Freud*. Chicago.

Leonard, M. (2015). *Tragic Modernities*. Cambridge, MA.

Lepeyre-Desmaison, C. (2001). *Pascal Quignard le solitaire*. Paris.

Lessing, G. E. (1985). *Werke und Briefe in zwölf Bänden*, ed. W. Barner, K. Bohnen, et al. Frankfurt am Main.

Lewis, C. (2011). 'Boileau and "Longinus" in Hölderlin's Sophokles-Anmerkungen', *Germanic Review*, 86/2: 114–33.

Lewis, T. (2011). *Religion, Modernity and Politics in Hegel*. Oxford.

Liébert, G. (2004). *Nietzsche and Music*, trans. D. Pellauer and G. Parkes. Chicago.

Loraux, N. (1999). *La Voix endeuillée: Essai sur la tragédie grecque*. Paris.

Loraux, N. (2002). *The Mourning Voice: An Essay on Greek Tragedy*, trans. E. T. Rawlings. Ithaca, NY.

Louth, C. (1998). *Hölderlin and the Dynamics of Translation*. Oxford.

McCall, T. (1988). 'The Case of the Missing Body', *Le pauvre Holterling*, 8: 53–72.

McCall, T. J. (2014). 'Wrathful Translation: The Sophocles of Hölderlin' <http://www.rc.umd.edu/praxis/mccall>. Unpaginated.

McFarland, J. (2013). *Constellation: Friedrich Nietzsche and Walter Benjamin in the Now-Time of History*. New York.

Mali, J. (1999). 'The Reconciliation of Myth: Benjamin's Homage to Bachofen', *Journal of the History of Ideas*, 60/1: 165–87.

Marchetti, A. (2000) (ed.). *Pascal Quignard: La Mise au silence*. Seysell.

Martindale, C. (2010). 'Performance, Reception, Aesthetics: Or Why Reception Studies Need Kant', in Hall and Harrop (2010), 71–84.

Marx, K. (2000). 'The Eighteenth Brumaire of Louis Bonaparte', trans. Terell Carver, in *Marx's Eighteenth Brumaire: (Post-)modern Interpretations*, ed. Mark Cowling and James Martin. London, 19–109.

Melville, H. (1852). *Pierre: or, The Ambiguities*. New York.

Menke, C. (1991). *Die Souveränität der Kunst: Ästhetische Erfahrung nach Adorno und Derrida*. Frankfurt am Main.

Menke, C. (1996). *Tragödie im Sittlichen: Gerechtigkeit und Freiheit nach Hegel*. Frankfurt am Main.

Menke, C. (2005). *Die Gegenwart der Tragödie: Versuch über Urteil und Spiel*. Frankfurt am Main.

Menke, C. (2009). *Tragic Play: Irony and Theater from Sophocles to Beckett*. New York.

Mills, P. (1996a). 'Hegel's *Antigone*', in Mills (1996b), 59–88.

Mills, P. (1996b) (ed.). *Feminist Interpretations of Hegel*. University Park, PA.

Momigliano, A. (1969). 'Prospettiva 1967 della storia greca', in *Quarto Contributo alla storia degli studi classici e del mondo antico*. Rome, 43–58.

Montani, P. (2001) (ed.). *Antigone e la filosofia* (Rome).

Morley, N. (2008). *Antiquity and Modernity*. Oxford.

Most, G. (2002). 'Heidegger's Greeks', *Arion*, 10/1: 83–98.

Mueller, C. (1996). 'Die Thebanische Trilogie des Sophokles und ihre Aufführung im Jahre 401: Zur Frühgeschichte der antiken Sophoklesrezeption und der Überlieferung des Textes', *Rheinisches Museum*, 139: 193–224.

Müller, A. (1967). *Über die dramatische Kunst*, in *Schriften*, ed. W. Schroeder and W. Siebert. Neuwied, i. 141–291.

Müller, K. O. (1833). *Aeschylos, Eumeniden: Griechisch und Deutsch mit erläuternden Abhandlungen über die äussere Darstellung und über den Inhalt und die Composition dieser Tragödie*. Göttingen.

Munteanu, D. L. (2012). *Tragic Pathos: Pity and Fear in Greek Philosophy and Tragedy*. Cambridge.

Neer, R. (2011). 'Poussin's Useless Treasures', in Kessler and Nirenberg (2011), 328–57.

Neske, G., and Kettering, E. (1990) (eds). *Martin Heidegger and National Socialism: Questions and Answers*, trans. L. Harries and J. Neugroschel. New York.

Newman, J. O. (2011). *Benjamin's Library: Modernity, Nation, and the Baroque.* Ithaca, NY.

Nietzsche, F. (1966). *Beyond Good and Evil,* trans. W. Kaufmann. New York.

Nietzsche, F. (1967). *The Case of Wagner,* trans. W. Kaufmann. New York.

Nietzsche, F. (1967–). *Werke (Kritische Gesamtausgabe),* ed. G. Colli and M. Montinari. 30 vols. Berlin.

Nietzsche, F. (1974). *The Gay Science,* trans. W. Kaufmann. New York.

Nietzsche, F. (1980). *Sämtliche Werke (Kritische Studienausgabe),* ed. G. Colli and M. Montinari, 15 vols. Munich.

Nietzsche, F. (1997). *Daybreak: Thoughts on the Prejudices of Morality* (1881/1887), trans. R. J. Hollingdale. Cambridge.

Nietzsche, F. (1998). *Philosophy in the Tragic Age of the Greeks.* Washington

Nietzsche, F. (1999). *The Birth of Tragedy and Other Writings,* trans. R. Speirs. Cambridge.

Nietzsche, F. (2006). *On the Genealogy of Morals,* trans. C. Diethe. Cambridge.

Nooter, S. (2012). *When Heroes Sing: Sophocles and the Shifting Soundscape of Tragedy.* Cambridge.

Nussbaum, M. (1986). *The Fragility of Goodness: Luck and Ethics in Greek Tragedy and Philosophy.* Cambridge.

Nussbaum, M. (2001). *The Fragility of Goodness: Luck and Ethics in Greek Tragedy and Philosophy.* Rev. edn. Cambridge.

O'Neill, E. (2003). *Mourning Becomes Electra.* London.

Ott, H. (1988). *Martin Heidegger: Unterwegs zu seiner Biographie.* Frankfurt.

Pan, David (2009). 'Afterword: Historical Event and Mythic Meaning in Carl Schmitt's *Hamlet or Hecuba*', in Schmitt (2009), 69–119.

Pan, D., and Reinhard Lupton, J. (2010). 'Introduction', *Telos,* 153 (special issue on Carl Schmitt's *Hamlet or Hecuba*), 3–7.

Paolucci, A., and Paolucci, H. (1962). *Hegel on Tragedy.* New York.

Pautrot, J.-L. (2004). 'La Musique de Pascal Quignard', *Études françaises,* 40: 55–76.

Pedrick, V., and Oberhelman, S. (2005) (eds). *The Soul of Tragedy: Essays on Athenian Drama* (Chicago).

Pinkard, T. (2002). *German Philosophy 1750–1860: The Legacy of Idealism.* Cambridge.

Pinkard, T. (2012). *Hegel's Naturalism: Mind, Nature, and the Final Ends of Life.* Oxford.

Pippin, R. (1988). *Hegel's Idealism: The Satisfactions of Self-Consciousness.* Cambridge.

Pippin, R. (1999). *Modernity as Philosophical Problem,* 2nd edn. Malden.

Pippin, R. (2002). 'What Was Abstract Art? (From the Point of View of Hegel)', *Critical Inquiry,* 29/1: 1–24.

Pippin, R. (2006). 'Introduction', in F. Nietzsche, *Thus Spoke Zarathustra*, ed. R. Pippin and A. del Caro. Cambridge, pp. viii–xxxv.

Pippin, R. (2007). 'Review, *In the Beginning Was the Deed*, by Bernard Williams', *Journal of Philosophy*, 104/10: 533–8.

Pippin, R. (2010a). *Hollywood Westerns and American Myth: The Importance of Howard Hawks and John Ford for Political Philosophy*. New Haven.

Pippin, R. (2010b). *Nietzsche, Psychology, and First Philosophy*. Chicago.

Pippin, R. (2012). *Fatalism in American Film Noir: Some Cinematic Philosophy*. Charlottesville.

Plumptre, E. (1865). *The Tragedies of Sophocles*. London.

Polt, R., and Fried, G. (2001) (eds). *A Companion to Heidegger's Introduction to Metaphysics*. New Haven.

Porter, J. I. (2000). *The Invention of Dionysus*. Stanford.

Porter, J. I. (2007). 'Lucretius and the Sublime', in *The Cambridge Companion to Lucretius*, ed. S. Gillespie and P. Hardie. Cambridge, 167–84.

Porter, J. I. (2010). *The Origins of Aesthetic Thought in Ancient Greece: Matter, Sensation, and Experience*. Cambridge.

Porter, J. I. (2015). *The Sublime in Antiquity*. Cambridge.

Potts, A. (1994). *Flesh and the Ideal: Winckelmann and the Origins of Art History*. New Haven.

Potts, A. (2006). 'Introduction', in J. J. Winckelmann, *History of the Art of Antiquity*. Los Angeles, 1–53.

Pucci, P. (1992). *Oedipus and the Fabrication of the Father*. Baltimore.

Quignard, P. (1990). *Albucius*. Paris.

Quignard, P. (1995). *Rhétorique speculative*. Paris.

Quignard, P. (1997). *Petits Traités II*. Paris.

Quignard, P. (2002a). *La Leçon de musique*. Paris. (First published 1987.)

Quignard, P. (2002b). *La Haine de la musique*. Paris. (First published 1996.)

Quignard, P. (2002c). *Le Nom sur le bout de la langue*. Paris. (First published 1993.)

Quignard, P. (2007). *Le Sexe et l'effroi*. Paris. (First published 1994.)

Rehm, R. (2002). *The Play of Space: Spatial Transformation in Greek Tragedy*. Princeton.

Reinhardt, K. (1961). 'Hölderlin und Sophokles', in A. Kelletat (ed.), *Hölderlin: Beiträge zu seinem Verständnis in unserem Jahrhundert*. Tübingen, 287–303.

Reiss, T. (1980). *Tragedy and Truth: Studies in the Development of a Renaissance and Neoloclassical Discourse*. New Haven.

Reiz, F. W. (1776) (ed.). Ἐκ τῶν Ἀριστοτέλους Πολιτικῶν. Leipzig.

Ritzer, M. (2012). '"Gewalt über unsre Leidenschaften?": Pathos und Pathetik der Emotion in der Tragödienästhetik der Aufklärung', *KulturPoetik*, 12: 1–40.

Roberts, D. (1998). 'Arte e mito. Adorno e Heidegger', *Nuova Corrente*, 45: 43–70.

Rockmore, T. (1992). *On Heidegger's Nazism and Philosophy*. London.

Rose, P. (1976). 'Sophocles' *Philoctetes* and the Teachings of the Sophists', *Harvard Studies in Classical Philology*, 80: 49–105.

Rosen, R., and Farrell, J. (1993) (eds). *Nomodeiktes: Greek Studies in Honor of Martin Oswald*. Ann Arbor.

Rosenfield, K. H. (1999). 'Getting inside Sophocles' Mind through Hölderlin's *Antigone*', *New Literary History*, 30/1: 107–27.

Rosenzweig, F. (2005). *The Star of Redemption*, trans. B. Galli. Madison.

Rousseau, J.-J. (1997). *Les Rêveries du promeneur solitaire*, ed. E. Leborgne (Paris).

Rudnytsky, P. (1987). *Freud and Oedipus*. New York.

Rutter, B. (2011). *Hegel on the Modern Arts*. Cambridge.

Sallis, J. (2002). *On Translation*. Bloomington.

Salzani, C. (2010). 'Purity (Benjamin with Kant)', *History of European Ideas*, 3: 438–47.

Santner, E. L. (2010). 'The Royal Remains: Carl Schmitt's *Hamlet or Hecuba*', *Telos* 153 (special issue on Carl Schmitt's *Hamlet or Hecuba*), 30–50.

Santner, E. L. (2012). *The Royal Remains: The People's Two Bodies and the Endgames of Sovereignty*. Chicago.

Schadewaldt, W. (1929). 'Sophokles, Aias und Antigone', *Neue Wege zur Antike*, 8: 61–109.

Schadewaldt, W. (1970 [1955]). 'Furcht und Mitleid? Zur Deutung des Aristotelischen Tragödiensatzes', in *Hellas und Hesperien: Gesammelte Schriften zur Antike und zur neueren Literatur*, ed. K. Bartels, R. Thurow and E. Zinn. 2nd rev. and enlarged edn. Zurich and Stuttgart, i. 194–236. (First published in *Hermes*, 83.)

Schadewaldt, W. (1966). 'Hölderlins Übersetzung des Sophokles', in *Antike und Gegenwart: Über die Tragödie*. Munich, 113–76.

Schein, S. (2005). 'Divine and Human in Sophocles' *Philoctetes*', in Pedrick and Oberhelman (2005), 27–47.

Schelling, F. W. J. (1976). *Philosophie der Kunst*. Darmstadt.

Schelling, F. W. J. (1978). *System of Transcendental Idealism* (1800), trans. P. Heath. Virginia.

Schelling, F. W. J. (1985). *Ausgewählte Schriften*, ed. M. Frank. Frankfurt am Main.

Schelling, F. W. J. (1989). *The Philosophy of Art*, trans. D. Stott. Minneapolis.

Schiller, F. (1838). *Sämmtliche Werke in zwölf Bänden*. Stuttgart.

Schiller, F. (1943-). *Werke. (Nationalausgabe)*. 36 vols. Weimar.

Schiller, F. (1988–2004). *Werke und Briefe in zwölf Bänden*. 12 vols. Frankfurt am Main.

Schiller, F. (1993). *Essays*, ed. W. Hinderer and D. O. Dahlstrom. New York.

Schlegel, A. W. (1923). *Vorlesungen über dramatische Kunst und Literatur*, ed. G. V. Amoretti. Bonn and Leipzig.

Schlegel, F. (1958–). *Kritische Friedrich-Schlegel-Ausgabe*, ed. E. Behler. Munich.

Schlegel, F. (2001). *On the Study of Greek Poetry*, ed. and trans. S. Barnett. Albany, NY.

Schmidt, D. (2001). *On Germans and Other Greeks: Tragedy and the Ethical Life*. Bloomington.

Schmitt, C. (2009). *Hamlet or Hecuba: The Intrusion of the Time into the Play*, trans. D. Pan and J. Rust. New York.

Schulte, M. (1992). *Die 'Tragödie im Sittlichen': Zur Dramentheorie Hegels*. Munich.

Scodel, R. (2012). *An Introduction to Greek Tragedy*. Cambridge.

Seaford, R. (1995). 'Historicizing Tragic Ambivalence', in Goff (1995), 202–22.

Segal, C. (1981). *Tragedy and Civilization: An Interpretation of Sophocles*. Cambridge, MA.

Segal, C. (1986). *Interpreting Greek Tragedy. Myth, Poetry, Text*. Ithaca, NY.

Segal, C. (1996). 'Catharsis, Audience and Closure in Greek Tragedy', in Silk (1996), 149–72.

Segal, C. (2001). *Oedipus Tyrannus: Tragic Herosim and the Limits of Knowledge*. 2nd edn. New York and London.

Shanks, A. (1991). *Hegel's Political Theology*. Cambridge.

Shanks, A. (2011). *Hegel and Religious Faith: Divided Brain, Atoning Spirit*. London.

Sharpe, L. (1991). *Schiller: Drama, Thought, and Politics*. Cambridge.

Sheehan, T. (2001). 'A Paradigm Shift in Heidegger Research', *Continental Philosophy Review*, 32/2: 1–20.

Shuttleworth, S. (1996). *Charlotte Brontë and Victorian Psychology*. Cambridge.

Silk, M. S. (1988). 'Pathos in Aristophanes', *Bulletin of the Institute of Classical Studies*, 34: 78–111.

Silk, M. S. (1996) (ed.). *Tragedy and the Tragic: Greek Tragedy and Beyond*. Oxford.

Silk, M. S. (2000). *Aristophanes and the Definition of Comedy*. Oxford.

Silk, M. S. (2001). 'Pindar Meets Plato: Theory, Language, Value, and the Classics', in S. J. Harrison (ed.), *Texts, Ideas, and the Classics: Scholarship, Theory, and Classical Literature*. Oxford, 26–45.

Silk, M. S., and Stern, J. P. (1981). *Nietzsche on Tragedy*. Cambridge.

Silk, M. S., Gildenhard, I., and Barrow, R. (2014). *The Classical Tradition: Art, Literature, Thought*. Chichester.

Sitze, A. (2012). 'The Tragicity of the Political: A Note on Carlo Galli's Reading of Carl Schmitt's *Hamlet or Hecuba*', in Hammill and Lupton (2012), 48–59.

Smerick, C. M. (2009). ' "And G-d Said": Language, Translation, and Scripture in Two Works by Walter Benjamin', *Shofar: An Interdisciplinary Journal of Jewish Studies*, 27/2: 48–68.

Soffer, G. (1996). 'Heidegger, Humanism, and the Destruction of History', *Review of Metaphysics*, 49/3: 547–76.

Solger, K.W.F. (1826). *Nachgelassene Schriften und Breifwechsel*, ed. L. Tieck and F. Raumer. 2 vols. Leipzig.

Sophocles (1885). *The Oedipus Tyrannus*, ed. R. C. Jebb. Cambridge.

Sophocles (1887). *The Oedipus Tyrannus*, trans. R. C. Jebb. 2nd edn. Cambridge.

Sophocles (1947). *Theban Plays*, trans. E. F. Watling. London.

Sophocles (1970). *Three Tragedies*, trans. H. D. F. Kitto. Oxford.

Sophocles (1974). *Sophokles Antigone*, trans. W. Schadewaldt. Frankfurt.

Sophocles (1989). *Antigone*, trans. Ezio Savino. Milan.

Sophocles (1989). *Antigone*, trans. F. Hölderlin, adapted by M. Walser and E. Selge. Frankfurt am Main.

Sophocles (1999). *Antigone*, ed. M. Griffith. Cambridge.

Sophocles (2003). *Dramen*, trans. W. Willige. Düsseldorf.

Speight, A. (2001). *Hegel, Literature and the Problem of Agency*. Cambridge.

Spengel, L. (1859). *Ueber die κάθαρσις τῶν παθημάτων: Ein Beitrag zur Poetik des Aristoteles*. Munich.

Stahr, A. (1840). 'Rev. of F. Ritter, *Aristotelis Poetica* (Renard, 1839)', *Ergänzungsblätter zur Allgemeiunen Literatur-Zeitung*, 69, 545–75.

Stahr, A. (1859). *Aristoteles und die Wirkung der Tragödie*. Berlin.

Steinberg, M. P. (1991). 'The Incidental Politics of Mendelssohn's *Antigone*', in R. L. Todd (ed.), *Mendelssohn and his World*. Princeton, 137–57.

Steinberg, M. P. (2004). *Listening to Reason: Culture, Subjectivity, and Nineteenth-Century Music*. Princeton.

Steiner, G. (1961). *The Death of Tragedy*. London.

Steiner, G. (1986). *Antigones*. Oxford.

Steiner, G. (1996). 'Tragedy, Pure and Simple', in Silk (1996), 534–46.

Stern, J. P. (1995). *The Dear Purchase: A Theme in German Modernism*. Cambridge.

Strathausen, C. (2010). 'Myth or Knowledge? Reading Carl Schmitt's *Hamlet or Hecuba*', *Telos* 153 (special issue on Carl Schmitt's *Hamlet or Hecuba*), 7–29.

Szondi, P. (1974). *Poetik und Geschichtsphilosophie*. 2 vols. Frankfurt am Main.

Szondi, P. (2002). *An Essay on the Tragic*, trans. P. Fleming. Stanford.

Tabachnick, D. (2006). 'The Tragic Double Bind of Heidegger's Techne', *PhaenEx*, 1/2: 94–112.

Taplin, O. (1978). *Greek Tragedy in Action*. London.

Taxidou, O. (2004). *Tragedy, Modernity and Mourning*. Edinburgh.

Taylor, C. (1991). *The Malaise of Modernity* (Ontario).

Taylor, J. B., and Shuttleworth, S. (1998) (eds). *Embodied Selves: An Anthology of Psychological Texts, 1830–1890*. Oxford.

Thibodeau, M. (2012). *Hegel and Greek Tragedy*. Plymouth.

Thirlwall, C. (1833). 'On the Irony of Sophocles', *Philological Museum*, 2: 483–537.

Thulstrup, N. (1980). *Kierkegaard's Relation to Hegel*. Princeton.

Treml, M. (1997). 'Zum Verhältnis von Jacob Bernays und Sigmund Freud', *Luzifer-Amor: Zeitschrift zur Geschichte der Psychoanalyse*, 10/19: 7–32.

Trüstedt, K. (2010). 'Hecuba against Hamlet: Carl Schmitt, Political Theology, and the Stake of Modern Tragedy', in *Telos*, 153 (special issue on Carl Schmitt's *Hamlet or Hecuba*), 94–112.

Veloso, C. W. (2007). 'Aristotle's *Poetics* without *Katharsis*, Fear, or Pity', *Oxford Studies in Ancient Philosophy*, 33: 255–84.

Vernant, J.-P. (1978). 'Ambiguity and Reversal: On the Enigmatic Structure of *Oedipus Rex*', *New Literary History*, 9/3: 475–501.

Vernant, J.-P., and Vidal-Naquet, P. (1972). *Mythe et tragédie en Grèce ancienne*. Paris.

Vernant, J.-P., and Vidal-Naquet, P. (1981). *Myth and Tragedy in Ancient Greece*, trans. J. Lloyd. New York.

Vietor, K. (1952). *Geist und Form: Aufsätze zur deutschen Literaturgeschichte*. Bern.

Vischer, F. T. (1967). *Über das Erhabene und das Komische und andere texte zur Aesthetik*. Frankfurt am Main.

Vohler, M. (1992–3). 'Hölderlins Longin-Rezeption', *Hölderlin-Jahrbuch*, 28: 152–72.

Wagner, R. (1983). *Dichtungen und Schriften. Jubiläumsausgabe*, ed. D. Borchmeyer. 10 vols. Frankfurt am Main.

Warminski, A. (1987). *Readings in Interpretation: Hölderlin, Hegel, Heidegger*. Minneapolis.

Weber, M. (1992). *The Protestant Ethic and the Spirit of Capitalism*, trans. T. Parsons. London.

Weber, S. (2004). *Theatriciality as Medium*. New York.

Weber, S. (2008). *Benjamin's –abilities*. Cambridge, MA.

Weil, H. (1848). 'Über die Wirkung der Tragödie nach Aristoteles', in *Verhandlungen der zehnten Versammlung deutscher Philologen, Schulmänner und Orientalisten in Basel, den 29. und 30. September und 1. und 2. October 1847*. Basle, 131–41.

Weil, H. (1859). 'Erklärung die aristotelische κάθαρσις betreffend', *Neue Jahrbücher für Philologie und Paedagogik*, 79: 159.

Whitlock Blundell, M. (1989). *Helping Friends and Harming Enemies: A Study in Sophocles and Greek Ethics*. Cambridge.

Whitman, C. (1951). *Sophocles: A Study of Heroic Humanism*. Cambridge, MA.

Wilamowitz-Möllendorff, U. von (1889). *Euripides Herakles I: Einleitung in die attische Tragödie*. Berlin.

Williams, B. (1986). *Ethics and the Limits of Philosophy*. Cambridge, MA.

Williams, B. (1993). *Shame and Necessity*. Berkeley and Los Angeles.

Williams, B. (1994). 'Nietzsche's Minimalist Moral Psychology', in R. Schacht (ed.), *Nietzsche, Genealogy, Morality*. Berkeley and Los Angeles, 237–50.

Williams, B. (2004). *Truth and Truthfulness*. Princeton.

Williams, B. (2005). *In the Beginning Was the Deed: Realism and Moralism in Political Argument*. Princeton.

Williams, R. (1979). *Modern Tragedy*. London.

Wilson, E. (2004). *Mocked with Death: Tragic Overliving from Sophocles to Milton*. Baltimore.

Winkler, J. J., and Zeitlin, F. (1990) (eds). *Nothing to Do with Dionysos? Athenian Drama in its Social Context*. Princeton.

Wise, J. (1998). *Dionysus Writes: The Invention of Theatre in Ancient Greece*. Ithaca, NY.

Witt, C. (2005). 'Tragic Error and Agent Responsibility', in *The Annual Proceedings of the Center for Philosophic Exchange*. Brockport, 1–22.

Young, J. (2002). *Heidegger's Later Philosophy*. Cambridge.

Zeitlin, F. (1965). 'The Motif of the Corrupted Sacrifice in Aeschylus' Oresteia', *Transactions of the American Philological Association*, 96: 463–505.

Zuckert, C. H. (1996). *Postmodern Platos: Nietzsche, Heidegger, Gadamer, Strauss, Derrida*. Chicago.

Index

Note: Bold entries refer to figures.

Printed and bound by CPI Group (UK) Ltd, Croydon, CR0 4YY